Rebellion in America

In a time of rising inequality and plutocratic government, citizens' movements are emerging with growing frequency to offer populist challenges to the declining living standards of masses of Americans, and to protest the conditions through which individuals suffer in poor communities across the country.

This book looks at the progression of modern social uprisings in the post-2008 period, including the Tea Party, Occupy Wall Street, Black Lives Matter, the Bernie Sanders "Revolution," Trump's populism, the anti-Trump revolt, and #MeToo. A key theme is that populism and mass anger at the political-economic status quo take different forms depending on whether the protests are progressive-left or right-wing in orientation.

Employing theories of elite politics and pluralism, and using a mixed-methods approach, Anthony DiMaggio harnesses his rich experience with movement politics and his engagement with a wide range of media and public opinion data to explain where we are today and how we got here – always with an eye on moving ahead. Aimed at courses on social movements wherever they're taught, this book also offers general readers insight into contemporary politics and protest.

Anthony DiMaggio is Associate Professor of Political Science at Lehigh University and author of a variety of books on mass media and politics, most recently *The Politics of Persuasion: Media Bias and Economic Policy in the Modern Era* (2017) and *Political Power in America: Class Conflict and the Subversion of Democracy* (2019). He has been an active participant in social movement politics for the last two decades, and is an avid social commentator.

Praise for *Rebellion in America*

"The world is aflame with popular uprisings, not least the United States. This careful study of the variety of recent movements, of how movements gain public support and the pitfalls and barriers they face, provides a very valuable guide to those committed to change the world – a critical necessity today."
—Noam Chomsky, *Emeritus Professor, Massachusetts Institute of Technology*

"Surveying the rapidly changing American political landscape from the Global Financial Crisis to the populist surge under Trump, Anthony DiMaggio offers a much-needed reappraisal of the role of social movements in promoting progressive societal transformation. Combining qualitative analysis with a wealth of empirical data, this landmark study focuses especially on the growing power of the social media and public opinion in shaping intersecting identities that drive popular protests on both the political Left and Right. Essential reading!"
—Manfred B. Steger, *University of Hawaiʻi, and Global Professorial Fellow, Western Sydney University*

"DiMaggio has written a compelling, deeply documented argument that popular social movements are the dominant force transforming the US political landscape. Read this book if you want to get hard evidence in a world of fake news about how social change really happens."
—Charles Derber, *Boston College*

Rebellion in America
Citizen Uprisings, the News Media, and the Politics of Plutocracy

Anthony DiMaggio

NEW YORK AND LONDON

First published 2020
by Routledge
52 Vanderbilt Avenue, New York, NY 10017

and by Routledge
2 Park Square, Milton Park, Abingdon, Oxon, OX14 4RN

Routledge is an imprint of the Taylor & Francis Group, an informa business

© 2020 Taylor & Francis

The right of Anthony DiMaggio to be identified as author of this work has been asserted by him in accordance with sections 77 and 78 of the Copyright, Designs and Patents Act 1988.

All rights reserved. No part of this book may be reprinted or reproduced or utilised in any form or by any electronic, mechanical, or other means, now known or hereafter invented, including photocopying and recording, or in any information storage or retrieval system, without permission in writing from the publishers.

Trademark notice: Product or corporate names may be trademarks or registered trademarks, and are used only for identification and explanation without intent to infringe.

Library of Congress Cataloging-in-Publication Data
A catalog record for this title has been requested

ISBN: 978-0-815-37121-2 (hbk)
ISBN: 978-0-815-37122-9 (pbk)
ISBN: 978-1-351-24722-1 (ebk)

Typeset in Sabon
by Integra Software Services Pvt. Ltd.

Contents

Acknowledgments   viii

Introduction: Social Movements and Rebellion in a Time of Plutocracy   1
Understanding Social Movements 2
Hegemony, Plutocracy, and Social Movements 4
Mainstream Scholarly Theories of Social Movements 4
Social Movements and the "Outside" Lobbying Strategy 10
Populism and Modern Social Movements 11
Research Design 11
Plan of the Book 12
    Chapter 1: The Tea Party and the Rise of Right-Wing Rebellion 12
    Chapter 2: The Economic Justice Movement: Challenging Plutocracy and Inequality 13
    Chapter 3: Black Lives Matter: and the Struggle against Color-Blind Racism 14
    Chapter 4: Populism in the 2016 Election 14
    Chapter 5: The Anti-Trump Uprising and beyond 15
Notes 15

1   The Tea Party and the Rise of Right-Wing Rebellion   24
A History of the Tea Party 25
Tea Partiers: What They Believed 26
Tea Party Bigotry? 29
Selling the Apocalypse: The Tea Party's Conspiracy Politics 31
Intersectional Identities: Tea Party Racism, Xenophobia, and Health-Care Protests 32
Intersectional Sexism and the Tea Party 33
Media and Scholarly Discourse on the Tea Party 35
Challenging Conventional Wisdom on the Tea Party 42

What Motivated the Tea Party? Socio-Cultural Versus Economic Attitudes? 45
Conclusion 50
Notes 55

2 **The Economic Justice Movement: Challenging Plutocracy and Inequality** 64

Inequality and Politics: What We Know 65
The Madison Uprising 68
Madison's Impact on Political Discourse 71
Media Effects 72
Occupy Wall Street: The Fight for Economic Justice Continues 80
Occupy Wall Street Emerges 81
The Occupiers: Who They Were, What They Believed 82
Occupy's Radical Politics 83
The Limits of Occupy 84
Occupy, Social Media, and the News 86
Media Effects 87
Occupy's Radical Appeal 91
Fight for $15 94
Chronology of the Protests 95
Conclusion 102
Notes 103

3 **Black Lives Matter: And the Struggle against Color-Blind Racism** 120
WITH SAKURA SHINJO

Intersectionality and BLM 121
What Can Be Learned from BLM? 121
Police Violence: A Background 122
Racism in America: What We Know 124
Ferguson: The Early Development of BLM 126
Social Media and the Ferguson Protests 128
The Media and Ferguson 129
Intersectionality and Ferguson 134
Freddie Gray and the Baltimore Uprising 136
Social Media, the News Media, and Baltimore 137
Intersectionality and Baltimore 141
Assessing the Impact of BLM 143
The Strengths (and Limits) of BLM 149
Policy Change 152
Conclusion 153
Notes 154

4 Populism in the 2016 Election — 166

Populism: A Background 167
Bernie Sanders and the 2016 Election 169
Sanders and the Media 173
Assessing Sanders' Appeal 174
Assessing Sanders' "Political Revolution" 183
Populism on the Right: The Rise of Trump 184
Populism and Plutocracy 186
Reactionary Populism in the Culture War 189
Trump and the Media 189
Trump and the Public: Right-Wing Populism and Its Supporters 197
The Myth of Trump's Economic Populism 204
Trump and "the Fascist Creep" 213
Conclusion 215
Notes 216

5 The Anti-Trump Uprising and Beyond — 229

A Second Renaissance of Protest 231
The 2017 Women's Marches 231
Opposing Trump's Travel Ban and the DACA Repeal 234
Tax Day Protests and the March(es) for Science 236
Opposing "Obamacare" Repeal 241
The Strengths and Limits of the Anti-Trump Protests 246
Beyond the Anti-Trump Protests: #MeToo 251
Conclusion 262
Notes 263

Conclusion — 274

Elections as an Instrument of Democracy? 275
Social Movements and Democracy 276
Notes 277

Index — 279

Acknowledgments

This book is the culmination of a research project that has been ongoing for the last five years, and has occupied countless hours. I want to thank my wife Mary, and sons Frankie and Tommy, for their patience and love during this challenging time. Your love and company have sustained me all these years. I'd also like to thank the rest of my family for their longstanding support throughout my academic career, including my parents and siblings. I also want to reach out to my academic colleagues, and thank them for all their support during my time in school and beyond, and in nurturing my development as a progressive scholar and intellectual. You all have helped me in my journey more than you'll ever know: Manfred Steger, Amentahru Wahlrab, Carlos Parodi, Ali Riaz, Jamal Nassar, John Vinzant, Stephen Caliendo, Andrew Rojecki, Andy McFarland, Henry Giroux, Robert McChesney, Christian Parenti, Lauren Langman, Noam Chomsky, Frances Fox Piven, Richard Matthews, Ted Morgan, Holona Ochs, Laura Olson, Vera Fennell, Chad Kautzer, Sakura Shinjo, and the rest of my colleagues at Lehigh University. This book would not have been possible if not for the support of my Lehigh colleagues, and the resources committed to my intellectual development from the university itself. Finally, I want to thank Mark Major for all his support over the years: including his advocacy for my academic work, his friendship, and his invaluable scholarly and intellectual contributions to *Political Science and Political Communication*. Your friendship over the years has enriched my life in countless ways.

Introduction
Social Movements and Rebellion in a Time of Plutocracy

The early twenty-first century is a time of instability and change. The decade following the 2008 economic collapse witnessed protest after protest by Americans who were tired of the status quo. This period represented a renaissance of protest unseen since the demonstrations of the 1960s. Protest was mainstreamed amidst record mass anger with government. By 2018, 57 percent of Americans said they were upset enough over an issue that they were willing to protest.[1] Such sentiment differed greatly from mass opinion during the 1960s, when most held unfavorable views of civil rights and anti-war protesters.[2]

Americans in 2018 were angry about many issues. Twenty-eight percent said protests over "sexual harassment and gender inequality in the workplace" were the most important movement to them, while another 27 percent cited the movement for "racial equality" via Black Lives Matter. Twenty-four percent cited the campaign against climate change as most important, while 9 percent identified most with the gay and lesbian rights movement. Some Americans were captivated by right-wing causes, as 24 percent listed the Trump-supported push to "protect borders and limiting immigration," and 23 percent cited "maintaining the right for all adults to purchase firearms" as the most important movements of the time.[3]

I offer four main arguments in this book. First, leftist social movements, not political parties or government institutions, are primarily responsible for promoting progressive societal transformation. By "progressive," I am referring to left-wing attitudes on political, social, and economic matters, including support for worker rights, and opposition to racism, sexism, and other forms of discrimination.

Second, I document how social transformation occurs through mass movements that utilize the media to communicate their values and shift public opinion. Despite a long-standing bias favoring official sources in the news, activists and social movements at times take advantage of windows of opportunity to reach large numbers of Americans.

Third, I find that grassroots populism during the 2010s was primarily a leftist phenomenon. The alliance between the American right and concentrated corporate and political power suggests a dominant role for political and business elites in leading far-right populism. This does not mean that conservative citizens fail to protest. But when conservatives do protest, movements such as the Tea Party are quickly co-opted by right-wing political, economic, and media elites. Some rightist "movements" are entirely dependent on top-down leadership, as with Trump's populism. In contrast, progressive movements oppose concentrated power, so they are forced to build mass support to pressure political officials for change.

Finally, the study of identities – and the intersections of various identities – is central to understanding movements on the left and right. "Intersectionality" theory is articulated primarily by leftist scholars. This research paradigm is overwhelmingly ignored in mainstream Political Science and Sociology. It is also dismissed by many on the left as "identity politics" – as directing attention away from economically centered forms of political analysis. Some academics within the "postmodernist" tradition also dismiss intersectionality, claiming it is not possible to talk about individuals as sharing "essential" identities.[4] These attacks reveal how out of touch some on the left are regarding the centrality of intersectional identities to the formation of social movements. It is difficult to understand social movement protests without understanding identities and intersectionality, which are central to protest movements and to understanding how race, ethnicity, class, geography, and age influence how Americans see the world. I make use of numerous public opinion surveys in order to understand how those residing at various intersecting identities respond to modern social movements.[5]

Understanding Social Movements

Social movements are based on the articulation of collective claims and grievances in their appeals to the public.[6] Occupy Wall Street embraced its identity as representing the "99 percent," and against the "1 percent" of business elites in an economy marked by rising inequality. Black Lives Matter activists offered an identity stressing equal rights for all.

Mass movements involve large numbers of people acting in regional, national, or global capacities, challenging established ideologies and power structures. They rely on protest, seeking to unify large numbers of people and establish "dense informal networks" in pursuit of common goals.[7]

Social movements engage in public outreach via demonstrations, protests, pamphleteering, civil disobedience, and community canvassing.[8] Outreach efforts gain public attention via media exposure – to communicate movement values with large numbers of people. By committing to a cause, movements generate opposition from those holding contrary values.[9] Despite this conflict, successful movements build support by relying on an "activist core" of full-time leaders, in addition to part-time participants who attend planning meetings, protests, and other events, and with the support of a sympathetic public.[10] This cultural transformation is vital to pressure political institutions to address social movements' demands.

Karl Marx and Friedrich Engels argued in *The Communist Manifesto* that "the history of all hitherto existing society is the history of class struggles."[11] They laid out a "materialist conception of history" – or "historical materialism," which placed economic factors above all others in guiding the course of history. Marx referred to historical materialism as driving "different theoretical products and forms of consciousness, religion, philosophy, [and] ethics."[12] He maintained that these forces operate within a system in which the economic "base" of society – defined by capitalist ownership of the means of production – determines how other societal institutions function.[13] Upon this "base" sits a "superstructure," including educational entities, the media, religious organizations, and the entertainment industry, among other institutions. Under orthodox Marxism, these institutions operate in service of capitalism.

Marxian language is embraced by many on the left. Marxist scholars recognize there are other factors outside economics that impact life outcomes, political systems, and behavior.[14] But much commentary on the left draws on orthodox Marxism, treating economics as if it is of sole importance, while analyses of gender, race, sexual orientation/identity, and intersectional identities are dismissed as diversionary and elitist "identity politics."[15] Orthodox Marxism has limited value in helping us understand social movements. Individual identities matter to the development of our values and priorities.

Engels wrote that "systems of dogma" – including those described by Marx as part of the societal "superstructure" – drive behavior, beliefs, and social outcomes. As Engels reflected, "younger people sometimes lay more on the economic side than is due to it." Other institutions in society "also play a part" in driving history.[16] Engels' recognition that non-economic ideological forces "may, within certain limits," play an independent role in impacting history helps us to understand how movements operate.[17]

Progressive movements, including the Madison protests of Republican Governor Scott Walker, Occupy Wall Street, Fight for $15, Black Lives Matter, and #MeToo, are motivated by economics, in addition to other factors. The concerns of Occupy, Madison, and Fight for $15 were primarily economic. But the Black Lives Matter movement – driven by anger over racism and police brutality – was also economic in orientation, as reflected in frustrations with a lack of resources in communities populated by poor people of color. #MeToo is a coordinated effort to fight sexism in the workplace and in society, but it is concerned with uneven economic power relations within corporate and political institutions dominated by affluent men.

Marx claimed "men make their own history, but they do not make it as they please; they do not make it under self-selected circumstances, but under circumstances existing already, given and transmitted from the past."[18] Following this logic, social movements are not manifestations of "free will," but the product of decisions to resist oppression within predetermined circumstances. We could refer to such protests as reflecting *constrained will*, in that activists rebel in response to long-standing grievances against exploitation.

Hegemony, Plutocracy, and Social Movements

Italian Marxist Antonio Gramsci developed a theory of "hegemony," describing capitalist elites as manipulating popular consciousness through indoctrination. He rejected as "primitive infantilism" the idea that "every fluctuation of politics and ideology can be presented and expounded as an immediate expression of the [economic] structure."[19] Gramsci saw intellectuals as vital to disseminating hegemonic values. He wrote of the power of elite-driven socialization in building "consent" for capitalist institutions that concentrate power in the hands of business elites.[20] Gramsci recognized the power of ideology to mold minds. Individuals support elitist belief systems, viewing them as common-sensical due to indoctrination.[21] But Gramsci also conceded that social control by elites could be preserved during periods of instability by granting concessions to dispossessed groups.[22] During periods of mass anger at the status quo, many Americans fight back, representing the interests of common people.[23]

In the 2010s, American politics became increasingly plutocratic. By plutocracy, I mean dominance of politics by business interests and the top 1 to 20 percent of income earners. Various studies now document how these affluent Americans dominate policy outcomes; the preferences of "average" Americans have little policy impact.[24]

Regarding plutocracy, Gramsci's discussion of hegemony and rebellion provides a useful guide for understanding social movements. Americans have grown angry with elite dominance of politics, and look to protest movements to express their displeasure with plutocracy. Many Americans are rejecting hegemonic claims that "free markets" provide for the needs of the people.[25] Progressive social movements seek to reclaim politics from elite interests, and these uprisings have succeeded in building critical public consciousness and promoting political change. But the co-optation of progressive forces, as Gramsci warned, may also mean the establishment of a new hegemonic system in which concessions are granted to protesters, while capitalism continues with a more human face.

Mainstream Scholarly Theories of Social Movements

Early scholarly depictions of social movements were not always kind. Academics saw them as fatalistic, populated by irrational individuals with little insight to add to political discourse.[26] Research that emphasized the value of social movements in representing citizens did not upend the negative view scholars held of mass protest.[27] But the pessimistic view of social movements was also challenged by those in the "pluralist" intellectual school, which saw mass political participation as central to democracy.[28] David Truman established a "disturbance theory" to predict when citizens are more likely to engage in political action. Organized groups of individuals seek out "equilibrium" through the well-being of their members. Perceived threats to a group disrupt this equilibrium. Truman was not clear on how severe a disturbance must be before citizens rise up in protest. But he believed disturbances provoked action from citizens set on restoring the pre-disturbance status quo.[29]

Truman's work falls within "strain theory," which predicts increased citizen action due to rising anger over perceived injustices.[30] Strain theory has received support from various social scientists.[31] Gurr's "relative deprivation" theory maintains that citizens rebel when there is a mismatch between their quality of life expectations and life outcomes. Violence is more likely when assessing individuals' positions in society, relative to what they believe they should achieve.[32] While Gurr's theory focuses on political violence, Truman's theory does not assume that strain produces violence.[33]

Although pluralism and strain theory were prominent in the mid-twentieth century, they were challenged in later years. While pluralism portrayed humans as "social animals" and citizen activism as natural, "resource mobilization" theory was less optimistic.[34] McCarthy and Zald rejected the assumption that individuals with grievances will organize to make their concerns known. Instead, they saw the rise and fall of movements as contingent upon the resources they build.[35] Of particular importance was "legitimacy," with a movement more likely to succeed if it "has at its disposal the power and resources of some established elite group."[36]

Resource mobilization theory drew on the work of Mancur Olson, who maintained that small, organized groups of business producers prevail over large groups of citizens. Large groups, Olson argued, struggle to impact policy because of a "free rider problem," with group members seeking free benefits without contributing to the group. In contrast, smaller producer groups find it easier to act because of the smaller number of people involved in them, the greater peer pressure they exert on members, and the larger benefits per person small groups provide. For these reasons, Olson believed, the privileged few would defeat the many.[37] There was little room for social movements in Olson's account, which he referred to as irrationally committed to "lost causes."[38] Other "elite theorists" agreed that business interests dominated American politics over citizens groups.[39] This skepticism about average citizens' impact was shared by many intellectuals over the years portraying citizens as incapable of forming wise decisions, as reliant on elites to form their opinions.[40]

Numerous sociologists have modified resource mobilization theory. Tilly, Tarrow, McAdam, and others offer a "political process" theory, which depicts movement success as a function of three factors: the level of organizational resources movements have access to; the degree to which movements benefit from a favorable "political opportunity structure," defined by support from government; and the degree of "cognitive liberation" within movements via their ability to develop critical consciousness to challenge the status quo.[41] Cognitive liberation includes "strategic efforts by groups of people to fashion shared understandings of the world and of themselves that legitimate and motivate collective action."[42]

Movements are also driven by "identity," across multiple dimensions, including gender, religious, nationalistic, geographical, racial, ethnic, and class distinctions.[43] With intersectionality, we see how identities form through interactions of class, gender, race, sexual orientation, gender identity, and physical impairment.[44] The theory was developed to shed light on how disadvantaged individuals experience the world.[45] But poorer Americans, blacks, lesbians, and women have long been marginalized in academia and the pioneers of intersectionality often share(d) radical socialist values, further contributing to their marginalization.[46] Still, intersectionality adds nuance and depth to the study of identities and their relationship to social movements. As I document, it has much to tell us about how social movements form and whether they succeed in their public appeals.

Each theory above assists in understanding why movements emerge. But each theory is also limited: classical pluralism falsely assumes that different social groups receive equal representation in politics, and that citizens restrict the power of business interests.[47] Numerous studies document growing plutocratic power in American politics.[48] Still, Truman's disturbance theory explains the origins of movements that are motivated by the grievances of members, combined with catalyst events that impel people to action. These events include: Barack Obama's election galvanizing the Tea Party and the rise of Trump's populism; rising inequality for Occupy Wall Street, Fight for $15, and Bernie Sanders' populism; the attacks on collective bargaining by Scott Walker for the Madison protests; and the deaths of black Americans by police for Black Lives Matter. Catalyst events are vital when responding to scholarly claims that disadvantaged groups often remain inactive despite their displeasure with the status quo. These events motivate individuals to action who otherwise remain passive.

Resource mobilization and policy process theories contribute to our understanding of social movements by emphasizing the role of elite support in enabling the success of protests. Scholars emphasize the importance of framing in the news to the success of movements.[49] Activists can "set the public agenda" for what issues Americans consider relevant, influence "how" they think about these issues, and impact their political attitudes.[50] Without a high volume of sympathetic media coverage, social movements struggle to influence public consciousness.

But resource mobilization and policy process theories do not fully recognize the power of movements to transform discourse, public opinion, and politics. They depict movements as reliant on elite actors. Political opportunity structures matter a great deal, but they are not everything. Radical social movements throughout history struggled to impact American society, *without* the support (initially) of elites. The anti-Vietnam War movement was initially dismissed by both parties, although the sustained vigilance of activists helped them gain public attention.[51] The civil rights movement had little support from Democrats and Republicans until the mid-1960s, when it found an ally in the executive branch.[52]

Finally, "identity politics" are vital to social movements. Race and class oppression drove the rise of Black Lives Matter protests. #MeToo drew upon the victimization of women in subordinate occupational positions, subject to sexual harassment and assault. But much of modern "identity politics" has devolved into discussions of individual identities divorced from class concerns, thereby limiting its value to the study of movements fighting American plutocracy. This development is acute within the Democratic Party establishment.

I draw from each of the four theories above, situating them within a hegemonic framework emphasizing rebellion against plutocratic politics and other forms of oppression. Leftist uprisings challenge hegemonic discourses that stigmatize poor whites, poor men and women, and poor people of color as "failures," and reactionary rhetoric that celebrates "free markets" and sees disadvantaged groups as morally degenerative and dangerous. Adopting hegemonic theory, I recognize the role of economics in driving social movements, while acknowledging – as Engels did – the importance of other components of identity.

Most political scientists ignore social movements. The discipline journals concentrating on American politics privilege the three branches of the federal government, political parties, and elections as mediums of representation. To demonstrate these biases, I reviewed all the scholarly articles from these journals from 2008 through 2018. Articles were classified based on the title, subtitle, and abstracts, including a reference to one of the areas of focus included in Figure I.1. Social movements receive little attention. Furthermore, populist campaigns, such as Bernie Sanders' 2016 Presidential run, the Tea Party, and Donald Trump's campaign to "Make America Great Again," are also marginalized. The media receive some scholarly attention, but are heavily neglected. Intersectionality is also ignored in establishment journals. Much of political

8   Introduction

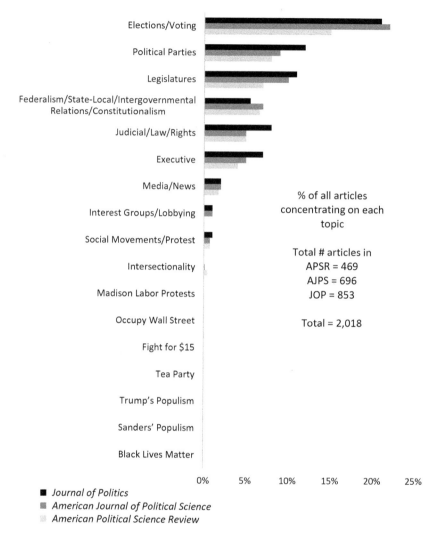

Figure I.1 Research Priorities in American Political Science (1/2008–5/2018)

scientists' time is devoted to elections and voting, political parties and legislatures, federalism, state and local politics, intergovernmental relations, Constitutionalism, judicial and legal politics, and executive politics.

An analysis of Sociology reveals a similar trend. The emphasis on movements has not occurred in establishment journals. A review of the *American Sociological Review* finds only one article on Occupy Wall Street, the 2011 Madison labor protests, and Black Lives Matter.[53] An inspection of the *American Journal of Sociology* finds no articles featuring Black Lives Matter, Occupy Wall Street, the Madison protests, or Fight for $15.

Elitism in Political Science means a focus on institutions of government over extra-institutional forces such as social movements. The fixation on parties and elections speaks to a hegemonic bias within a discipline that sees electoralism as the center of "democratic" politics.

Some scholars address the vital political importance of social movements. Piven, Cloward, Gillion, Lee, and Morgan examine the civil rights movement, documenting its impact on political values and politics. Piven and Cloward portray it as an example of disruption of the status quo, which won political and civil rights for its supporters.[54] Morgan finds that, despite much negative media attention toward 1960s-era protests, the civil rights movement broke into mass discourse to make its demands heard.[55] Gillion documents how increased media attention to civil rights protests produced growing awareness of racial segregation and discrimination. Increased media attention was associated with favorable policy responses from government.[56] Finally, Lee documents how public identification with the civil rights movement was a stronger predictor of support for civil rights legislation than was identification with the Democratic Party.[57] Lee's findings reveal the power of the civil rights movement, beyond its affiliation with the Democratic Party.

Other studies yield similar results. Steger, Goodman, and Wilson's examination of the global justice movement reveals that its activists offer a coherent social justice narrative that puts people first over business profits, and that this movement is a serious alternative to corporate globalization.[58] Woodly's shows that gay and lesbian activists have drawn favorable media attention, thereby building public support for same-sex marriage.[59] Weldon argues that social movements are *more* effective at representing disadvantaged groups than are political parties.[60] Her research on women's rights and labor activism suggests that movements prioritizing intersectional identities – including economic-, gender-, and race-based concerns – help secure policies that benefit disadvantaged peoples. States with women's rights campaigns that include a larger number of groups focusing on women of color produce stronger movements and greater policy responsiveness to women, and women of color.[61] This finding undermines attacks on intersectional activism for allegedly fragmenting the left.[62]

Perhaps most important to this book is Piven's *Challenging Authority*. Piven is hardly starry eyed when it comes to prospects for political change arising from social movements. She and Cloward claim political systems grant largely cosmetic concessions to progressive movements.[63] Still, Piven argues that periods of mass uprising produce significant change:

ordinary people exercise power in American politics mainly at those extraordinary moments when they rise up in anger and hope, defy the rules that ordinarily govern their daily lives, and by doing so, disrupt the workings of the institutions in which they are enmeshed.[64]

Her analysis includes examples throughout history, including the Revolutionary War, the abolitionist movement, and protests during the Great Depression and the 1960s.[65] Echoing Piven, I find we have again entered an "extraordinary moment" in history of mass disruption, with protests seriously challenging the status quo.

Social Movements and the "Outside" Lobbying Strategy

Social scientists agree the communication of grievances is important for social movements.[66] And how the media "frame" the news also matters for shaping political discourse.[67] But there is disagreement about how effective movements are in cultivating media attention, and regarding how biased the media are toward official and business interests over those of ordinary Americans. Many studies emphasize that there is an official source bias in the media that privileges official voices over those of the people.[68] Social movements are said to struggle in gaining news attention.[69] Other scholarship points to a pro-business or pro-upper-class bias in the news, and a hegemonic privileging of advertiser and corporate interests.[70] Some depict the media as privileging liberal voices.[71] Still others emphasize a negativity bias aimed at attracting audiences.[72] Some believe the media are pluralistic, making room for citizens' voices.[73]

Walker's *Mobilizing Interest Groups in America* popularized the notion of "the outside lobbying strategy." This strategy can be interpreted to include citizens groups utilizing the media to gain mass attention. Citizens groups use their strength in numbers to cultivate news coverage, showing there is room in media discourse for citizens to influence political discourse.[74] But social movements attract coverage, within specific limits. While many studies document the biases in the media in favor of political officials and business interests, there are also periods of historical flux when progressive movements exploit "cracks in the system" and break into media discourse. My case studies do *not* provide evidence that movements are on an equal footing with government officials. Far from playing a dominant role in the news, social movements compete in a crowded landscape, and they face an uphill battle when confronting governmental dominance of the news. But during times when citizens *succeed* in influencing news narratives, they cultivate growing public support as a result of their widening reach.

Populism and Modern Social Movements

McNall argues that movements are characterized by anger and outrage.[75] This includes a commitment to protest and other forms of political expression, such as voting or even violence. Populism is marked by trust in the masses, who are seen as virtuous and wise, and distrust of the political establishment, which is viewed as corrupt and unresponsive. Populist campaigns are typically based around strong personalities that provide leadership in the charge against "elites," while inflaming the passions of "the people." But not all forms of populism are equal. Some are elite-based, despite ironically attacking "elites." Others are based on grassroots protest. I document how left social movements draw their power from bottom-up pressures, seeking to uproot centers of concentrated power. Black Lives Matter, the Madison labor protests, Occupy Wall Street, and Fight for $15 are examples of progressive populism. In contrast, right-wing populism is more anemic. It is heavily dependent on corporate power and white patriarchal power structures, while claiming to speak for "the average man." This populism is top-down, as seen in the Tea Party and Trump's populism.

One consequence of right-wing populism is that it removes power from citizens' hands, while stifling direct democracy, and empowering elites. By working upon the prejudices of conservatives, these movements embrace authoritarianism, while flirting with fascism. I define authoritarianism as a commitment to centralized leadership and to undemocratic, repressive politics that demands citizens' obedience to authority and punishes those withholding obedience. I define fascism as a political system that depends on a dictatorial political leader, and utilizes nationalism, prejudice, and violence to cultivate citizen support. There is overlap between these two definitions, and I use them both to refer to Trump's populism. While left-wing populism over the last decade was primarily grassroots, right-wing populism during the 2010s was heavily reliant on corporate and Republican power.

Research Design

This book analyzes the stories of modern social movements – if such stories were told by a political sociologist who relies on empirical research methods. I selected my case studies not based on whether a movement succeeded or failed. Rather, I selected some of the most salient uprisings of the 2010s as related to the rise of American plutocracy.[76] I rely on participant observation in movements, which I took part in throughout the 2010s in the Midwest and on the east coast. I rely on participation in protests to understand what values motivate activists. My observations include experiences with the Tea

Party, in which I attended rallies, participated in online group communications, and went to planning meetings in the Chicago metropolitan region throughout 2010, when the Tea Party reached a high-point of attention in the news. On the left, observations include my travels to Madison, Wisconsin in February of 2011 in the labor uprising against Republican Governor Scott Walker and his efforts to eliminate collective bargaining for public-sector employees. These observations included conversations with protesters, to identify what beliefs drove demonstrators. Finally, I participated in nearly two-dozen rallies, organizing meetings, workshops, marches, and other events from late 2016 through late 2017, with the rise of the anti-Trump protests. These events were in Eastern Pennsylvania and Washington, D.C. They included protest of Trump's electoral victory, his inauguration, the 2017 travel ban on Muslim immigrants, his repeal of DACA protections for undocumented immigrants, the 2017 March for Science and Tax Day protest, and protests of Trump's efforts to repeal the Affordable Care Act.

My research utilizes content analyses of media coverage of protests. I use *Lexis Nexis* and *Nexis Uni* databases to examine stories from 2010 through 2018, overlapping with the rise and fall of various social movements. I used these databases to assess the successes and failures of movements in gaining favorable coverage. Archival analysis allows me to construct political histories for movements, tracing out timelines, including their rise and fall. In total, I analyze more than 35,000 news-related articles, and hundreds of news outlets, coupled with closer analyses of a dozen news sources. These include national and regional newspapers, newswire services, radio news, internet news, broadcast television, and cable news. I provide more information for how I analyzed news stories related to each social movement throughout each chapter and in my endnotes.

Finally, my research includes statistical examinations of public opinion via "regression" analyses, to measure the impact of media coverage and demographic and attitudinal factors on opinions of social movements. I examine surveys from Princeton's *Pew Research Center*, and from other polling organizations. By including these surveys, I speak more authoritatively about how movements win public support.

Plan of the Book

This book is divided into five separate chapters, examining various case studies of social movements and mass populism on the left and right. I include summaries of those chapters below.

Chapter 1: The Tea Party and the Rise of Right-Wing Rebellion

Tea Partiers were motivated by opposition to President Barack Obama and by an "anti-government" philosophy. This group was reactionary in its cultural outlook, depicting Obama as an exotic and dangerous "other," via supporters' embrace of the conspiracy that Obama was not a U.S. citizen. The movement rejected Democratic economic policies, while attacking the "undeserving poor" as lazy and gaming the system for "free" welfare benefits. The Tea Party cultivated significant public support through sympathetic media coverage due to the backing it received from the Republican Party. Tea Party protests were never as large as depicted in the media. It was a relatively small movement, whose messages were amplified by journalists and Republican Congressional candidates in the 2010 elections. Despite the collapse of the Tea Party protest following these elections, it pulled the Republican Party to the right, reinforcing plutocratic political interests.[77]

Chapter 2: The Economic Justice Movement: Challenging Plutocracy and Inequality

Modern leftist economic movements challenge plutocracy in politics. The 2011 Madison protests opposed Republican proposals to strip labor unions of collective bargaining rights. In line with Truman's disturbance theory, the protests were motivated by concerns that the assault on unions would harm Wisconsin workers. Madison protesters drew on sympathetic media coverage to build public support for their protests of Governor Scott Walker's anti-union agenda. The movement failed in rolling back his anti-union reforms. Still, Wisconsin unions' campaign fed into a larger progressive uprising that pulled the Democratic Party to the left, via the rise of the Bernie Sanders wing of the party.

This chapter continues with Occupy Wall Street, which won sympathetic media coverage for its grievances, including anger over record inequality and Wall Street's power in politics. Occupy never developed policy reforms to market to a political party. Still, the movement popularized discourse on inequality and "the 1 percent" of wealthy Americans who have seen their fortunes grow at the expense of "the 99 percent." Occupy fed into an emerging populist wave within the Democratic Party in the 2016 and 2020 elections.

Finally, this chapter examines Fight for $15. This movement drew support from organized labor, while pursuing a higher minimum wage. It benefitted from significant public support, drawing on the popular belief that those who work should earn a wage that pays for all basic needs. Fight for $15 received little national news attention and struggled to break into mass political discourse. But it inspired an uprising within the Democratic Party – evident in Sanders' and Elizabeth Warren's embrace of the movement.

The economic justice movement reinforces Truman's disturbance theory, demonstrating how public anger over changes in the economy impel citizens to action. Occupy reflected mass anger at record inequality;

14 *Introduction*

Madison represented mounting resentment of a political system that assaults union protections; and Fight for $15 included critical acts of civil disobedience from those suffering poor working conditions via low pay and benefits.

Chapter 3: Black Lives Matter: and the Struggle against Color-Blind Racism

The Black Lives Matter (BLM) movement emerged from protests of the Trayvon Martin shooting in 2012, and intensified with the protests in Ferguson, Missouri in 2014, the death of Freddie Gray in Baltimore in 2015, and in response to other killings of black men. These protests demonstrate Truman's disturbance theory in that they constitute a mass rebellion against a law-enforcement system discriminating against people of color. This discrimination is "color-blind," in that law enforcement discriminates against people of color, despite police claiming to abhor racism.

BLM was also motivated by economics. Much of protestors' anger was driven by anxiety over enduring poverty in poor minority neighborhoods. Public support for protests of racial profiling and police brutality were strongest among younger, poorer, urban, black Americans, a finding that speaks to the economic foundation of BLM.

BLM cultivated positive media attention through major protests in Ferguson and elsewhere. This coverage helped build support for the movement's cause of fighting structural racism in America.

Chapter 4: Populism in the 2016 Election

Chapter 4 examines the rise of competing forms of electoral populism, via the campaigns of Bernie Sanders and Donald Trump. Sanders' support was derived from younger, lower-income whites struggling with college debt and health-care costs. Trump's rise, in contrast, was mainly due to the rising salience of reactionary cultural attitudes.

Trump's supporters expressed little interest in inequality and displayed few signs of economic insecurity. Instead, they drew on a general notion of lost "greatness," calling back to a history in which white men openly discriminated against women, people of color, and immigrants.

The media covered Sanders and Trump differently. Sanders was marginalized, while Trump's populism was indulged. Sanders' strong showing in the 2016 primaries related to his platform, which spoke to younger, less affluent Americans who were tired of establishment Democrats.

Trump was a media darling during the 2016 election. He dominated the news over competitors and won support from millions of Americans because of his appeal to reactionary segments of the population embracing racism, sexism, and xenophobia; and because of his populist rhetoric, which stoked anger among conservatives convinced that their best economic days were behind them. Neither Trump nor Sanders received majority public support. But their competing forms of populism mobilized millions of anxious Americans.

Chapter 5: The Anti-Trump Uprising and Beyond

The anti-Trump movement quickly gained public acceptance following his rise to power. Opposition to Trump included protests of his foreign and domestic policy, and of his leadership of an increasingly reactionary political system. Opposition to Trump reached a high watermark with protests of his inauguration in January 2017, although demonstrations continued into 2018. The anti-Trump protests were reactive, rather than progressive. Because of its concentration on one individual, and due to its alliance with the Democratic Party, the movement struggled to develop an agenda for change. Throughout 2017, the anti-Trump protests were mildly successful in impacting federal policy outcomes, but impacted political discourse and mass consciousness. Chapter 5 ends with an analysis of #MeToo, which heightened awareness of sexual harassment and assault in the workplace.

Notes

1 Hart Research Associates/Public Opinion Strategies, "Study #18164: Social Trends Survey," *NBC/Wall Street Journal*, March 2018, https://www.wsj.com/public/resources/documents/wsjnbcpoll0314final.pdf.
2 Terry Anderson, *The Movement and the Sixties: Protest in America from Greensboro to Wounded Knee* (New York: Oxford University Press, 1996).
3 Hart Research Associates, "Study #18164," 2018.
4 For a discussion of the ways in which academics and intellectuals dismiss intersectionality, see the discussions in: Patricia Hill Collins and Sirma Bilge, *Intersectionality* (Cambridge: Polity, 2016); and S. Laurel Weldon, *When Protest Makes Policy: How Social Movements Represent Disadvantaged Groups* (Ann Arbor, MI: University of Michigan Press, 2012). For a discussion on the left of intersectionality and identity politics as artificial elitist constructs, see: Todd Gitlin, "The Left, Lost in the Politics of Identity," *Harpers*, September 1993, https://harpers.org/archive/1993/09/the-left-lost-in-the-politics-of-identity/; Chris Hedges, "The Bankruptcy of the American Left," *Truthdig*, February 5, 2018, https://www.truthdig.com/articles/bankruptcy-american-left/; Bruce Dixon, "Intersectionality Is a Hole. Afro-Pessimism Is a Shovel. We Need to Stop Digging, Part 1 of 3," *Black Agenda Report*, January 25, 2018, https://www.blackagendareport.com/intersectionality-hole-afro-pessimism-shovel-we-need-stop-digging-part-1-3; Julian Vigo, "From Identity Politics to Academic Masturbation," *Truthdig*, March 28, 2018, https://www.truthdig.com/articles/from-identity-politics-to-academic-masturbation/; Mark Lilla, "The End of Identity Liberalism," *New York Times*, November 18, 2016, https://www.nytimes.com/2016/11/20/opinion/sunday/the-end-of-identity-liberalism.html; Michael K. Smith, "Class Dismissed:

16 *Introduction*

  Identity Politics without the Identity," *Counterpunch*, December 5, 2017, https://www.counterpunch.org/2017/12/05/class-dismissed-identity-politics-without-the-identity/; Vincent Emanuele, "The Curse and Failure of Identity Politics," *Counterpunch*, February 8, 2016, https://www.counterpunch.org/2017/12/05/class-dismissed-identity-politics-without-the-identity/.
5 One concern regarding the study of intersectionality in surveys is that various identity groups, for example, lower-income black women, represent a relatively small subsample within polls with only 1,000 or 2,000 people. To address this problem, survey firms provide "survey weights" to compensate for the under-sampling, and to provide more effective measures for public opinion related to small, under-represented demographic groups. I include survey weights in all my "regression" analyses, in my analyses of all intersectional identity groups discussed in this book.
6 Charles Tilly and Lesley J. Wood, *Social Movements: 1768–2008* (Boulder, CO: Paradigm Publishers, 2009); Donatella Della Porta and Mario Diani, *Social Movements: An Introduction* (Malden, MA: Wiley Blackwell Publishing, 2006); Riley E. Dunlap and Aaron M. McCright, "Social Movement Identity: Validating a Measure of Identification with the Environmental Movement," *Social Science Quarterly* 89, no. 5 (2008): 1045–1065; William A. Gamson, "Commitment and Agency in Social Movements," *Sociological Forum* 6, no. 1 (1991): 27–50; Anthony Oberschall, *Social Movements: Ideologies, Interests, and Identities* (Piscataway, NJ: Transaction Publishers, 1996).
7 Porta and Diani, *Social Movements*, 2006.
8 Tilly and Wood, *Social Movements*, 2009; Porta and Diani, *Social Movements*, 2006.
9 Porta and Diani, *Social Movements*, 2006; Charles Tilly and Sidney Tarrow, *Contentious Politics* (New York: Oxford University Press, 2015); Sidney Tarrow, *Power in Movement: Social Movements and Contentious Politics* (Cambridge: Cambridge University Press, 2011); Doug McAdam, Sidney Tarrow, and Charles Tilly, *Dynamics of Contention* (Cambridge: Cambridge University Press, 2001); Sidney Tarrow, *The Language of Contention: Revolutions in Words 1688–2012* (Cambridge: Cambridge University Press, 2013).
10 Oberschall, *Social Movements*, 1996.
11 Karl Marx and Friedrich Engels, *The Communist Manifesto* (New York: Bantam Classics, 1993).
12 Karl Marx, "A Critique of the German Ideology," *Marx/Engels Internet Archive*, 1845, https://www.marxists.org/archive/marx/works/download/Marx_The_German_Ideology.pdf.
13 Karl Marx, "A Contribution to the Critique of Political Economy," *Marx/Engels Internet Archive*, 1859, https://www.marxists.org/archive/marx/works/1859/critique-pol-economy/.
14 Terry Eagleton, *Why Marx Was Right* (New Haven, CT: Yale University Press, 2018); Bertell Ollmann, *Alienation: Marx's Conception of Man in a Capitalist Society* (Cambridge: Cambridge University Press, 1977); Terrell Carver, *The Cambridge Companion to Marx* (Cambridge: Cambridge University Press, 1991); Ernest Mandel, *Marxist Economic Theory* (New York: Monthly Review Press, 1971); August Nimtz, *Marx and Engels: Their Contribution to the Democratic Breakthrough* (Albany, NY: State University of New York Press, 2000); Shlomo Avineri, *The Social and Political Thought of Karl Marx* (Cambridge: Cambridge University Press, 1970); John McMurtry, *The Structure of Marx's World-View* (Princeton, NJ: Princeton University Press, 1971).

15 Gitlin, "The Left, Lost in the Politics of Identity," 1993; Hedges, "The Bankruptcy of the American Left," 2018; Dixon, "Intersectionality is a Hole," 2018; Vigo, "From Identity Politics to Academic Masturbation," 2018; Lilla, "The End of Identity Liberalism," 2016; Smith, "Class Dismissed: Identity Politics without the Identity," 2017; Emanuele, "The Curse and Failure of Identity Politics," 2016.
16 Friedrich Engels, "Engels to J. Bloch in Konigsberg," *Marx/Engels Internet Archive*, September 21, 1890, https://www.marxists.org/archive/marx/works/1890/letters/90_09_21.htm.
17 Friedrich Engels, "Engels to Conrad Schmidt in Berlin," *Marx/Engels Internet Archive*, October 27, 1890, https://www.marxists.org/archive/marx/works/1890/letters/90_10_27.htm.
18 Karl Marx, "The Eighteenth Brumaire of Louis Bonaparte," *Marx/Engels Internet Archive*, 1852, https://www.marxists.org/archive/marx/works/download/pdf/18th-Brumaire.pdf.
19 David Forgacs, ed. *The Antonio Gramsci Reader: Selected Writings 1916–1935* (New York: New York University Press, 2000).
20 Forgacs, *The Antonio Gramsci Reader*, 2000.
21 Forgacs, *The Antonio Gramsci Reader*, 2000.
22 Forgacs, *The Antonio Gramsci Reader*, 2000.
23 Forgacs, *The Antonio Gramsci Reader*, 2000.
24 Martin Gilens, *Affluence and Influence: Economic Inequality and Political Power in America* (Princeton, NJ: Princeton University Press, 2014); Martin Gilens and Benjamin Page, "Testing Theories of American Politics: Elites, Interest Groups, and Average Citizens," *Perspectives on Politics* 12, no. 3 (2014): 564–581; Daniel M. Butler, *Representing the Advantaged: How Politicians Reinforce Inequality* (Cambridge: Cambridge University Press, 2014); Nicholas Carnes, *White Collar Government: The Hidden Role of Class in Economic Policy Making* (Chicago: University of Chicago Press, 2013); Jacob S. Hacker and Paul Pierson, *Winner-Take-All Politics: How Washington Made the Rich Richer – and Turned its Back on the Middle Class* (New York: Simon & Schuster, 2011); Larry M. Bartels, *Unequal Democracy: The Political Economy of the New Guiled Age* (Princeton, NJ: Princeton University Press, 2010); Larry M. Bartels, Hugh Heclo, Rodney E. Hero, and Lawrence R. Jacobs, "Inequality and American Governance," in *Inequality in American Democracy: What We Know and What We Need to Learn*, eds. Theda Skocpol and Lawrence R. Jacobs (Thousand Oaks, CA: Sage Publications, 2005): 156–213; Thomas J. Hayes, "Responsiveness in an Era of Inequality: The Case of the U.S. Senate," *Political Research Quarterly* 66, no. 3 (2013): 585–99; Elizabeth Rigby and Gerald C. Wright, "Political Parties and Representation of the Poor in the American States," *American Journal of Political Science* 57, no. 3 (2013): 552–565; Jeffrey R. Lax and Justin H. Phillips, "The Democratic Deficit in the States," *American Journal of Political Science* 56, no. 1 (2012): 148–166.
25 Donatella Della Porta, *Social Movements in Times of Austerity* (Cambridge: Polity, 2015).
26 Henry Blumer, "Collective Behavior," in *New Outline of the Principles of Sociology*, Alfred M. Lee, ed. (New York: Barnes & Noble, 1951): 166–222; Robert Michels, *Political Parties: A Sociological Study of the Oligarchical Tendencies of Modern Democracy* (New York: Free Press, 1962); Mancur Olson, *The Logic of Collective Action: Public Goods and the Theory of Groups* (Cambridge, MA: Harvard University Press, 1971).

18 Introduction

27 Seymour Martin Lipset, *Union Democracy: The Inside Politics of the International Typographical Union* (New York: Free Press, 1977).
28 Robert Dahl, *Who Governs? Democracy and Power in an American City* (New Haven, CT: Yale University Press, 2005); Arthur Bentley, *The Process of Government: A Study of Social Pressures* (Hoboken, NJ: Transaction Publishers, 1995); Matt Grossmann, *The Not So Special Interests: Interest Groups, Public Representation, and American Governance* (Palo Alto, CA: Stanford University Press, 2012); Jeffrey M. Berry, *The New Liberalism: The Rising Power of Citizen Groups* (Washington D.C.: Brookings Institution Press, 1999); Eric Montpetit, *In Defense of Pluralism: Policy Disagreement and its Media Coverage* (Cambridge: Cambridge University Press, 2016).
29 See David B. Truman, *The Governmental Process: Political Interests and Public Opinion* (Berkeley, CA: University of California Press, 1993): ch. 2.
30 For classic works in the area of strain theory, see: Marx and Engels, *The Communist Manifesto*, 1993; Ted Robert Gurr, *Why Men Rebel* (New York: Routledge, 2011); Truman, *The Governmental Process*, 1993; James C. Davies, "Toward a Theory of Revolution," *American Sociological Review* 27, no. 1 (1962): 5–19; and Neil J. Smelser, *Theory of Collective Behavior* (New York: Free Press, 1965). For more recent works on strain theory, see: David Snow, Daniel Cress, Liam Downey, and Andrew Jones, "Disrupting the 'Quotidian': Reconceptualizing the Relationship between Breakdown and the Emergence of Collective Action," *Mobilization: An International Quarterly* 3, no. 1 (1998): 1–22; Robert S. Erikson and Laura Stoker, "Caught in the Draft: The Effects of Vietnam Draft Lottery Status on Political Attitudes," *American Political Science Review* 105, no. 2 (2011): 221–237; and Justin Gest, *The New Minority: White Working Class Politics in an Age of Immigration and Inequality* (New York: Oxford University Press, 2016).
31 Gurr, *Why Men Rebel*, 2011; Davies, "Toward a Theory of Revolution," 1962.
32 Gurr, *Why Men Rebel*, 2011: 24.
33 Chapter 2 of Truman's *The Governmental Process* does not explicitly say that disturbance theory leads to violence.
34 Bentley, *The Process of Government*, 1995; Truman, *The Governmental Process*, 1993.
35 John D. McCarthy and Mayer N. Zald, "Social Movement Organizations," in *The Social Movements Reader: Cases and Concepts*, eds. Jeff Goodwin and James M. Jasper (Malden, MA: Wiley Blackwell, 2015): 159–174.
36 McCarthy and Zald, "Social Movement Organizations," 2015.
37 Olson, *The Logic of Collective Action*, 1971.
38 Olson, *The Logic of Collective Action*, 1971: 161–162.
39 Floyd Hunter, *Community Power Structure: A Study of Decision Makers* (Chapel Hill, NC: University of North Carolina Press, 1969); C. Wright Mills, *The Power Elite* (New York: Oxford University Press, 2000); Theodore Lowi, *The End of Liberalism: Ideology, Policy, and the Crisis of Public Authority* (New York: W.W. Norton, 1969).
40 Adam J. Berinsky, *In Time of War: Understanding American Public Opinion from World War II to Iraq* (Chicago: University of Chicago Press, 2009); John R. Zaller, *The Nature and Origins of Mass Opinion* (Cambridge: Cambridge University Press, 1992); Gabriel S. Lenz, *Follow the Leader? How Voters Respond to Politicians Policies and Performance* (Chicago: University of Chicago Press, 2012); Scott L. Althaus, *Collective Preferences in Democratic Politics: Opinion Surveys and the Will of the People* (Cambridge: Cambridge University Press, 2003); Phillip Converse, "The Nature of Belief

Systems in Mass Publics," in *Ideology and Its Discontents*, ed. David E. Apter (New York: The Free Press, 1964): 206–261; Philip Converse, "Information Flow and the Stability of Partisan Attitudes," *Public Opinion Quarterly* 26, no. 4 (1962): 578–599; Gabriel Almond, *The American People and Foreign Policy* (Westport, CT: Praeger, 1965); James N. Rosenau, *Public Opinion and Foreign Policy* (New York: Random House, 1961); George F. Kennan, *American Diplomacy* (Chicago: University of Chicago Press, 1985).

41 Doug McAdam, *Political Process and the Development of Black Insurgency, 1930–1970* (Chicago: University of Chicago Press, 1999); Charles Tilly and Sidney Tarrow, *Contentious Politics* (New York: Oxford University Press, 2015); Sidney Tarrow, *Power in Movement: Social Movements and Contentious Politics* (Cambridge: Cambridge University Press, 2011); Doug McAdam, Sidney Tarrow, and Charles Tilly, *Dynamics of Contention* (Cambridge: Cambridge University Press, 2001); Michael T. Heaney and Fabio Rojas, *Party in the Street: The Antiwar Movement and Democratic Party after 9/11* (Cambridge: Cambridge University Press, 2015); Daniel Schlozman, *When Movements Anchor Parties: Electoral Alignments in American History* (Princeton, NJ: Princeton University Press, 2015).

42 Doug McAdam, John D. McCarthy, and Mayer N. Zald, eds., *Comparative Perspectives on Social Movements: Political Opportunities, Mobilizing Structurers, and Cultural Framings* (Cambridge: Cambridge University Press, 1996).

43 Manuel Castells, *The Power of Identity* (Malden, MA: Wiley Blackwell, 2010).

44 Kimberle Crenshaw, "Demarginalizing the Intersection of Race and Sex: A Black Feminist Critique of Antidiscrimination Doctrine, Feminist Theory, and Antiracist Politics," *University of Chicago Legal Forum* 140 (1989): 137–167; Kimberle Crenshaw, "Mapping the Margins: Intersectionality, Identity Politics, and Violence against Women of Color," *Stanford Law Review* 43, no. 6 (1991): 1241–1299; Alexander-Floyd Nikol, "Disappearing Acts: Reclaiming Intersectionality in the Social Sciences in a Post-Black Feminist Era," *Feminist Formations* 24, no. 1 (2012): 1–25; Angela Y. Davis, *Women, Race, and Class* (New York: Vintage, 1983); Evelyn Higginbotham, "African-American Women's History and the Metalanguage of Race," *Signs* 17, no. 2 (1992): 251–274; Patricia Hill Collins, "Learning from the Outsider within: The Sociological Significance of Black Feminist Thought," *Social Problems* 33, no. 6 (1986): S14–S32; Kimberly Springer, "The Interstitial Politics of Black Feminist Organizations," *Meridians: Feminism, Race, Transnationalism* 1, no. 2 (2001): 155–191; Patricia Hill Collins, *Black Feminist Thought: Knowledge, Consciousness, and the Politics of Empowerment* (New York: Routledge, 1990); Patricia Hill Collins and Sirma Bilge, *Intersectionality* (Cambridge: Polity, 2016); bell hooks, *Feminism Is for Everybody* (New York: Routledge, 2015); bell hooks, *Feminist Theory from Margin to Center* (New York: Routledge, 2015); Benita Roth, *Separate Roads to Feminism: Black, Chicana, and White Feminist Movements in America's Second Wave* (Cambridge: Cambridge University Press, 2004); Iris House, Inc., *History & Mission*, Bronx, New York, 1992; Julia S. Jordan-Zachery, *Shadow Bodies: Black Women, Ideology, Representation, and Politics* (New Brunswick, NJ: Rutgers University Press, 2017); Julia S. Jordan-Zachery, *Black Women, Cultural Images, and Social Policy* (New York: Routledge, 2010).

45 The Combahee River Collective, "A Black Feminist Statement," in *The Black Feminist Reader*, eds. Joy James and Tracy Denean Sharpley-Whiting (Malden, MA: Blackwell Publishers, 2000): 261–270.

46 The Combahee River Collective, "A Black Feminist Statement," 2000; Third World Viewpoint, "Challenging Capitalism and Patriarchy: Third World Viewpoint Interview with bell hooks," *Z Magazine*, December 1995: 36–39.
47 E.E. Schattsneider, *The Semisovereign People: A Realist's View of Democracy in America* (New York: Wadsworth Publishing, 1975); Andrew S. McFarland, *Neopluralism: The Evolution of Political Process Theory* (Lawrence, KS: University Press of Kansas, 2004).
48 Martin Gilens, *Affluence and Influence: Economic Inequality and Political Power in America* (Princeton, NJ: Princeton University Press, 2014); Martin Gilens and Benjamin I. Page, "Testing Theories of American Politics: Elites, Interest Groups, and Average Citizens," *Perspectives on Politics* 12, no. 3 (2014): 564–581; Benjamin I. Page and Martin Gilens, *Democracy in America: What Has Gone Wrong and What We Can Do about It* (Chicago, IL: University of Chicago Press, 2017). For a more detailed review of the plutocracy literature in Political Science, see Chapter 2.
49 Todd Gitlin, *The Whole World Is Watching: Mass Media in the Making and Unmaking of the New Left* (Berkley, CA: University of California Press, 1980); William Gamson, Bruce Fireman, and Steven Rytina, *Encounters with Unjust Authority* (Homewood, IL: Dorsey, 1982); Hank Johnston and John A. Noakes, eds., *Frames of Protest: Social Movements and the Framing Perspective* (Lanham, MD: Rowman & Littlefield, 2005).
50 For studies of media agenda setting, see: James W. Dearing and Everett M. Rogers, *Agenda-Setting* (Thousand Oaks, CA: Sage, 1996); Frank R. Baumgartner and Bryan D. Jones, *Agendas and Instability in American Politics*, 2nd edn. (Chicago, IL: Chicago University Press, 1993); John W. Kingdon, *Agendas, Alternatives, and Public Policies* (New York: Longman, 2003); Maxwell McCombs, *Setting the Agenda: Mass Media and Public Opinion* (Cambridge: Polity, 2014); and Shanto Iyengar and Donald R. Kinder, *News that Matters: Television and American Public Opinion* (Chicago, IL: University of Chicago Press, 2010). For studies of media priming, see: Shanto Iyengar, *Is Anyone Responsible? How Television Frames Political Issues* (Chicago, IL: University of Chicago Press, 1994); Dietram A. Scheufele and David Tewksbury, "Framing, Agenda Setting, and Priming: The Evolution of Three Media Effects Models," *Journal of Communication* 57, no. 1 (2007): 9–20; and Frank D. Gilliam and Shanto Iyengar, "Prime Suspects: The Influence of Local Television News on the Viewing Public," *American Journal of Political Science* 44, no. 3 (2000): 560–567.
51 Edward P. Morgan, *What Really Happened to the 1960s: How Mass Media Culture Failed American Democracy* (Lawrence, KS: University Press of Kansas, 2010).
52 Daniel Q. Gillion, *The Political Power of Protest: Minority Activism and Shifts in Public Policy* (Cambridge: Cambridge University Press, 2013).
53 Ruth Milkman, "A New Political Generation: Millennials and the Post-2008 Wave of Protest," *American Sociological Review* 82, no. 1 (2017): 1–31.
54 Frances Fox Piven and Richard A. Cloward, *Poor People's Movements: Why They Succeed, How They Fail* (New York: Vintage, 1977).
55 Morgan, *What Really Happened to the 1960s*, 2010.
56 Gillion, *The Political Power of Protest*, 2013.
57 Taeku Lee, *Mobilizing Public Opinion: Black Insurgency and Racial Attitudes in the Civil Rights Era* (Chicago, IL: University of Chicago Press, 2002).
58 Manfred B. Steger, James Goodman, and Erin K. Wilson, *Justice Globalism: Ideology, Crises, Policy* (Thousand Oaks, CA: Sage, 2013).

59 Deva R. Woodly, *The Politics of Common Sense: How Social Movements Use Public Discourse to Change Politics and Win Acceptance* (New York: Oxford University Press, 2015).
60 Weldon, *When Protest Makes Policy*, 2012.
61 Weldon, *When Protest Makes Policy*, 2012.
62 Gitlin, "The Left, Lost in the Politics of Identity," 1993.
63 Piven and Cloward, *Poor People's Movements*, 1977.
64 Francis Fox Piven, *Challenging Authority: How Ordinary People Change America* (Lanham, MD: Rowman & Littlefield, 2006).
65 Piven, *Challenging Authority*, 2006. For a second analysis of the abolition movement, see: Margaret E. Keck and Kathryn Sikkink, *Activists beyond Borders: Advocacy Networks in International Politics* (Ithaca, NY: Cornell University Press, 1998).
66 Sidney Tarrow, *The Language of Contention: Revolutions in Words 1688–2012* (Cambridge: Cambridge University Press, 2013); Charles J. Stewart, Craig Allen Smith, and Robert E. Denton Jr., *Persuasion and Social Movements* (Long Grove, IL: Waveland Press, 2012); Manuel Castells, *Networks of Outrage and Hope: Social Movements in the Internet Age* (Cambridge: Polity, 2015); Zeynep Tufekci, *Twitter and Tear Gas: The Power and Fragility of Networked Protest* (New Haven, CT: Yale University Press, 2018); Philip N. Howard and Muzammil M. Hussain, *Democracy's Fourth Wave? Digital Media and the Arab Spring* (New York: Oxford University Press, 2013).
67 Robert M. Entman, "Framing: Toward Clarification of a Fractured Paradigm," *Journal of Communication* 43, no. 4 (1993): 51–58; Robert M. Entman, *Projections of Power: Framing News, Public Opinion, and U.S. Foreign Policy* (Chicago: University of Chicago Press, 2003); Erving Goffman and Bennett Berger, *Frame Analysis: An Essay on the Organization of Experience* (Lebanon, NH: Northeastern University Press, 1986); Karen S. Johnson-Cartee, *News Narratives and News Framing: Constructing Political Reality* (Lanham, MD: Rowman & Littlefield, 2004); Maria Elizabeth Grabe and Erik Page Bucy, *Image Bite Politics: News and Visual Framing of Elections* (Oxford: Oxford University Press, 2009); Pippa Norris, ed., *Framing Terrorism: The News Media, the Government, and the Public* (New York: Routledge, 2003); Diana Kendall, *Framing Class: Media Representations of Wealth and Poverty in America* (Lanham, MD: Rowman & Littlefield, 2011); Mark Major, *The Unilateral Presidency and the News Media: The Politics of Framing Executive Power* (New York: Palgrave, 2014).
68 W. Lance Bennett, Steven Livingston, and Regina Lawrence, *When the Press Fails: Political Power and the News Media from Iraq to Katrina* (Chicago, IL: University of Chicago Press, 2007); Scott L. Althaus, Jill A. Edy, Robert M. Entman, and Patricia Phalen, "Revising the Indexing Hypothesis: Officials, Media, and the Libya Crisis," *Political Communication* 13, no. 4 (1996): 407–421; Daniel C. Hallin, *The Uncensored War: The Media and Vietnam* (New York: Oxford, 1986); Jonathan Mermin, *Debating War and Peace: Media Coverage of U.S. Intervention in the Post-Vietnam Era* (Princeton, NJ: Princeton University Press, 1999); John Zaller and Dennis Chiu, "Government's Little Helper: U.S. Press Coverage of Foreign Policy Crises, 1945–1991," *Political Communication*, 13, no. 4 (1996): 385–405; W. Lance Bennett, *News: The Politics of Illusion* (New York: Longman, 2006); Edward S. Herman and Noam Chomsky, *Manufacturing Consent: The Political Economy of the News Media* (New York: Pantheon, 2002); Robert W. McChesney, *Rich Media, Poor Democracy: Communication*

Politics in Dubious Times (New York: New Press, 1999); David Domke, *God Willing: Political Fundamentalism in the White House, the "War on Terror" and the Echoing Press* (Ann Arbor, MI: Pluto Press, 2004); Major, *The Unilateral Presidency and the News Media*, 2014; Danny Hayes and Matt Guardino, *Influence from Abroad: Foreign Voices, the Media, and U.S. Public Opinion* (Cambridge: Cambridge University Press, 2013); Scott A. Bonn, *Mass Deception: Moral Panic and the U.S. War on Iraq* (New Brunswick, NJ: Rutgers University Press, 2010); Brigitte L. Nacos, Yaeli Bloch-Elkon, and Robert Y. Shapiro, *Selling Fear: Counterterrorism, the Media, and Public Opinion* (Chicago, IL: University of Chicago Press, 2011).

69 Jules Boykoff, "Framing Dissent: Mass-Media Coverage of the Global Justice Movement," *New Political Science* 28, no. 2 (2006): 201–228; Jules Boykoff, *The Suppression of Dissent: How the State and Mass Media Squelch US American Social Movements* (New York: Routledge, 2006); Morgan, *What Really Happened to the 1960s*, 2010; Trevor Thrall, "The Myth of the Outside Strategy: Mass Media News Coverage of Interest Groups," *Political Communication* 23, no. 4 (2006): 407–420; Anthony DiMaggio, *When Media Goes to War: Hegemonic Discourse, Public Opinion, and the Limits of Dissent* (New York: Monthly Review Press, 2010); Andrew Rojecki, *Silencing the Opposition: Antinuclear Movements and the Media in the Cold War* (Champaign, IL: University of Illinois Press, 1999); David Croteau and William Hoynes, *By Invitation Only: How the Media Limit Political Debate* (Monroe, ME: Common Courage, 1994).

70 For the large literature covering the issue of pro-business and hegemonic biases in U.S. media, see the literature review chapter in: Anthony R. DiMaggio, *The Politics of Persuasion: Economic Policy and Media Bias in the Modern Era* (Albany, NY: State University of New York Press, 2017).

71 For the literature covering the issue of liberal bias in U.S. media, see the literature review chapter in DiMaggio, *The Politics of Persuasion*, 2017.

72 For the large literature covering the issue of a negative or bad news biases in U.S. media, see the literature review chapter in DiMaggio, *The Politics of Persuasion*, 2017.

73 For the literature on media pluralism, see the literature review chapter in DiMaggio, *The Politics of Persuasion*, 2017.

74 Jack Walker Jr., *Mobilizing Interest Groups in America: Patrons, Professions, and Social Movements* (Ann Arbor, MI: University of Michigan Press, 1991); Thrall, "The Myth of the Outside Strategy," 2006; Grossmann, *The Not So Special Interests*, 2012; Berry, *The New Liberalism*, 1999; Deana A. Rohlinger, *Abortion Politics, Mass Media, and Social Movements in America* (Cambridge: Cambridge University Press, 2014); Deepa Kumar, *Outside the Box: Corporate Media, Globalization, and the UPS Strike* (Champaign, IL: University of Illinois Press, 2007); Anthony R. DiMaggio, *The Rise of the Tea Party: Political Discontent and Corporate Media in the Age of Obama* (New York: Monthly Review Press, 2011); Michael Lipsky, "Protest as a Political Resource," *American Political Science Review* 62, no. 4 (1968): 1144–1158; Harvey Molotch, "Media and Movements," in *The Dynamics of Social Movements: Resource Mobilization, Social Control, and Tactics*, John D. McCarthy and Mayer N. Zald, eds. (Cambridge, MA: Winthrop, 1979): 71–93.

75 Scott G. McNall, *Cultures of Defiance and Resistance: Social Movements in 21st-Century America* (New York: Routledge, 2018).

76 I have not included some social movements, such as Antifa and the rise of the "Alt-Right" white supremacy movement, since these movements were

much smaller than the case studies examined in this text, although I agree that they are significant to the study of American politics and society. Other social movements, such as the gay and lesbian rights movement and the environmental movement, are heavily social in orientation, having to do with issues of human sustainability and equal rights, but not directly tied to the economic insecurity of the American public. Clearly, environmentalism is indirectly related to plutocracy, since environmental activists are driven by efforts to draw attention to climate change and fossil fuel interests' success in rolling back environmental regulations. But the environmental movement represents a particularly unique challenge, in that it is not a well-contained social movement, as are those examined throughout this book. Rather, the movement has developed in waves over the decades, rising and falling in relation to issues such as environmental pollution, protection of the ozone layer, opposition to nuclear power, and the fight against climate change, the latter of which persists across the decades. There is only so much space in any research project, and a full account of all modern social movements (unfortunately) is simply not possible.

77 The Tea Party can be included within scholar Isaac Martin's larger discussion of "Rich People's Movements," those committed to reinforcing the privilege and power of affluent white males and business elites, through the promotion of conservative and "free market" policies. See: Isaac William Martin, *Rich People's Movements: Grassroots Campaigns to Untax the One Percent* (New York: Oxford University Press, 2013). For more on conservative movements in defense of privilege, see: David R. Dietrich, *Rebellious Conservatives: Social Movements in Defense of Privilege* (New York: Palgrave, 2014); and Isaac William Martin, *The Permanent Tax Revolt: How the Property Tax Transformed American Politics* (Palo Alto, CA: Stanford University Press, 2008).

1 The Tea Party and the Rise of Right-Wing Rebellion

I present five main claims in this chapter. First, the Tea Party was an elitist movement and was concerned with enhancing corporate political power, displaying little concern with inequality or aiding disadvantaged groups. Tea Partiers' support for deregulation and tax cuts for the wealthy suggested they were committed to enhancing plutocracy. The Tea Party depended on organizing from the top down, with help from Republican candidates committed to a pro-business agenda.

Second, the Tea Party was not independent of the Republican Party, and it was not a *mass* movement.[1] This uprising was anemic compared to larger movements, including the 2003 anti-Iraq war protests and the anti-Trump protests. Local chapters were infrequently active, and the movement lacked enough grassroots participation to sustain itself over time.

Third, because the Tea Party was embraced by the Republican Party, it received extensive news attention. Social movements traditionally operate on the "outside" of politics looking in, influencing government indirectly by influencing discourse and public opinion, pressuring for change. But the Tea Party depended on support from Tea Party Republican candidates. Despite failing to become a mass movement, it pulled political discourse to the right, while cultivating support from the public.

Fourth, "identity politics" was central to the Tea Party, regarding its expressions of classism, racism, sexism, xenophobia, and Islamophobia. The Tea Party symbolized a rising conservative backlash against change. This was personified in its disruptive opposition to America's first black President – Barack Obama. Tea Party prejudice manifested itself through classism, sexism, and racism, and at the intersections of these identities. Tea Partiers were committed to intersectional sexism. Some scholars claim it "empowered" women, since many served in leadership positions in the movement. However, the Tea Party was committed to empowerment only among conservative white women. Liberal women and women of color were treated with hostility by a movement that embraced racial prejudice.

Finally, the Tea Party embraced a conservative backlash against demographic change. Tea Partiers felt the "real America" (as in conservative middle-class whites) was under assault from various "threats." They sought to spotlight the "dangers" posed by immigrants, the "drain" on societal resources resulting from "overly generous" welfare programs for "lazy" poor people of color, and the Muslim fifth column "threat."

Truman's disturbance theory depicts citizens as mobilizing when their perceived well-being is in danger. With the Tea Party, the disturbance was evident in its opposition to national demographic shifts. But the Tea Party's backlash populism was anemic due to the reluctance of sympathizers to sustain organizing efforts over time. Still, Tea Partiers benefitted from a favorable "political opportunity structure," with Republican officials adopting the "Tea Party" brand.[2]

The Tea Party's populism was *not* defined by economic insecurity, of which its supporters revealed little. Their anxiety was more general, lamenting the poor state of the economy under Obama. The Tea Party was defined by patriarchal, "white identity politics," serving as a precursor to the rise of Donald Trump's populist politics in 2016.[3] However, while Trump's supporters were strongly concerned with sociocultural issues, Tea Partiers were more focused on economics.

My findings are drawn from two sources. First, I provide personal reflections, based on my participant-observation in Tea Party events and meetings throughout the Chicago metro area in 2010. Since Illinois elected more Tea Party Republicans to office than any other state in the 2010 elections, it represents an ideal place for observing Tea Partiers. Second, I supplement my first-person reflections with survey data, demonstrating how my personal observations relate to national trends. I discuss how the movement impacted the news, and how sympathetic coverage impacted political discourse and public opinion.

A History of the Tea Party

The Tea Party was active from 2009 to 2010. Its members demonstrated in numerous cities, favoring conservative economic policies. They drew inspiration from the Boston Tea Party of 1773, when revolutionaries dumped tea into Boston Harbor in protest of British taxes under the banner of "no taxation without representation." This claim gained popularity with Tea Partiers who rejected Obama's economic policies.

The Tea Party was centered on a few personalities. One was Keli Carender, a conservative activist who called in February 2009 for Seattle residents to protest against the Democrats' stimulus bill, allocating hundreds of billions to revive the economy following the 2008 economic collapse.[4] Carender referred to the legislation as the "porkulus," drawing on criticisms of Congressional spending bills as laden with "pork" barrel spending projects.

Coinciding with Carender's protest was a "rant heard round the world" from *CNBC* analyst Rick Santelli on February 19, 2009, in which he called on the floor of the Chicago Mercantile Exchange for a Tea Party protest in Chicago.[5] Protesting "big government" policies, Santelli railed against allocating hundreds of billions of dollars to help families avoid foreclosure.[6] Santelli complained Obama was "promoting bad behavior" by helping "subsidize the losers' mortgages" following the housing market crash.[7] Santelli's position reflected that of many conservatives who blamed home owners for making poor financial decisions, rather than focusing on banks engaged in predatory lending.[8]

Shortly following Carender's and Santelli's statements, Tea Party protests began to emerge. On April 15, 2009, Tea Party events occurred in more than 200 cities, drawing tens of thousands of demonstrators.[9] In August 2009, Tea Party activists attended Democratic "town hall" meetings across the country, protesting against the Democrats' health-care reform.[10] These activists' opposition fueled critical media coverage of health-care reform.[11]

The Tea Party attracted high profile supporters, including former Republican House Majority Leader and *Freedom Works* Chairman Dick Armey, former Republican Alaskan Governor and vice-presidential candidate Sarah Palin, and media pundit Glenn Beck. Beck's September 2009 "9/12" rally drew on Tea Party support, attracting tens of thousands to Washington D.C., seeking to unite Americans as they came together after the September 11 terror attacks. The 9/12 project coincided with the September 12 "Taxpayer March on Washington," attended by various Tea Party activists. By 2010, the Tea Party emerged as a phenomenon in American politics. Its first national convention in Nashville in February drew national media attention, cementing the Tea Party as a political force. The Tea Party's second annual "Tax Day" protests occurred on April 15, drawing thousands of participants across 150 cities.[12]

The media referred to the Tea Party as social movement from 2010 onward.[13] But its grassroots elements dissipated by the end of 2010. Tea Party rallies no longer took place across many cities. The Tea Party was heavily reliant on top-down support from the Republican Party, media, and elite political groups, and once these actors had achieved their goal – returning Republicans to Congressional power – the movement quickly disappeared. Such is the nature of anemic, top-down populism.

Tea Partiers: What They Believed

Many polls were conducted to understand Tea Partiers' ideology, which was described by *Bloomberg News* as "Super Republican" because of its supporters' partisan leanings.[14] Tea Partiers were relatively affluent. The April 2010 *CBS–New York Times* national poll of Tea Party supporters showed they were more likely to come from middle-to-upper income backgrounds.[15] Tea Partiers were disproportionately white, male, middle-aged to older, Republican, conservative, college educated, married, Protestant, and regular church attenders. And they were more likely to represent these groups when compared to the public, with limited support from less privileged social groups.

My observations of Tea Partiers, supplemented by national polls, suggest they represented the far right, and were more conservative than the public on every political question surveyed in the April 2010 *CBS–New York Times* poll and the *Pew Research Center*'s March 2011 poll. The most commonly expressed goal of Tea Partiers was reducing the size of the federal government. Most (53 percent) said they were "angry" when describing their "feelings about the way things are going in Washington."[16] Tea Partiers' attendance of rallies spoke to their passion in protesting government. That passion manifested itself in anger against Obama. More than any other figure, his policies were criticized in the rallies and meetings I attended. Most Tea Partiers disapproved of Obama's job handling the economy, health care, and budget deficit.[17] Only a small minority approved of the Democrats' 2009 stimulus.[18]

Large majorities of Tea Party supporters preferred a "smaller government" with "fewer services." They agreed government is "wasteful and inefficient," and government regulation of business "does more harm than good." I met many protesters who felt the Democratic health-care reform would unfairly tax hard-working Americans and redistribute the benefits to poor people and illegal immigrants. At one Chicago rally, speakers railed against the "mental midgets" who run the party, who "confiscate" working Americans' incomes via taxes, spending them on the poor. In my time observing Tea Party rallies and meetings, I never heard anyone discuss inequality or poverty as serious problems.

Classism was apparent in surveys. Large majorities of Tea Partiers agreed "poor people have it easy because they get government benefits without doing anything in return," that "Obama's policies favor the poor," and that "government can't afford to do much more to help the needy." While 60 percent of Americans believed government should seek to reduce inequality in America, only 43 percent of Tea Party supporters felt the same.[19] Tea Partiers' conservative attitudes toward welfare were coupled with individualistic views of success in America. A large majority believed "most people who want to get ahead can make it if they're willing to work hard." With the notion that laziness was the primary impediment to success, three-quarters of Tea Partiers agreed "government benefits encourage the poor to remain poor."

Tea Partiers' call for limited government, however, was belied by most supporters' embrace of welfare programs from which they benefitted. Most agreed Medicare and Social Security are worth the cost. A majority agreed the taxes they paid were "fair," suggesting they were not anti-tax, but rather opposed to the poor. Programs for the poor were a waste, since they encouraged laziness. But Social Security and Medicare were worth it, since they benefitted Tea Partiers.

Tea Partiers demonstrated bias toward the wealthy. Most opposed raising taxes on those earning more than $250,000 a year to help Americans purchase health insurance via the "Affordable Care Act" (ACA). Most agreed Obama's policies favored the poor.[20] As I observed in Tea Party protests, this conclusion was driven by the ACA's provisions to expand Medicaid for the poor and provide assistance to working Americans purchasing insurance.

Tea Partiers were driven by an embrace of "free markets." A regular theme I observed during demonstrations was the notion that the government meddles in peoples' lives, stifling personal freedom and business innovation. Most Tea Partiers I spoke with, and most supporters in the April 2010 CBS–New York Times survey, refused to blame Wall Street for contributing to the 2008 economic meltdown and recession, and most said the economy would have recovered without the federal bank bailout. Most Tea Partiers polled said "Wall Street helps the economy more than it hurts it," and that "corporations make a fair and reasonable amount of profit." At Tea Party rallies, a "free market" approach was proclaimed, with placards reading: "No More Bailouts!" and "Give Me Liberty, Not Bailouts and Debt!"

Despite investment banks' role in creating the housing bubble by investing in complex financial instruments that fueled unsustainable lending, the Tea Party's "free market" politics led them to emphasize other targets. A plurality of Tea Partiers surveyed blamed Congress for the country's economic troubles.[21] One could blame Congress for deregulating the banking industry, enabling them to engage in risky financial housing investments. But to exempt Wall Street from blame meant Tea Partiers defended elite economic institutions that were the dominant symbol of American plutocracy.

Tea Partiers I conversed with insisted they opposed bailouts. But this position was limited as a measure of anti-establishment politics. While most Tea Partiers opposed the bailout, they embraced the discredited belief that markets operate efficiently without regulation. This belief was dealt a severe blow by the 2008 crash and the reckless investments pursued by Wall Street. The Tea Party's embrace of "free market" politics reveals it was not anti-establishment, but pro-Wall Street. The movement sought to enhance corporate power through business deregulation. Without regulations following the 2008 bailout, investment banks were free to create more economic bubbles via speculative investing, and could expect to be bailed out again by taxpayers, since they were deemed "too big to fail."

Finally, Tea Partiers demonstrated their commitment to pro-business policies via attacks on organized labor. A common theme I observed among Tea Partiers was a disdain for unions, which were seen as preventing corporations from remaining "competitive." One organizer encouraged activists to deride the Democratic Party for relying on unions, and to cultivate resentment against union members, who "earn more than you do" and "have a stranglehold" on Democratic politics. Most Tea Partiers polled held an unfavorable view of unions and a favorable view of corporations, believed that union workers benefitted from unfair advantages over non-union workers, agreed states should cut government employee pensions, and sided with businesses over unions in labor disputes.[22]

Tea Partiers' beliefs were well outside the mainstream.[23] A comprehensive review of economic attitudes across two-dozen questions surveyed by *Pew*, CBS, and the *New York Times* in their April 2010 and March 2011 surveys found that Tea Partiers' economic attitudes were outside the mainstream, and were more conservative than the public by double digits for 23 of the 24 questions. Some Tea Partiers were aware their beliefs fell outside the mainstream. In meetings I observed in Chicago, organizers told recruits that when activists canvassed neighborhoods during the 2010 election season, they should avoid references to the movement as Republican. One organizer said: "get them to embrace conservative positions on political issues, and they'll end up voting the right way without you telling them to vote Republican." Electoral candidates speaking at rallies consistently marketed the movement as non-partisan. Chicago Tea Party activists and leaders referred to themselves as "ordinary folks" who were concerned with good government. Many Tea Partiers concealed their political affiliations, contributing to the normalization of far-right politics in political discourse.

Tea Partiers did not care only about economics, but also embraced conservative social positions. A review of the 2010 *CBS–New York Times* and 2011 *Pew* surveys finds Tea Partiers were more conservative than the public on immigration, opposition to same-sex marriage, homophobia, abortion, and gun control laws, and in recognizing the institutional barriers that perpetuate racial inequality. In all, supporters of the Tea Party ranged from 7 to 27 percentage points more conservative than the public across 11 questions surveyed. Clearly, Tea Party hostility toward minorities was directed against those who were not white heterosexual conservatives. Right-wing social attitudes were tied to the movement's Christian contingent. Forty-two percent of Tea Party supporters identified with the "conservative Christian movement."[24] Most Tea Partiers saw the U.S. as a Christian, not secular, nation.[25]

Tea Party Bigotry?

Most Tea Partiers would probably disagree they were racist. Large majorities claimed blacks and whites have an equal chance of succeeding, denied that racial discrimination is why many blacks "can't get ahead," and that blacks who cannot "get ahead" are "responsible for their own condition." These views are not racist in the traditional sense, as are claims that minorities are inferior or less intelligent. But modern racism often works in subtler ways than in the past. Today, many express implicit forms of racism, such as refusing to recognize that societal institutions engage in racial discrimination.

As discussed in Chapter 3, the criminal justice system is marked by racial profiling, police brutality, and other forms of discrimination against people of color. Media perpetuate stereotypes against African Americans as disproportionately poor and criminal.[26] Educational institutions discriminate based on varied funding levels of schools, depriving poor minority communities of vital educational resources.[27] Banks are more likely to deny loans and job interviews to black applicants with comparable records to white applicants.[28] By denying these trends, Tea Partiers engaged in a type of racism – "color-blind racism" – manifested via willful ignorance to institutional discrimination.

Color-blind racism refers to beliefs that are derogatory against people of color expressed by those who do not see themselves as racist.[29] By refusing to recognize institutional racism and by attributing inequality to the "laziness" of minorities, color-blind racism is a subtler version of prejudice that perpetuates discrimination against people of color, while blaming the victims for their lot in life.

Racism within the Tea Party is not a new idea.[30] The Tea Party's embrace of white identity politics speaks to a reactionary backlash that operated at the intersections of various forms of prejudice. The racism of the Tea Party was captured via their refusal to recognize historic barriers to racial equality: 73 percent of Tea Partiers disagreed that "generations of slavery and discrimination have created conditions that make it difficult for blacks to work their way out of the lower-class," while an equal number agreed that "it's really a matter of some people not trying hard enough; if blacks would only try harder, they could be just as well off as whites."

Other metrics also revealed prejudice: 57 percent of Tea Partiers agreed blacks are not "trustworthy," while only 45 percent agreed blacks are "intelligent," and only 35 percent agreed blacks are "hardworking."[31] These results suggest significant openness to racial stereotypes from Tea Party supporters.

Some scholars place Tea Party racism at the center of their analyses. Parker and Barreto find the Tea Party was driven by opposition to growing racial and ethnic diversity.[32] Attacks on Muslims and unauthorized immigrants were common from what I observed among Chicago-area Tea Partiers. Much of the opposition to immigrants centered on "Obamacare" and claims that unauthorized immigrants take advantage of it, while draining taxpayer resources. Attacks on Muslims as a subversive threat were also common among Chicago Tea Partiers.

Despite these beliefs, Tea Partiers did not emphasize their reactionary social beliefs or place them on an equal footing with their economic attitudes. There was little effort among Chicago Tea Partiers to discuss white–black relations, gender-related issues, or homosexuality. Rather, the Tea Party agenda focused on the deficit, government spending, taxes, and social welfare. Tea Partiers' choice to emphasize economics over social issues, however, does not mean that the two can be separated. As I argue in this chapter, Tea Party prejudice operated at the intersection of classism and racism.

Selling the Apocalypse: The Tea Party's Conspiracy Politics

Tea Partiers embraced a variety of conspiracy theories. I commonly heard Chicago Tea Partiers engage in apocalyptic, end-times warnings about the end of the republic and the rise of authoritarianism. They conveyed the impression that the U.S. was in danger of collapsing into violence, chaos, and dictatorship. Tea Partiers' commitment to apocalyptic conspiracies often centered on Obama, via the perception that he was not a U.S. citizen. This point was expressed at Chicago rallies, on placards claiming Obama was born in Kenya and secretly a Muslim. Nationally, 30 percent of Tea Party adherents believed Obama was born in another country, and another 29 percent were unsure, meaning 59 percent fell into some version of the "birther" conspiracy.[33] Conservative media personalities such as Donald Trump, Sean Hannity, and Rush Limbaugh trafficked in alternate versions of the theory.

Bigotry was also apparent regarding attitudes toward Muslims. One Chicago Tea Party chapter I observed devoted workshops to discussing an all-encompassing threat of Muslims to national security, with special speakers and documentaries, and from alleged experts discussing the "threat" of Islam. These negative depictions were based on out-group stereotypes, since no Muslims were present at meetings.

Islamophobia was common nationally. Two-thirds of Republicans agreed in 2011 that Islamic values run contrary to American values.[34] A 2011 poll found 67 percent of Tea Partiers felt Islam is more violent than other religions.[35] The belief that Muslims are a fifth column threat is referred to as "Orientalism."[36] This prejudice is rejected in studies demonstrating the vast majority of Muslim Americans abhor violence, are patriotic, view American society positively, and are ideologically moderate.[37]

Tea Partiers' attitudes toward Muslims suggest a paranoid thinking that sees immigrants, non-Christians, and people of color as threats. This "paranoid style" of politics, as it was called by historian Richard Hofstadter, was applied to other "out-group" individuals, such as Obama, who did not fit the Tea Party profile of a white, middle-aged-to-older conservative.[38] In Obama, Tea Partiers found their ultimate foil. Demonizing the president, they combined fears endemic in white-identity politics. Attacks on Obama were defined by intersectional prejudice, combining classism, xenophobia, racism, and Islamophobia.

As a black, "closet Muslim" and "socialist" "foreigner," Obama's rise to political power embodied Tea Partiers' worst fears about "change."

Tea Partiers' susceptibility to conspiracy theories likely related to their heavy reliance on *Fox News*, right-wing talk radio, and far-right pundits such as Glenn Beck.[39] These sources trafficked in conspiracy theories, such as claims that "Obamacare" was a "government takeover" of health care, that Obama was not a U.S. citizen, and that he was socialist. As the April 2010 *CBS–New York Times* poll found, 92 percent of Tea Partiers believed "Obama's policies are moving the country more toward socialism."

One conspiracy among Tea Partiers was the belief that Obama was creating government "death panels" to deny care to the sick. This claim was wrong with respect to the ACA, which contained no such provision. The "death panels" claim was popularized when Republican Sarah Palin promoted it on Facebook, and it gained media attention. It caught on among Tea Partiers, who were already willing to believe the worst about Obama. As NPR reflected on the conspiracy: "The specter of 'death panels' became an instant rallying cry for the still-new Tea Party movement, whose supporters crowded into town hall meetings and shouted down Democratic lawmakers considering support for the ACA."[40]

Chicago-area Tea Partiers commonly referenced "death panels." Placards warning about the deteriorating quality of health care were routine at demonstrations. Meetings were dominated by discussions of health-care reform. One informational "town hall" session in the summer of 2010 sponsored by Tea Party Republican Congressional candidate Joe Walsh hosted panelists who warned about a government takeover of health care, while lamenting government "death panels."

Intersectional Identities: Tea Party Racism, Xenophobia, and Health-Care Protests

Tea Partiers were critical of demographic diversification and welfare policies assisting poor people of color. Prejudice among Tea Partiers was significantly associated with opposition to welfare policies such as "Obamacare." My analysis of *Pew*'s March 2011 survey finds that Tea Party supporters who agreed that immigrants are a "burden" on society were significantly more likely to oppose "Obamacare," as were Tea Partiers who agreed that "our country has made the changes needed to give blacks equal rights with whites." The predictive power of each variable listed in Figure 1.1 is measured on a scale from "0" to "1," with a "0" representing no association between each variable and opinions of health-care reform, and a "1" representing a perfect association. My analysis allows me to isolate the predictive power of each factor, while holding every other factor constant at its average value.[41]

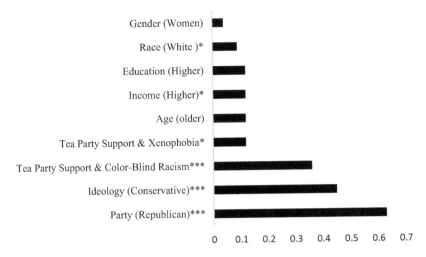

Figure 1.1 Opposition to Health Care Reform: Xenophobia and Color-Blind Racism

Source: *Pew Research Center*, March 2011 poll
Statistical Significance Levels: *** = 0.1% ** = 1% * = 5%
Controls: gender, age, education, race, income, political party, ideology

Color-blind racism, manifested in the erroneous belief that blacks and whites are treated equally in the U.S., mattered when it came to Tea Partiers' attitudes toward welfare policy. But it appeared to exert a stronger impact on opinions of "Obamacare" than did suspicion of immigrants. Xenophobia and color-blind racism were significant predictors of ACA attitudes, after controlling for respondents' party, ideology, age, income, education level, gender, and race.[42]

Truman's "disturbance theory" argued that citizens are more likely to organize due to perceived external threats to their well-being. For Tea Partiers, Obama's rise to power was a serious threat to conservative, white, Christian America. Obama symbolized a changing country, via the opening of the political establishment to people of color. Furthermore, Tea Partiers saw immigrants and people of color as taking advantage of the welfare system. These prejudices were apparent with the racial undertones characterizing Tea Partiers' resistance to "Obamacare."

Intersectional Sexism and the Tea Party

Some scholarship frames the Tea Party as dedicated to "conservative feminism," since many women played leadership roles in the movement.[43] Women in Tea Party groups felt empowered by pursuing their conservative and libertarian principles.[44] I observed women in prominent political roles throughout Chicago. I saw little evidence of overt sexism during my discussions with activists.

It is not surprising that women feel empowered in groups providing them with leadership positions. But with the Tea Party's opposition to government policies aimed at reducing gender inequality, referring to the movement as "feminist" is questionable. Feminism is historically defined by support for government action in fighting patriarchal societal institutions and behavior. But the Tea Party has no commitment to these positions, instead holding contempt for them.[45]

The "empowerment" narrative also selectively emphasizes the impact of some women – white, middle-to-upper-class conservative women – at the expense of less privileged groups. Tea Party activists I spoke with drew inspiration from conservative-Republican leaders like Michele Bachmann and Sarah Palin, but the movement also indulged in an intersectional sexism operating at the junction of gender, race, and ideology. Sexism emerged in attacks against specific groups of women from major movement figures such as Rush Limbaugh, who expressed contempt for politically active liberal-Democratic women and liberal women of color.

As I document later in this chapter, consumption of Limbaugh's radio program was a significant predictor of Tea Party support. Limbaugh held a symbolic position as a public face of the movement. His commitment to intersectional sexism demonstrates the role prejudice played in the Tea Party. Limbaugh is notorious for his attacks on liberal women, such as reproductive rights activist Sandra Fluke, who he claimed was a "slut" and "prostitute" who "wants to be paid for sex" after she advocated that insurance companies provide women with contraceptive coverage.[46] Limbaugh praised Sarah Palin for her Tea Party activism, but he also embraced misogyny by attacking liberal women like Fluke.

Limbaugh attacks liberal women as "feminazis," claiming that "feminism allows unattractive women access to the mainstream of society."[47] He denigrates female journalists writing for "liberal" outlets as "infobabes," and attacked black Democratic woman Carol Mosely Braun – the first black woman elected to the U.S. Senate – by drawing on stereotypical racial imagery from "The Jeffersons" television program depicting Braun as "movin' on up" by raising the profile of black women.[48] Limbaugh depicts black women as exotic, foreign others in their dress and eating habits.[49] Many Tea Partiers – 44 percent of movement supporters, and 39 percent of Tea Party women – were followers of Limbaugh's radio program.[50] And Tea Party women were significantly more likely than other Americans to listen to Limbaugh's program, after controlling for respondents' political party, ideology, age, education, income, and race.[51] Their willingness to follow him despite his misogynist behavior reveals a tolerance for sexism against liberal women.

The failure to recognize sexism within the Tea Party speaks to the limits of mainstream social science. This silence on intersectional sexism speaks to a hegemonic bias in higher education, in which white women hold the dominant position in the study of politics and identity.

Media and Scholarly Discourse on the Tea Party

Scholars emphasize how citizens groups and movements use the media to amplify their messages, cultivating support from the public.[52] Some research claims the Tea Party received favorable coverage; some suggests coverage varied depending on the news outlet.[53] It helped that the Tea Party received support from Republican officials and "citizens" groups such as "Freedom Works" and "Americans for Prosperity," which are funded by business interests. Groups with greater financial resources receive more media attention.[54] And with the official source bias in the news, movements with a significant top-down component like the Tea Party draw significant attention. Scholars argue that a major predictor of movement success is the extent to which activists benefit from openings within the political system to further their interests.[55] The Tea Party used Republican support to gain saturation-level media attention. With dozens of Congressional candidates claiming the Tea Party brand, the movement became an "inside" lobbying political force, while adopting an "outside" protest strategy.[56]

Media support for the Tea Party was widespread. The *New York Times* coverage was sympathetic to the movement. The paper amplified Tea Party positions, including claims that the movement was grassroots, decentralized, non-partisan, and driven by economic anxieties:

> The Tea Party movement has become a platform for conservative populist discontent ... At the grass-roots level, it consists of hundreds of autonomous Tea Party groups, widely varying in size and priorities, each influenced by the peculiarities of local history ... The ebbs and flows of the Tea Party ferment are hardly uniform. It is an amorphous, factionalized uprising with no clear leadership and no centralized structure.

The paper described Tea Partiers with "families upended by lost jobs, foreclosed homes and depleted retirement funds" who "wanted to know why it happened and whom to blame."[57] The *Washington Post* depicted the Tea Party as "noisy" and "anti-government," and "preparing to shake up the 2010 elections by channeling money and supporters to conservative candidates set to challenge both Democrats and Republicans."[58] The paper reported: "many gave voice to their outrage in nearly identical phrasing, complaining about Obama's efforts to 'redistribute wealth' [and] about the 'offshoring' of U.S. jobs."[59] *Time* magazine wrote: "At a time of historic economic insecurity, the Tea Party movement has stolen the hearts of conservatives."[60]

Conservative pundits argued the Tea Party was a "mainstream" movement with mass appeal.[61] Pollsters claimed it was "one of the most powerful and extraordinary movements in recent American history," and "potentially strong enough to elect senators, governors, and congressmen."[62] They dismissed as "obviously false" claims that it was "just an adjunct to the Republican Party," and that it "represents a bunch of right wing extremists and racists ... despite ample evidence that Tea Party members are part of the American mainstream."[63]

Progressives also sought to appeal to the movement. An article in *The Nation*, "How to Talk to a Tea Party Activist," sought "common ground" with the movement: "Many participants have seen their personal economic security devastated by the economic meltdown. They are worried about their tax bills, national debt, and the economy their children will inherit. They feel isolated and the Tea Party is a community."[64] *The Nation* advocated that progressives work with Tea Partiers to "build a broad-based coalition for economic change."[65]

Scholars depicted the Tea Party as an independent force, as a "conservative populist movement" that had a significant "influence" on the 2010 midterms.[66] It transcended partisan motivations: "Their goal was not to give the Republicans a majority but to elect people who stood for what they believe in."[67] The movement was "anti-government" – displaying "fierce independence" and "anti-elite sentiment."[68] The Tea Party was eclectic: "Considered in its entirety," it "is neither a top-down creation nor a bottom-up explosion," instead including a "grassroots" element of "energized" and "angry, conservative-minded citizens," a conglomeration of "national funders and ultra-free market advocacy groups that seek to highlight and leverage grassroots efforts to further their long-term goal of remaking the Republican Party"; and an array of "conservative media-hosts who openly espouse and encourage the cause."[69] Other scholarship claimed that financial insecurity in predominantly white neighborhoods produced greater Tea Party support, suggesting the movement represented poorer whites.[70]

A review of media coverage using the *Nexis Uni* database, and including broadcast news, national print, cable news, and radio sources, suggests the Tea Party benefitted from a large volume of favorable coverage. It garnered significant attention in the news relative to other protests and social movements, and journalists emphasized its concerns as an authentic populist revolt. Table 1.1 shows the Tea Party appeared daily in each news outlet examined, ranging from a low of one story per day on *CBS News* to eight segments on *CNN*. Regardless of venue, the Tea Party was a fixture of reporting.

Table 1.1 also documents Tea Party coverage compared to other movements. It tallies the total articles in the *New York Times* covering

Table 1.1 The Tea Party and the News Media

The Tea Party's Salience in the News (4/15–12/31/2010)

News organization	# of stories per day	# stories per month
New York Times	4.5	135
ABC News	1.2	36
CBS News	0.9	27
NBC News	1.3	39
NPR	2	60
Fox News	4.1	123
CNN	7.9	237
MSNBC	2.8	84

Comparing New York Times *Coverage of the Tea Party to Other Movements*

Protest movement	# of stories per month	# Congressional references to movement per month
Tea Party (4/15–12/31/2010)	135	8.5
Tea Party (2011)	120	36.3
Madison Labor Protests (2/14–3/31/2011)	33	2
Occupy Wall Street (9/17–12/31/2011)	324	9.7
Occupy Wall Street (2012)	57	1.3
Black Lives Matter (2015)	27	1.7
Black Lives Matter (2016)	75	1.9
Black Lives Matter (2017)	54	1
Fight for $15 (2015)	3	.3
Fight for $15 (2016)	3	0

Source: *Nexis Uni* academic database

the Tea Party from April 2010, during the height of the movement's activism via "tax day" rallies across the country, through December 2010, after the midterm elections, and from January through December 2011, when the Tea Party became a force in Congress. The Tea Party was covered more often than the Madison protests, Black Lives Matter (BLM), and Fight for $15. It received less coverage than Occupy Wall Street (Occupy) did in late 2011, although more coverage than Occupy did in 2012. In sum, simplistic notions of the "liberal media" downplaying conservative movements, while prioritizing left-wing ones, are unsubstantiated. The Tea Party received more attention than most left movements did in the 2010s.

Movements are more likely to succeed when they exploit supportive elements of the political structure. If a major party favors a movement, it is likely to receive more news attention. The Tea Party, supported by Republican elites, cultivated more coverage than movements with less party support. I measure political support by analyzing Congress' attention to each movement, via the Congressional Record's database of legislator statements on the House and Senate floors.[71] In Table 1.1, of the five periods in which Congress paid greatest attention to a movement, the Tea Party was the first and third most discussed. Similarly, the Tea Party received the second and third most news coverage of all movements examined. The Tea Party in 2010 and 2011, Occupy in 2011, and Madison in 2011 were the most likely movements to be discussed in Congress, and were four of the five most heavily covered movement periods. In contrast, BLM (2015 and 2017) and Fight for $15 (2015–2016) received the least attention from Congress and were four of the five least covered movements.

As I document in Chapter 3, BLM, despite being much more active over a longer period than the Tea Party, received much less news attention. And as I find in Chapter 2, Fight for $15, despite attracting thousands of protesters and tens of millions of supporters, was not embraced by either major party, and struggled to attract media attention. BLM, at least initially, resided outside the ideological boundaries of Democratic politics, attracting little attention from Democrats until after high-profile protests in Ferguson and Baltimore. In contrast, the Tea Party was linked to establishment politics, and was discussed alongside references to the Republican Party in 69 percent of the *New York Times* articles covering the movement in 2010, and 71 percent in 2011. The findings here and in coming chapters suggest that progressive movements have a harder time attracting coverage than rightist movements, as the former often reside outside the ideological boundaries of the two-party system.

One might argue the cause and effect relationship between government and media attention is reversed. That is, increased media attention to movements causes political leaders to pay greater attention to them, and to talk about them more in the House and Senate. But there is no apparent reason why reporters would pay more attention to some movements than others. Why pay more attention to the Tea Party and Occupy than Fight for $15 and BLM, when the latter two saw participation by larger numbers of activists over longer periods? Alternatively, an official source bias explains the observed coverage of the Tea Party.[72] Rather than the greater "newsworthiness" of some movements over others, journalistic deference to government voices explains why Occupy and the Tea Party were privileged over other movements.

Salience counts reveal much about coverage of movements, but they do not reveal how movements are framed. To measure how sympathetic the media were to the Tea Party, I analyzed "positive" and "negative" frames, with positive references discussing it as "grassroots," "populist," a "movement," as a "rebellion" or an "uprising." These terms emphasize the Tea Party as a bottom-up, mass phenomenon. In contrast, media coverage was negative if it criticized the Tea Party, including references to the movement as "Astroturf," "extremist," "racist," "right-wing," or "reactionary." These classifications depict the Tea Party as fake, prejudiced, and extremist.

Additional measures assessed coverage of Tea Partiers' grievances, including:

- a "health-care" frame, with references to the Tea Party and "Obama-care," health-care reform, or the ACA;
- a "tax" frame, with references to concerns with taxes or tax cuts;
- a "libertarian" frame, with discussion of "small government," the "free market," opposition to the 2008 bailout, or concerns about "big government" "spending";
- an "economic distress" frame, with references to concerns about "jobs," "free trade" and "outsourcing," the post-2008 "recession," "inequality," or "economic insecurity."[73]

Table 1.2 demonstrates that coverage was sympathetic to the movement. Positive frames were present in most of the articles and segments in every outlet examined. In all but one outlet, positive framing appeared in two-thirds to more than three-quarters of articles. Negative framing was less frequent. In only two outlets, *CNN* and *MSNBC*, did negative frames appear in most segments. Negative pieces appeared between a quarter to less than half of the time for seven of nine outlets. Additionally, other research finds positive characteristics of reporting. References to the Tea Party as an independent force fighting the "Republican establishment" appeared in two dozen to five dozen articles per month for each outlet, or in one to two pieces per day.[74] The health-care frame was common, appearing in a third to three-quarters of pieces for eight of the nine outlets, and in most articles for three of nine outlets. The tax frame appeared a third to three-quarters of the time in eight of nine outlets, and most of the time in four of nine outlets. Libertarian themes were present from a third to three-quarters of the time in eight of nine news outlets, and more than half the time in four of nine outlets. The economic distress frame was the least frequent, never appearing most of the time in any of the outlets. In summary, although coverage varied, the Tea Party benefitted from a large volume of positive attention.

When most information Americans receive is filtered through the media, journalists have significant power over mass discourse. Most Americans were unlikely to be in contact with a Tea Party protester in 2010. Only

Table 1.2 Framing the Tea Party in the News (4/1–11/30/2010)

News Outlet	Positive Frames (% of all stories appearing in)	Negative Frames (% of all stories appearing in)	Health Care Frame (% of all stories appearing in)	Tax Frame (% of all stories appearing in)	Libertarian Frame (% of all stories appearing in)	Economic Distress Frame (% of all stories appearing in)
New York Times	78	24	33	34	39	15
Associated Press	81	20	33	35	43	16
ABC News	82	18	18	19	27	14
CBS News	55	39	41	52	64	20
NBC News	77	24	17	35	39	14
NPR	77	27	32	31	46	13
Fox News	67	43	54	59	63	16
CNN	74	53	51	57	66	19
MSNBC	75	78	75	78	77	31

Source: Lexis Nexis academic database

a small number of Americans engaged in such activities. Due to positive coverage, those paying closer attention to the news should be more likely to hold favorable opinions of the movement. This expectation is validated in the June and September 2010 *Pew* surveys, for which I generated statistical values to measure the power of various factors in predicting support for the Tea Party.[75] Statistical findings fall on a scale from "0" to "1," with "0" suggesting no relationship between attention to the Tea Party and support, while a "1" suggests a perfect relationship. Figure 1.2 shows the power of each factor in predicting support for the Tea Party, after statistically controlling for other factors listed. Partisanship and ideology were the strongest predictors of support, although attention to the Tea Party in the news was significant as well. The relationship between media consumption and Tea Party support was statistically significant, after controlling for the other factors in Figure 1.2.[76]

Pew's March 2011 poll surveyed Americans about other media consumption habits, including attention to conservative sources such as Rush Limbaugh's radio program, Glenn Beck's program on *Fox News*, and *Fox News*. Conservative media consumption was significantly associated with Tea Party support. As can be seen in Figure 1.3, consumption of Limbaugh's and Beck's programs and *Fox News*, although not as powerful in predicting Tea Party support as ideology, were more powerful than party, age, income, gender, race, and education.[77] These results suggest that positive Tea Party coverage was instrumental in spreading the movement's message.

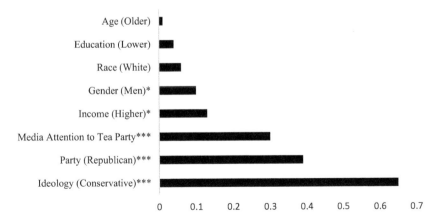

Figure 1.2 Media Consumption and Tea Party Support
Source: *Pew Research Center*, June 2010 poll
Statistical Significance Levels: *** = 0.1% ** = 1% * = 5%
Controls: gender, age, education, race, income, political party, ideology

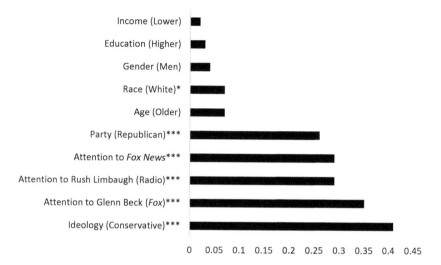

Figure 1.3 Tea Party Support and Right-Wing Media Consumption
Source: *Pew Research Center*, March 2011 poll
Statistical Significance Levels: *** = 0.1% ** = 1% * = 5%
Controls: gender, age, education, race, income, political party, ideology

Challenging Conventional Wisdom on the Tea Party

Tea Party boosters claimed it was independent of partisan politics, mainstream, populist, a reflection of economic insecurity, and a grassroots rebellion against political elites. But these claims were exaggerated or inaccurate. My examination of Tea Party supporters' beliefs demonstrated they were *not* mainstream, but well to the right of the public. Furthermore, partisanship was a core component driving Tea Party support.[78] *Pew's* September 2010 poll allows for an examination of which factors were most strongly associated with Tea Party support. In Figure 1.4, I analyze the power of each factor, after controlling for all factors listed, in predicting Tea Party support.

A preference for Republican candidates to win the 2010 elections and respondents' ideology were the dominant factors accounting for Tea Party support. This contradicts the claim that Tea Partiers were independent of the Republican Party, or that they valued ideology more than winning elections. Both factors were equal considerations. Most Republicans who ran in the 2010 midterms were *not* Tea Partiers, demonstrating that Tea Partiers were happy to vote Republican, even when the candidate did not embrace the movement.

What about claims that the Tea Party was a mass movement? It seems clear that the Tea Party was a social movement. Estimates suggest that

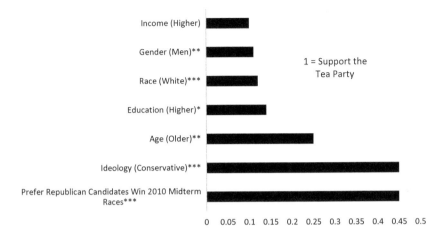

Figure 1.4 Tea Party Support: Republican Electoral Motivations
Source: *Pew Research Center*, September 2010 poll
Statistical Significance Levels: *** = 0.1% ** = 1% * = 5%
Controls: gender, age, education, race, income, political party, ideology

membership across local chapters ranged from a low of 67,000 nationally to a quarter of a million.[79] Active members were estimated at 160,000, with more than 160 chapters holding meetings, with members attending rallies, contacting officials, giving campaign donations, and working on Republican campaigns.[80] But these numbers are radically lower than the size of the Tea Party, as depicted in the media. Thirteen percent of Tea Party supporters claimed to be actively attending meetings or rallies. But out of a country (in 2010) of 235 million adults, with 18 percent (42 million people) claiming to be Tea Party supporters, and 13 percent of those supporters claiming to be active in the party, this would mean nearly 5.5 million protesters.[81] A review of local chapters showed active participation in the movement was radically lower, reaching a maximum of a quarter of a million people. If 5.5 million claimed to be active, compared to actual findings of 160,000 to 250,000, this suggests an exaggeration of activism 22 to 34 times over. Exaggeration was also evident in estimates of chapter activity. Twenty-one percent of Americans said the Tea Party was "active" in their community.[82] But with just over 160 active chapters and 804 Tea Party groups with some web presence, compared to more than 19,000 municipalities in the U.S., Americans' estimates of Tea Party activity were severely exaggerated.[83] Based on the above numbers, the number of Tea Party groups represented just 4 percent of all municipalities, with active chapters representing less than 1 percent of municipalities.

Other data reinforce the above findings on the inflated nature of the movement. The 2009 and 2010 tax day rallies saw participation in the thousands or tens of thousands, not millions.[84] Tea Party turnouts paled in comparison to real mass movements. The 2003 anti-war movement was global in its structure, and attracted 10 to 15 million people protesting the invasion of Iraq.[85] Protests of Donald Trump's inauguration in January 2017 occurred in approximately 550 cities, attracting 3 to 5 million people.[86]

Although the Tea Party included a few hundred thousand members, my observation of local chapters found movement activism was anemic. Activists exhibited little interest in regular meetings. Participation in national conventions was weak to non-existent. The Tea Party's February 2010 national convention had just 600 attendees.[87] And in the run-up to the 2010 midterms, the Tea Party convention in Las Vegas was cancelled due to low interest.[88] Support for the Tea Party collapsed overnight following the 2010 elections, suggesting the movement was driven by short-term electoral concerns. This electoral focus was conceded by Chicago organizers with whom I spoke, and was confirmed in polls demonstrating that the goal of electing Republicans was the main driver of Tea Party support.

Why did the Tea Party disappear so quickly following the midterms? Investigations of the movement provided an answer: its supporters were never strongly committed to activism. Most got their information about the Tea Party from the media – especially from *Fox News* – not from attending rallies.[89] In canvassing "hundreds of local Tea Party groups," the *Washington Post* "reveal[ed] a different sort of organization" than commonly portrayed – "one that is not so much a movement as a disparate band of vaguely connected gatherings that do surprisingly little to engage in the political process." The report found little evidence of Tea Partiers committed to campaigning for candidates, as they remained disinterested in direct action geared at influencing politics.[90]

My observations of the Chicago area revealed similar findings to the *Post*'s. Few municipalities formed chapters. The ones that did suffered from weak meeting turnouts, and a common complaint from organizers was the lack of active members outside of individuals signing up for email listservs. One local Chicago leader boasted having more than 1,000 members in his chapter, but perhaps a dozen attended planning meetings. One organizer for this local bragged that, through the listserv, he "generated a lot of noise" through "email blasts," but that he was stepping down from his leadership role due to lack of interest in face-to-face meetings.

In my Chicago case study, rallies were also characterized by elitism and anemic participation. Most speakers were not local organizers or chapter members, but Republican candidates. Attendance rates were thin. Despite Chicago being the birthplace of the Tea Party, only about 2,000 Tea Partiers attended the April 2010 tax day rally in downtown Chicago. By comparison, the anti-Trump protests in January 2017 in Chicago saw an estimated 150,000-person turnout. The problems of Chicago were apparent across other cities where Tea Party chapters organized. My review of more than 150 local chapters that participated in a tax day rally in April 2010 found that 92 percent displayed no evidence of regular meetings – defined as at least one meeting a month, for two consecutive months – in 2010.

If Tea Party activism was anemic locally, this was not the case nationally. Numerous Tea Party umbrella organizations operated, many funded by business interests. The Koch brothers, billionaire industrialists from Texas, became infamous for funding national Tea Party groups. *Americans for Prosperity* and *Freedom Works* spoke for the Tea Party in national media, and these groups received much of their funding from business interests. Their leadership role in the Tea Party was spotlighted by critics viewing the movement as Astroturf.[91]

What Motivated the Tea Party? Socio-Cultural Versus Economic Attitudes

Portrayals from the media and scholars depicted Tea Party supporters as frustrated due to mounting financial insecurity. But not everyone agreed this was a motivating factor. Parker and Barreto argued the movement was a function of white rage at a changing America:

> people are driven to support the Tea Party from the anxiety they feel as they perceive the America they know, the country they love, slipping away, threatened by the rapidly changing face of what they believe is the 'real' America: a heterosexual, Christian, middle-class, (mostly) male, white country."[92]

Tea Partiers "wish[ed] to turn the clock back" to when people of color, Muslims, women, immigrants, and gay and lesbian Americans had not yet asserted themselves in fighting for equal rights.[93] Reactionaries have long opposed equality for disadvantaged groups. In this sense, Parker and Barreto argue, the Tea Party is "nothing new," but "an extension of right-wing movements of the past."[94] They find that Tea Partiers' beliefs were driven by stereotypes, anxiety, fear, and paranoia against minority groups.[95] Obama's election was a watershed moment that sparked the Tea Party and its opposition to demographic "change." This change, Tea Partiers believed, meant "the erosion" of their "social position," and "the displacement of the white, Christian, male-dominated, native-born Americans."[96] Parker and Barreto document the rise of conspiratorial rhetoric on Tea Party-affiliated websites, and find that Tea Partiers held negative views toward illegal immigrants and racist beliefs.[97]

I provided evidence that racism and xenophobia were underlying Tea Partiers' opposition to health-care reform. Most Tea Partiers embraced racism toward blacks, classism against the poor, homophobia, xenophobia, and Islamophobia. These results validate Parker and Barreto's claims that Tea Partiers held prejudiced attitudes.

But the Tea Party was driven by more than social prejudice. They were also motivated by far-right economic values. And contrary to media claims, Tea Partiers were not generally economically disadvantaged or significantly harmed by free trade. The movement's supporters were largely middle- to middle-upper-class, and had little interest in state assistance for the needy.

Economic attitudes were more prominent drivers of Tea Party support than socio-cultural attitudes. Tea Partiers felt "economic issues like taxes and jobs" were more important than "social issues like abortion and same-sex marriage." Seventy-eight percent of Tea Partiers preferred to focus on economic issues; only 14 percent were interested primarily in social issues.[98] My examination of numerous polls from *Pew* in 2010 and 2011 confirms this conclusion. I measured the strength of associations between various social and political-economic attitudes and Tea Party support. A value of "0" suggests no relationship between an attitude and Tea Party support, while "1" suggests a perfect relationship.

The September 2010 *Pew* poll included economic attitudes concerning corporations, size of government, health care, government spending, and perceived opportunities for societal advancement. In Figure 1.5, we see that economic concerns were consistently significant predictors of Tea Party support, including: agreement that most corporations make reasonable profits, opposition to the ACA, support for smaller government providing fewer services, and agreement that government is wasteful and inefficient.

In contrast, social attitudes were weaker or insignificant in predicting Tea Party support, including: disagreement with claims that the U.S. is marred by racial inequality, opposition to same-sex marriage, and feelings that immigrants are a societal burden. Other significant predictors of support include approval of the Iraq war and anger at the government, which for Tea Partiers was linked to opposition to government spending. Only one social position – opposition to gun regulation – was a significant predictor of Tea Party support, and this attitude has little directly to do with racial prejudice.

Subsequent survey data provides for similar findings. In the February 2011 *Pew* survey represented in Figure 1.6, only one social attitude – support for an Arizona immigration law empowering local police to detain undocumented immigrants – was a significant predictor of Tea Party support. The other three significant predictors were economic, including: unfavorable attitudes toward unions; support for cutting state

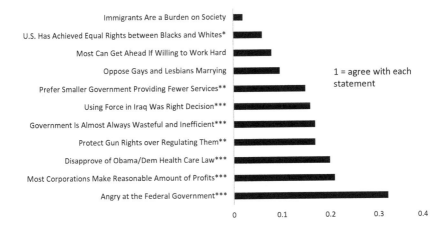

Figure 1.5 Attitudinal Predictors of Tea Party Support: Economic Policy, Foreign Policy, and Social Attitudes
Source: *Pew Research Center*, September 2010 poll
Statistical Significance Levels: *** = 0.1% ** = 1% * = 5%
Controls: gender, age, education, race, income, political party, ideology

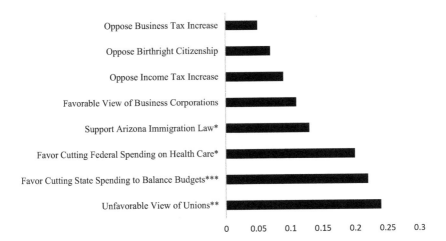

Figure 1.6 Attitudinal Predictors of Tea Party Support: Immigration v. Political-Economic Factors
Source: *Pew Research Center*, February 2011 poll
Statistical Significance Levels: *** = 0.1% ** = 1% * = 5%
Controls: gender, age, education, race, income, political party, ideology

spending to balance budgets; and support for cutting federal spending on health care. Agreement that birthright citizenship should be repealed for undocumented immigrants' children was not associated with Tea Party support.

The March 2011 *Pew* survey included additional measures of public opinion, shown in Figure 1.7. Concerns driving Tea Partiers were primarily economic. Significant predictors of Tea Party support included: a preference for smaller government with fewer services, agreement that reducing the federal deficit is a top priority, and the feeling that Wall Street helps the economy more than it hurts it. Social attitudes were weaker predictors of support, including opposition to a path to citizenship for unauthorized immigrants, preference for stronger border enforcement, and the feeling that same-sex couples raising children harms society. In contrast, social attitudes about inter-racial marriage and dislike of non-Christians were not significant predictors of Tea Party support. The findings from these surveys suggest that both social and economic attitudes accounted for Tea Party support, although economic factors were stronger.

The conclusion that economic factors primarily drove Tea Party support is further validated by Figure 1.2 and the September 2010 *Pew* poll, with gender and race being weaker predictors of support. If the Tea Party was primarily driven by concern with demographic change and social issues, we might expect respondents' gender and race to be more powerful predictors of support. But this is not the case. The Tea Party was not primarily defined by racial or gender-based characteristics.[99]

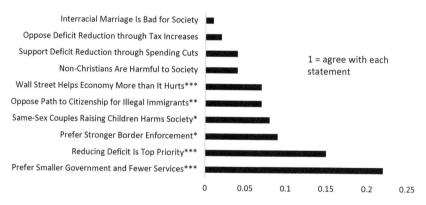

Figure 1.7 Attitudinal Predictors of Tea Party Support: Economic and Socio-Cultural Factors

Source: *Pew Research Center*, March 2011 poll
Statistical Significance Levels: *** = 0.1% ** = 1% * = 5%
Controls: gender, age, education, race, income, political party, ideology

The Tea Party and the Right-Wing Rebellion 49

What about claims that Tea Party support was motivated by growing economic anxiety? A review of *Pew*'s survey questions reveals little evidence that Tea Partiers were motivated by economic insecurity. In two of the six surveys examined from June 2010 through March 2011, there was no link between income and support for the Tea Party. In the other surveys, higher-income Americans were more likely to embrace the movement. For measures of employment status appearing in two of the surveys (September and December 2010), unemployment was unrelated to Tea Party support. Additionally, Tea Partiers described their economic situations positively. Seventy-eight percent described their "financial situation" as "very" or "fairly good," compared to 73 percent of all Americans.[100] Other measures of insecurity were also not associated with Tea Party support, including:

- worries about "problems" in "financial and housing markets" (9/2010);
- worries about "rising prices" in the economy (9/2010);
- worries about "the job situation" in America (9/2010);
- feelings that free trade had hurt oneself and one's family (11/2010);
- recognition that jobs were "difficult to find" where one lived (12/2010);
- having someone in one's household who was out of a job or looking for work in the past year (12/2010);
- recognition that real estate in one's community lost value in the past year (12/2010);
- recognition that one struggled to "afford things in life" that one wanted (12/2010);
- rating one's personal finances as "only fair" or "poor" (12/2010; 2/2011);
- recognition that the late-2000s recession "had a major effect" on one's finances (2/2011);
- dissatisfaction with one's financial situation (3/2011); and
- concern that one did not have enough money to "make ends meet" (3/2011).

Disadvantaged groups of whites were also no more likely to support the Tea Party. In the September 2010 *Pew* survey, these included poorer whites (households making less than $50,000 a year), poorer men, poorer women, poorer white men, and poorer white women. Considering the popularity of claims that Tea Partiers were suffering from economic troubles, it is striking that movement support was not associated with a single item above.

There were three survey items related to perceptions of economic insecurity associated with Tea Party support. These were: (1) the perception that the U.S. was making progress in addressing the gap between rich and poor (12/2010); (2) the perception that the country was not making progress in making available well-paying jobs (12/2010); and (3) concerns that the economy was "only fair" or "poor" (12/2010; 2/2011). The first attitude is no indication of economic anxiety. It is well documented that inequality has grown since the 1980s and in the post-2008 economic period, so the claim that inequality is declining reveals how out of touch Tea Partiers were with the problems faced by poor Americans.

Tea Party defenders might focus on the second and third findings as examples of empathy with the poor and disadvantaged. But this is difficult to take seriously. These concerns are not directly related to disadvantaged groups, and as already documented, most Tea Partiers were hostile to minority and disadvantaged groups, including blacks, immigrants, Muslims, the uninsured, and the poor. The movement's upper-class bias and prejudice on socio-cultural issues meant that it sided with the wealthy over the poor.

Although movement supporters were more likely to hold negative perceptions of the economy, perceptions of the condition of respondents' home state economies were *not* associated with Tea Party support in *Pew*'s February 2011 survey. If Tea Partiers were in tune with the condition of the national economy as a motivator for embracing populist revolt, they should also be aware of the happenings in their home states. If individuals recognize economic suffering as a national problem, they should be able to identify it in their own backyard. This was not the case. Tea Partiers expressed a generic concern with the economy and jobs, at a time when these concerns were prominent in Republican rhetoric (the Obama years). Whatever the reason for their anger over the economy and jobs, it had little connection to Tea Partiers' economic situations, to dire conditions in their home states, or to the suffering of disadvantaged groups.

Conclusion

What is the significance of the Tea Party to American politics? The media depicted the movement as central to the outcome of the 2010 elections. The *New York Times* claimed it "helped shift the balance of power in Washington, with the Republican Party's takeover of the House of Representatives." The movement was

> propelled by deep economic worries and a forceful opposition to the Democratic agenda of health care and government spending ... Most voters said they believed Mr. Obama's policies would hurt the country in the long run, rather than help it, and a large share of voters said they supported the Tea Party movement, which has backed insurgent candidates all across the country.[101]

The *Washington Post* wrote: "The Tea Party celebrated decisive victories ... proving it has matured from a protest movement into a powerful force for political change."[102] CNN reported that "an energized conservative electorate, fueled by the anti-establishment Tea Party movement ... helped Republicans to what could be their biggest gain in congressional elections in decades."[103]

Despite claims about the Tea Party's role in the midterms, the evidence in favor of this was weak. Tea Partiers were more likely to say they followed the 2010 election season, more likely to say they had contacted a political official in the run-up to the election and given money to a campaign, and Tea Party groups' endorsements of various candidates helped elect Tea Party candidates in Republican primary elections.[104] But Tea Partiers were no more likely to register to vote in any of the pre-general election *Pew* polls, and no more likely than non-Tea Partiers to claim they vote most or all of the time, or that they were likely to vote in the midterms.[105] Actually, the Tea Party turned voters *off* in the 2010 elections; according to *Pew*'s September survey, only 21 percent of Americans said a candidate being a Tea Party supporter made them "more likely" to vote for that candidate; 32 percent said being a Tea Party supporter made them "less likely" to vote for a candidate; and 39 percent said a candidate's position toward the movement made "no difference either way."[106] So 71 percent were either unaffected by the Tea Party or turned off by it, and being a Tea Party supporter did not increase one's likelihood of voting.

If the Tea Party was as powerful as many argued, there should be evidence that it fueled conservative attitudes in the early 2010s. To test this claim, I examined the September 2010 *Pew* poll to assess whether Tea Party support was a significant driver of attitudes on issues important to the movement, including opinions of Obama, the ACA, and government. Figures 1.8, 1.9, and 1.10 provide little evidence of the primary role of the Tea Party in driving political attitudes. For opinions of the ACA (Figure 1.8), Tea Party support, while significant, was half as strong as Republican partisanship in predicting opposition to health-care reform. Similarly, partisanship was about twice as powerful as Tea Party support in predicting disapproval of Obama (Figure 1.9). For opinions about the size of government (Figure 1.10), Tea Party support was slightly more powerful a predictor than Republican partisanship. In sum, the Tea Party was a significant force in predicting conservative attitudes; it was just a much weaker factor than partisanship. As I show in subsequent chapters, this is the opposite of what we see with progressive movements. For BLM, the Madison protests, and Occupy, movement identification was a stronger predictor of progressive attitudes than partisanship. These findings speak to anemic populism at work in the Tea Party. In contrast, leftist movements, which typically combat organized political and business interests, rely on grassroots organization to break into the news, impact public opinion, and influence policy.

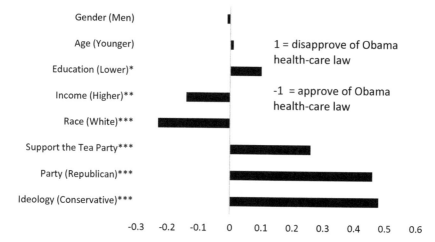

Figure 1.8 Tea Party Support and the Affordable Care Act
Source: *Pew Research Center*, September 2010 poll
Statistical Significance Levels: *** = 0.1% ** = 1% * = 5%
Controls: gender, age, education, race, income, political party, ideology

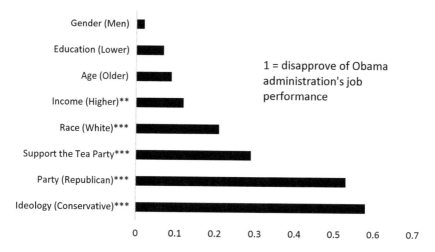

Figure 1.9 Tea Party Support and Attitudes Toward Obama
Source: *Pew Research Center*, September 2010 poll
Statistical Significance Levels: *** = 0.1% ** = 1% * = 5%
Controls: gender, age, education, race, income, political party, ideology

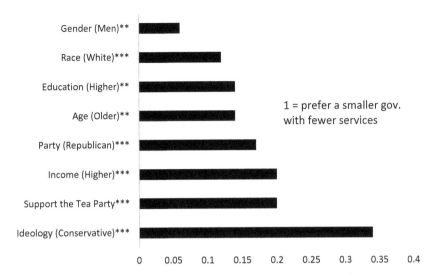

Figure 1.10 Tea Party Support and Opinions of Size of Government
Source: *Pew Research Center*, September 2010 poll
Statistical Significance Levels: *** = 0.1% ** = 1% * = 5%
Controls: gender, age, education, race, income, political party, ideology

We might question to what extent the above findings demonstrate the Tea Party impacted political attitudes. Is it not just as plausible that opposition to Obama, preference for smaller government, and opposition to health-care reform drove Tea Party support? I argue that both of these processes appear to be at work. It was obvious from my interactions with Tea Partiers that conservative values and opposition to Obama drove movement support. But the data in this chapter also suggest that the Tea Party fueled growing conservatism. Coverage of the Tea Party produced growing support, as media consumers were exposed to the protesters' grievances.

Furthermore, large numbers of Americans believed the Tea Party impacted politics and society. In September 2010, 70 percent of Americans said they supported the Tea Party and the major political stances it had raised related to smaller government.[107] That same month, 42 percent said the Tea Party "has been a good thing for the American political system," while 18 percent felt it had been a "bad thing," meaning 60 percent recognized the movement had an effect on society.[108] In another poll from October 2010, 32 percent of Americans said the Tea Party would "make the Republican Party stronger," while 28 percent agreed it would make the party weaker, and 24 percent felt it would have no impact. So 60 percent of Americans felt the Tea Party had an impact on

Republican politics.[109] During this same month, 55 percent of Americans agreed the Tea Party could "effectively bring about major changes in the way the government operates."[110] By early 2011, and after dozens of Tea Partiers won seats in Congress following the 2010 elections, 26 percent of Americans agreed the Tea Party was gaining "too much attention" from Republicans in Congress, compared to 29 percent who felt the movement was getting the "right amount" of attention. Just 17 percent felt the movement received "too little" attention. In other words, 55 percent of Americans believed the Tea Party was having some kind of impact on Congressional politics.[111] As I document below, these feelings were vindicated by a review of Tea Party Republicans' voting records, showing they were significantly to the right of the rest of the party.

On two other levels, the Tea Party played an important role in politics. First, it utilized the media to shift the national discourse toward an anti-government mood and to encourage resistance to health-care reform. And as previous research documented, attention to news on the Tea Party was associated with growing opposition to the Obama administration's health-care reform.[112] This relationship was significant, after controlling for respondents' partisanship, ideology, gender, age, education, income, and race. The Tea Party pulled political discourse to the right, with Tea Partiers opposed to the ACA.

Second, the Tea Party played a symbolic political role. Its rise suggested a rightward polarization of society. This was evident in the Tea Party's backlash against "change," via its resistance to Obama's election and demographic change.[113] The Tea Party should be remembered not only for its reactionary economics, but for its commitment to white identity politics. Rightward polarization in America has been occurring for decades. But the Tea Party intensified this polarization. Racial prejudice and xenophobia were not the primary drivers of the Tea Party, but were significant, nonetheless.

Much of Tea Partiers' anger centered on an intersectional prejudice against Obama, drawing on racist, xenophobic, Islamophobic, and classist prejudices. And Tea Partiers embraced negative stereotypes against many minorities and the poor via their support for the Arizona immigration law, which was a significant factor driving Tea Party support. Finally, Tea Partiers' opposition to the ACA was driven by xenophobia and racism.

The rightward shift of the public via the Tea Party's rise was significant, as it was a precursor to another wave of right-wing populism – seen in the rise of Trump – which also fused reactionary social and economic attitudes. That the Tea Party received support from as much as a third of Americans, and that public support remained at nearly a fifth of Americans years after its collapse, both speak to the power of right-wing populism.[114]

Finally, the rise of the Tea Party was important because it fueled polarization in Congressional politics. Tea Party Congressional Republicans were more conservative than non-Tea Party Republicans, as measured by their voting records.[115] Party polarization manifested itself, via rising legislative obstructionism with the filibuster, and in opposition to tax increases on the wealthy and negotiations over deficit reduction. Tea Partiers also played a prominent role in the 2013 government shutdown, which was motivated by efforts to repeal the ACA.

Despite its anemic populism, the Tea Party mobilized hundreds of thousands of Americans. It garnered positive media coverage, dominating news cycles for more than a year and shifting discourse to the right. Sympathetic coverage helped shift public opinion to the right and encourage mass support for the Tea Party. Although the impact of the Tea Party on the 2010 elections was minimal, the rise of Tea Party Republicans in Congress meant further polarization of national politics.

Notes

1 Scott Rasmussen and Doug Schoen, *Mad as Hell: How the Tea Party Movement Is Fundamentally Remaking Our Two-Party System* (New York: Harper, 2010); CNN polling found that most Tea Party supporters referred to themselves as "independents." For more, see: CNN, "Who Are the Tea Party Activists?", February 18, 2010, http://www.cnn.com/2010/POLITICS/02/17/tea.party.poll/index.html.
2 Sidney G. Tarrow, *Power in Movement: Social Movements and Contentious Politics* (Cambridge: Cambridge University Press, 2011); Doug McAdam, Sidney G. Tarrow, and Charles Tilly, *Dynamics of Contention* (Cambridge: Cambridge University Press, 2001); Doug McAdam, *Political Process and the Development of Black Insurgency, 1930–1970* (Chicago: University of Chicago Press, 1999).
3 Public intellectual, activist, and commentator Eric Draitser took to popularizing the term "white identity politics" during the rise of Donald Trump to political power, although the term is also applicable to the Tea Party movement. For more on Draitser's writing, see: Eric Draitser, "Donald Trump and the Triumph of White Identity Politics," *Counterpunch*, March 24, 2017, https://www.counterpunch.org/2017/03/24/donald-trump-and-the-triumph-of-white-identity-politics/.
4 Kate Zernike, "Unlikely Activist Who Got to the Tea Party Early," *New York Times*, February 27, 2010, http://www.nytimes.com/2010/02/28/us/politics/28keli.html.
5 The Week Staff, "The Tea Party's Road to Legitimacy: A Timeline," *The Week*, April 15, 2010, http://theweek.com/articles/495258/tea-partys-road-legitimacy-timeline.
6 The Week Staff, "The Tea Party's Road to Legitimacy," 2010.
7 Andrew Kirell, "'This Is America!' When CNBC Created the Tea Party," *The Daily Beast*, October 30, 2015, http://www.thedailybeast.com/when-cnbc-created-the-tea-party.
8 Kirell, "'This Is America!'" 2015.

9. CNN, "Nationwide 'Tea Party' Protests Blast Spending," April 15, 2009, http://www.cnn.com/2009/POLITICS/04/15/tea.parties/.
10. Alex Isenstadt, "Town Halls Gone Wild," *Politico*, July 31, 2009, http://www.politico.com/story/2009/07/town-halls-gone-wild-025646; Lee Fang, "Rightwing Harassment Strategy against Dems Detailed in Memo: 'Yell,' 'Stand Up and Shout Out,' 'Rattle Him,'" *Think Progress*, July 31, 2009, https://thinkprogress.org/right-wing-harassment-strategy-against-dems-detailed-in-memo-yell-stand-up-and-shout-out-rattle-him-94e9af741078/.
11. Mark Jurkowitz, "Town Hall Showdowns Fuel Health Care Coverage," *Project for Excellence in Journalism*, August 10, 2009, http://www.journalism.org/2009/08/10/pej-news-coverage-index-august-39-2009/.
12. Anthony R. DiMaggio, *The Rise of the Tea Party: Political Discontent and Corporate Media in the Age of Obama* (New York: Monthly Review Press, 2011); Amy Gardner and Michael E. Ruane, "'Tea Party' Protesters Gather in Washington to Rally against Taxes, Spending," *Washington Post*, April 16, 2010, http://www.washingtonpost.com/wp-dyn/content/article/2010/04/15/AR2010041503344.html.
13. Paul Steinhauser and Kevin Bohn, "Budget Deal Doesn't Thrill Some in the Tea Party Movement," *CNN.com*, April 9, 2011, http://politicalticker.blogs.cnn.com/2011/04/09/budget-deal-doesnt-thrill-some-in-the-tea-party-movement/; Amy Gardner and Rosalind S. Helderman, "Newt Gingrich Using Energy, Power of Tea Party Movement," *Washington Post*, January 24, 2012, https://www.washingtonpost.com/politics/newt-gingrich-using-energy-power-of-tea-party-movement/2012/01/24/gIQAs7WnOQ_story.html?utm_term=.f6d4bb9b6a1c; Associated Press, "Five Years Later, an Evolving Tea Party Movement Wades into the 2014 Elections," *Foxnews.com*, August 4, 2013, http://www.foxnews.com/politics/2013/08/04/five-years-later-evolving-tea-party-movement-wades-into-2014-elections.html.
14. Paul L. Street and Anthony R. DiMaggio, *Crashing the Tea Party: Mass Media and the Campaign to Remake American Politics* (New York: Routledge, 2011).
15. *New York Times*, "Polling the Tea Party," April 14, 2010, https://archive.nytimes.com/www.nytimes.com/interactive/2010/04/14/us/politics/20100414-tea-party-poll-graphic.html.
16. Kate Zernike, *Boiling Mad: Inside Tea Party America* (New York: Times Books, 2010); *New York Times*, "Polling the Tea Party," 2010.
17. *New York Times*, "Polling the Tea Party," 2010.
18. *New York Times*, "Polling the Tea Party," 2010.
19. Langer Research, "ABC News/Washington Post Poll: Income Inequality," November 9, 2011, http://www.langerresearch.com/wp-content/uploads/1129a5IncomeInequality.pdf.
20. *New York Times*, "Polling the Tea Party," 2010.
21. *New York Times*, "Polling the Tea Party," 2010.
22. This survey finding is based on the *Pew Research Center*'s February 2011 national survey.
23. Charles F. Andrain, *Political Power and Economic Inequality: A Comparative Policy Approach* (Lanham, MD: Rowman & Littlefield, 2014).
24. Scott Clement and John C. Green, "The Tea Party and Religion," *Pew Research Center: Religion and Public Life*, February 23, 2011, http://www.pewforum.org/2011/02/23/tea-party-and-religion/.
25. Ruth Braunstein and Malaena Taylor, "Is the Tea Party a 'Religious' Movement? Religiosity in the Tea Party Versus the Republican Right," *Sociology of Religion* 78, no. 1 (2017): 33–59.

26 Robert M. Entman and Andrew Rojecki, *The Black Image in the White Mind: Media and Race in America* (Chicago: University of Chicago Press, 2001); Martin Gilens, *Why Americans Hate Welfare: Race, Media, and the Politics of Antipoverty Policy* (Chicago: University of Chicago Press, 2000).
27 Lyndsey Layton, "Connecting School Spending and Student Achievement," *Washington Post*, July 9, 2014, https://www.washingtonpost.com/local/education/connecting-school-spending-and-student-achievement/2014/07/09/cfc82cf6-06fd-11e4-bbf1-cc51275e7f8f_story.html?utm_term=.8a3e980e0a1d; Steve Aos and Annie Pennucci, "K-12 Education Spending and Student Outcomes: A Review of the Evidence," *Washington State Institute for Public Policy*, October 2012, http://www.wsipp.wa.gov/ReportFile/1108/Wsipp_K-12-Education-Spending-and-Student-Outcomes-A-Review-of-the-Evidence_Full-Report.pdf.
28 Peter Eavis, "Race Strongly Influences Mortgage Lending in St. Louis, Study Finds," *New York Times*, July 19, 2016, https://www.nytimes.com/2016/07/19/business/dealbook/race-strongly-influences-mortgage-lending-in-st-louis-study-finds.html; Drew DeSilver and Kristen Bialik, "Blacks and Hispanics Face Extra Challenges in Getting Home Loans," *Pew Research Center*, January 10, 2017, http://www.pewresearch.org/fact-tank/2017/01/10/blacks-and-hispanics-face-extra-challenges-in-getting-home-loans/; Marianne Bertrand and Sendhil Mullainathan, "Are Emily and Greg More Employable than Lakisha and Jamal? A Field Experiment on Labor Market Discrimination," *The American Economic Review* 94, no. 4 (2004): 991–1013.
29 Eduardo Bonilla-Silva, *Racism without Racists: Color-Blind Racism and the Persistence of Racial Inequality in America* (Lanham, MD: Rowman & Littlefield, 2017).
30 Christopher S. Parker and Matt A. Barreto, *Change They Can't Believe in: The Tea Party and Reactionary Politics in America* (Chicago: University of Chicago Press, 2014); Alan Abramowitz, "Grand Old Tea Party: Partisan Polarization and the Rise of the Tea Party Movement," in *Steep: The Precipitous Rise of the Tea Party*, eds. Lawrence Rosenthal and Christine Trost (Berkeley, CA: University of California Press, 2012): 195–211; Darrel Enck-Wanzer, "Barack Obama, the Tea Party, and the Threat of Race: On Racial Neoliberalism and Born-Again Racism," *Communication, Culture, and Critique* 4, no. 1 (2011): 23–30.
31 Christopher S. Parker, "2010 Multi-State Survey of Race and Politics," *University of Washington Institute for the Study of Ethnicity, Race, and Sexuality*, 2010, https://depts.washington.edu/uwiser/racepolitics.html.
32 Parker and Barreto, *Change They Can't Believe in*, 2014.
33 *New York Times*, "Polling the Tea Party," 2010.
34 Ali Gharib, "Poll: Two-Thirds of Republicans, Tea Partiers and Fox News Viewers Think Islam Is Incompatible with American Values," *Think Progress*, September 6, 2011, https://thinkprogress.org/poll-two-thirds-of-republicans-tea-partiers-and-fox-news-viewers-think-islam-is-incompatible-with-49a614bcdf30.
35 Russell Heimlich, "Does Islam Encourage Violence?", *Pew Research Center*, April 6, 2011, http://www.pewresearch.org/fact-tank/2011/04/06/does-islam-encourage-violence/.
36 Edward Said, *Orientalism* (New York: Vintage Books, 1979); Zachary Lockman, *Contending Visions of the Middle East: The History and Politics of Orientalism* (Cambridge: Cambridge University Press, 2009).

37 Tom Rosentiel, "Muslim Americans: Middle Class and Mostly Mainstream," *Pew Research Center*, May 22, 2007, http://www.pewresearch.org/2007/05/22/muslim-americans-middle-class-and-mostly-mainstream/; Jeff Diamant, "American Muslims Are Concerned – But Also Satisfied with Their Lives," *Pew Research Center*, July 26, 2017, http://www.pewresearch.org/fact-tank/2017/07/26/american-muslims-are-concerned-but-also-satisfied-with-their-lives/.
38 Richard Hofstadter, *The Paranoid Style in American Politics* (New York: Vintage, 2008).
39 Tea Partiers' heavy reliance on these media outlets was revealed in numerous national surveys, including the 2010 *CBS–New York Times* poll, and the March 2011 *Pew* survey.
40 Don Gonyea, "From the Start, Obama Struggled with Fallout from a Kind of Fake News," *National Public Radio*, January 10, 2017, http://www.npr.org/2017/01/10/509164679/from-the-start-obama-struggled-with-fallout-from-a-kind-of-fake-news.
41 In this chapter and throughout this book, I utilize binary and ordered logistic regression to analyze public opinion data that is dichotomous and ordinal in nature. I utilize first differences analysis via the Clarify statistical program to generate predicted values for each independent variable, after holding all other variables constant at their mean values.
42 I created an interactive variable between opinions about immigration and opinions of the Tea Party. This variable is statistically significant at the 0.1 percent level in predicting attitudes toward health-care reform, after controlling for survey respondents, sex, education, age, income, race, political party, and ideology.
43 Meghan A. Burke, *Race, Gender, and Class in the Tea Party: What the Movement Reflects about Mainstream Ideologies* (Lanham, MD: Lexington Books, 2016): 3.
44 Melissa Deckman, *Tea Party Women: Mama Grizzlies, Grassroots Leaders, and the Changing Face of the American Right* (New York: New York University Press, 2016).
45 Deckman, *Tea Party Women*, 2016.
46 Maggie Fazeli Fard, "Sandra Fluke, Georgetown Student Called a 'Slut' by Rush Limbaugh, Speaks Out," *Washington Post*, March 2, 2012, https://www.washingtonpost.com/blogs/the-buzz/post/rush-limbaugh-calls-georgetown-student-sandra-fluke-a-slut-for-advocating-contraception/2012/03/02/gIQAvjfSmR_blog.html?utm_term=.d2c0f6153153.
47 Margaret Carlson, "An Interview with Rush Limbaugh," *Time*, October 26, 1992, http://content.time.com/time/magazine/article/0,9171,976829,00.html
48 Emily Atkin, "The Revenge of Rush Limbaugh's 'Infobabes,'" *The New Republic*, August 11, 2017, https://newrepublic.com/article/144232/revenge-rush-limbaughs-infobabes; Steve Rendall, "Limbaugh: A Color Man Who Has a Problem with Color?" *Fairness & Accuracy in Reporting*, June 7, 2000, http://fair.org/article/limbaugh-a-color-man-who-has-a-problem-with-color/.
49 Claire Suddath, "Conservative Radio Host Rush Limbaugh," *Time*, March 4, 2009, http://content.time.com/time/nation/article/0,8599,1882947,00.html; Mikki Kendall, "22 Times Michele Obama Endured Rude, Racist, Sexist, or Plain Ridiculous Attacks," *Washington Post*, November 16, 2016, https://www.washingtonpost.com/posteverything/wp/2016/11/16/22-times-michelle-obama-endured-rude-racist-sexist-or-plain-dumb-attacks/?utm_term=.349e674f7521.

50 *Pew Research Center*, March 2011 Political Typology Survey, March 29, 2011.
51 In the *Pew* March 2011 survey, Tea Party-supporting women are significantly more likely to consume Rush Limbaugh's radio program, compared to other groups of Americans. The relationship remains statistically significant at the 5 percent level, after controlling for respondents' political party, ideology, age, education, race, and income.
52 Daniel Q. Gillion, *The Political Power of Protest: Minority Activism and Shifts in Public Policy* (Cambridge: Cambridge University Press, 2013); Deva R. Woodly, *The Politics of Common Sense: How Social Movements Use Public Discourse to Change Politics and Win Acceptance* (Oxford: Oxford University Press, 2015); Matt Grossmann, *The Not So Special Interests: Interest Groups, Public Representation, and American Governance* (Palo Alto, CA: Stanford University Press, 2012); Jeffrey M. Berry, *The New Liberalism: The Rising Power of Citizens Groups* (Washington, DC: Brookings Institution Press, 2000).
53 For claims that coverage of the Tea Party varied by news outlet, see: David A. Weaver and Joshua M. Scacco, "Revisiting the Protest Paradigm: The Tea Party as Filtered through Prime-Time Cable News," *The International Journal of Press/Politics* 18, no. 1 (2013): http://journals.sagepub.com/doi/abs/10.1177/1940161212462872; Patrick Rafail and John D. McCarthy, "Making the Tea Party Republican: Media Bias and Framing in Newspapers and Cable News," *Social Currents*, March 1, 2018, http://journals.sagepub.com/doi/pdf/10.1177/2329496518759129; for studies suggesting that media coverage of the Tea Party was positive, see: Jules Boykoff and Eulalie Laschever, "The Tea Party Movement, Framing, and the U.S. Media," *Social Movement Studies* 10, no. 4 (2011): 341–366; DiMaggio, *The Rise of the Tea Party*, 2011; Daniel Skinner, "'Keep Your Government Hands Off My Medicare!' An Analysis of Media Effects on Tea Party Health Care Politics," *New Political Science* 34, no. 4 (2012): 605–619; Matt Guardino and Dean Snyder, "The Tea Party and the Crisis of Neoliberalism: Mainstreaming New Right Populism in the Corporate News Media," *New Political Science* 34, no. 4 (2012): 527–548.
54 Trevor A. Thrall, "The Myth of the Outside Strategy: Mass Media News Coverage of Interest Groups," *Political Communication* 23, no. 4 (2006): 407–420.
55 McAdam, Tarrow, and Tilly, *Dynamics of Contention*, 2001; Tarrow, *Power in Movement*, 2011.
56 Jack L. Walker Jr., *Mobilizing Interest Groups in America: Patrons, Professions, and Social Movements* (Ann Arbor, MI: University of Michigan Press, 1991); Thrall, "The Myth of the Outside Strategy," 2006; Grossmann, *The Not So Special Interests*, 2012.
57 David Barstow, "Tea Party Lights Fuse for Rebellion on Right," *New York Times*, February 15, 2010, http://www.nytimes.com/2010/02/16/us/politics/16teaparty.html?pagewanted=all.
58 Dan Eggen and Perry Bacon Jr., "Tea Party Conservatives Gear up to Affect 2010 Elections with Fundraising, PACs," *Washington Post*, December 10, 2009, http://www.washingtonpost.com/wp-dyn/content/article/2009/12/09/AR2009120904637.html.
59 Gardner and Ruane, "'Tea Party' Protesters Gather in Washington to Rally against Taxes, Spending," 2010.

60 Michael Scherer, "Tea Party Time: The Making of a Political Uprising," *Time*, September 16, 2010, http://content.time.com/time/magazine/article/0,9171,2019608,00.html.
61 Peggy Noonan, "Why It's Time for a Tea Party: The Populist Movement Is More a Critique of the GOP than a Wing of It," *Wall Street Journal*, September 17, 2010, https://www.wsj.com/articles/SB10001424052748703440604575496221482123504; Juan Williams, "Tea Party Anger Reflects Mainstream Concerns: Dissatisfaction with the Economy and the Country's Direction Cuts across Racial Lines," *Wall Street Journal*, April 2, 2010, https://www.wsj.com/articles/SB10001424052702304252704575155942054483252.
62 Rasmussen and Schoen, *Mad as Hell*, 2010: 1.
63 Rasmussen and Schoen, *Mad as Hell*, 2010: 6.
64 Chuck Collins, "How to Talk to a Tea Party Activist," *The Nation*, April 14, 2010, https://www.thenation.com/article/how-talk-tea-party-activist/.
65 DiMaggio, *The Rise of the Tea Party*, 2011: 121.
66 Rory McVeigh, "What's New about the Tea Party Movement," in *Understanding the Tea Party Movement*, eds. Nella Van Dyke and David S. Meyer (New York: Routledge, 2014): 15–34. For a second quote from McVeigh discussing the allegedly independent power of the Tea Party, see: Patrik Jonsson, "Occupy Wall Street Movement Intrigues, Confounds the Tea Party," *Christian Science Monitor*, October 19, 2011, https://www.minnpost.com/christian-science-monitor/2011/10/occupy-wall-street-movement-intrigues-confounds-tea-party.
67 John C. Berg, "President Obama, the Tea Party Movement, and the Crisis of the American Party System," *Suffolk University*, April 29, 2011, https://ssrn.com/abstract=1879523.
68 Ronald P. Formisano, *The Tea Party: A Brief History* (Baltimore, MD: Johns Hopkins University Press, 2012): 6–8, 20.
69 Theda Skocpol and Vanessa Williamson, *The Tea Party and the Remaking of Republican Conservatism* (Oxford: Oxford University Press, 2016): 12.
70 Abby Scher and Chip Berlet, "The Tea Party Moment," in *Understanding the Tea Party*, eds. Nella Van Dyke and David S. Meyer (New York: Routledge, 2014): 108.
71 The search included any news stories, op-eds, editorials, letters to the editor, and other features that referenced the following words: "Tea Party," "Occupy Wall Street," "Black Lives Matter," and "Scott Walker," alongside references to "Madison," and "protest(s)," "protester(s)," or "demonstration(s)." For the Congressional Record, the searches were the same, with the exception of the Madison protests, in which I searched simply for references to "Scott Walker" as related to collective bargaining, pensions, and Wisconsin state workers.
72 Gaye Tuchman, *Making News: A Study in the Construction of Reality* (New York: Free Press, 1979); Herbert J. Gans, *Deciding What's News: A Study of CBS Evening News, NBC Nightly News, Newsweek, and Time* (New York: Vintage, 1980).
73 The economic distress frame included any stories that referenced the Tea Party within 50 words of any of the key words included in this analysis.
74 DiMaggio, *The Rise of the Tea Party*, 2011: 118.
75 The specific question surveyed by the *Pew Research Center* was: "How much, if anything, have you heard or read about the Tea Party movement that has been involved in campaigns and protests in the U.S. over the

past year?" This question, is not a perfect measurement of media attention, since it also asks about how much individuals had "heard" about the Tea Party, which could be in reference to television news, radio news, and conversations with others. Still, the question does measure how closely Americans were paying attention to news on the Tea Party, and as mentioned in this chapter, it is highly unlikely that the vast majority of Americans knew an individual who had been directly involved in Tea Party protests, considering how few were active in such activities. This means that even conversations with other Americans about the Tea Party were likely to originate from those individuals engaging in media coverage of the social movement.

76 In the June 2010 *Pew Research Center* monthly poll, the relationship between media consumption and support for the Tea Party is statistically significant at the 0.1 percent level, after controlling for respondents' sex, age, education, race, political party, ideology, and income.

77 In my modeling, I completed two separate binary logistic regression analyses: one for consumption of Beck and Limbaugh's programs and one for *Fox News* more generally, since there was a high correlation between *Fox News* consumption on the one hand, and Beck and Limbaugh consumption on the other. For both regressions, I controlled for political party, ideology, gender, age, education, race, and income.

78 Michael T. Heaney and Fabio Rojas, *Party in the Street: The Antiwar Movement and the Democratic Party after 9/11* (Cambridge: Cambridge University Press, 2015).

79 Devin Burghart and Leonard Zeskind, "Tea Party Nationalism: A Critical Examination of the Tea Party Movement and the Size, Scope, and Focus of its National Factions," *Institute for Research and Education on Human Rights*, Fall 2010, http://dig.abclocal.go.com/wtvd/docs/IREHR_Report_102010.pdf; Shannon Travis, "Counting Tea Party Activists Causes Conflict," *CNN.com*, April 22, 2010, http://politicalticker.blogs.cnn.com/2010/04/22/counting-tea-party-activists-causes-conflicting-numbers/.

80 Skocpol and Williamson, *The Tea Party and the Remaking of Republican Conservatism*, 2016; Abramowitz, "Grand Old Tea Party," 2012; *New York Times*, "Polling the Tea Party," 2010.

81 *New York Times*, "Polling the Tea Party," 2010; United States Census Bureau, "Population Estimates, July 1, 2017," 2018, https://www.census.gov/quickfacts/fact/table/US/PST045216.

82 *New York Times*, "Polling the Tea Party," 2010.

83 Brian Lavin, "Census Bureau Reports There Are 89,004 Local Governments in the United States," *United States Census Bureau*, August 30, 2012, https://www.census.gov/newsroom/releases/archives/governments/cb12-161.html.

84 Associated Press, "Thousands of Anti-Tax 'Tea Party' Protesters Turn Out in U.S. Cities," *FoxNews.com*, April 15, 2009, http://www.foxnews.com/politics/2009/04/15/thousands-anti-tax-tea-party-protesters-turn-cities.html; Ben Smith, "The Tea Party's Exaggerated Importance," *NBCNews.com*, April 22, 2010, http://www.nbcnewyork.com/news/politics/The_tea_party_s_exaggerated_importance-91798119.html; Kate Zernike, "With Tax Day as Theme, Tea Party Groups Demonstrate," *New York Times*, April 15, 2009, http://www.nytimes.com/2010/04/16/us/politics/16rallies.html.

85 Ishaan Tharoor, "Viewpoint: Why Was the Biggest Protest in World History Ignored?" *Time*, February 15, 2013, http://world.time.com/

2013/02/15/viewpoint-why-was-the-biggest-protest-in-world-history-ignored/.
86 Kaveh Waddell, "The Exhausting Work of Tallying America's Largest Protest," *The Atlantic*, January 23, 2017, https://www.theatlantic.com/technology/archive/2017/01/womens-march-protest-count/514166/.
87 Kate Zernike, "Tea Party Convention is Canceled," *New York Times*, September 24, 2010, https://thecaucus.blogs.nytimes.com/2010/09/24/tea-party-convention-is-canceled/.
88 Brian Montopoli, "Tea Party Convention in Las Vegas Canceled," *CBS News*, September 24, 2010, http://www.cbsnews.com/news/tea-party-convention-in-las-vegas-cancelled/.
89 *New York Times*, "Polling the Tea Party," 2010.
90 Amy Gardner, "Gauging the Scope of the Tea Party Movement in America," *Washington Post*, October 24, 2010, http://www.washingtonpost.com/wp-dyn/content/article/2010/10/23/AR2010102304000.html.
91 George Monbiot, "The Tea Party Movement: Deluded and Inspired by Billionaires," *The Guardian*, October 25, 2010, https://www.theguardian.com/commentisfree/cifamerica/2010/oct/25/tea-party-koch-brothers; Thom Hartmann, "There Is No Such Thing as the Tea Party; There Is Only a Collection of Billionaires," *Truthout*, October 2, 2013, https://truthout.org/articles/there-is-no-such-thing-as-the-tea-party-there-is-only-a-collection-of-billionaires/.
92 Parker and Barreto, *Change They Can't Believe in*, 2014: 3.
93 Parker and Barreto, *Change They Can't Believe in*, 2014: 3.
94 Parker and Barreto, *Change They Can't Believe in*, 2014: 13.
95 Parker and Barreto, *Change They Can't Believe in*, 2014: 29, 32.
96 Parker and Barreto, *Change They Can't Believe in*, 2014: 34, 39.
97 Parker and Barreto, *Change They Can't Believe in*, 2014: 54, 92.
98 *New York Times*, "Polling the Tea Party," 2010.
99 Parker and Barreto do not primarily look at economic attitudes as major predictors of Tea Party support, which explains why they fail to find that such attitudes are stronger predictors than social attitudes.
100 *New York Times*, "Polling the Tea Party," 2010.
101 Jeff Zeleny, "G.O.P. Captures House, But Not Senate," *New York Times*, November 2, 2010, http://www.nytimes.com/2010/11/03/us/politics/03elect.html?pagewanted=all; Jim Rutenberg and Jeff Zeleny, "Democrats Outrun by a 2-Year G.O.P. Comeback Plan," *New York Times*, November 3, 2010, http://www.nytimes.com/2010/11/04/us/politics/04campaign.html.
102 Krissah Thompson and Amy Gardner, "Victories Give Force to Tea Party Movement," *Washington Post*, November 3, 2010, http://www.washingtonpost.com/wp-dyn/content/article/2010/11/02/AR2010110201301.html.
103 CNN Wire Staff, "GOP Roars Back to Take U.S. House; Democrats Cling to Senate Majority," *CNN.com*, November 3, 2010, http://www.cnn.com/2010/POLITICS/11/02/election.main/index.html.
104 For more on Tea Partiers' greater likelihood of contacting officials and giving money to campaigns, see: Abramowitz, "Grand Old Tea Party," 2012; for more on Tea Partiers' attention to the election season, see: *Pew Research Center*, June 2010 Poll, 2010. Tea Partiers were statistically more likely to pay attention to 2010 election news, after controlling for respondents' party, ideology, income, gender, age, education, and race. The relationship between Tea Party support and election attention was significant at the 0.01 percent level.

105 These two survey questions were pulled from the September 2010 and March 2011 *Pew Research Center* surveys. Likelihood of voting and frequency of voting were not significantly associated with Tea Party support, after controlling for respondents' political party, ideology, sex, age, education, race, and income.
106 *Pew Research Center*, "Pew Research Center/National Journal Congressional Connection Poll," September 2010; Christopher F. Karpowitz, J. Quin Monson, Kelly D. Patterson, and Jeremy C. Pope, "Tea Time in America? The Impact of the Tea Party Movement on the 2010 Midterm Elections," *PS: Political Science and Politics* 44, no. 2 (2011): 303–309.
107 *Fox News*/Opinion Dynamics, "Fox News/Opinion Dynamics Poll: September 2010," *iPoll*, 2010.
108 *NBC News/Wall Street Journal*, "NBC News/Wall Street Journal Poll: September 2010," *iPoll*, 2010.
109 *CBS News*, "CBS News Poll: October 2010," *iPoll*, 2010.
110 *ABC News/Yahoo News*, "ABC News/Yahoo News Poll: October 2010," *iPoll*, 2010.
111 *CBS News*, "CBS News Poll: February 2011," *iPoll*, 2011.
112 DiMaggio, *The Rise of the Tea Party*, 2011: 199.
113 The idea of polarization on the American right in general, and among Tea Partiers, has been documented in numerous studies, including: Abramowitz, "Grand Old Tea Party," 2012; and *Pew Research Center*, "Political Polarization in the American Public," June 12, 2014, http://www.people-press.org/2014/06/12/political-polarization-in-the-american-public/.
114 Jim Norman, "In U.S., Support for Tea Party Drops to New Low," *Gallup*, October 26, 2015, http://www.gallup.com/poll/186338/support-tea-party-drops-new-low.aspx; Peter Steinhauser, "Poll: Tea Party Movement Fails to Make Any Impression on 4 out of 10," *CNN.com*, February 5, 2010, http://www.cnn.com/2010/POLITICS/02/05/poll.tea.party/index.html.
115 Jordan M. Ragusa and Anthony Gaspar, "Where's the Tea Party? An Examination of the Tea Party's Voting Behavior in the House of Representatives," *American Politics Research* 69, no. 2 (2016): 373–383; Michael A. Bailey, Jonathan Mummolo, and Hans Noel, "Tea Party Influence: A Story of Activists and Elites," *American Politics Research* 40, no. 5 (2012): 769–804; Stephen Pettigrew and Jamie Carson, "Strategic Politicians, Partisan Roll Calls, and the Tea Party: Evaluating the 2010 Midterm Elections," *Electoral Studies* 32, no. 1 (2013): 26–36; DiMaggio, *The Rise of the Tea Party*, 2011; Street and DiMaggio, *Crashing the Tea Party*, 2011.

2 The Economic Justice Movement
Challenging Plutocracy and Inequality

Over the last four decades, the U.S. economy has increasingly served the wealthy, contributing to growing inequality. Despite labor productivity doubling between 1980 and 2016, and family work hours increasing by about a quarter, incomes for the middle fifth and second lowest fifth of earners increased by just 10 and 6 percent respectively, and fell by 1 percent for the poorest fifth.[1] In contrast, the top 20 percent saw their incomes increase by more than 50 percent, and the top 5 percent by 77 percent.[2] The top 1 percent increased their incomes by 190 percent.[3]

Coupled with the growth of health-care and higher education costs beyond inflation, most Americans were in a worse position by the 2010s than in previous decades.[4] Between 2003 and 2013, the median household lost a third of its net worth, largely due to losses following the 2008 housing crash.[5] By the mid-2010s, the poorest 40 percent of Americans held zero financial wealth, while the middle fifth held just 3 percent. Sixty percent held almost no wealth.[6] In contrast, the wealthiest 1 percent controlled nearly 40 percent of wealth, while the wealthiest 20 percent owned nearly 90 percent.[7]

The 2010s saw a level of income inequality higher than at any time in the past century.[8] This period of transition produced increasingly progressive attitudes among most Americans. As captured in Figure 2.1, whether it was increased recognition of tension between rich and poor, growing popularity of unions, or intensifying demands that government address inequality, Americans became more disillusioned with an economy and government seen as failing to provide for the peoples' needs.[9] Many Americans mobilized to combat growing inequality, low-pay work, and rising worker insecurity. The rise of progressive beliefs was related to major events of the time, including the 2011 Madison demonstrations against Governor Scott Walker, the appearance of Occupy Wall Street (Occupy), the Fight for $15, and Bernie Sanders' presidential campaign. Public opinion across most issues is remarkably stable over the years.[10] But as Page and Shapiro find, significant events produce shifts in mass attitudes.[11] The 2008 economic crash was one such event.

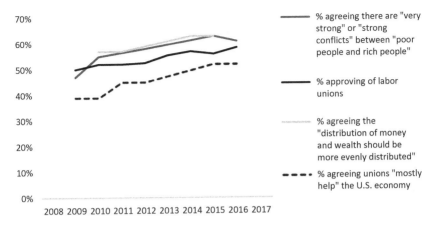

Figure 2.1 Progressive Economic Attitudes in an Era of Rising Protest
Sources: *Gallup* and *Pew* polls, 2009–2016

Inequality and Politics: What We Know

The history of inequality has long been a focus for scholars.[12] And the study of inequality received growing attention following the 2008 economic crisis.[13] Studies demonstrate that government policies that protect unions and allocate greater resources to welfare spending contribute to income growth and well-being for lower- and middle-class families, reducing poverty and inequality, and increasing happiness and satisfaction.[14]

Social scientists warn about inequality in political representation via upper-class and business dominance of government.[15] The United States is known for unequal political participation by education level and income – which feed into unequal representation.[16] The affluent are more likely to vote and lower voter turnout among the poor produces weaker pressure for government to reduce inequality.[17]

For many years, Political Science placed little emphasis on inequality. Many assumed the political system democratically represented the people. But studies now find that higher-income earners are better represented in policy outcomes than other Americans.[18] Inequality reinforces plutocracy in politics, with higher inequality in some states being associated with lower spending on welfare benefits for the needy.[19] This finding holds across wealthy countries.[20]

The U.S. political system enables gridlock via empowerment of the minority party in the Senate.[21] This obstruction prevents the passage of policies aimed at inequality reduction.[22] Americans are subject to discipline by the marketplace, which depresses wages and gouges consumers (for profit) on items such as health care. Americans "drift" along without assistance, subject to the effects of market forces.[23]

Government's siding with the affluent, and its contribution to growing inequality via inaction, have consequences. Americans are increasingly insecure via the rise of low-wage work, growing costs of living, and declining health.[24] Poverty and inequality are associated with growing obesity, poor health outcomes, decreased life satisfaction, and increased stress and anger.[25] Increased inequality produces poorer quality of life, with more unequal societies producing poorer educational outcomes, health outcomes, lower life expectancy, and rising violence.[26] With growing inequality, plutocracy becomes a growing concern.[27] Rising inequality produces increased disillusionment and distrust of government, and depresses voting among disadvantaged groups.[28] And high inequality is harmful to democracy.[29]

Growing economic insecurity produces resentment toward plutocratic political systems. Economic insecurity and lower-class status are associated with progressive-leftist values, and higher-class status and incomes with conservative beliefs.[30] Lower-income Americans are more likely to vote for liberal candidates, even among lower-income whites who are sometimes portrayed as supporting Republicans.[31] Some scholars hypothesize that growing inequality produces increased support for redistributing wealth from rich to poor.[32] Other research documents the relationship between rising inequality and support for redistribution and labor unions, which reduce inequality via collective bargaining.[33]

Growing inequality can impact voting patterns and fuel progressive movements. "Retrospective voting" finds that economic insecurity, increasing unemployment, and rising inflation contribute to resentment toward incumbents and the party of the president.[34] Movements stimulate critical consciousness against plutocratic politics and inequality.[35] Social scientists – via strain theory – acknowledge as much.[36] Personal grievances motivate disadvantaged groups to demand better representation from government via mobilization of social movements. Citizens suffer from "cognitive dissonance" when their expected life outcomes do not match actual outcomes, and they blame the political and economic systems for this "status inconsistency."[37] When this happens, the formation of social movements may be more likely.

Many scholars maintain that insecurity and inequality encourage conservative beliefs. Teixeira and Rogers documented the flocking of white working-class voters away from the Democrats in the 1990s, due to perceptions that the party had failed to represent citizens.[38] Journalist Thomas Frank popularized the "What's the Matter with Kansas?" thesis, claiming Republicans promote conservative positions to voters on social issues such as school prayer and abortion, while pursuing economic policies that harm most people.[39]

The notion that working-class whites form conservative attitudes and prefer Republicans is defended in various studies.[40] Cramer finds poorer rural whites are more likely to resent liberals and government employees, viewing them as out of touch with working-class Americans. This resentment drove the popularity of Wisconsin Republican Governor Scott Walker.[41] Hochschild argues poorer southern Tea Partiers feel like "strangers in their own land" due to mounting economic anxieties, leading them to oppose "special" treatment for minorities via affirmative action and welfare.[42] Other studies claim growing inequality produces a conservative shift in public opinion and increased opposition to welfare programs.[43]

Some scholars maintain that differences between higher-, middle-, and lower-income Americans are minimal.[44] They declare the death of class consciousness, citing Americans' reluctance to think of themselves in class terms.[45] Shifts in public opinion over time are parallel across income groups, suggesting minimal distinctions between more and less affluent Americans.[46] Other studies find growing inequality is not associated with demands for redistribution from wealthier to poorer Americans.[47] In a nation that values individualism, feelings about personal responsibility for economic success and failure are a better predictor of political beliefs than one's economic position.[48] And some find that unemployment and displeasure with one's personal finances are not associated with voting behavior.[49] Others conclude growing inequality and economic insecurity depress political participation.[50] Some findings suggest Americans are unified across income groups in preferring policies that reduce poverty and inequality.[51] These studies suggest income and class are not predictors of political beliefs or behavior.

In this chapter, I argue that economically motivated movements stimulate opposition to inequality and plutocratic policies, via the rise of the Madison and Occupy protests of 2011, and Fight for $15. I label them "the economic justice movement." As Americans grew increasingly strained following the 2008 economic crash, economically insecure Americans became "disturbed" – to borrow Truman's terminology – rejecting the political-economic status quo. Despite the strength of a hegemonic ideology demonizing unions, the minimum wage, and inequality reduction strategies, disadvantaged Americans rose up to protest their economic insecurity. They used the media to cultivate public support. These findings contradict studies claiming that poverty and insecurity produce support for conservative policies, and arguments that class divisions do not influence beliefs and behavior.

This chapter's case studies reinforce the Marxian position that economic circumstances determine one's ideological orientation. But contrary to orthodox Marxism, economics is not the only factor impacting beliefs and actions. Gender, race, ethnicity, sexual identity, and geographic location matter, as do the intersections of these identities.

Madison, Occupy, and Fight for $15 benefitted from varied levels of support from intersecting identity groups. Race, ethnicity, gender, and income interact to impact political values, and intersectional analyses of economic movements are central to understanding why some are more or less appealing to the public.

Piven and Cloward wrote that grassroots insurgencies of the poor force political elites to grant policy concessions.[52] Severe disturbances – particularly economic ones – pressure the political system, as poor people's movements engage in disruptive tactics vital to "challenging political authority."[53] Piven and Cloward argue: "extraordinary disturbances in the larger society are required to transform the poor from apathy to hope."[54] This transformation is at play in all three movements: Madison, Occupy, and Fight for $15, which provided the foundation for Bernie Sanders' 2016 and 2020 progressive insurgencies. Participants in these movements were not always poor, but all worked toward aiding the economically stressed in a time of growing inequality.

The Madison Uprising

In February 2011, a mass protest emerged against Wisconsin Governor Scott Walker. Walker proposed a "budget repair bill" to reduce the state's deficit following the 2008 economic collapse. The bill prohibited collective bargaining for state employees for raises above changes in the consumer price index. This meant workers could not collectively negotiate for raises, since cost of living adjustment increases are not "raises." The bill mandated that state employees contribute 50 percent of the costs of pensions, and at least 12.6 percent of the costs for health-care premiums.[55] This meant as much as a 12 percent pay cut, and an average reduction of 8 percent.[56]

Citing a $137 million deficit, Walker insisted the changes were necessary to right the state's financial ship.[57] He had "to do what is necessary to bring the state's spending in line with our taxpayers' ability to pay ... the bottom line is we are trying to balance our budget and there really is no room to negotiate on that because we're broke."[58] Walker threatened to lay off 1,500 state workers if his bill was not passed.[59]

Despite Walker's warnings, critics took issue with his claims. There is no significant correlation between state unionization rates and state budget deficits, which undermines the claim that unions were bankrupting Wisconsin.[60] Then there was Walker's claim that Wisconsin was "broke," which *Politifact* deemed "false":

> Experts agree the state faces financial challenges in the form of deficits. But they also agree the state isn't broke. Employees and bills are being paid. Services are continuing to be performed. Revenue continues to roll in. A variety of tools – taxes, layoffs, spending cuts, debt shifting – is available to make ends meet.[61]

Public sector employees took to the streets in Madison, set on disrupting politics-as-usual on the capitol. Thousands occupied the capitol building, and tens of thousands protested daily, with as many as 100,000 on weekends in February and March.[62] Demonstrators hailed from various occupations: police officers, teachers, firefighters, social workers, electricians, highway repair crew workers, college teaching assistants, and other government workers, friends, and family.[63]

In February 2011, I traveled to Madison to observe and support union workers protesting Walker's "budget repair bill." Through my conversations with protesters, I witnessed several developments that spoke to demonstrators' motives. The protests were non-violent, and received support from unions, including the American Federation of State, County, and Municipal Employees (AFSCME), the Service Employees International Union (SEIU), the University of Wisconsin Madison's Teachers Assistants Union, and various locals throughout the state. The primary message was that Walker was pursuing a union-busting strategy, independent of deficit concerns. This was conveyed by demonstrators mentioning that Walker claimed collective bargaining changes were necessary to reduce the budget deficit, despite passing tax cuts for businesses that year reducing revenues by $140 million. Tax cuts for the wealthy, they maintained, were balanced on the backs of public-sector workers.

Other grievances were also articulated. One was that the anti-union bill was part of a stealth agenda against state workers, since Walker never campaigned on assaulting unions. Another was that Walker was anti-family, since his bill harmed public-sector employees. The bill was deemed anti-student, since teachers endured pay cuts in a state where public employees earned an average of only $48,348 a year – less than the national median income of $50,502.[64] With an 8 percent average cut in income under Walker's bill, state employees saw their average incomes decline by $3,868, to $44,480 a year.

I observed a symbolic element to the protests through various expressions of solidarity. There was anger at Walker's assault on Wisconsin's labor heritage, considering the state was the first to protect collective bargaining in 1959. The symbolic value of the protests was apparent across occupations affected in different ways by Walker's bill. Protesters were united, as seen in the police and firefighters' participation, despite both being exempt from collective bargaining restrictions.[65] Their participation spoke to the solidarity among state workers. Third, demonstrators understood what collective bargaining meant for their identities. The chant "United we bargain, divided we beg," revealed a unification that went beyond bargaining for incomes and benefits. The protests suggested a sense of class consciousness; government employees were unified in their commitment to raising the living standards of the working-class.

Finally, there was also an international symbolic component via comparisons between the Arab uprisings against Middle Eastern dictators and government employees' resistance to Walker. Protesters made comparisons between Egyptian dictator Hosni Mubarak, who was overthrown by a revolution in 2011, and Walker's assault on public sector workers. The attempt to link corruption in the Middle East with corruption at home spoke to a solidarity expressed by Wisconsin workers with citizens of another country suffering under political repression.

Despite the uprising, the protests failed in preventing the elimination of collective bargaining. Initially, Democratic Senators fled to Illinois, delaying a vote on Walker's bill. Since only 19 Republicans remained, the chamber was unable to vote on budgetary legislation, as 20 Senators are required to establish a quorum.[66] But by stripping elements from the bill relating directly to state finances, the Senate passed the bill by a vote of 18:1 on March 9, followed by a vote for the bill of 53:42 in the Wisconsin Assembly.[67] Walker signed the bill in June, although legal challenges followed. But the Wisconsin Supreme Court and a federal district court ruled the law was constitutional, with decisions on whether to recognize collective bargaining falling on states.

Calls for a general strike were voiced by some protestors, but union leaders settled on a recall strategy. Some progressives attacked this approach, maintaining that union leaders were too timid in fighting Walker, while others were sympathetic.[68] The recall campaign was in full swing by late year in 2011, with union activists collecting more than the half-million signatures needed.[69] Ultimately, the recall failed. The election, which took place in June 2012, saw Walker prevail over Democratic challenger Tom Barrett, with Walker receiving 53 percent of the vote.[70] In a sign of the declining solidarity among union workers, 39 percent of those from union households voted for Walker. This trend mirrored other states during the 2012 presidential election, with Barack Obama only modestly outperforming Mitt Romney with union households in rustbelt states.[71]

Viewed simply as a state-level union campaign, the protests against Walker failed. But as part of a larger economic justice movement, the protests were the first battle in a larger conflict aimed at improving the living standards of working Americans. As labor activist Connor Donegan explained:

> The Wisconsin rebellion was the result of accumulated grievances – declining wages and benefits, cuts to education, unemployment and underemployment, bank bailouts, and record corporate profits – pushed over the edge by an assault on the only remaining organized segment of the working-class.[72]

Following the 2008 crash, the battle for economic justice did not end in Wisconsin. It *began* there, spreading with the Occupy protests, Fight for $15, and the teachers' strikes in Chicago (2012) and West Virginia (2018). As Lee Sustar reflects: "Wisconsin became a touchstone for workers who were searching for both inspiration and strategies for their own similar struggles."[73] And the disruptive tactics adopted in Wisconsin – specifically the sit-in at the state's capitol, inspired other activists, as seen in the civil disobedience of Occupy and the strikes by service workers via Fight for $15.

Madison's Impact on Political Discourse

The Madison protests received sustained attention in the news. This attention was largely positive, privileging the grievances of state employees, while discounting Walker's assertions. To generalize about news coverage, I examined national and local news sources, including 1,116 articles, drawing on a local source: the *Wisconsin State Journal*, radio (*NPR*), a wire service (the *Associated Press*), broadcast news (*ABC*, *CBS*, *NBC*), cable (*CNN*, *Fox News*, *MSNBC*), online news (*CNN.com*), and national news (*New York Times*). I examined every story or segment, op-ed, editorial, and letter to the editor referencing Walker, Madison, and the protests.[74]

I drew on three frameworks from each side of the conflict. On the protesters' side, I included the following:

- References to Walker's efforts to eliminate collective bargaining. Such references were favorable to demonstrators I spoke with, considering Walker's rhetoric claiming his budget bill left collective bargaining "fully intact."[75] This was not the case, as Walker spoke of "changes to limit collective bargaining to the base pay rate" for public sector employees.[76]
- Discussions of the increases in pension and health-care costs for public employees, which were unpopular with most Americans and with protesters.[77]
- References to Walker's $140 million in tax cuts for businesses, which were seen by protesters a "class war" in which the governor cut public employee benefits, while enriching corporations.[78] This point was common among demonstrators with whom I engaged.

On the pro-Walker side, I included the following:

- References to Walker's claim that his legislation was necessary to balance the budget, to deal with the deficit "crisis," and budget problems, and discussions of proposed budget cuts or gaps in the budget.[79] Such references reinforced Walker's attempts to link deficits with collective bargaining.
- Walker's efforts to discredit protesters. This framework included references to them as disruptive and harming the capitol related to his

72 The Economic Justice Movement

claim that protesters were responsible for $7.5 million in property damages. This assertion received a "pants on fire" rating from *Politifact*, which estimated damages at less than $350,000.[80] The framework also includes Walker's discredited claim that 100,000 protesters in Madison were shipped into the state by outside agitators.[81]
- References to Walker's false claim that his bill left collective bargaining "fully intact."

Table 2.1 suggests that media coverage of the protests was favorable. References to Walker's bill as an assault on collective bargaining appeared in most stories for 10 of the 11 outlets. The business tax cuts framework – which spoke to the idea of class war against unions, did not appear nearly as often, and was observed in a majority of stories for none of the 11 outlets. However, references to rising health-care and pension costs appeared in most stories for 8 of the 11 outlets. Partisan patterns were also apparent. *Fox News* was among the least likely to discuss Walker's business tax cuts or his imposition of additional pension and health-care costs on workers. In contrast, *MSNBC* was one of the most likely to stress Walker's tax cuts and his attack on collective bargaining.

While most media outlets regularly conveyed two of the three frameworks favoring protesters, they downplayed many of Walker's claims. Almost no attention was devoted to his claims that protesters "almost all" came from out of state, that they caused property damage, and that his bill left collective bargaining intact. On the other hand, most stories repeated Walker's claim that limiting collective bargaining would reduce the state's deficit. This was an important win for Walker, even if his other claims were ignored, because the hegemonic notion that unions are bad for society was routinely reinforced in Madison coverage. Overall, however, these findings suggest the Madison uprising succeeded in impacting media discourse on an issue of major importance – unionization. One might expect that, because of coverage that disrupted Walker's anti-union agenda, attention to reporting on Madison would produce growing support for unions and collective bargaining.

Media Effects

The Madison protests teach us about the impact of movements as related to the media and intersectionality. Figure 2.2 speaks to both points. Regarding the media, it draws from the *Pew Research Center*'s late-February poll on the protests, which measured how closely citizens followed "news" on "Disputes in Wisconsin between state governments and public employee unions," while asking whether one "side[d] more with the governor or the public employee unions." Media consumption was a significant predictor of protest support, after controlling for race,

Table 2.1 Competing News Frames and the Madison Protests: February 14–March 10, 2011

News Outlet	Favorable Frames (% of stories appearing in)		Critical Frames (% of stories appearing in)		
	Walker Is Attacking Collective Bargaining[1]	Business Tax Cuts[2]	Attack on Pensions / Health Insurance[3]	Deficit Concerns / Budget Repair[4]	Collective Bargaining Intact[5]	Discrediting Protesters[6]
New York Times	92	13	61	56	0	0
ABC News	50	0	60	50	0	0
NBC News	84	0	58	63	0	0
CBS News	83	0	58	79	0	0
CNN	92	7	64	87	<1	1
Fox News	86	4	36	64	0	0
MSNBC	95	38	33	89	0	2
Associated Press	91	11	54	54	0	0
CNN.com	100	16	100	88	0	0
NPR	88	4	65	58	0	0
Wisconsin State Journal	76	4	35	84	0	0

Source: Nexis Uni academic database

Notes

1 This frame included any stories that referenced Governor "Walker" and "collective bargaining" for all news sources examined.
2 This frame included any stories that referenced Governor "Walker" or "protest" or "Madison" within 100 words of references to a "tax break" or "tax breaks" or a "tax cut" or "tax cuts."
3 For all print, broadcast news, online, newswire, and radio transcripts, I examined references to "health care" or "pension(s)" in stories on Governor Walker and the protests. For cable transcripts, I examined references to "Walker" or "protest" or "Madison" within 50 words of "health care" or "pension(s)."
4 For all print, broadcast news, online, newswire, and radio transcripts, I examined references to the Wisconsin "budget" within five words of "repair," or to the need for "balance," a "balanced" budget, or "balancing" the budget, or to references to a "crisis," "gap(s)," or "problem(s)," or "cut(s)" or to a "deficit." For cable transcripts, I examined references to "Walker" within 100 words of "budget." In that sub-sample of articles, I examined articles that referenced the other terms described immediately above.
5 This frame included references to "Walker" and discussions of "collective bargaining" as left "fully intact."
6 For all print, broadcast news, online, newswire, and radio transcripts, I examined references to "property" within five words of references to "damage" or "damaged" property. For cable transcripts, I examined references to "Walker" within 50 words of references to "property" or "damage" or "damaged" property or "property damage."

74   *The Economic Justice Movement*

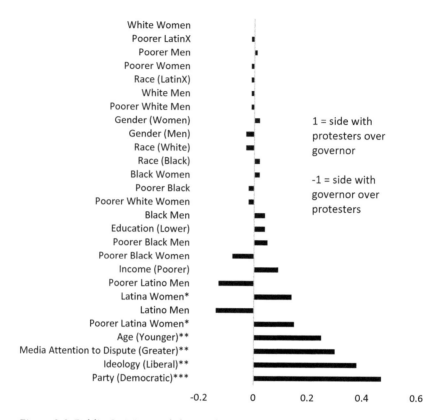

Figure 2.2 Public Opinion and the Madison Protests
Source: *Pew Research Center*, February 24–27, 2011 poll
Controls: gender, age, education, race, income, political party, ideology, media attention
Significance levels: *** = 0.1% ** = 1% * = 5%

income, education, partisanship, ideology, gender, and age. Media consumption was a stronger predictor of attitudes than other variables, with the exceptions of ideology and partisanship.

Regarding intersectionality, one could conclude from Figure 2.2 that the concept holds little significance for Madison.[82] There are few interactions between race, gender, and income that are significant predictors of attitudes toward the conflict. Only Latina women and poorer Latina women were significantly more likely to express an opinion in favor of the protesters, and the relationships are weaker than for age, media consumption, ideology, and partisanship. But this interpretation is a limited reading of public opinion. Taking a more holistic view, we see most Americans expressed favorable views of unions in early 2011. Figure 2.3 provides a summary of

The Economic Justice Movement 75

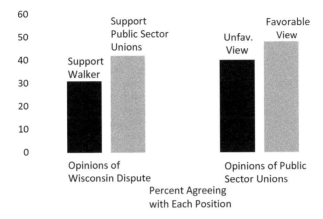

Figure 2.3 Public Opinion of Labor Unions and Wisconsin
Source: *Pew Research Center*, February 3, 2011 poll

findings from *Pew*'s February survey, with a plurality of Americans siding with the unions over Walker and holding favorable views of unions.

Furthermore, intersectionality worked to impact attitudes as related to opinions toward unions. Figure 2.4 draws on a second February 2011 *Pew* poll asking respondents whether they believed union agreements "give union workers unfair advantages" over non-union workers, or if they "ensure union workers are treated fairly." Intersectional identities were significant in predicting attitudes toward unions.

Intersections of race, gender, and class were significant for whites (poorer white men/women and poorer men) and blacks (poorer black men/women and black men/women), although not for LatinX Americans (poorer LatinX men/women, and LatinX men/women). The intersections of race, gender, and income were more powerful predictors of attitudes compared to race or gender alone. Income, although not a significant predictor of opinions toward the protests, was among the most powerful predictors of opinions of unions more generally.

These findings tell us much about public opinion. Protests played an instrumental role in early 2011 in cultivating public support – by garnering sympathetic exposure in the media. The Madison uprising (Figure 2.2) spoke to younger Americans, Democrats, liberals, heavier media consumers, and various LatinX subgroups. In other words, the protests brought many Americans together in favor of worker rights. But the movement struggled to draw support from poorer Americans, women, and black and Latino men. This does not suggest that unions are irrelevant to less privileged groups. As documented in Figure 2.4,

76 The Economic Justice Movement

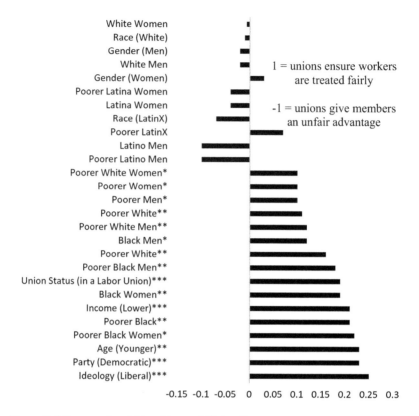

Figure 2.4 Intersectional Identities and Union Support
Source: *Pew Research Center*, February 3, 2011 poll
Controls: gender, age, education, race, income, political party, ideology, union status
Significance levels: *** = 0.1% ** = 1% * = 5%

poorer Americans and disadvantaged groups at the intersections of class, race, and gender identities were more likely to favor unions.

These findings speak to the strengths and weaknesses of Madison. The movement gained news attention and was supported by many Americans. However, the regional, white nature of protests did not speak directly to poorer people of color. This limitation could be addressed via a national resurgence of organized labor, by building a mass movement speaking to diverse groups of Americans.

How central was the union movement to driving public support for progressive politics? The simple answer is that Madison had a significant impact on public opinion. To measure the movement's impact, I examined the second February 2011 *Pew* survey, asking Americans whether they identified with public sector unions in their disputes with state and local governments. This question serves as a proxy measure for assessing the public's attachment to the Madison protests. I examine the predictive power of attachment to the union protest on public attitudes for two survey questions: (1) whether respondents believed unions have a "positive" or "negative" effect on "salary and benefits" for workers; and (2) whether unions have a "positive" or "negative" impact on "the availability of good jobs in America." I assess how strong the public attachment to unions is, relative to the power of a more elitist factor – attachment to the Democratic Party – in predicting support for organized labor.

Figure 2.5 assesses the association between identification with union protesters and support for collective bargaining. Protest support is a stronger predictor of support for collective bargaining than partisanship, after controlling for gender, age, education, race, income, union status (in a union or not), and ideology. This same pattern is revealed in Figure 2.6, for the power of union attachment over partisanship, on recognition that unions protect "good paying jobs."

One might question claims about an impact of Madison on public opinion by arguing that the cause-and-effect relationship is reversed. It could be beliefs that unions protect good jobs and have a positive impact on salaries and benefits are driving public identification with labor protesters, rather than identification with protesters driving opinions about unions' impact. I argue both processes are at work. On the one hand, my time with demonstrators in Madison made it clear protestors were driven by beliefs that unions have a positive impact on

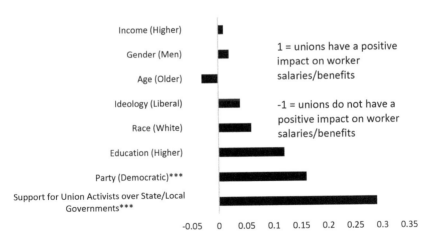

Figure 2.5 Union Support, Partisanship, and Collective Bargaining
Source: *Pew Research Center*, February 3, 2011 poll
Controls: gender, age, education, race, income, ideology, union status
Significance levels: *** = 0.1% ** = 1% * = 5%

78 *The Economic Justice Movement*

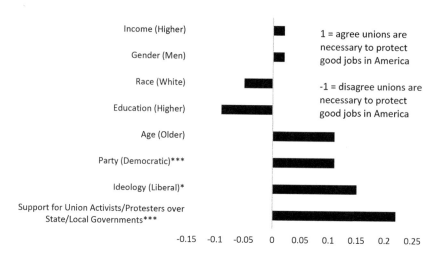

Figure 2.6 Union Support, Partisanship, and Good Jobs in America
Source: *Pew Research Center*, February 3, 2011 poll
Controls: gender, age, education, race, income, political party, ideology, union status
Significance levels: *** = 0.1% ** = 1% * = 5%

working conditions. But this is not the entire story. The protesters were united in solidarity. This solidarity took on a power of its own, inspiring activists and strengthening their commitment to worker rights.

Participants understood that collective action and solidarity were vital to winning benefits for workers. In other words, union identification, and identification with the protests drove protesters to improve the lives of fellow workers.

Furthermore, the Madison protests resonated with the public beyond a utilitarian commitment to collective bargaining. Most Americans approved of the movement and what it stood for; polling from June 2011 found 52 percent sided with teacher unions in disputes with state governors, while polling from February 2011 found a plurality sided with Madison protestors over Walker.[83] Most Americans hold favorable views of unions in general, agreeing they have a positive impact on the pay and benefits received by their members.[84] In other words, there is strong evidence organized labor has had an independent impact on public consciousness. This conclusion is validated by my finding that attention to news on Madison (which favored the protesters) helped to cultivate public support for protesters. Clearly, the movement itself made an impression on the public.

Many who study movements will recognize the power of unions, outside of clientelistic notions that collective bargaining delivers monetary benefits. Americans embrace unions because of the material benefits they bring members. But union support extends beyond that. There is a solidarity component to unionism; rank-and-file members recognize the importance of joining together to exercise a democratic role in the workplace. This solidarity was at work in Madison. Solidarity was apparent via the mass turnout of demonstrators in favor of working-class empowerment. Support for unions extends beyond a mechanistic concern with benefits. It is also driven by empathy with fellow workers and a joint concern for the welfare of working people.

There is also evidence of union solidarity with the public. More than 4 in 10 Americans in February 2011 who were not in a union shared a favorable view of unions.[85] These individuals recognized the value of unions in representing their members, supporting unions independent of self-gain. Nearly half of Americans in March 2011 shared "sympathy" with unions engaged in disputes with employers.[86] While not as strong as "empathy," this sympathy for unions suggests many Americans support organized labor. A second survey question that month found 40 percent of Americans believed "public sector unions that represent employees of local, state, and the federal government" are "more helpful" than "harmful to society."[87] This response measures the importance of unions to the public good, and to a communitarian-style thinking. Finally, 43 percent of Americans in March 2011 agreed "government employee unions help the country" by giving "dedicated public employees like teachers, police, and firefighters the leverage they need to negotiate reasonable pay and benefits packages," in contrast to feelings that "government employee unions hurt the country" because "they demand pay and benefits packages that break our budgets, hurt our fiscal standing, and place an unreasonable burden on the taxpayers who pay the bills."[88] References to unions "helping the country" are an example of the public recognizing the broad societal value of unionization.

The above findings can be interpreted independently of causal processes. The association between attitudes about unions' impact and identification with union protesters exists independently of partisanship. So the labor movement cannot be reduced to a one-dimensional manifestation of elite power over mass consciousness. Democratic Party politics and organized labor are not synonymous. Many working Americans have lost faith in the party. Democratic presidents did much to harm unions. Bill Clinton endorsed the North American Free Trade Agreement, enabling the outsourcing of union jobs. In 2008, Obama promised to pass the Employee Free Choice Act, to streamline the process through which workers vote on forming a union. But Obama abandoned this promise, leaving unions to continue a membership decline that has occurred for decades. The Madison protests, in contrast, sought to disrupt the anti-labor status quo of the modern Democratic Party.

Madison represented a moment in history when workers challenged a political system contributing to their long-term deterioration. The union movement of early 2011 symbolized collective solidarity among working people pursuing their rights. While many scholars neglect the centrality of movements in promoting social change, Madison fueled the campaign for workplace economic justice. If the protests failed to roll back Walker's anti-union agenda, they raised consciousness in support of a pro-labor agenda. The protests inspired a disruptive, insurgent movement in the Democratic Party – via the 2016 and 2020 Sanders campaigns – for the resurgence of organized labor.

Occupy Wall Street: The Fight for Economic Justice Continues

Occupy emerged in the fall of 2011, in the wake of the 2008 economic crash. The movement gave voice to millions who faced an economy marked by stagnant-to-declining incomes, manufacturing outsourcing, and the rise of temporary employment. It spotlighted political and economic systems seen as corrupt and ignorant to the needs of the many. Occupy impacted politics, not in pushing policy reforms, but in raising awareness of poverty, inequality, and plutocratic politics.

While economic grievances drove Occupy, the Canadian magazine *Adbusters* was the spark that lit the protest. On June 9, 2011, the magazine tweeted a call for mobilization, centering on a #OccupyWallStreet initiative, to begin on September 17. As inspiration, *Adbusters* drew on the 2011 uprisings in Tahrir Square, Egypt, resulting in a revolution against Dictator Hosni Mubarak. *Adbusters* cited the Indignados protest movement in Spain, which opposed anti-worker "free market" political reforms following the 2008 global economic crash.[89] The Egyptian revolution was a non-violent uprising that drew support from a broad base of many different activist groups, including Egyptian youth, protesting unemployment, poverty, food insecurity, political repression, and torture.[90] Many Occupy demonstrators drew inspiration from the Egyptian revolution, as well as from the Madison protests, reflected in their chant: "We will fight! We will win! Cairo, New York, Wisconsin!"[91]

The Indignados youth movement (also called the "encampment" movement) was a wave of radical protest that emerged in mid-2011, emphasizing the failure of the Spanish government to provide for citizens' needs in a time of economic crisis. The movement held a radical commitment to disrupting everyday life and politics in Spanish cities, seen in the occupation of, and camping out in, public squares, in addition to demonstrations and other symbolic actions.[92] Grievances driving the protests included anger at the lack of government accountability to the people, concern with rising unemployment, opposition to cuts in public services, resentment toward the government for bailing out banks following the 2008 collapse, and anger at mass home foreclosures. The movement was radical in its rejection of consumer-driven capitalism, reflected in its slogan "we are not commodities in the hands of politicians and bankers," and in its support for nationalized health care, adequate housing-for-all, nationalization of the banks, and demands for direct democracy.[93] The movement relied on *Twitter* and *Facebook*, with tens of thousands mobilizing across 80 cities in 2011, and with hundreds of thousands protesting across 57 cities against cuts in social spending and collective bargaining rights.[94] An estimated 8 million people participated in the Indignados movement, revealing a mass uprising against conservative reforms.[95]

Occupy Wall Street Emerges

Drawing on the aforementioned uprisings, *Adbusters* called for a "revolutionary" movement to challenge Wall Street and disrupt American "business-as-usual" in the nation's leading financial district:

> America needs its own Tahrir acampada. Imagine 20,000 people taking over Wall Street indefinitely ... Are you ready for a Tahrir moment? September 17th, flood into lower Manhattan, set up tents, kitchens, peaceful barricades and occupy Wall Street.[96]

A thousand people responded to the call, occupying Zuccotti Park in New York City, which is a privately owned space in Lower Manhattan's financial district.[97] On September 17, a few hundred activists slept overnight in the park; that number grew to thousands by October.[98] Castells referred to Occupy as "a largely spontaneous expression of outrage," spotlighting the economic suffering of "the 99 percent" of Americans, compared to "the 1 percent" of financial elites.[99]

Within a week of September 17, thousands of marchers were active in Zuccotti Park.[100] Occupiers marched uptown on September 24, resulting in 80 demonstrators being arrested, as police pepper sprayed a group of women, earning the movement significant coverage.[101] Daily marches on Wall Street became the norm, while acts of civil disobedience drew a heavy-handed police response. On October 1, thousands marched on the Brooklyn Bridge, shutting down traffic, leading to 700 arrests.[102] On October 5, 15,000 protesters marched from Foley Square to Zuccotti Park. Although the march was peaceful, 200 were pepper sprayed and arrested after trying to push through barricades that blocked them from entering Wall Street.[103] Protests in New York spread to other cities. Over 951 cities in 82 counties had Occupy encampments, with more than 7,700 arrests across 114 cities.[104]

The Occupiers: Who They Were, What They Believed

Survey work across two of the Occupy chapters – New York and Chicago – determined who the Occupiers were and what they believed. They were more likely to be male (61 percent in NYC; 70 percent in Chicago), college educated (52 percent in NYC; 47 percent in Chicago), younger (average age 33 in NYC; 58 percent were 18–29 in Chicago), white (68 percent in NYC; 71 percent in Chicago) rather than black or LatinX (20 percent in both cities), unemployed (28 percent in NYC; 27 percent in Chicago), from union households (40 percent in NYC), and with bifurcated incomes (63 percent earning less than $100,000 a year, compared to 77 percent of all NYC residents, but with 37 percent earning more than $100,000 a year compared to 24 percent of NYC residents).[105] So Occupy activists were an eclectic mix, with many having higher and lower incomes and with many being unemployed. The group was a fusion of younger, poorer millennials and older, unionized Americans, considering the movement's support from the American Federation of Teachers, the United Federation of Teachers, the SEIU, AFSCME, the AFL-CIO, and the New York Local Transport Workers Union of America.[106]

Occupy activists were progressive-left to radical in their beliefs. Most described themselves as liberal or extremely liberal (72 percent in NYC and Chicago), while 60 percent voted for Obama in 2008 (in NYC). But most were critical of Obama after his promises of "hope" and "change" were accompanied by economic decline, high unemployment, significant losses in household wealth, and growing inequality. Seventy-three percent in New York disapproved of the job Obama was doing as president, compared to 67 percent in Chicago. Three-quarters of Chicago Occupiers said Obama's policies favored the wealthy. For New York activists, 97 percent disapproved of the job Congress was doing; 54 percent said they would not vote Democrat or Republican in 2012; and 73 percent aligned with neither the Democrats nor the Republicans. Just 6 percent in New York said they trusted the government.[107]

In New York City, activists cited economic grievances as motivating their protests. These included anger at Wall Street banks and financial firms bailed out following the 2008 crash; concern with homeowners who were foreclosed on, and disgust with the subprime predatory loan mortgages sold to the consumers, which caused the economic crash; concerns about unemployment and student loan debts; rejection of "trickle down" rhetoric idealizing "free markets," and discontent with the poor state of democracy and the few opportunities for direct forms of political participation.[108] When asked about the biggest concerns driving Occupy, New York activists cited in descending order of importance: (1) concern with growing inequality and the political power of the "1 percent"; (2) frustration with the dominant role of money in politics; (3) concern with corporate greed; (4) concern with student loan debt; (5) support for organized labor; (6) health-care concerns; and (7) concern with unemployment.[109]

Occupy's Radical Politics

Occupy was driven by principles of egalitarianism and participatory democracy. It rejected "vertical authority" structures, favoring "horizontal" decision-making, in which participants were supposed to be equals.[110] The General Assembly of Occupy New York – meeting daily in fall 2011 – was a place for democratic deliberation, with motions requiring 90 percent approval to pass.[111]

The movement was radical in its disruptive tactics. The occupation of Zuccotti Park – a privately owned space, and the occupation of the Brooklyn Bridge, were acts of civil disobedience, as was what they symbolized – the envisioning of an alternative society free of corporate power in politics, culture, and society. New York Occupy sought to build an alternative community with tents, toilets, a "people's kitchen," childcare assistance, spaces for play and a community garden, a "people's library," medical assistance, and security.[112] Occupy's tactics were "performative," via public displays of protest, which spoke to acts of historical civil disobedience such as the sit-in civil rights protests of the 1960s and the theatrical antics of anti-Vietnam War demonstrators.[113] These protests were radical and disruptive in that they sought to uproot the political status quo. Occupy rejected the hegemonic norms of capitalism that were driving American politics.

Other radical disruptive acts occurred outside New York. The "Occupy Our Homes" day of action (December 6, 2011), organized in 25 cities, protested a political system that bailed out banks, but allowed Americans to lose their residences to foreclosure. Occupy action centered on (1) efforts to prevent the foreclosures by camping out at homes; (2) disruption of courthouse hearings on properties under foreclosure; and (3) campaigns to reclaim vacant homes for homeless people and others in need.[114]

The most militant of all chapters, Occupy Oakland, engaged in radical protest, met by police violence after demonstrators were forced out of Frank Ogawa Plaza. The incident received heavy attention after an 84-year-old retired schoolteacher was pepper sprayed, and the *YouTube* video of the incident gained exposure.[115] Roughly 30,000 protesters pushed back against police to re-establish the camp. Civil disobedience was used when Occupy shut down the port of Oakland, the second largest on the west coast, through a general strike on December 12, 2011.[116] Occupy efforts to shut down other ports occurred in Los

Angeles, San Diego, Tacoma, Longview, and Seattle, partly in solidarity with the International Longshoreman Workers Union in its dispute with EGT corporation in Longview, Washington.[117]

The Limits of Occupy

Occupy was not without critics. Political officials viewed it as an embarrassing eyesore that polluted "public" places. Police suppression in cities and on college campuses such as University of California, Davis, where non-violent occupiers were pepper sprayed, sent the message that disruptive occupations were unwelcome. Political officials shut down encampments throughout the fall of 2011, citing safety concerns, litter, unsanitary conditions, and public health hazards to evict protesters.[118] Despite these pretexts, it was clear that Occupy's ideology and its disruptive tactics were a threat to the established order.[119] Aggressive clearing tactics, coupled with the growing cold of winter, led to Occupy's downfall.[120] The Chicago Grant Park camp was shut down by police shortly after it was established. In Philadelphia, Boston, and Los Angeles, camps were shut down by police by late November to December.[121] Camps in Oakland and New York were closed in mid-November.[122]

Occupy was criticized for its almost exclusive focus on economics, marginalizing racist and sexist discrimination. Despite some evidence the movement attempted to develop solidarity across class, race, and gender lines, Occupiers often dismissed concerns that were not explicitly economic.[123] Reports emphasized the lack of concern within Occupy over misogyny and racism, pointing to these shortcomings as reasons why women and people of color failed to embrace the movement.[124] Gould-Wartofsky recounts his experiences in the New York camp, and on the white male privilege that defined Occupy.

> Bearded white men quickly assumed positions of power, influence, and informal leadership as the "coordinators." They had done so by way of an unspoken division of labor that ran through the working groups, and increasingly, through the General Assembly itself.[125]

Occupiers claimed they were building a "post-racial" society; therefore, little attention was devoted to racism.[126] This position meant that funds "flowed freely to every [working] group but the People of Color [group]. Many who came to the occupation to speak out" about racism "found their voices silenced, their views sidelined by facilitators and the drafters of key documents."[127]

Occupy pioneered a unique means of communicating in encampments with large numbers of people, without use of amplification, via the "People's Mic." By yelling "Mic Check," individuals and groups were ceded time to deliberate, and messages were spread throughout the camp by word of mouth. But the People of Color working group struggled to gain attention, as their messages were muffled, marginalizing their concerns.[128] The New York camp was defined by misogynist behavior, as Wartofsky reflects on the aggressive white, radical "young men," pejoratively labeled "manarchists or mactivists" who

> vied with one another for personal prestige, political influence, and sexual partners among their peers. They jockeyed for position in the social order of Occupy, jostled for a place at the front lines of the action, and loudly asserted their masculinity in the guise of 'radical autonomy.'[129]

The white male privilege phenomenon was not anecdotal. A survey of New York Occupy found little interest in understanding intersecting forms of discrimination across class, color, and gender lines. Nowhere in the list of concerns motivating activists was sexism found. Concerns with immigrant rights and racism were weak, appearing near the bottom of a list of issues that led activists to support Occupy.[130] Considering these findings, one can see why critics dismissed the movement as dominated by "white guys hanging out in parks," large numbers of whom dismissed the problems of women and people of color.

A second criticism emphasized Occupy's unwillingness to offer reform proposals. Gitlin described Occupy as "more disruptive, more utopian" than other movements.[131] It was an "apolitical" movement, avoiding political advocacy, but wanting to transform the political-economic system.[132] Occupy intellectuals voiced support for "stay[ing] out of politics," while agreeing that "achieving reforms is important."[133] The fear of being perceived as mainstream motivated them to avoid political engagement, with Occupiers more likely to see themselves as "independent" of parties, compared to Tea Party supporters, who were closely affiliated with the Republican Party.[134]

The aversion to political engagement was confirmed in the New York General Assembly's announcement that "Occupy Wall Street does not make demands," and their call to "occupy everything, [and] demand nothing."[135] The reluctance to articulate a vision resulted from a split between Occupy's radical and reformist elements. As one account from the New York camp reflected: "Anarchists and horizontalists pushed for a process of unanimous consensus, while democratic socialists, populists, and pragmatists favored some form of majority vote."[136] The New York camp required 90 percent of the General Assembly to vote for a proposal for adoption, making it difficult to organize for change. As Gould-Wartofsky explains, "the would-be occupiers came to a decision, early on, to eschew any and all demands, not because they knew better, but because they could not come to a consensus on what demands to make."[137]

Occupy, Social Media, and the News

Occupy's pioneering of social media activism received significant attention.[138] And although the movement was analyzed by sociologists, it got little recognition from mainstream political scientists. Scant attention was paid to how media covered Occupy, and research that was done only looked at how the movement was negatively portrayed.[139] Previous research finds Occupy activists relied heavily on social media and in-person communication to articulate their goals.[140] Social media venues such as *Facebook*, *YouTube*, *Tumblr*, and *Twitter* aided activists in disseminating messages, coordinating protests, and spotlighting police repression.[141] Most camps had a *Facebook* page, and members of New York Occupy sent out 120,000 tweets a day in November 2011.[142]

Social media were instrumental in spreading Occupy's "99 percent" slogan regarding growing inequality.[143] But at its core, Occupy was a face-to-face movement.[144] The New York encampment relied on in-person communication, with General Assembly meetings occurring twice a day.[145] Other cities heavily depended on face-to-face dialogue. Occupy New York primarily relied on in-person networking. Of New York Occupiers, 82 percent reported visiting the camp at Zuccotti Park and marching in at least one Occupy protest, while 64 percent participated in at least one General Assembly meeting. By comparison, 66 percent posted about Occupy on *Facebook*, *Twitter*, or other social media. While online networking was central to the movement, it did not replace direct communications.[146]

How did Occupy fare in the news? This question is central to identifying the impact of a movement seeking to shift political discourse. I analyzed 10 national media sources, including any story, analysis, segment, op-ed, editorial, or letter to the editor during the fall of 2011 and early 2012 mentioning "Occupy Wall Street." I utilized the *Lexis Nexis* database, analyzing more than 3,400 articles, spanning online news, radio, cable, broadcast news, and print, from September 17, 2011 (the first day of the protests in New York City), through January 15, 2012, when protesters attempted to re-occupy Zuccotti Park after being expelled.

I included three frames speaking positively to Occupy, with messages drawn from activists' grievances, including:

- references to Occupy and the 2008 bailout – a central grievance of the movement, and references to corporate greed;[147]
- references to class discrepancies or conflict between the top 1 percent of income earners and the 99 percent, or references to rich or the upper-class in contrast the middle-class, or to poverty, the poor, or lower-class Americans;[148]
- references to Occupy's concerns with jobs, the economy/financial crisis, unemployment, and capitalism.[149]

In contrast, I also examined three critical frames:

- comments referring to violence as related to Occupy, including rape, assaults, or sexual assaults in the camps, and to police reliance on tear gas, pepper spray, and arrests;[150]
- discussions of Occupy as a leaderless or anarchist movement – used by critics to argue the movement lacked viability;[151]
- references to Occupy raising questions about its agenda, goals, or demands.[152] These points were made by critics, including leftists.[153]

Although the movement was subject to regular criticism in the media, it received more positive coverage than not. Table 2.2 provides estimates for the 10 outlets. References to corporate greed and the bailout appeared in most stories for only 4 of 10 news outlets, but appeared in 29 to 50 percent of stories for the other six.

The class conflict frame materialized in most stories for 6 of the 10 outlets and appeared in 30 to 47 percent of stories for the other four. References to economic anxiety appeared most of the time for 3 of 10 outlets, but regularly in other venues, 31 to 50 percent of the time. Critical frames were less frequent. "Law and order" references, concerning discussion of Occupy violence and police management of protests, were reported most of the time for 4 of 10 news organizations. References to Occupy's lack of formal leadership and its lack of an agenda were more infrequent, failing to appear in most stories for any of the 10 outlets.

Occupy, despite its radical politics, broke into political discourse via sustained media coverage of its grievances. Public anger over corporate greed was common following the 2008 crash. Occupy capitalized on that sentiment. It drew attention to class conflict and inequality, focusing on American anxieties in a depressed economy. With 40 percent of Americans in 2012 holding negative perceptions of capitalism, Occupy's criticisms of the economic system found a sympathetic audience.[154]

Coverage of Occupy highlighted the allegedly deviant nature of the protests, emphasizing arrests and confrontations with police. But this trend is hardly unique to Occupy, as scholarship documents media marginalization of other progressive movements.[155] The lack of attention to criticisms of Occupy, related to its lack of an agenda or leaders, is noteworthy. These criticisms could have been emphasized if journalists sought to undermine Occupy. That would not have been difficult, especially if journalists emphasized the radical politics of anarchist organizers.

Media Effects

As with Madison, Occupiers utilized the media to garner favorable attention. Although the media are known for an official source and hegemonic

Table 2.2 Media Coverage of Occupy (9/17/2011–1/15/2012)

Favorable Frames					Critical Frames	
	Corporate Greed (% of stories appearing in)	Class Conflict	Economic Anxiety	Law and Order (% of stories appearing in)	Leadership?	Agenda?
New York Times	36	52	36	39	9	12
Associated Press	52	54	31	57	9	8
National Public Radio	50	67	50	36	5	7
ABC News	30	36	47	48	1	7
CBS News	48	47	59	56	5	9
NBC News	29	30	33	42	2	4
CNN	51	51	71	59	9	17
MSNBC	53	82	75	39	7	26
Fox News	32	42	43	41	10	10
CNN.com	52	65	48	59	16	21

Source: Lexis Nexis academic database

biases, Occupy forced its way into the media spotlight. This was likely due to the large nature of the protests, making it more difficult for reporters to ignore. One would expect that, considering the positive coverage, greater public attention to news on Occupy produced growing sympathy. To measure media effects, I examined two *Pew* polls from October and December 2011, during the rise and fall of Occupy. *Pew* surveyed Americans on their attention to news on "anti-Wall Street protests in New York and other cities" and their "opinions of the Occupy Wall Street movement" and "the concerns" the movement raised. Figure 2.7 documents the impact of the media, and intersecting group identities, on public opinion. Those paying closer attention to Occupy in October and December were significantly more likely to support the movement, after

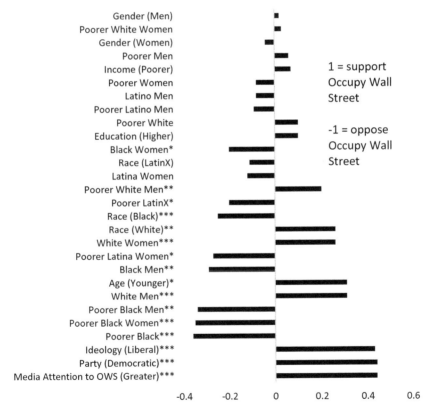

Figure 2.7 Public Opinion of Occupy Wall Street
Source: *Pew Research Center*, October 2011 poll
Controls: gender, age, education, race, income, ideology, party
Significance levels: *** = 0.1% ** = 1% * = 5%

controlling for respondents' gender, age, education, race, income, ideology, and political party. These findings reinforce the power of movements to gain media attention and public support.

Figure 2.7 reveals the strengths and weaknesses of Occupy in appealing to Americans of intersecting identities, and to relatively disadvantaged groups. On the one hand, the movement significantly appealed to white men and women and to poorer white men and women. So the movement appealed to disadvantaged Americans, within limits. But it was less successful in cultivating support from other groups, including black men and women, poorer LatinX Americans, poorer blacks, poorer Latina women, and poorer black men and women. These findings, aside from demonstrating the relevance of an intersectional analysis of Occupy, reveal that the intersecting identity group variables listed in Figure 2.7 were more powerful than single identity groups (for gender, race, and income) in predicting opinions of Occupy. In other words, intersectional analysis provides significant "value added" when analyzing how identity impacts social movement attitudes. What do we make of Occupy's struggle to resonate with people of color and poor people of color? These findings are not surprising when we consider the criticisms of the movement – that it was disinterested in the problems facing minorities and poor people of color, and that it exhibited misogynist tendencies, reflected in the gendered power dynamics of the NYC encampment. Occupy was a significant movement for change, offering radical critiques of the U.S. political-economic system, and those messages gained attention in the news and the ear of the public. Occupy captivated tens of millions with its critiques of American capitalism, raising hopes that another political and economic system was possible. But by failing to target racism and sexism, the movement struggled to gain traction among poorer people of color. Appealing to these groups was necessary if Occupy wished to flower into a larger movement representing economically disadvantaged Americans across class, gender, and color lines.

Despite Occupy's limits, the movement gained mass support. By December 2011, 44 percent supported Occupy, while 39 percent were opposed.[156] My analysis of *Pew*'s October 2011 survey also found the movement was more likely to be supported by lower-income whites, younger Americans, the more highly educated, liberals, and Democrats.

Although income was not a significant predictor of support in the October *Pew* poll, the December *Pew* poll found the movement made inroads with poorer Americans. Americans identifying as "lower-class" were 13 percentage points more likely to support Occupy than those identifying as "upper-middle-class," and 25 percentage points more likely to support it than members of the "upper-class." Americans from households earning less than $10,000 a year and from $10,000 to $20,000 were 18 and 21 percentage points respectively more likely to support Occupy than those earning more than $150,000. These findings were statistically significant after controlling for respondents' race, gender, education, age, party, and ideology.[157]

Occupy's Radical Appeal

Occupy's politics were radical, via its attempt to construct alternative communities, challenging hegemonic individualistic notions of identity under capitalism. Occupy's concern with growing inequality and plutocratic politics put it at odds with capitalism. But how strongly did Occupy's politics resonate with the public? To answer this question, I examined survey data on Occupy supporters to gauge how closely attachment to the movement was tied to leftist political-economic views. Figure 2.8, drawn from the December 2011 *Pew* survey, suggests the movement's radical, counter-hegemonic politics spoke to many Americans. While a concern with the threat posed by financial and banking institutions was not a significant predictor of Occupy support, all other political views examined helped account for why many embraced the movement. The strongest factors associated with embracing Occupy were support for socialism, and the feeling that the rich and corporations have too much power. By comparison, less radical assessments of the political-economic system were not as strongly associated with Occupy support – including feelings that the wealthy are not paying

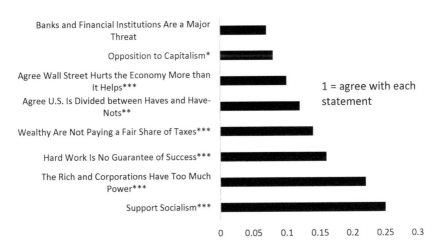

Figure 2.8 Economic Attitudes and Support for Occupy Wall Street
Source: *Pew Research Center*, December 2011
Significance levels: *** = 0.1% ** = 1% * = 5%

92 The Economic Justice Movement

their fair share of taxes, that hard work is no guarantee of economic success, and that Wall Street has hurt the economy more than helped it. All three of these views are potentially compatible with a reformist political approach seeking to rein in corporate power. In contrast, feelings that the rich and corporations have too much power – when coupled with support for socialism – suggest a foundational rejection of the political-economic system, and of hegemonic notions that Americans should be self-reliant, without expecting government assistance, in a "free market" system. It was Occupy's leftist politics that awakened a radical spirit among millions who were increasingly disillusioned with the economy, and politics, thereby disrupting a political culture that had long celebrated the "virtues" of the "free market" system.

Despite Political Science downplaying social movements' importance, the evidence with Occupy suggests it was more a force in driving public support for progressive government policies, compared to attachment to the Democratic Party. As Figure 2.9 suggests, support for Occupy was more than twice as powerful a predictor of support for government helping unemployed Americans find jobs, and more powerful than age, education, ideology, income, gender, and race. As documented in Figure 2.10, Occupy support was a slightly stronger predictor than partisanship of support for the notion that government should reduce inequality between rich and poor.

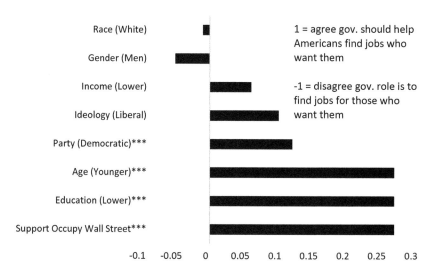

Figure 2.9 Occupy Wall Street and Economic Policy Attitudes: Jobs
Source: *Pew Research Center*, July 2012 poll
Controls: gender, age, education, race, income, ideology, party
Significance levels: *** = 0.1% ** = 1% * = 5%

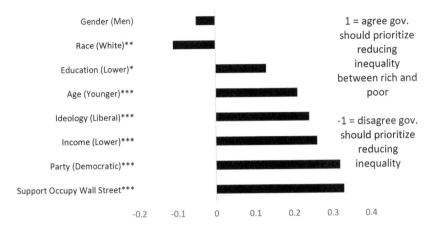

Figure 2.10 Occupy Wall Street and Economic Policy Attitudes: Inequality
Source: *Pew Research Center*, July 2012 poll
Controls: gender, age, education, race, income, ideology, party
Significance levels: *** = 0.1% ** = 1% * = 5%

The results, when coupled with the Madison findings, reveal that social movements stand at the forefront of driving public opinion toward progressive change.

The above findings can be interpreted in two ways. One can argue that Occupy support drove progressive attitudes, as related to government action on creating jobs and reducing inequality. Or one could claim that support for government action on creating jobs and reducing inequality drove support for Occupy. I argue both processes were at work. It is clear from examining surveys of Occupy demonstrators that they were motivated by concerns with inequality and growing economic insecurity in America. But the movement took on a life of its own, inspiring Americans and galvanizing public support. It reinforced the notion that Americans could join in solidarity to disrupt a political-economic system deemed corrupt and failing the masses.

For example, one survey in the months following the fall of Occupy found more than 40 percent of Americans identified with the movement and its notion of solidarity among "the 99 percent."[158] This power of the collective should not be downplayed by simply emphasizing the movement as driven by individual grievances.

As a representation of collective identity, Occupy's appeal was apparent from numerous surveys. Polling data from October 2011 found 46 percent of Americans believed "the views of people involved in the movement generally reflect the views of most Americans."[159]

That same month, 47 percent saw Occupy as a "positive force" due to the negative effects of Wall Street greed on "ordinary Americans." By comparison, 37 percent agreed Occupy was "a negative force," made up of "left-wing activists" who hated "free markets."[160] Either way, 84 percent of Americans agreed that Occupy had an effect on society. In December 2011, 48 percent agreed "with the concerns Occupy protests have raised."[161] And despite the demise of Occupy, 39 percent of Americans believed in April 2012 that the movement served "a vital and important purpose" by "protesting against the conduct of large corporations and wage inequality between workers and executives."[162] The concern with wage inequality was a sign of solidarity with the poor. This concern was present among higher-income earners who participated in the movement, and higher-income Americans supporting Occupy. For example, Pew's October 2011 poll found 52 percent of Americans earning $100,000 a year or more supported Occupy, even though they were unlikely to suffer from economic insecurity.

Figures 2.9 and 2.10 can also be interpreted to suggest the importance of Occupy, without calling on notions of causality. Support for Occupy and for government action on jobs and inequality were strongly associated, and this relationship persisted after controlling for partisanship and its relationship to economic policy attitudes. Occupy was fiercely independent in its politics and disassociated itself from the Democratic Party – even if many Democrats supported the movement. Occupy operated outside the bipartisan spectrum of opinions in Washington D.C. To say the movement was an adjunct of the Democratic Party is to severely misunderstand it. At a time of mass distrust of government and anger at rising inequality, Occupy spoke to tens of millions who shared its concerns. The movement exercised independent power by utilizing the media to build public support. As I discuss in Chapter 4, it also impacted Democratic politics, via the Bernie Sanders electoral campaign.

Fight for $15

Little scholarship has examined social movement efforts to promote a higher minimum wage, or a "living wage" empowering workers to provide for basic needs.[163] A few journalistic accounts examined the labor movement's recent push for a higher minimum wage, but these inquiries do not explore the ways the movement was covered in the news or how it was viewed by the public.[164]

Fight for $15 has its roots in the 1990s and 2000s, in municipal politics. Labor and community groups organized for living wage ordinances covering city employees, private sector employees, or both.[165] This movement met with initial success, with 140 cities establishing living wage ordinances by 2007, despite flying under the radar of national discourse.[166] Against plutocratic dominance of government,

Fight for $15 sought to reassert citizen influence over politics. It challenged the hegemonic notion that "free markets" best provide for workers, and that labor organizing is harmful to the working poor.

The living wage movement shifted its focus by the 2010s to establishing higher minimum wages in states and nationally. It advocated for higher pay for service workers, and better health care and other benefits. These workers found an ally in organized labor, particularly the Service Employees International Union (SEIU). But protests were planned by union activists, community activists, immigrant rights groups, religious leaders and faith-based groups, and women's rights organizations.[167] All of this is to say the movement was driven by solidarity among different activist groups working together to achieve change.

Fight for $15 drew on the grievances and vigilance of food service workers. They had grown increasingly frustrated at an industry employing workers in high-stress environments, earning low wages, and offering the average worker just 24 hours of work a week to circumvent legal requirements to provide health insurance to full-time workers.[168] These grievances were the impetus for the disruptive strikes employed by service workers throughout the 2010s.

Activist accounts of Fight for $15 trace its rise to the disruptive successes of Occupy Wall Street. As labor activist David Rolf explained about the food service protests: "we are operating in a changed public opinion environment post-Occupy, when income inequality and wage stagnation are finally becoming among the principal moral issues of our time. After forty years of stagnant and declining wages, people have had enough."[169] Fight for $15 and Occupy drew on support from unions, which saw the uprisings as vital to the fight against the impoverishment of American workers.

Chronology of the Protests

With Fight for $15, employees organized within low-wage service industries, including fast food and retail chains. The movement emerged in the early 2010s, with service workers protesting a minimum wage that had fallen in value greatly since its highest value of nearly $11 an hour (in 2018 dollars) in 1969.[170] The first action occurred in November 2012, when workers from New York Communities for Change organized a walk-out strike of workers from McDonalds, Wendy's, Taco Bell, KFC, and Burger King, demanding a $15 minimum wage.[171] Protests continued in July 2013, when hundreds of restaurant workers walked out of dozens of establishments in Chicago, Detroit, and St. Louis, and in August when workers in 60 cities walked out demanding higher pay.[172] These disruptions continued into December, when thousands in more than 100 cities walked out.[173] For Wal-Mart employees, walk-outs and protests in 2012 occurred in a dozen

96 *The Economic Justice Movement*

cities, provoking a retaliatory response from the company, as workers were illegally fired for labor organizing.[174] In 2013, Wal-Mart employees took part in a "Ride for Respect" in which 100 traveled to the corporation's headquarters in Bentonville, Arkansas to attend a shareholders meeting demanding better treatment.[175] Additional fast-food protests occurred in September 2014 in more than 100 cities, and in December in over 190 cities.[176] May 2015 saw turnouts in hundreds of cities, including Boston, New York, Atlanta, and Los Angeles, with estimates of 60,000 fast food, home care, retail, academic, and airport workers supporting higher wages and benefits.[177] In 2017, demonstrations included Midwestern hospital workers, who joined hundreds of food service workers across the country in walk-out strikes on Labor Day.[178] Even larger numbers protested in February 2018, when 50 cities saw demonstrations demanding a $15 wage and the right to form a union.[179]

Calls for higher pay were supported by some political leaders. Bernie Sanders adopted a $15 minimum wage in his policy platform when he ran for president in 2016 and 2020.[180] Elizabeth Warren also supported a $15 wage in her 2020 presidential campaign, as did Beto O'Rourke, Kamala Harris, Joe Biden, and others. In total, 19 Democratic Presidential candidates supported the $15 wage – a sign of the impact of the Fight for $15 on mainstream Democratic electoral politics.[181]

Fight for $15 commanded little attention, struggling to break into media discourse. Fight for $15 (Figure 2.11) did not receive as much coverage in the *New York Times* during the 2010s, compared to the Tea Party and Black Lives Matter.

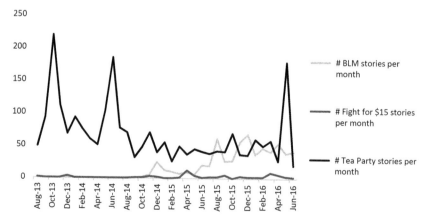

Figure 2.11 Fight for $15 Coverage in Comparative Context (8/1/2013–6/30/2018)

Source: *Nexis Uni* academic database

Utilizing *Nexis Uni*, I find Fight for $15 averaged just 0.2 stories a day in 2014, 0.5 stories a day in 2015, and 0.2 stories a day in 2016. By comparison, the Tea Party appeared in 3.6 stories a day in 2010. The Madison protests appeared in 1.7 stories a day in February and March 2011, while Occupy appeared in 9.7 stories a day in late 2011. The Ferguson protests were referenced in 8.5 stories a day in August 2014, while Black Lives Matter was referenced in 0.7 to 1.7 stories a day in 2015 and 2016.

Coverage of Fight for $15 was meager across many news sources, as documented in Table 2.3. Depending on the venue, the ratio of stories referencing BLM compared to Fight for $15 ranged from 9:1 to 81:1, while the ratio for Tea Party to Fight for $15 spanned from 35:1 to 209:1.

The discrepancy between coverage of BLM and Fight for $15 *could* be explained by the differences in the protests, with the labor strikes being short daily episodes, compared to the sustained period of protests for BLM in Ferguson, Baltimore, and elsewhere. But this fails to explain why Fight for $15 received less attention than the Tea Party, which was also defined by short, daily protest episodes. To explain unequal coverage, we should look to the difference between the Tea Party and Fight for $15, based on their varied

Table 2.3 A Marginalized Movement: Comparative Coverage of Fight for $15 (8/1/2013–6/30/2016)

News Outlet	Fight for $15	Black Lives Matter	Tea Party	Ratio of BLM to Fight for $15 Stories	Ratio of Tea Party to Fight for $15 Stories
New York Times	23	210	806	9:1	35:1
ABC News	0.7	26	69	37:1	99:1
NBC News	0	18	59	–	–
CBS News	1	29	97	29:1	97:1
CNN	23	560	1,388	24:1	60:1
Fox News	3.4	111	439	33:1	129:1
MSNBC	5.8	102	585	18:1	101:1
Associated Press	56	818	3,649	15:1	65:1
CNN.com	2.7	111	108	41:1	40:1
NPR	0.7	57	146	81:1	209:1

Source: *Nexis Uni* database

98 *The Economic Justice Movement*

support from political officials. While the Tea Party was embraced by Republican leaders, Fight for $15 received little initial Democratic support. Outside of Presidential candidate Bernie Sanders, few high-profile officials called for a $15 minimum wage during the early to mid-2010s, and the movement was marginalized in media discourse.

Compared to Hillary Clinton, Sanders' campaign received significantly less news attention during the primary season.[182] This was likely the result of journalists seeing Sanders and his "democratic socialism," as non-mainstream. Despite complaints about a "Bernie blackout," Sanders was the primary competition for Clinton in the primaries, and his status as a presidential candidate could be expected to produce greater coverage for Fight for $15, considering he embraced the movement.

Reporters were more likely to discuss a $15 minimum wage in the context of the Sanders campaign than in relation to Fight for $15. In Figure 2.12, I measure during the 2016 primary season the discrepancy between the stories covering Sanders and a $15 minimum wage, compared to coverage of Fight for $15. For every month but one, Sanders stories outnumbered Fight for $15 stories by 2:1 to 6:1. While Fight for $15 received little attention, the $15 minimum wage was more "newsworthy" when attached to Sanders' campaign.

Despite the lack of media attention, the public was sympathetic to Fight for $15's push for higher wages. In 2015, 73 percent supported a minimum wage raise.[183] And Pew found in August 2016 that

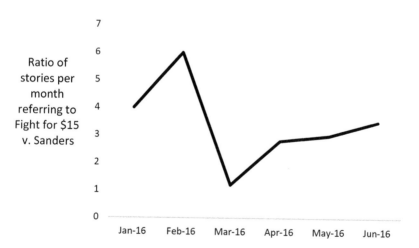

Figure 2.12 Sanders' Impact on $15 Minimum Wage Coverage in the *New York Times*

Source: *Nexis Uni* academic database

58 percent of Americans supported a $15 minimum wage.[184] By 2019, two-thirds supported this wage.[185]

Protests from service workers pressured states to raise minimum wages. American states were more likely in the mid-to-late 2010s to raise the minimum wage – at the height of Fight for $15 – than in the early-to-mid 2000s. During the first five years of the new millennium, the nation typically saw five to seven states raise the minimum wage per year. In contrast, 20 states raised their minimum wage in 2015, while 14 did so in 2016, 21 in 2017, and 18 in 2018.[186] These raises occurred in Democratic and Republican states.

Looking to New York and California, where both states announced plans for a $15 minimum wage, it is clear Fight for $15 had an impact. In New York, Governor Andrew Cuomo declared a "Drive for $15" tour across the state, as part of the broader "Campaign for Economic Justice."[187] In April 2016, he announced a raise in the state's minimum wage from $9 to $15 by 2020 before an audience of labor activists, labor leaders, and fast-food workers.[188] Cuomo's efforts were an example of a politician reaching out to constituents in his re-election campaign. Officials appeal to interest groups and social movements to improve their electoral prospects. And workers were courted throughout Cuomo's campaign at rallies and in the legislative process. As the *New York Times* reported:

> When lawmakers in Albany balked at the idea [of raising the minimum wage], Mr. Cuomo convened a board to look at wages in the fast-food industry, which is one of the biggest employers of low-wage workers in the state, with about 180,000 employees. After hearing testimony from dozens of fast-food workers, the board members decided the state should mandate that fast-food chains pay more.[189]

A similar scenario played out in California. Democratic Governor Jerry Brown was reluctant to consider a large minimum wage increase, but pressure from service workers and the public changed his mind. As the Sacramento Bee reported:

> Brown, a fiscal moderate, had previously expressed reservations about a wage increase. But amid growing concern about income inequality in California and the national thrust of the labor-backed 'Fight for 15' campaign, his hand was forced. Public opinion polls showed strong support for increasing the state's mandatory minimum beyond its current $10.[190]

The cases of New York and California suggest that progressive reforms are possible when movements pressure officials for change. Minimum wage raises are popular with the public, and Democratic leaders seek to cultivate votes from service workers and union members in their political base. These electoral pressures, coupled with protests from organized labor, suggest officials had an electoral incentive to represent poorer Americans.

The gains of Fight for $15 are also visible nationally. Sanders staked out a progressive presidential campaign drawing on organized labor and Fight for $15. He explicitly referenced the movement in his electoral efforts.[191] Although he did not win the 2016 Democratic primary race, his populist campaign directed attention to a minimum wage increase. And Hillary Clinton's adoption of a $12 minimum wage was an obvious nod to pressure from Sanders.[192] While Clinton lost the election, her support for a wage increase suggested Fight for $15 was pushing the Democratic Party to the left. That commitment continued, with Senate and House Democratic leaders Chuck Schumer and Nancy Pelosi introducing a "Better Deal" legislative proposal in 2017, supporting a $15 minimum wage.[193]

The Fight for $15 succeeded in mainstreaming its political demands. From 2013 to 2016, the *New York Times* printed 434 articles referencing a $15 minimum wage, which is just 12 stories a month, or 0.4 stories a day. In the 2016 primary and election (January through November), references to a $15 minimum wage appeared in only 0.5 stories a day. But by 2019, the issue had gained wider acceptance, with 19 Democratic Presidential candidates embracing it, and House Democrats passing legislation supporting a $15 minimum wage. This growing acceptance overlapped with increased coverage of the $15 wage, as the *New York Times* ran 286 articles on the subject in the first eight months of the year alone, averaging 36 articles a month, and 1.2 per day. This represents a tripling of coverage compared to from 2013 to 2016, reflecting the rising popularity of Fight for $15's political agenda.

At the time of writing (September 2019), Fight for $15 had not yet initiated a mass wave of organization across the nation by galvanizing laborers to protest or strike for a higher minimum wage or for re-unionization. Protests and strikes occurred once or a few times a year in the 2010s. And labor continued its long decline in this period, via the falling unionization rate. However, Fight for $15 demonstrated that its demand for higher wages was widely supported by the mass public, and by the Democratic Party.

We see the potential of Fight for $15 in opinion surveys. Figure 2.13 documents support for a $15 minimum wage across demographic groups. Fight for $15's cause does not suffer from the same limitations as the Madison protests and Occupy. The $15 minimum wage is supported by disadvantaged groups, including lower-income Americans, blacks and black women, LatinX men and women, and poorer LatinX men and women. Additionally, the movement draws

The Economic Justice Movement 101

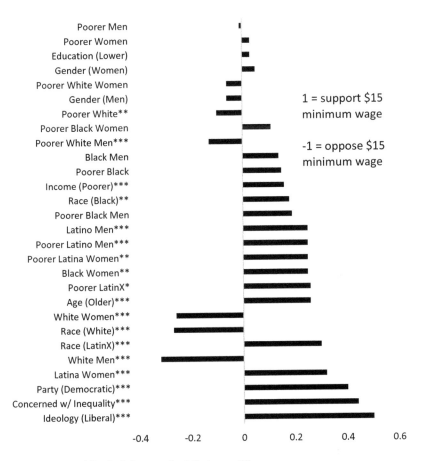

Figure 2.13 Public Opinion on the Minimum Wage
Source: *Pew Research Center*, August 2016 poll
Controls: gender, age, education, race, income, ideology, party
Significance levels: *** = 0.1% ** = 1% * = 5%

support from older Americans, Democrats, liberals, and those concerned with inequality.

Although a $15 minimum wage is more likely to be opposed by poorer whites and poorer white men, these findings are misleading. Right-wing politics are not driving white men and poorer white men to oppose raising the minimum wage. Poorer white men are more likely to support a higher minimum wage, just not $15. According to *Pew*'s December 2015 survey, 71 percent of poorer white men (earning under $50,000 a year) favored raising the minimum wage. A plurality favored a raise to $10 to $10.99 an hour, while 65 percent said they favored a raise to higher than $7.25 to as much as $10.99.

Fight for $15 did not suffer from the limits of other progressive movements. While Occupy and Madison struggled to cultivate support among women, people of color, and poorer women and poorer people of color, Fight for $15 did not have this problem. It had not succeeded by the late 2010s in doubling the national minimum wage. But it does benefit from majority support and draws support from poor communities and poor people of color. This is likely due to the inclusive nature of a higher minimum wage, which benefits poor whites, blacks, and LatinX individuals. Despite challenges, Fight for $15 saw its greatest successes in not only the $15 minimum wage raises in New York and California, but also its pressuring Democrats to embrace the movement.

Conclusion

The Madison protests failed to stop Walker's anti-labor agenda, but were part of a larger progressive resurgence, when coupled with Occupy and Fight for $15. Two of these movements attracted positive news coverage, which they used to build public support. The other – Fight for $15 – saw state and national successes. All these movements influenced Democratic politics, even if by the late 2010s they had not yet achieved their goals regarding protecting labor rights, reducing inequality, and raising the minimum wage.

The economic justice movement shifted public opinion to the left, directing attention to the grievances of working Americans. Plutocratic politics privileges business interests, but these movements shifted the conversation toward the grievances of the disadvantaged. They disrupted hegemonic "free market" politics-as-usual thinking, which assumes there is little government can do to aid the working-class.

The economic justice movement saw varied success in speaking to disadvantaged Americans. Occupy was most successful among poorer white men, but struggled with poor people of color. The Madison protests lacked support from poor whites and people of color, although unions drew support from poorer whites and blacks. Fight for $15 gained support among poor service workers, and has the potential to unite poor people and poor people of color. It received less support from poorer whites and poorer white men, but most in these groups supported raising the minimum wage.

The economic justice movement united tens of millions of Americans in solidarity against rising worker insecurity. It is more than just the sum of its parts. It is about more than mechanistically serving individuals' economic interests. These movements appeal to millions because of their messages, and because the movements as collective entities reveal it is possible to fight for progressive change. We should view these movements as more than transactional entities providing material benefits to supporters. They reveal a public commitment to collective identity, solidarity and empathy in pursuit of larger democratic causes and against plutocracy.

Notes

1 Sarah A. Donovan, Marc Labonte, and Joseph Dalaker, "The U.S. Income Distribution: Trends and Issues," *Congressional Research Service*, December 8, 2016, https://fas.org/sgp/crs/misc/R44705.pdf; United States Census Bureau, "Historical Income Tables: Households," 2018, https://www.census.gov/data/tables/time-series/demo/income-poverty/historical-income-households.html; FRED Economic Data, "Nonfarm Business Sector: Real Output Per Hour of All Persons," *St. Louis Federal Reserve*, March 7, 2018, https://fred.stlouisfed.org/series/OPHNFB; The Hamilton Project, "Median Earnings and Annual Hours Worked for Two-Parent Families," *The Hamilton Project*, July 8, 2011, http://www.hamiltonproject.org/charts/median_earnings_and_annual_hours_worked_for_two-parent_families; Ellen R. McGrattan and Richard Rogerson, "Changes in the Distribution of Family Hours Worked since 1950," *Federal Reserve of Minneapolis*, April 2008, https://www.minneapolisfed.org/research/SR/SR397bw.pdf.
2 United States Census Bureau, "Historical Income Tables: Households," 2018.
3 Davie Gilson and Edwin Rios, "Charts that Show Income Inequality Isn't Getting Better Anytime Soon," *Mother Jones*, December 22, 2016, https://www.motherjones.com/politics/2016/12/america-income-inequality-wealth-net-worth-charts/.
4 John W. Schoen, "Why Does a College Degree Cost So Much?", *CNBC.com*, June 16, 2015, https://www.cnbc.com/2015/06/16/why-college-costs-are-so-high-and-rising.html; Jeanne Sahadi, "Warren Buffett Is Right. Health Care Costs Are Swallowing the Economy," *CNNMoney*, January 30, 2018, http://money.cnn.com/2018/01/30/news/economy/health-care-costs-eating-the-economy/index.html.
5 Gilson and Rios, "Charts that Show Income Inequality Isn't Getting Better Anytime Soon," 2016.
6 Christopher Ingraham, "If You Thought Income Inequality Was Bad, Get a Load of Wealth Inequality," *Washington Post*, May 21, 2015, https://www.washingtonpost.com/news/wonk/wp/2015/05/21/the-top-10-of-americans-own-76-of-the-stuff-and-its-dragging-our-economy-down/?utm_term=.5bcc64248551.
7 Matt Egan, "Record Inequality: The Top 1% Controls 38.6% of America's Wealth," *CNNMoney*, September 27, 2017, http://money.cnn.com/2017/09/27/news/economy/inequality-record-top-1-percent-wealth/index.html; Ingraham, "If You Thought Income Inequality was Bad, Get a Load of Wealth Inequality," 2015.
8 Drew DeSilver, "U.S. Income Inequality, on Rise for Decades, Is Now Highest Since 1928," *Pew Research Center*, December 5, 2013, http://www.pewresearch.org/fact-tank/2013/12/05/u-s-income-inequality-on-rise-for-decades-is-now-highest-since-1928/; Jeff Guo, "Income Inequality Today May Be Higher than in Any Other Era," *Washington Post*, July 1, 2016, https://www.washingtonpost.com/news/wonk/wp/2016/07/01/income-inequality-today-may-be-the-highest-since-the-nations-founding/?utm_term=.3ff5209ee576.

9 Gallup, "Labor Unions," *Gallup.com*, 2017, http://news.gallup.com/poll/12751/labor-unions.aspx; Frank Newport, "Americans Continue to Say U.S. Wealth Distribution Is Unfair," *Gallup.com*, May 4, 2015, http://news.gallup.com/poll/182987/americans-continue-say-wealth-distribution-unfair.aspx. The findings for the *Pew Research Center*'s polls on the conflict between the rich and poor can be found through a question search of *Pew*'s website, which reveals poll results for August 2009, December 2011, December 2012, December 2016, and December 2017.
10 Benjamin I. Page and Robert Y. Shapiro, *The Rational Public: Fifty Years of Trends in Americans' Policy Preferences* (Chicago: University of Chicago Press, 1992).
11 Page and Shapiro, *The Rational Public*, 1992.
12 Sean Wilentz, *The Politicians and the Egalitarians: The Hidden History of American Politics* (New York: W.W. Norton, 2017); Robert A. McGuire, *To Form a More Perfect Union: A New Economic Interpretation of the United States Constitution* (New York: Oxford University Press, 2003); Michael J. Thompson, *The Politics of Inequality: A Political History of the Idea of Economic Inequality in America* (New York: Columbia University Press, 2012); Charles A. Beard, *An Economic Interpretation of the Constitution of the United States* (Mineola, NY: Dover Publications, 2004); Michael J. Klarman, *The Framer's Coup: The Making of the United States Constitution* (New York: Oxford University Press, 2016); Clement Fatovic, *America's Founding and the Struggle over Economic Inequality* (Lawrence, KS: University Press of Kansas, 2015); Luke Mayville, *John Adams and the Fear of American Oligarchy* (Princeton, NJ: Princeton University Press, 2016).
13 Edward Royce, *Poverty and Power: The Problem of Structural Inequality* (Lanham, MD: Rowman & Littlefield, 2015); Scott R. Sernau, *Social Inequality in a Global Age* (Thousand Oaks: CA: Sage Publications, 2016); Early Wysong and Robert Perrucci, *The New Class Society: Goodbye American Dream?* (Lanham, MD: Rowman & Littlefield, 2013); Matthew P. Drennan, *Income Inequality: Why It Matters and Why Most Economists Didn't Notice* (New Haven, CT: Yale University Press, 2015); Dennis L. Gilbert, *The American Class Structure in an Age of Growing Inequality* (Thousand Oaks, CA: Sage Publications, 2014); Jeff Manza and Michael Sauder, *Inequality and Society: Social Science Perspectives on Social Stratification* (New York: W.W. Norton, 2009); Stephen J. McNamee and Robert K. Miller Jr., *The Meritocracy Myth* (Lanham, MD: Rowman & Littlefield, 2013); Stephen M. Caliendo, *Inequality in America: Race, Poverty, and Fulfilling Democracy's Promise* (Boulder, CO: Westview Press, 2017); David Grusky and Tamar Kricheli-Katz, eds. *The New Gilded Age: The Critical Inequality Debates of Our Time* (Palo Alto, CA: Stanford University Press, 2012); Marcia J. Carlson and Paula England, eds. *Social Class and Changing Families in an Unequal America* (Palo Alto, CA: Stanford University Press, 2011); Peter Temin, *The Vanishing Middle Class: Prejudice and Power in a Dual Economy* (Cambridge, MA: MIT Press, 2018).
14 Larry M. Bartels, *Unequal Democracy: The Political Economy of the New Gilded Age* (Princeton, NJ: Princeton University Press, 2010); Nathan J. Kelly, *The Politics of Income Inequality in the United States* (Cambridge: Cambridge University Press, 2011); David Brady, *Rich Democracies, Poor People: How Politics Explains Poverty* (New York: Oxford University Press, 2009); Carsten Jensen and Kees Van Kersbergen, *The Politics of Inequality* (New York: Palgrave, 2016); Drew

DeSilver, "Global Inequality: How the U.S. Compares," *Pew Research Center*, December 19, 2013, http://www.pewresearch.org/fact-tank/2013/12/19/global-inequality-how-the-u-s-compares/; Lane Kenworthy, "Do Social-Welfare Policies Reduce Poverty? A Cross-National Assessment," *Social Forces* 77, no. 3 (1999): 1119–1139; Stephanie Moller, Evelyne Huber, John D. Stephens, David Bradley, and Francois Nielsen, "Determinants of Relative Poverty in Advanced Capitalist Democracies," *American Sociological Review* 68, no. 1 (2003): 22–51; Timothy Smeeding, "Poor People in Rich Nations: The United States in Comparative Perspective," *Journal of Economic Perspectives* 20, no. 1 (2006): 69–90; Benjamin Radcliff, *The Political Economy of Human Happiness: How Voters' Choices Determine the Quality of Life* (Cambridge: Cambridge University Press, 2013); Thomas J. Hayes and D. Xavier Medina Vidal, "Fiscal Policy and Economic Inequality in the U.S. States: Taxing and Spending from 1976 to 2006," *Political Research Quarterly* 68, no. 2 (2015), http://journals.sagepub.com/doi/abs/10.1177/1065912915578461?journalCode=prqb.

15 C. Wright Mills, *The Power Elite* (New York: Oxford University Press, 2000); G. William Domhoff, *Who Rules America? The Triumph of the Corporate Rich* (New York: McGraw Hill, 2013); Theodore J. Lowi, *The End of Liberalism: The Second Republic of the United States* (New York: W.W. Norton, 2009); Mancur Olson, *The Logic of Collective Action: Public Goods and the Theory of Groups* (Cambridge, MA: Harvard University Press, 1971); E. E. Schattsneider, *The Semisovereign People: A Realist's View of Democracy in America* (Belmont, CA: Wadsworth, 1975); Floyd Hunter, *Community Power Structure: A Study of Decision Makers* (Chapel Hill, NC: University of North Carolina Press, 1969).

16 Kay Lehman Schlozman, Sidney Verba, and Henry E. Brady, *The Unheavenly Chorus: Unequal Political Voice and the Broken Promise of American Democracy* (Princeton, NJ: Princeton University Press, 2013); Kay Lehman Schlozman, Henry E. Brady, and Sidney Verba, *Unequal and Unrepresented: Political Inequality and the People's Voice in the New Gilded Age* (Princeton, NJ: Princeton University Press, 2018); Jan E. Leighley and Jonathan Nagler, *Who Votes Now? Demographics, Issues, Inequality, and Turnout in the United States* (Princeton, NJ: Princeton University Press, 2013).

17 Vincent A. Mahler, David K. Jesuit, and Piotr R. Paradowski, "Electoral Turnout and State Redistribution: A Cross-National Study of Fourteen Developed Countries," *Political Research Quarterly* 67, no. 2 (2014), http://journals.sagepub.com/doi/abs/10.1177/1065912913509306.

18 Martin Gilens, *Affluence and Influence: Economic Inequality and Political Power in America* (Princeton, NJ: Princeton University Press, 2014); Martin Gilens and Benjamin Page, "Testing Theories of American Politics: Elites, Interest Groups, and Average Citizens," *Perspectives on Politics* 12, no. 3 (2014): 564–581; Daniel M. Butler, *Representing the Advantaged: How Politicians Reinforce Inequality* (Cambridge: Cambridge University Press, 2014); Nicholas Carnes, *White Collar Government: The Hidden Role of Class in Economic Policy Making* (Chicago: University of Chicago Press, 2013); Jacob S. Hacker and Paul Pierson, *Winner-Take-All Politics: How Washington Made the Rich Richer – and Turned Its Back on the Middle Class* (New York: Simon & Schuster, 2011); Bartels, *Unequal Democracy*, 2010; Larry M. Bartels, Hugh Heclo, Rodney E. Hero, and Lawrence R. Jacobs, "Inequality and

American Governance," in *Inequality in American Democracy: What We Know and What We Need to Learn*, eds. Theda Skocpol and Lawrence R. Jacobs (Thousand Oaks, CA: Sage Publications, 2005), pp. 156–213; Thomas J. Hayes, "Responsiveness in an Era of Inequality: The Case of the U.S. Senate," *Political Research Quarterly* 66, no. 3 (2013): http://journals.sagepub.com/doi/abs/10.1177/1065912912459567; Elizabeth Rigby and Gerald C. Wright, "Political Parties and Representation of the Poor in the American States," *American Journal of Political Science* 57, no. 3 (2013): 552–565; Jeffrey R. Lax and Justin H. Phillips, "The Democratic Deficit in the States," *American Journal of Political Science* 56, no. 1 (2012): 148–166.

19 Lyle Scruggs and Thomas J. Hayes, "The Influence of Inequality on Welfare Generosity: Evidence from the U.S. States," *Politics and Society* 45, no. 1 (2017): http://journals.sagepub.com/doi/abs/10.1177/0032329216683165.

20 Erling Barth, Henning Finseraas, and Karl O. Moene, "Political Reinforcement: How Rising Inequality Curbs Manifested Welfare Generosity," *American Journal of Political Science* 59, no. 3 (2015): 565–577.

21 For research on political leaders' refusal to pander to public opinion, see: Lawrence R. Jacobs and Robert Y. Shapiro, *Politicians Don't Pander: Political Manipulation and the Loss of Democratic Responsiveness* (Chicago: University of Chicago Press, 2000). For research on mass public preferences for progressive redistribution, see: Benjamin I. Page and Lawrence R. Jacobs, *Class War? What Americans Really Think about Economic Inequality* (Chicago: University of Chicago Press, 2009).

22 Peter K. Enns, Nathan J. Kelly, Jana Morgan, Thomas Volscho, and Christopher Witko, "Conditional Status Quo Bias and Top Income Shares: How U.S. Political Institutions Have Benefitted the Rich," *Journal of Politics* 76, no. 2 (2014): 289–303.

23 Benjamin I. Page and Martin Gilens, *Democracy in America?: What Has Gone Wrong and What We Can Do About It* (Chicago: University of Chicago Press, 2018); Hacker and Pierson, *Winner-Take-All Politics*, 2011; Walter Lippmann, *Drift and Mastery* (Madison, WI: University of Wisconsin Press, 1986).

24 Jacob S. Hacker, Gregory A. Huber, Austin Nichols, Philipp Rehm, Mark Schlesinger, Rob Valletta, and Stuart Craig, "The Economic Security Index: A New Measure for Research and Policy Analysis," *Review of Income and Wealth* 60, no. 1 (2014): 5–32.

25 James A. Levine, "Poverty and Obesity in the U.S.," *Diabetes* 60, no. 11 (2011): 2667–2668; Steven H. Woolf, Laudan Aron, Lisa Dubay, Sarah M. Simon, Emily Zimmerman, and Kim X. Luk, "How Are Income and Wealth Linked to Health and Longevity?" *Urban Institute*, April 2015, https://www.urban.org/sites/default/files/publication/49116/2000178-How-are-Income-and-Wealth-Linked-to-Health-and-Longevity.pdf; Carol Graham, *Happiness for All? Unequal Hopes and Lives in Pursuit of the American Dream* (Princeton, NJ: Princeton University Press, 2017).

26 Simon Reid-Henry, *The Political Origins of Inequality: Why a More Equal World Is Better for Us All* (Chicago: University of Chicago Press, 2015); Goran Therborn, *The Killing Fields of Inequality* (Cambridge: Polity, 2013); Pablo Fajnzylber, Daniel Lederman, and Norman Loayza, "Inequality and Violent Crime," *Journal of Law and Economics* 45, no. 1 (2002): https://www.journals.uchicago.edu/doi/abs/10.1086/338347.

27 Thompson, *The Politics of Inequality*, 2012.

28 For the impact of inequality on political participation, see: Frederick Solt, "Economic Inequality and Democratic Political Engagement," *American Journal of Political Science* 52, no. 1 (2008): 48–60; Frederick Solt, "Does Economic Inequality Depress Electoral Participation? Testing the Schattschneider Hypothesis," *Political Behavior* 32, no. 2 (2010): 285–301. For growing economic inequality and insecurity's effect on trust of government, see: Alberto Alesina and Romain Wacziarg, "The Economics of Social Trust," in *Disaffected Democracies: What's Troubling the Trilateral Countries?*, eds. Susan J. Pharr and Robert D. Putnam (Princeton, NJ: Princeton University Press, 2000), pp. 149–170; Andrew Wroe, "Economic Insecurity and Political Trust in the United States," *American Politics Review* 44, no. 1 (2016): 131–163.

29 Carles Boix, *Political Order and Inequality: Their Foundations and Their Consequences for Human Welfare* (Cambridge: Cambridge University Press, 2015).

30 Michael Hout, "How Class Works: Objective and Subjective Aspects of Class since the 1970s," in *Social Class: How Does It Work?* eds. Annette Laureau and Dalton Conley (Thousand Oaks, CA: Sage Publications, 2008), pp. 25–64; Michael D. Grimes, "Class and Attitudes toward Structural Inequalities: An Empirical Comparison of Key Variables in Neo- and Post-Marxist Scholarship," *The Sociological Quarterly* 30, no. 3 (1989): 441–463; Richard Centers, *The Psychology of Social Classes: A Study of Class Consciousness* (Princeton, NJ: Princeton University Press, 1949); Mary R. Jackman and Robert W. Jackman, *Class Awareness in the United States* (Berkeley, CA: University of California Press, 1983); Anthony R. DiMaggio, "Class Sub-Conscious: Hegemony, False Consciousness, and the Development of Political and Economic Policy Attitudes," *Critical Sociology* 41, no. 3 (2015): 549–563; Jeff Manza and Clem Brooks, *Social Cleavages and Political Change: Voter Alignment and U.S. Party Coalitions* (New York: Oxford University Press, 1999); William Franko, Caroline J. Tolbert, and Christopher Witko, "Inequality, Self-Interest, and Public Support for 'Robin Hood' Tax Policies," *Political Research Quarterly* 66, no. 4 (2013): 923–937; Jacob S. Hacker, Philipp Rehm, and Mark Schlesinger, "The Insecure American: Economic Experiences, Financial Worries, and Policy Attitudes," *Perspectives on Politics* 11, no. 1 (2013): 23–49; Alberto Alesina and Eliana La Ferrera, "Preferences for Redistribution in the Land of Opportunities," *Journal of Public Economics* 89 (2015): 897–931; Yeheskel Hasenfeld and Jane Rafferty, "The Determinants of Public Attitudes toward the Welfare State," *Social Forces* 67, no. 4 (1989): 1027–1048.

31 Bartels, *Unequal Democracy*, 2010; Andrew Gelman, *Red State, Blue State, Rich State, Poor State: Why Americans Vote the Way They Do* (Princeton, NJ: Princeton University Press, 2008).

32 Allan H. Meltzer and Scott F. Richard, "A Rational Theory of the Size of Government," *Journal of Political Economy* 89, no. 5 (1981): 914–927.

33 Benjamin J. Newman and John V. Kane, "Economic Inequality and Public Support for Organized Labor," *Political Research Quarterly* 70, no. 4 (2017): 918–932; Christopher D. Johnston and Benjamin J. Newman, "Economic Inequality and U.S. Public Policy Mood across Space and Time," *American Politics Review* 44, no. 1 (2016): 164–191; Noam Lupu and Jonas Pontusson, "The Structure of Inequality and the Politics of Redistribution," *American Political Science Review* 105, no. 2 (2011): 316–336; Benjamin J. Newman, Christopher D. Johnston, and

Patrick L. Lown, "False Consciousness or Class Awareness? Local Income Inequality, Personal Economic Position, and Belief in American Meritocracy," *American Journal of Political Science* 59, no. 2 (2015): 326–340.

34 Morris P. Fiorina, *Retrospective Voting in American National Elections* (New Haven, CT: Yale University Press, 1981); Selim Erdem Aytac, "Relative Economic Performance and the Incumbent Vote: A Reference Point Theory," *Journal of Politics* 80, no. 1 (2018): 16–29; Lynn Vavreck, *The Message Matters: The Economy and Presidential Campaigns* (Princeton, NJ: Princeton University Press, 2009); Gary C. Jacobson and Samuel Kernell, *Strategy and Choice in Congressional Elections* (New Haven, CT: Yale University Press, 1983); Edward R. Tufte, *Political Control of the Economy* (Princeton, NJ: Princeton University Press, 1978); Neil Malhotra and Yotam Margalit, "Expectation Setting and Retrospective Voting," *Journal of Politics* 76, no. 4 (2014): 1000–1016; James E. Campbell, Bryan J. Dettrey, and Hongxing Yin, "The Theory of Conditional Retrospective Voting: Does the Presidential Record Matter Less in Open-Seat Elections?" *Journal of Politics*, 72, no. 4 (2010): 1083–1095; Michael Becher and Michael Donnelly, "Economic Performance, Individual Evaluations, and the Vote: Investigating the Causal Mechanism," *Journal of Politics* 75, no. 4 (2013): 968–979; Barry C. Burden and Amber Wichowsky, "Economic Discontent as a Mobilizer: Unemployment and Voter Turnout," *Journal of Politics* 76, no. 4 (2014): 887–898; Andrew Healy and Neil Malhotra, "Retrospective Voting Reconsidered," *Annual Review of Political Science* 16, no. 1 (2013): 285–306; Bradley Dickerson, "Economic Perceptions, Presidential Approval, and Causality: The Moderating Role of the Economic Context," *American Politics Review* 44, no. 6 (2016): 1037–1065.

35 Frances Fox Piven and Richard Cloward, *Poor People's Movements: Why They Succeed, How They Fail* (New York: Vintage, 1978); Frances Fox Piven, *Challenging Authority: How Ordinary People Change America* (Lanham, MD: Rowman & Littlefield, 2008); Edward P. Morgan, *What Really Happened to the 1960s: How Mass Media Culture Failed American Democracy* (Lawrence, KS: University Press of Kansas, 2010); Daniel Q. Gillion, *The Political Power of Protest: Minority Activism and Shifts in Public Policy* (Cambridge: Cambridge University Press, 2013); Deva R. Woodly, *The Politics of Common Sense: How Social Movements Use Public Discourse to Change Politics and Win Acceptance* (New York: Oxford University Press, 2015); Taeku Lee, *Mobilizing Public Opinion: Black Insurgency and Racial Attitudes in the Civil Rights Era* (Chicago: University of Chicago Press, 2002).

36 For classic works in the area of strain theory, see: Karl Marx and Friedrich Engels, *The Communist Manifesto* (London: Pluto Press, 2017); Ted Robert Gurr, *Why Men Rebel* (New York: Routledge, 2011); David B. Truman, *The Governmental Process: Political Interests and Public Opinion* (Berkeley, CA: University of California Press, 1993); James C. Davies, "Toward a Theory of Revolution," *American Sociological Review* 27, no. 1 (1962): 5–19; Neil J. Smelser, *Theory of Collective Behavior* (New York: Free Press, 1965). For more recent works on strain theory, see: David Snow, Daniel Cress, Liam Downey, and Andrew Jones, "Disrupting the 'Quotidian': Reconceptualizing the Relationship between Breakdown and the Emergence of Collective Action," *Mobilization: An International Quarterly* 3, no. 1 (1998): 1–22; Robert

S. Erikson and Laura Stoker, "Caught in the Draft: The Effects of Vietnam Draft Lottery Status on Political Attitudes," *American Political Science Review* 105, no. 2 (2011): 221–237.

37 James A. Geschwender, "Continuities in Theories of Status Consistency and Cognitive Dissonance," *Social Forces* 46, no. 2 (1967): 160–171; James A. Geschwender, "Explorations in the Theory of Social Movements and Revolutions," *Social Forces* 47, no. 2 (1968): 127–135; Gerhard E. Lenski, "Status Crystallization: A Non-Vertical Dimension of Social Status," *American Sociological Review* 19, no. 4 (1954): 405–413.

38 Ruy Teixeira and Joel Rogers, *America's Forgotten Majority: Why the White Working Class Still Matters* (New York: Basic Books, 2001).

39 Thomas Frank, *What's the Matter with Kansas? How Conservatives Won the Heart of America* (New York: Holt, 2005).

40 Justin Gest, *The New Minority: White Working Class Politics in an Age of Immigration and Inequality* (New York: Oxford University Press, 2016); Anthony Mughan, Clive Bean, and Ian McAllister, "Economic Globalization, Job Insecurity, and the Populist Reaction," *Electoral Studies* 22, no. 4 (2003): 617–633.

41 Katherine Cramer Walsh, "Putting Inequality in Its Place: Rural Consciousness and the Power of Perspective," *American Political Science Review* 106, no. 3 (2012): 517–532; Katherine J. Cramer, *The Politics of Resentment: Rural Consciousness in Wisconsin and the Rise of Scott Walker* (Chicago: University of Chicago Press, 2016).

42 Arlie Russell Hochschild, *Strangers in Their Own Land* (New York: The New Press, 2018).

43 Matthew Luttig, "The Structure of Inequality and Americans' Attitudes toward Redistribution," *Public Opinion Quarterly* 77, no. 3 (2013): 811–821; Nathan J. Kelly and Peter K. Enns, "Inequality and the Dynamics of Public Opinion: The Self-Reinforcing Link between Economic Inequality and Mass Preferences," *American Journal of Political Science* 54, no. 4 (2010): 855–870; Karl Ove Moene and Michael Wallerstein, "Inequality, Social Insurance, and Redistribution," *American Political Science Review*, 95, no. 4 (2001): 859–874; Roland Benabou, "Unequal Societies: Income Distribution and the Social Contract," *American Economic Review* 90, no. 1 (2000): 96–129.

44 Joseph Daniel Ura and Christopher R. Ellis, "Income, Preferences, and the Dynamics of Policy Responsiveness," *PS: Political Science and Politics* 41, no. 4 (2008): 785–794; Stuart N. Soroka and Christopher Wlezien, "On the Limits to Inequality in Representation," *PS: Political Science and Politics* 41, no. 2 (2008): 319–327.

45 Terry N. Clark and Seymour Martin Lipset, "Are Social Classes Dying?" *International Sociology* 6, no. 4 (1991): 397–410; Robert Nisbet, "The Decline and Fall of the Concept of Social Class," *Pacific Sociological Review* 2, no. 1 (1959): 11–17; Jan Pakulski and Malcolm Waters, *The Death of Class* (Thousand Oaks, CA: Sage Publications, 1996); Paul Kingston, *The Classless Society* (Palo Alto, CA: Stanford University Press, 2000).

46 Page and Shapiro, *The Rational Public*, 1992.

47 Lane Kenworthy and Leslie McCall, "Inequality, Public Opinion, and Redistribution," *Socio-Economic Review* 6, no. 1 (2008): 35–68.

48 Stanley Feldman, "Economic Self-Interest and Political Behavior," *American Journal of Political Science* 26, no. 3 (1982): 446–466.

49 Donald R. Kinder and D. Roderick Kiewiet, "Economic Discontent and Political Behavior: The Role of Personal Grievances and Collective

Economic Judgments in Congressional Voting," *American Journal of Political Science* 23, no. 3 (1979): 495–527.
50 Adam Seth Levine, *American Insecurity: Why Our Economic Fears Lead to Political Inaction* (Princeton, NJ: Princeton University Press, 2015); Steve Fraser, *The Age of Acquiescence: The Life and Death of American Resistance to Organized Wealth and Power* (Boston, MA: Little, Brown, & Company, 2015).
51 Page and Jacobs, *Class War?*, 2009.
52 Piven and Cloward, *Poor People's Movements*, 1978, pp. xxii, 33.
53 Piven and Cloward, *Poor People's Movements*, 1978, pp. 12, 28, 96; Piven, *Challenging Authority*, 2008.
54 Piven and Cloward, *Poor People's Movements*, 1978, p. 14.
55 State Journal Staff, "Highlights of Gov. Walker's Budget Repair Bill," *Wisconsin State Journal*, February 11, 2011, http://host.madison.com/wsj/news/local/govt-and-politics/highlights-of-gov-walker-s-budget-repair-bill/article_3d93e6aa-363a-11e0-8493-001cc4c002e0.html.
56 Steven Greenhouse, "Wisconsin's Legacy for Unions," *New York Times*, February 22, 2014, https://www.nytimes.com/2014/02/23/business/wisconsins-legacy-for-unions.html; Cenk Uygur, "MSNBC Live with Cenk Uygur," *MSNBC*, February 28, 2011, 6:00 PM EST.
57 Monica Davey and Steven Greenhouse, "Angry Demonstrations in Wisconsin as Cuts Loom," *New York Times*, February 16, 2011, http://www.nytimes.com/2011/02/17/us/17wisconsin.html.
58 Scott Walker, "Budget Repair Bill Message from Governor Walker to UW Employees," *University of Wisconsin-Madison News*, February 11, 2011, https://news.wisc.edu/budget-repair-bill-message-from-governor-walker-to-uw-employees/; James B. Nelson, "Wisconsin Gov. Scott Walker Says Wisconsin is Broke," *Politifact*, March 3, 2011, http://www.politifact.com/wisconsin/statements/2011/mar/03/scott-walker/wisconsin-gov-scott-walker-says-wisconsin-broke/.
59 Erik Kain, "Wisconsin Governor Scott Walker Threatens Layoffs, $1 Billion in Cuts to Schools," *Forbes*, February 28, 2011, https://www.forbes.com/sites/erikkain/2011/02/28/wisconsin-governor-scott-walker-threatens-layoffs-1-billion-in-cuts-to-schools-if-democrats-dont-return-to-vote/#3dd422024b22.
60 Sylvia A. Allegretto, Ken Jacobs, and Laurel Lucia, "The Wrong Target: Public Sector Unions and State Budget Deficits," *UC Berkeley Labor Center*, October 13, 2011, http://laborcenter.berkeley.edu/the-wrong-target-public-sector-unions-and-state-budget-deficits/; Richard B. Freedman and Eunice Han, "The War against Public Sector Collective Bargaining in the U.S.," *Journal of Industrial Relations* 54, no. 3 (2012): 386–408; John Sides, "The Relationship between Union Membership and State Budget Deficits," *The Monkey Cage*, February 21, 2011, http://themonkeycage.org/2011/02/the_relationship_between_union/.
61 Nelson, "Wisconsin Gov. Scott Walker Says Wisconsin is Broke," 2011.
62 James B. Kelleher, "Up to 100,000 Protest Wisconsin Law Curbing Unions," *Reuters*, March 13, 2011, https://www.reuters.com/article/us-wisconsin-protests/up-to-100000-protest-wisconsin-law-curbing-unions-idUSTRE72B2AN20110313; John Nichols, "Tens of Thousands Protest Move by Wisconsin's Governor to Destroy Public Sector Unions," *The Nation*, February 16, 2011, https://www.thenation.com/article/tens-thousands-protest-move-wisconsins-governor-destroy-public-sector-unions/.

The Economic Justice Movement   111

63 Lee Sustar, "Who Were the Leaders of the Wisconsin Uprising," in *The Wisconsin Uprising*, ed. Michael Yates (New York: Monthly Review Press, 2012), p. 60.
64 Davey and Greenhouse, "Angry Demonstrations in Wisconsin as Cuts Loom," 2011; Amanda Noss, "Household Income for States: 2010 and 2011: American Community Survey Briefs," *United States Census Bureau*, September 2012, https://www2.census.gov/library/publications/2012/acs/acsbr11-02.pdf.
65 Tom Kertscher, "Wisconsin Gov. Scott Walker Says His Budget-Repair Bill Would Leave Collective Bargaining 'Fully Intact,'" *Politifact*, February 18, 2011, http://www.politifact.com/wisconsin/statements/2011/feb/18/scott-walker/wisconsin-gov-scott-walker-says-his-budget-repair-/.
66 Bill Glauber, Jason Stein, and Patrick Marley, "Democrats Flee State to Avoid Vote on Budget Bill," *Journal Sentinel*, February 17, 2011, http://archive.jsonline.com/news/statepolitics/116381289.html.
67 Mary Spicuzza and Clay Barbour, "Budget Repair Bill Passes Senate, Thursday Vote Set in Assembly," *Wisconsin State Journal*, March 10, 2011, http://host.madison.com/wsj/news/local/govt-and-politics/budget-repair-bill-passes-senate-thursday-vote-set-in-assembly/article_8747fa04-4a74-11e0-8e6b-001cc4c03286.html.
68 Connor Donegan, "Disciplining Labor, Dismantling Democracy: Rebellion and Control in Wisconsin," in *The Wisconsin Uprising*, ed. Michael Yates (New York: Monthly Review Press, 2012), p. 38; John Nichols, *Uprising: How Wisconsin Renewed the Politics of Protest, from Madison to Wall Street* (New York: Nation Books, 2012), p. 130.
69 Jason Stein, Tom Tolan, and Daniel Bice, "Recall Group Says It Has More than 500,000 Signatures," *Journal Sentinel*, December 15, 2011, http://archive.jsonline.com/news/statepolitics/recall-group-says-it-has-more-than-500000-signatures-5u3f3mt-135670858.html/.
70 Monica Davey and Jeff Zeleny, "Walker Survives Wisconsin Recall Vote," *New York Times*, June 5, 2012, http://www.nytimes.com/2012/06/06/us/politics/walker-survives-wisconsin-recall-effort.html.
71 Steven Greenhouse, "Can Labor Still Turn Out the Vote?", *New York Times*, March 4, 2016, https://www.nytimes.com/2016/03/06/opinion/sunday/can-labor-still-turn-out-the-vote.html.
72 Donegan, "Disciplining Labor," 2012, p. 39.
73 Sustar, "Who Were the Leaders of the Wisconsin Uprising," 2012, pp. 83–84.
74 I used the *Nexus Uni* database, and populated my list of articles with a key word search for each source that included the words "Scott Walker," "Madison," and/or "protest," "protests," "protester," or "protesters."
75 Kertscher, "Wisconsin Gov. Scott Walker Says His Budget-Repair Bill Would Leave Collective Bargaining 'Fully Intact,'" 2011.
76 Walker, "Budget Repair Bill Message from Governor Walker to UW Employees," 2011.
77 Anthony DiMaggio, "Rightwing Manipulation of the Wisconsin Revolt," *Counterpunch*, February 25, 2011, https://www.counterpunch.org/2011/02/25/rightwing-manipulation-of-the-wisconsin-revolt/.
78 Chris Bury and Olivia Katrandjian, "Protesters Take State Capital in Wisconsin," *ABC News*, February 18, 2011, http://abcnews.go.com/US/protestors-state-capitol-wisconsin/story?id=12947666.
79 I looked at references to Governor Walker's claims that that his legislation was necessary to "repair" or "balance(ing)" the budget, to deal with the "deficit" or budget "crisis" or to deficit and budget "problem/problems," and

discussions of proposed budget "cut(s)" or "gap(s)" in the budget. I included any stories that referenced the Wisconsin "budget" within five words of "repair" or "balance" or "balanced" or "balancing" or "crisis" or "gap" or "gaps" or "problem" or "problems" or "cut" or "cuts" or "deficit."

80 James B. Nelson, "Wisconsin Officials Claim Cleaning up the State Capitol Will Cost $7.5 Million," *Politifact*, March 8, 2011, http://www.politifact.com/wisconsin/statements/2011/mar/08/mike-huebsch/wisconsin-officials-claim-cleaning-state-capitol-w/.

81 Tom Kertscher, "100,000 Pro-Union Protesters Were Shipping into Wisconsin, Scott Walker Says," *Politifact*, July 30, 2015, https://www.politifact.com/wisconsin/statements/2015/jul/30/scott-walker/pro-union-protesters-were-shipped-wisconsin-scott-/.

82 In Figure 2.2, "poorer" is defined as individuals from households earning less than $50,000 a year, which was about the median household income in the early 2010s.

83 Gallup, "Attitudes toward the Public Schools Survey," *iPoll*, June 4–13, 2011; *Pew Research Center*, "February 2011 Political Survey," February 3, 2011.

84 Gallup, "Gallup Poll, August 2017," *iPoll*, August 2–6, 2017; *Pew Research Center*, "Political Survey, February 2011," *iPoll*, February 2–7, 2011; *Pew Research Center*, "Political Survey, March 2011," *iPoll*, February 22–March 1, 2011.

85 *Pew Research Center*, "February 2011 Political Survey," 2011.

86 CNN/Opinion Research Corporation, "CNN/Opinion Research Corporation Poll, March 2011," *iPoll*, March 11–13, 2011.

87 Reason-Rupe, "Reason-Rupe Poll, March 2011," *iPoll*, March 24–April 9, 2011.

88 Resurgent Republic Survey, "Resurgent Republic Survey, March 2011," *iPoll*, March 1–3, 2011.

89 Victoria Carty, *Social Movements and New Technology* (New York: Routledge, 2015), p. 126.

90 Agence France-Presse, "Egypt Braces for Nationwide Protests," *France 24*, January 25, 2011, https://web.archive.org/web/20110201013309/http://www.france24.com/en/20110125-egypt-braces-nationwide-protests; Encyclopedia Britannica, "Egypt Uprising of 2011," *Encyclopedia Britannica*, 2018, https://www.britannica.com/event/Egypt-Uprising-of-2011; Yolande Knell, "Egypt's Revolution: 18 Days in Tahrir Square," *BBC News*, January 25, 2012, http://www.bbc.com/news/world-middle-east-16716089.

91 Michael Gould-Wartofsky, *The Occupiers: The Making of the 99 Percent Movement* (New York: Oxford University Press, 2015), pp. 27, 29, 39.

92 Carty, *Social Movements and New Technology*, 2015, pp. 127–128.

93 Wartofsky, *The Occupiers*, 2015, pp. 28, 30.

94 Carty, *Social Movements and New Technology*, 2015, pp. 128–129; Al Goodman, "Thousands in Spain Revive May 15 Protests to Rail against Cuts, Government," *CNN.com*, May 13, 2012, https://www.cnn.com/2012/05/12/world/europe/spain-protests/index.html.

95 Carty, *Social Movements and New Technology*, 2015, p. 129.

96 Adbusters, "America Needs Its Own Tahrir Acampada," *Twitter*, June 9, 2011, https://twitter.com/adbusters/status/78989903232376832?lang=en; Manuel Castells, *Networks of Outrage and Hope: Social Movements in the Internet Age* (Cambridge: Polity, 2015), p. 162.

97 Castells, *Networks of Outrage and Hope*, 2015, p. 165.

The Economic Justice Movement 113

98 Jason Kessler and Michael Martinez, "Wall Street Protests Grow after Unions' Endorsement," *CNN.com*, October 5, 2011, https://www.cnn.com/2011/10/05/politics/occupy-wall-street/index.html.
99 Castells, *Networks of Outrage and Hope*, 2015, p. 187.
100 Carty, *Social Movements and New Technology*, 2015, p. 140.
101 The Week Staff, "Occupy Wall Street: A Protest Timeline," *The Week*, October 7, 2011, http://theweek.com/articles/481160/occupy-wall-street-protest-timeline.
102 Wartofsky, *The Occupiers*, 2015, p. 71; The Week Staff, "Occupy Wall Street," 2011.
103 Castells, *Networks of Outrage and Hope*, 2015, p. 165; Christina Boyle, Emily Sher, Anjali Mullany, and Helen Kennedy, "Occupy Wall Street Protests: Police Make Arrests, Use Pepper Spray as Some Activists Storm," *New York Daily News*, October 6, 2011, http://www.nydailynews.com/new-york/occupy-wall-street-protests-police-arrests-pepper-spray-activists-storm-barricade-article-1.961645.
104 Scott G. McNall, *Cultures of Defiance and Resistance: Social Movements in 21st-Century America* (New York: Routledge, 2018), p. 70; Caroline Fairchild, "Occupy Arrests Near 8,000 as Wall Street Eludes Prosecution," *Huffington Post*, May 23, 2013, https://www.huffingtonpost.com/2013/05/23/occupy-wall-street-arrests_n_3326640.html; Carty, *Social Movements and New Technology*, 2015, p. 136.
105 Robert Sanchez, "Benedictine Survey: Occupy Protesters Unhappy with Obama," *Daily Herald*, November 14, 2011, http://www.dailyherald.com/article/20111114/news/711149921/; Costas Panagopoulos, "Occupy Wall Street Survey Results," *Fordham University*, October 2011, https://www.fordham.edu/download/downloads/id/2538/occupy_wall_street_survey.pdf; Ruth Milkman and Stephanie Luce, "Occupy Wall Street," in *The Social Movements Reader: Cases and Concepts*, eds. Jeff Goodwin and James M. Jasper (Malden, MA: Wiley Blackwell, 2015), p. 38.
106 Wartofsky, *The Occupiers*, 2015, pp. 27, 94; Carty, *Social Movements and New Technology*, 2015, p. 165; Milkman and Luce, "Occupy Wall Street," 2015, p. 38.
107 Sanchez, "Benedictine Survey," 2011; Panagopoulos, "Occupy Wall Street Survey Results," 2011.
108 Gitlin, *Occupy Nation*, 2012, p. 29; Wartofsky, *The Occupiers*, 2015, pp. 8, 17, 19, 44.
109 Milkman and Luce, "Occupy Wall Street," 2015, p. 42.
110 Charles F. Andrain, *Political Power and Economic Inequality: A Comparative Policy Approach* (Lanham, MD: Rowman & Littlefield, 2014), p. 125.
111 Wartofsky, *The Occupiers*, 2015, p. 50.
112 Castells, *Networks of Outrage and Hope*, 2015, pp. 172–173.
113 Charles Tilly and Sidney Tarrow, *Contentious Politics* (New York: Oxford University Press, 2015), p. 18.
114 Les Christie, "Occupy Protesters Take over Foreclosed Homes," *CNNMoney*, December 6, 2011, http://money.cnn.com/2011/12/06/real_estate/occupy_movement_spreads/index.htm; Wartofsky, *The Occupiers*, 2015, p. 171.
115 Carty, *Social Movements and New Technology*, 2015, p. 144.
116 Carty, *Social Movements and New Technology*, 2015, p. 146.

117 "Occupy Aims to Shut Down West Coast Ports – as It Happened," *The Guardian*, December 12, 2011, https://www.theguardian.com/world/blog/2011/dec/12/occupy-west-coast-ports-shut-down.
118 Wartofsky, *The Occupiers*, 2015, pp. 133–134.
119 Staff and Agencies, "Michael Bloomberg: Occupy Wall Street Is Trying to Destroy Jobs," *The Guardian*, October 8, 2011, https://www.theguardian.com/world/2011/oct/08/bloomberg-occupy-wall-street-jobs; "Rahm Emanuel Doesn't Agree with Occupy Movement's Solutions," *Huffington Post*, October 11, 2011, https://www.huffingtonpost.com/2011/10/11/rahm-emanuel-doesnt-agree_n_1005454.html.
120 MSNBC.com Staff and News Service Reports, "Occupy Chicago: At Least 30 Anti-Wall Street Protesters Arrested in Grant Park," *NBCnews.com*, October 23, 2011, http://www.nbcnews.com/id/45004483/ns/us_news-life/t/occupy-chicago-least-anti-wall-street-protesters-arrested-grant-park/.
121 Associated Press, "Police Clear Out Occupy Boston Camp," *CBSnews.com*, December 10, 2011, https://www.cbsnews.com/news/police-clear-out-occupy-boston-camp/; Adam Nagourney, "'Occupy' Protesters Evicted in Two Cities," *New York Times*, November 30, 2011, https://www.nytimes.com/2011/12/01/us/occupy-los-angeles-philadelphia-camps-cleared-by-police.html.
122 Malia Wollan, "Police Clear Occupy Oakland Encampment, But Protesters Return," *New York Times*, November 14, 2011, https://www.nytimes.com/2011/11/15/us/police-raid-occupy-oakland-camp.html; James Barron and Colin Moynihan, "City Reopens Park after Protesters Are Evicted," *New York Times*, November 15, 2011, https://www.nytimes.com/2011/11/16/nyregion/police-begin-clearing-zuccotti-park-of-protesters.html.
123 Kara Dellacioppa, "Rethinking Resistance and the Cultural Politics of Occupy," *New Political Science* 35, no. 3 (2013): 403–416.
124 Kenyon Farrow, "Occupy Wall Street's Race Problem," *American Prospect*, October 24, 2011, http://prospect.org/article/occupy-wall-streets-race-problem; Stacy Patton, "Why Blacks Aren't Embracing Occupy Wall Street," *Washington Post*, November 25, 2011, https://www.washingtonpost.com/opinions/why-blacks-arent-embracing-occupy-wall-street/2011/11/16/gIQAwc3FwN_story.html?utm_term=.9e9fabf37b32; Jillian Berman, "Occupy Wall Street Actually Not at All Representative of the 99 Percent, Report Finds," *Huffington Post*, January 29, 2013, https://www.huffingtonpost.com/2013/01/29/occupy-wall-street-report_n_2574788.html.
125 Wartofsky, *The Occupiers*, 2015, p. 73.
126 Wartofsky, *The Occupiers*, 2015, p. 98.
127 Wartofsky, *The Occupiers*, 2015, p. 99.
128 Wartofsky, *The Occupiers*, 2015, p. 98.
129 Wartofsky, *The Occupiers*, 2015, p. 178.
130 Milkman and Luce, "Occupy Wall Street," 2015, p. 42.
131 Gitlin, *Occupy Nation*, 2012, p. 41.
132 Gitlin, *Occupy Nation*, 2012, p. 21.
133 Gitlin, *Occupy Nation*, 2012, p. 141.
134 Gitlin, *Occupy Nation*, 2012, pp. 142, 151; Michael Heaney and Fabio Rojas, *Party in the Street: The Antiwar Movement and the Democratic Party after 9/11* (Cambridge: Cambridge University Press, 2016).
135 Wartofsky, *The Occupiers*, 2015: 51; Carty, *Social Movements and New Technology*, 2015: 190.
136 Wartofsky, *The Occupiers*, 2015: 48.

137 Wartofsky, *The Occupiers*, 2015: 51.
138 Ernesto Castañeda, "The Indignados of Spain: A Precedent to Occupy Wall Street," *Social Movement Studies* 11, no. 3–4 (2012): 309–319; Sarah Kerton, "Tahrir, Here? The Influence of the Arab Uprisings on the Emergence of Occupy," *Social Movement Studies* 11, no. 3–4 (2012): 302–308; Kevin M. DeLuca, Sean Lawson, and Ye Sun, "Occupy Wall Street on the Public Screens of Social Media: The Many Framings of the Birth of a Protest Movement," *Communication, Culture, and Critique* 5, no. 4 (2012): 483–509; Mark Tremayne, "Anatomy of Protest in the Digital Era: A Network Analysis of Twitter and Occupy Wall Street," *Social Movement Studies* 13, no. 1 (2014): 110–126; Benjamin Gleason, "#Occupy Wall Street: Exploring Informal Learning about a Social Movement on Twitter," *American Behavioral Scientist* 57, no. 7 (2013): 966–982; Michael J. Jensen and Henrik P. Bang, "Occupy Wall Street: A New Political Form of Movement and Community?" *Journal of Information Technology & Politics* 10, no. 4 (2013): 441–461.
139 Kaibin Xu, "Framing Occupy Wall Street: A Content Analysis of the New York Times and USA Today," *International Journal of Communication* 7 (2013): 2412–2432.
140 Sasha Costanza-Chock, "Mic Check! Media Cultures and the Occupy Movement," *Social Movement Studies* 11, no. 3–4 (2012): 375–385.
141 Carty, *Social Movements and New Technology*, 2015: 138, 142; David S. Meyer, *The Politics of Protest: Social Movements in America* (New York: Oxford University Press, 2014): 142.
142 Castells, *Networks of Outrage and Hope*, 2015: 174, 177.
143 W. Lance Bennett and Alexandra Segerberg, *The Logic of Connective Action: Digital Media and the Personalization of Contentious Politics* (Cambridge: Cambridge University Press, 2014): 163–164.
144 Bennett and Segerberg, *The Logic of Connective Action*, 2014: 203.
145 Milkman and Luce, "Occupy Wall Street," 2015: 33.
146 Milkman and Luce, "Occupy Wall Street," 2015: 33.
147 For this frame, I examined references to the "banks," to the 2008 "bailout" or banks being "bailed out," to Wall Street "greed" or "corporate greed," all in stories emphasizing Occupy Wall Street.
148 For this frame, I examined references to the "one percent," to "wealth," "inequality," to the "99 percent," to "poverty" or "the poor," "the rich," the "middle class," "upper class," and the "wealthy" that appeared in stories emphasizing Occupy Wall Street.
149 For this frame, I examined stories that referenced Occupy Wall Street within 100 words of references to "jobs," the "economy," the "economic crisis," the "financial crisis," the "unemployed" or "unemployment," and "capitalism" more broadly.
150 For this frame, I examined stories that referenced the "arrest" of protesters or "arrests," "violent" behavior or "violence," "rape," "assault," "sexual assault," the use of "tear gas" or "pepper spray" or individuals being "pepper sprayed," and those protesters who were "arrested," all in stories that emphasized Occupy Wall Street.
151 For this frame, I examined stories that referenced Occupy Wall Street as "leaderless" or "anarchist" or referenced "anarchism."
152 For this frame, I examined stories that emphasized Occupy Wall Street within 100 words of discussion of the movement's "agenda," "goal(s)," and "demand(s)."

153 Dan Schnur, "What Should Occupy Wall Street's Agenda Be?", *Washington Post*, October 21, 2011, https://www.washingtonpost.com/opinions/what-should-occupy-wall-streets-agenda-be/2011/10/21/gIQA5iTk4L_story.html?utm_term=.48c777ea6fe3; Julianne Pepitone, "Why Occupy Wall Street Isn't about a List of Demands," *CNNMoney*, October 12, 2011, http://money.cnn.com/2011/10/12/technology/occupy_wall_street_demands/index.htm.

154 Russell Heimlich, "Little Change in Public's Response to 'Capitalism,' 'Socialism,'" *Pew Research Center*, January 10, 2012, http://www.pewresearch.org/fact-tank/2012/01/10/little-change-in-publics-response-to-capitalism-socialism/.

155 Edward P. Morgan, *What Really Happened to the 1960s: How Mass Media Culture Failed American Democracy* (Lawrence, KS: University Press of Kansas, 2010); Anthony DiMaggio, *When Media Goes to War: Hegemonic Discourse, Public Opinion, and the Limits of Dissent* (New York: Monthly Review Press, 2010).

156 Castells, *Networks of Outrage and Hope*, 2015: 196.

157 Class status is a significant predictor of Occupy attitudes at the 5 percent level, and income is at the 1 percent level.

158 Ipsos-Public Affairs/Reuters, "Ipsos-Public Affairs/Reuters Poll," *iPoll*, September 7–10, 2012.

159 *CBS News/New York Times*, "CBS News/New York Times Poll, October 2011," *iPoll*, October 19–24, 2011.

160 Resurgent Republic, "Resurgent Republic Survey, October 2011," *iPoll*, October 30–November 4, 2011.

161 *Pew Research Center*, "Pew Research Center Poll, December 2011," *iPoll*, December 8–11, 2011.

162 *NBC News/Wall Street Journal*, "NBC News/Wall Street Journal Poll, April 2012," *iPoll*, April 13–17, 2012.

163 Woodly, *The Politics of Common Sense*, 2015.

164 David Rolf, *The Fight for $15: The Right Wage for a Working America* (New York: New Press, 2016); Jonathan Rosenblum, *Beyond $15: Immigrant Workers, Faith Activists, and the Revival of the Labor Movement* (New York: Beacon, 2017).

165 Woodly, *The Politics of Common Sense*, 2015.

166 Harry J. Holzer, "Living Wage Laws: How Much Do (Can) They Matter?" *The Urban Institute*, October 2008, https://www.urban.org/sites/default/files/publication/32126/411783-Living-Wage-Laws.PDF.

167 Laurel Weldon, *When Protest Makes Policy: How Social Movements Represent Disadvantaged Groups* (Ann Arbor, MI: University of Michigan Press, 2011); Rosenblum, *Beyond $15*, 2017: 5; Rolf, *The Fight for $15*, 2016: 123, 140.

168 Rolf, *The Fight for $15*, 2016: 124.

169 Rolf, *The Fight for $15*, 2016: 162.

170 Kate Rogers, "Adjusted for Inflation, the Federal Minimum Wage Is Worth Less than 50 Years Ago," *CNBC.com*, July 21, 2016, https://www.cnbc.com/2016/07/21/adjusted-for-inflation-the-federal-minimum-wage-is-worth-less-than-50-years-ago.html.

171 Alana Semuels, "Fast-Food Workers Walk Out in N.Y. amid Rising U.S. Labor Unrest," *Los Angeles Times*, November 29, 2012, http://articles.latimes.com/2012/nov/29/business/la-fi-mo-fast-food-strike-20121129.

172 Atossa Araxia Abrahamian, "U.S. Fast-Food Workers Protest, Demand a 'Living Wage,'" *Reuters*, August 29, 2013, https://www.

reuters.com/article/us-usa-restaurants-strike/u-s-fast-food-workers-pro test-demand-a-living-wage-idUSBRE97S05320130829; Ellyn Fortino, "Chicago Fast Food & Retail Workers Win Victories after April Strike," *Progress Illinois*, July 10, 2013, http://www.progressillinois. com/posts/content/2013/07/10/chicago-fast-food-retail-workers-win-vic tories-after-april-strike; Paul Harris, "Fast-Food Worker Wage Protests Spread to St Louis and Detroit," *The Guardian*, May 10, 2013, https://www.theguardian.com/world/2013/may/10/fast-food-worker-protest-detroit-st-louis.

173 Erika Eichelberger, "How Those Fast-Food Strikes Got Started," *Mother Jones*, December 6, 2013, https://www.motherjones.com/politics/2013/12/how-fast-food-strikes-started/; Adam Gabbatt, "U.S. Fast-Food Workers Strike over Low Wages in Nationwide Protests," *The Guardian*, December 5, 2013, https://www.theguardian.com/world/2013/dec/05/fast-food-workers-strike-minimum-wage.

174 Alice Hines, "Walmart's First-Ever Retail Worker Strike Spreads to 12 Cities," *Huffington Post*, October 9, 2012, https://www.huffingtonpost.com/2012/10/09/walmart-strike-dallas-arkansas-los-angeles-workers_n_1951867. html; Hadley Malcolm, "Judge Rules Walmart Unlawfully Fired Workers on Strike," *USA Today*, January 22, 2016, https://www.usatoday.com/story/money/2016/01/22/judge-rules-walmart-unlawfully-fired-workers-on-strike/79160730/.

175 Nathan Layne, "Wal-Mart Strikes Lawful, Must Reinstate Workers: NLRB Judge," *Reuters*, January 21, 2016, https://www.reuters.com/art icle/us-wal-mart-strike/wal-mart-strikes-lawful-must-reinstate-workers-nlrb-judge-idUSKCN0V001Z.

176 Bruce Horovitz, "Thousands of Fast-Food Workers Strike; Arrests Made," *USA Today*, September 4, 2014, https://www.usatoday.com/story/money/business/2014/09/04/fast-food-restaurants-strike-mcdonalds-wendys-burger-king-taco-bell/15058943/; CNN Wire, "Thousands of Fast Food Workers Strike in 190 Cities, Demand $15 an Hour Wage," *KLTA5*, December 4, 2014, http://ktla.com/2014/12/04/thousands-fast-food-workers-go-on-strike-in-190-cities-demand-15-an-hour-wage/.

177 Steven Greenhouse and Jana Kasperkevic, "Fight for $15 Swells into Largest Protest by Low-Wage Workers in U.S. History," *The Guardian*, April 15, 2015, https://www.theguardian.com/us-news/2015/apr/15/fight-for-15-minimum-wage-protests-new-york-los-angeles-atlanta-boston.

178 Paul Davidson, "Midwest Hospital Workers to Join Fight for $15 Hourly Wage," *USA Today*, September 1, 2017, https://www.usatoday.com/story/money/2017/08/31/midwest-hospital-workers-join-fight-15-hourly-wage/617395001/; Boston25, "Fast Food Workers Strike for $15 Minimum Wage," *Foxnews.com*, September 4, 2017, http://www.foxnews.com/us/2017/09/04/fast-food-workers-strike-for-15-minimum-wage.html; S. M. Chavey, "Fast Food Workers Strike and Rally on Labor Day in St. Paul for $15 Minimum Wage," *Twin Cities Pioneer Press*, September 4, 2017, https://www.twincities.com/2017/09/04/fast-food-workers-strike-and-rally-on-labor-day-in-st-paul-for-15-minimum-wage/; Natasha Bach, "Fast Food Workers Are Going on Strike on Labor Day," *Fortune*, September 4, 2017, http://fortune.com/2017/09/04/labor-day-fast-food-worker-strikes/.

179 Paul Davidson and Ryan Poe, "Workers Seek $15 Wage, Union Rights in Protests in Many Cities," *USA Today*, February 12, 2018, https://www.usatoday.com/story/money/2018/02/12/workers-seek-15-wage-union-rights-protests-many-cities/331481002/.

118   *The Economic Justice Movement*

180 Nicholas Fandos, "Bernie Sanders Proposes Federal Minimum Wage of $15 an Hour," *New York Times*, July 22, 2015, https://www.nytimes.com/politics/first-draft/2015/07/22/bernie-sanders-proposes-federal-minimum-wage-of-15-an-hour/.
181 Alexia Fernández Campbell, "Presidential Hopefuls Are Promising Workers a $15 Minimum Wage," *Vox.com*, April 30, 2019, https://www.vox.com/2019/4/30/18522505/candidates-position-15-dollar-minimum-wage.
182 Nik DeCosta-Klipa, "This Harvard Study Both Confirms and Refutes Bernie Sanders's Complaints about the Media," *Boston Globe*, June 14, 2016, https://www.boston.com/news/politics/2016/06/14/harvard-study-confirms-refutes-bernie-sanderss-complaints-media.
183 *Pew Research Center*, "December 2015 Political Survey," December 8–13, 2015, http://www.people-press.org/question-search/?qid=1871608&pid=51&ccid=51#top.
184 *Pew Research Center*, "August 2016 Political Survey," August 18–26, 2016, http://www.people-press.org/question-search/?qid=1884112&pid=51&ccid=51#top.
185 Leslie Davis and Hannah Hartig, "Two-Thirds of Americans Favor Raising Federal Minimum Wage to $15 an Hour," *Pew Research Center*, July 30, 2019, https://www.pewresearch.org/fact-tank/2019/07/30/two-thirds-of-americans-favor-raising-federal-minimum-wage-to-15-an-hour/.
186 David Cooper, "20 States Raise Their Minimum Wages While the Federal Minimum Continues to Erode," *Economic Policy Institute*, December 18, 2014, https://www.epi.org/blog/20-states-raise-their-minimum-wages-while-the-federal-minimum-continues-to-erode/; Will Kimball, "14 States Raised Their Minimum Wage at the Beginning of 2016, Lifting the Wages of More than 4.6 Million Working People," *Economic Policy Institute*, January 21, 2016, https://www.epi.org/blog/14-states-raised-their-minimum-wage-at-the-beginning-of-2016-lifting-the-wages-of-more-than-4-6-million-working-people/; Dan Caplinger, "2017 Minimum Wage Increases: These 21 States Are Paying Workers More," *USA Today*, December 30, 2016, https://www.usatoday.com/story/money/personalfinance/2016/12/30/2017-minimum-wage-increases-these-21-states-are-paying-workers-more/95741406/; Grace Donnelly, "The Minimum Wage Will Increase on January 1 for 18 States and 20 Cities," *Fortune*, December 20, 2017, http://fortune.com/2017/12/20/minimum-wage-increases-jan-2018/.
187 SEIU, "Campaign Touring the State to Push for a $15 Minimum Wage for All New Yorkers," *Service Employees International Union*, February 2016, https://www.1199seiu.org/mario_cuomo_campaign_for_economic_justice_kicks_off_drive_for_15_with_rallies_in_nyc_and_long_island.
188 Associated Press, "New York Oks $15 Minimum Wage for Fast-Food Workers," *USA Today*, September 11, 2015, https://www.usatoday.com/story/money/business/2015/09/11/ny-raises-minimum-wage-fast-food-workers/72049896/.
189 Patrick McGeehan, "New York Plans $15-an-Hour Minimum Wage for Fast Food Workers," *New York Times*, July 22, 2015, https://www.nytimes.com/2015/07/23/nyregion/new-york-minimum-wage-fast-food-workers.html.
190 David Siders, "Jerry Brown Signs $15 Minimum Wage in California," *The Sacramento Bee*, April 4, 2016, http://www.sacbee.com/news/politics-government/capitol-alert/article69842317.html.

191 Nadia Prupis, "Fifteen Bucks and a Union': Bernie Sanders Marches with Striking Workers," Billmoyers.com, November 11, 2015, https://billmoyers.com/2015/11/11/fifteen-bucks-and-a-union-bernie-sanders-marches-with-striking-workers/.
192 Jordan Weissmann, "Hillary Clinton Finally Explains What It Would Take for Her to Support a $15 Minimum Wage," *Slate.com*, April 18, 2016, http://www.slate.com/blogs/moneybox/2016/04/18/hillary_clinton_explains_her_position_on_a_15_minimum_wage.html.
193 Elana Schor and Heather Caygle, "Dems' New Pitch to Voters: A 'Better Deal,'" *Politico.com*, July 5, 2017, https://www.politico.com/story/2017/07/05/democrats-trump-congress-better-deal-240150.

3 Black Lives Matter

And the Struggle against Color-Blind Racism

With Sakura Shinjo

On February 26, 2012, Trayvon Martin was killed in a gated community in Sanford, Florida, walking home after buying snacks from a convenience store. He died in a confrontation with a neighborhood watch captain, George Zimmerman. Varying accounts of the conflict surfaced. Zimmerman claimed he was tracking a "suspicious person," and the shooting was in self-defense.[1] Others pointed out that Martin was unarmed (Zimmerman was armed with a handgun), that Zimmerman failed to identify himself as a neighborhood watchman, and followed and harassed Martin without cause.[2] While Zimmerman was charged with second-degree murder, he was acquitted, and the Department of Justice (DOJ) failed to pursue charges.[3]

The shooting received media attention for months and years to come. Martin's story demonstrated the U.S. was far from achieving the "post-racial" nirvana commentators celebrated following Barack Obama's election.[4] He quickly became a symbol for millions of African Americans, and his death spawned a social movement centered on the message that Black Lives Matter. Obama announced that Martin's death held emotional resonance for him: "If I had a son, he'd look like Trayvon … When I think about this boy, I think about my own kids."[5]

Civil rights activists reacted to Martin's death by seeking public support for a "Black Lives Matter" (BLM) movement. Alicia Garza, Patricia Cullors, and Opal Tometi, all progressive black activists, took to *Facebook* to establish a #BlackLivesMatter initiative, which went viral nationally. They sought to unify anti-racist, anti-sexist, anti-classist, queer-empowerment politics, while emphasizing the racially repressive nature of the U.S. police state.

Martin's death was the first of many organized under the BLM banner. Subsequent deaths of black men at the hands of the police became catalysts for protest in poor black communities, where the criminal justice system targets people of color. Garza, an organizer for the *National Domestic Workers Alliance*, spoke of Zimmerman's acquittal as a "gut" punch, reminding her that "black lives don't matter" in America.[6] Cullors, a prison reform activist, reflected that Martin's death "sparked a movement" against "white supremacist vigilante violence," which "demanded this nation confront its racist past and present."[7] Tometi, an organizer for *Black Alliance for Just Immigration*, called for a "human rights movement" to challenge systemic racism, demanding local governments address racial discrimination.[8]

Intersectionality and BLM

BLM was never simply about police brutality. It was about recognizing different dimensions of repression that define individuals' experiences, identities, and actions. Keeanga-Yamahtta Taylor writes of the "overlapping oppressions confronting black people in the struggle to end police violence and win justice."[9] She draws on an essay from Garza, which speaks to these intersections in radical terms:

> When we say Black Lives Matter, we are talking about the ways in which black people are deprived of our basic human rights and dignity ... It is an acknowledgement that one million black people are locked in cages in this country – one half of all people in prisons or jails – is an act of state violence. It is an acknowledgement that black women continue to bear the burden of a relentless assault on our children and our families and that assault is an act of state violence. Black queer and trans folks, bearing a unique burden in a hetero-patriarchal society that disposes of us like garbage and simultaneously fetishizes us and profits off of us is state violence ... the fact that black girls are used as negotiating chips during times of conflict and war is state violence.[10]

The founders of BLM articulated intersectional concerns as related to societal racism. Whether BLM succeeded in adopting an intersectional framework that speaks to people within disadvantaged groups is a question we address here.

What Can Be Learned from BLM?

Through analyzing historical case studies of protest against police brutality in Ferguson, Missouri and Baltimore, Maryland, we advance numerous arguments. First, we argue BLM shows how leftist movements are *the* central actor in promoting progressive change, more so than political leaders. Truman's disturbance theory is useful in explaining BLM's rise, with the deaths of Trayvon Martin and other black men serving as catalysts that sparked disruptive protests that spoke to grievances among people of color regarding police brutality, racial profiling, systemic racism, and anxieties about poverty in minority communities.

Second, these case studies speak to persistent racism and classism in America, via the maintenance of political institutions discriminating against poor people of color. Opposition to racism and to a political-economic system that favors affluent whites were major drivers of BLM. These concerns were reflected in the comments of the movement's founders, and in the rebellion against police in Ferguson – where government discriminated against poor people of color for monetary gain. In an era of growing inequality and plutocratic politics, poor communities of color lack economic resources to provide for vital services.

Third, we argue social movements are vital to disrupting racist and plutocratic systems, and the discourses sustaining them. The media are defined by hegemonic biases in favor of government and business interests. But with extraordinary effort, progressive movements do break into media discourse during periods of mass protest. These movements gain sustained, favorable coverage. In a heavily mediated society, Americans rely primarily on the press for information. It is unlikely most Americans knew someone active in the Ferguson or Baltimore protests, meaning the media seriously shaped perceptions of BLM. Through its use of the media, BLM cultivated support for their cause, pressuring governments to pass political reforms.

Finally, we document how identities are central to movements and politics. We experience the world at the intersections of multiple identities. Intersectionality speaks to meaningful categories of identity within the mass public. Here, we emphasize the intersections of age, geographical location, class, gender, and race.

Police Violence: A Background

It is no accident that waves of protests followed the killings of black males across the U.S. These deaths provoke feelings of anger and resentment, persisting in strained communities enduring the pressures of poverty and discrimination from law enforcement. Eric Garner's death at the hands of New York City police on July 17, 2014 was one example of a heavy-handed, racially discriminatory criminal justice system. Garner, suspected of selling cigarettes on the streets of Staten Island, was placed in an unlawful chokehold by police and pushed face-first to the ground by four officers, despite him warning them eleven times he could not breath.[11] After losing consciousness, Garner was brought to a hospital, but pronounced dead after arrival. The New York City Medical Examiner ruled the death a homicide.[12]

Garner's death provoked protests in New York and across the country, with demonstrators calling for the officers' prosecution.[13] Although none was convicted, the city paid a $5.9 million settlement to Garner's family. Mayor Bill de Blasio said he was "very troubled" by the video of the altercation: "fundamental questions are being asked, and rightfully so ... the way we go about policing has to change. People need to know that black lives and brown lives matter as much as white lives."[14]

A second example of deadly policing involved Chicagoan Laquan McDonald, who was gunned down in a police brutality cover-up. On October 20, 2014, Chicago police were called to the Archer Heights neighborhood after a report that a young man with a knife broke into numerous vehicles. Once confronted, McDonald used his knife to slash one of the police car's tires, and also damaged one of the officer's windshields.[15] One report recounts of the police version of the story:

> [McDonald] who had PCP in his system when he died, was behaving erratically and refusing police commands to drop the folding knife. At the time of the shooting, the police union maintained that the officer fired in fear of his life because the teen lunged at him and his partner with the knife.[16]

Chicago Police Department's version of the incident was refuted after a video was made public demonstrating it lied about that night's events. Contrary to the claim that officer Jason Van Dyke shot McDonald in self-defense, the video showed the officer shot him in the back as he walked away from police.[17] Thirty seconds after arriving on the scene, and 6 seconds after exiting his car, Van Dyke fired numerous shots that brought McDonald to the ground, after which the officer emptied his clip into the suspect, with McDonald in the fetal position. Van Dyke shot McDonald 16 times in 15 seconds, with the suspect on the ground for 13 of those seconds.[18] Van Dyke was charged with and convicted of murder, and Chicago paid $5 million to McDonald's family. The case gained attention after Mayor Rahm Emanuel refused to make the video public during a contested re-election season, then was forced to release it after a journalist sued for access.[19] The case demonstrated that corruption in Chicago politics reached the highest levels of government. McDonald's shooting incited protests from November 2015 through March 2016, with demonstrators demanding police Superintendent Garry McCarthy's and Mayor Emanuel's resignations.[20]

McDonald's and Garner's deaths were symbolically powerful, speaking to the problem of police brutality. They stoked mass anger in poor minority communities because of longstanding feelings that police abuse people of color. Police shootings of black men, including Michael Brown in Ferguson (2014), Freddie Gray in Baltimore (2015), Alton Sterling in Baton Rouge, Louisiana (2016), and Philando Castile in St. Paul, Minnesota (2016), all produced protests. Were these deaths isolated incidents of police violence, or did they reveal broader problems with police brutality? We address these questions, reviewing evidence of institutional racism and police brutality against poor people of color.

Racism in America: What We Know

In February 2017, 62 percent of Americans agreed "blacks who can't get ahead in this country are mostly responsible for their own condition."[21] This sentiment overlapped with claims that the U.S. was entering a "post-racial" era, with racial prejudice no longer a barrier to success.[22] This assertion was repeatedly repudiated in scholarship.[23] Whites and blacks retain different beliefs about the fairness of the criminal justice system, with blacks less trusting than whites.[24] Numerous inquiries document how racial prejudice motivated vote choices in the 2008 election.[25] Racial prejudice drove Republican and Tea Party policy attitudes on taxes, health care, and voter preferences, and racial animosity was a potent force after Obama's rise to power.[26]

Despite many Americans depicting themselves as "color blind" and free from prejudice, scholars document persistent institutional racism.[27] Communities remain racially segregated due to white resistance to desegregation.[28] Segregation matters because of its effects on education.[29] The relationship between community poverty and poorer academic performance suggests that racial and economic segregation perpetuate place-based educational inequalities between blacks and whites.[30] Inequalities between communities feed racial inequality in occupational outcomes, since schools in poor minority communities struggle to provide educational opportunities necessary to secure well-paying occupations.[31]

The criminal justice system perpetuates racial inequality. Alexander argues the "war on drugs" replaced previous racist efforts, via the Jim Crow system, to discriminate against minorities.[32] This war traces back to the Johnson, Nixon, Reagan, and George H. W. Bush administrations, and continued via heavy-handed policing tactics targeting poor minorities.[33] The "war on drugs" disproportionately targets people of color, and criminalized black males, a third of whom have felony convictions.[34] In the 2010s, non-violent drug possession arrests outnumbered those for violent crimes, signaling the ascendance of the "war on drugs."[35] Although whites and blacks use drugs at comparable rates, blacks account for 35 percent of drug arrests and 55 percent of drug convictions, despite being less than 15 percent of the population.[36] This suggests racial profiling of people of color.[37]

Conservatives claim that blacks are arrested at greater rates than whites because of higher crime rates in minority communities.[38] In 2014, the criminal justice system incarcerated 2.3 million blacks, a third of the imprisoned population, despite blacks comprising a quarter of criminal arrests.[39] And numerous studies that remove community entirely from consideration – via examination of highway stops – find that people of color are still disproportionately targeted.[40] And as the *New York Times* reports, across most states examined in traffic searches, police "consistently found drugs, guns, or other contraband more often if the driver was white."[41]

Race matters to policing in use of force incidents. One study of police stops in 11 cities found that accounting for varied violent crime rates among blacks and whites, the average use-of-force rate for blacks was 273 per 100,000 people, compared to 76 per 100,000 for whites, a 3.6:1 imbalance.[42] A study of seven large states found blacks were more often subject to violence, even in cases when they did not resist arrest.[43]

Systemic racism persists in capital punishment cases. It was spotlighted in the Supreme Court case of *McKleskey v. Kemp* (1987), with minorities in Georgia 70 percent more likely to receive a death sentence than whites. Death sentences were 4.3 times more likely when the victim was white.[44] Despite the court's plea to Georgia to address racism in death penalty cases, discrimination continues. The *New York Times* reported in the early 2010s that, in the three decades following *McKleskey*, racially discriminatory applications of the death penalty persisted.[45]

Scholarly works also document media perpetuations of racial stereotypes. The media marginalized and portrayed as extremist the civil rights movement.[46] Reporting on crime and poverty is heavily stereotypical. Blacks are more likely to be depicted as criminals or suspected perpetrators, more than the actual number of blacks committing crimes.[47] Blacks are more likely to be portrayed as poor, in higher numbers than is the case.[48] These trends reveal the hegemony of cultural racism in America.

Americans allow racism to define their thoughts and behavior.[49] Individuals "perform" for others by conforming to racial stereotypes of "whiteness" and "blackness."[50] Implicit racial biases in the news activate latent prejudices in the subconscious mind.[51] News stories, which regularly conflate "black" with "poverty," produce opposition to welfare, as many Americans see blacks as poor and undeserving of assistance.[52] As a result, opinions on welfare become heavily racialized.[53] Reporting on crime regularly associates "black" with "perpetrator," leading news consumers to support harsher "get tough on crime" laws. Television audiences are "primed" to associate "blackness" with negative emotional responses, as related to crime.[54] The racialization of crime coverage leads consumers to view violence as more morally heinous when committed by blacks.[55] Finally, racial prejudice is linked to anger on the right, with conservative outrage driving opposition to government policies benefitting poor people of color.[56]

Racial priming and racist stereotypes have consequences for public policy. Welfare programs are increasingly punitive toward the poor, driven by the assumption that the disadvantaged are morally deviant and lazy. This framework for "disciplining the poor" is linked to racial stereotypes, with sanctions against welfare recipients directed against minorities, despite whites receiving most benefits.[57] The linking of welfare and poverty to minorities, while not as prevalent in media discourse prior to the 1960s, was common in the post-civil rights era.[58]

Despite racial stereotyping, activists have made progress in fighting racism. The civil rights movement combatted discrimination and created pressure for democratic reforms.[59] Race continues to drive social movement activism in modern times.[60] But scholars are of varying minds regarding the impact of social movements on politics, with some emphasizing government's role in creating opportunities for them to succeed.[61] Others stress the dominant role of movements in forcing government to respond to demands for change.[62]

Despite racism in the news, stereotypical content has declined in election ads.[63] As a result, negative racial priming against people of color became less of a concern in elections, at least prior to the re-emergence of blatant racism in the 2016 presidential election with Trump. Other research finds that media were susceptible to pressure from the civil rights movement. During the 1960s, activists secured sympathetic news coverage, cultivating public support, translating into pressure on the executive, Congress, and the courts.[64] In modern times, activists utilize the media to direct attention to police brutality against minorities.[65]

While BLM transformed American politics and values, it received sparse attention in scholarly studies. Some work laid out a preliminary movement history, discussing its social and philosophical significance.[66] Some research emphasizes the symbolic power of black protests with nationalistic themes, while other work examines BLM as it applies to the Ferguson demonstrations.[67] Our chapter fleshes out BLM's role in impacting media and political discourse.

Ferguson: The Early Development of BLM

Michael Brown graduated from high school in the summer of 2014. Aged 18, he was days from entering a training program for heating and air conditioning repair. Late in the morning of August 9, he and a friend reportedly stole cigarillos from a market, leaving on foot. Officer Darren Wilson drove up to Brown as he walked home, and a struggle ensued. While witness reports vary, Brown was shot six times and died at the scene.

Conflicts emerged in eyewitness stories. Some accounts described Brown as holding his hands up to surrender after he fled from an initial confrontation with Wilson. Brown was depicted as stumbling toward Wilson after being shot numerous times, the implication being he was not a threat when killed.[68] Wilson maintained Brown reached for the officer's gun, prompting him to fire in self-defense.[69] After Brown fled, a second altercation resulted in what one eyewitness described as a "full charge at the officer," upon which Wilson killed Brown.[70] The *New York Times* reported three months after the shooting:

> a review of thousands of pages of testimony from the case, made public last week, shows the forensic evidence and some witness' accounts are consistent with Wilson's explanation of what happened: that he shot Brown because the teenager was charging forward in a threatening way, and that Brown's hands were not raised to the sky, but were at his sides.[71]

A grand jury did not bring criminal charges against Wilson.[72]

Brown's death was an important symbolic event. It sparked protests in Ferguson and, whatever the facts of the case, it spoke to longstanding grievances within Ferguson related to segregation, poverty, and anger over police brutality. The *New York Times* situated the protests within a historical context, stressing growing inequality in the St. Louis metro region:

> St. Louis has long been one of the nation's most segregated metropolitan areas, and there remains a high wall between black residents – who overwhelmingly have lower incomes – and the white power structure that dominates City Councils and police departments like the one in Ferguson.

The paper pointed to Ferguson's history of white flight, in which white residents fled the city and suburbs like Ferguson to avoid desegregation:

> As black families moved into Ferguson, whites fled. In 1980, the town was 85 percent white and 14 percent black; by 2010, it was 29 percent white and 69 percent black. But blacks did not gain political power as their numbers grew. The mayor and the police chief are white, as are five of the six City Council members. The school board consists of six white members and one Hispanic ... The disparity is most evident in the Ferguson Police Department, of which only three of the 53 officers are black. The largely white force stops black residents far out of proportion to their population. Blacks account for 86 percent of the traffic stops in the city, and 93 percent of the arrests after those stops.[73]

There was a disconnect between Ferguson's black population and the government and policing structures, which represented the city's white demographic. The protests made explicit the gulf between the white power structure and black residents.

Anger over racial discrimination was documented in the DOJ's report on Ferguson, following an investigation into the city's policing practices.

The report spotlighted a pattern of racial profiling, suppression of dissent against police critics, excessive force, routine violations of the right to privacy, and failure to respond to community complaints against officers accused of misconduct. The report concluded that black residents in Ferguson were twice as likely as whites to be searched by police and 2.37 times more likely to be arrested after a stop, with discrimination the product of officers embracing the revenue scheme from city officials, utilizing the Ferguson Police Department as a de facto taxation agency against people of color. Such harassment prompted the city to elevate monetary concerns over due process and equal protection under the law. Ferguson police's harassment of black residents fostered distrust of law enforcement.[74] This resentment drove protests of Brown's shooting. Black Ferguson residents, cut out of economic prosperity due to the effects of segregation, were also being harassed by the white power structure.

In this emotionally charged environment, protests following Brown's death were violent and non-violent. Looting of a dozen business establishments resulted in dozens of arrests, prompting Governor Jay Nixon to call in the National Guard and impose a curfew.[75] Nixon proclaimed: "We will not allow a handful of looters to endanger the rest of this community. If we're going to achieve justice, we must first have and maintain peace."[76] Nixon's comments revealed that the violence was the province of a small number of malcontents. And rioters had no monopoly on violence, as reports highlighted aggressive police and National Guard tactics via use of tear gas and rubber bullets against protesters.[77] The suppression extended beyond looters, as 132 protesters were arrested in the 12 days of protests after Brown's death under "failure to disperse" charges unrelated to vandalism or rioting.[78]

Many grievances drove the protests, as interviews with community members revealed. These included: anger with the perceived immunity of Ferguson police who shoot black residents; distrust of the city's white power structure; demands for an in-depth investigation of the shooting; anger over the suppression of protests against police brutality; demands that the city respect civil rights of black residents; feelings of futility regarding citizen–police relations; anger over the struggles within black communities related to poverty, drug abuse, and poor educational opportunities; and outrage over Ferguson police's leaving Brown's dead body on the sidewalk for hours in the hot summer sun.[79] These points do not suggest vague, unarticulated anger. Rather, black residents held serious grievances against a repressive local political system.

Social Media and the Ferguson Protests

BLM was birthed via social media, with the online networking of Cullors, Garza, and Tometti via their #BlackLivesMatter rallying cry. They met through "Black Organizing for Leadership and Dignity"

(BOLD), a national networking group for community organizing. While these activists sought a broader uprising, the BLM movement took time to gain notoriety. Protests in Ferguson (2014), New York City (2014), Chicago (2014), Baltimore (2015), and other cities raised attention for the movement's cause. These protests reveal the power of social media, via citizens' phone recordings of altercations between police and black men spread virally through *Facebook*, *Twitter*, and elsewhere, fueling anger over police brutality and demonstrations.

Social media played a vital role in Ferguson. *Facebook*, *Twitter*, and other venues informed community members and others about how the protests unfolded, in part circumventing traditional news media. Activists in Ferguson utilized social media to disseminate images of police violence against protesters, encouraging others to be more vigilant in recording police–citizen interactions.[80] They used these venues to communicate information about planned demonstrations.[81] Social media allowed Americans to engage in discourses on the Ferguson protests, racism, and police violence. BLM supporters engaged in formidable organizing online, giving voice to millions of people across the country frustrated with police brutality.

Social media were a double-edged sword. They were utilized by federal authorities to monitor protesters in Ferguson and beyond. The Ferguson and Baltimore police departments tracked protesters' *Twitter*, *Facebook*, and *Instagram* profiles following the deaths of Michael Brown (Ferguson) and Freddie Gray (Baltimore), using that information in their crowd-control efforts.[82] The American Civil Liberties Union protested the surveillance, which they deemed as having a chilling effect on protests.[83] The spying confirmed longstanding community concerns about heavy-handed law enforcement tactics.

The Media and Ferguson

The Ferguson protestors were able to attract favorable coverage from the news media. We examined the period from August 9 (2014), when Brown was killed, through August 25, when the final protests occurred, and after the state withdrew National Guard troops.[84] We included various print, television, online, and radio sources – 11 in total – and more than 2,200 stories, television segments, and other articles, including op-eds, editorials, and letters to the editor referencing "Michael Brown" and "Ferguson." We included mostly national sources, and those serving local newspaper markets, including the *Associated Press* and *St. Louis Post-Dispatch*. We used *Nexis Uni* to conduct a comprehensive analysis of Ferguson content.

We constructed six major frames through which reporting could have conveyed main themes related to Brown's shooting and subsequent protests, drawing on: (1) community concerns in Ferguson from protesters, discussed earlier in this chapter; and (2) official voices, which were critical of the protesters. We describe these frames, and the justification for adopting each, below. Critical frames with the potential to undermine protests include the following:

- A "police protect and serve" frame, depicting Ferguson police and the National Guard as playing a stabilizing role in response to protests, providing safety and order. This frame included: references to efforts from police to protect Ferguson residents; references to the importance of community safety; discussion of the National Guard operating in Ferguson, and its (and Ferguson police's) efforts to pacify violence via a curfew and martial law, reliance on tear gas, rubber bullets, and other riot gear and body armor used in crowd control; and reporting of individuals arrested in policing the protest zones.[85] This frame is grounded in the statements of city officials, who ordered the curfew, imposed martial law, and justified these actions by referring to the danger posed by looters and rioters.[86] This frame is negative in its depictions of the protests, in that the police are seen as an inherently stabilizing force, working against protests in the name of the common good.
- A "protester violence" frame, suggesting protesters were extremists. By directing attention to a small number of deviant individuals, such coverage drew attention away from the grievances of protesters, and from the fact that the vast majority of protesters were non-violent. This frame included: discussion of riots and looting in Ferguson; violence by city residents; vandalism; discussion of chaos, anarchy, and anarchist protesters set on destabilizing Ferguson; and references to unrest.[87] As with the previous frame, this one was based on the statements of city and state officials who warned of criminal elements in the protests.[88] Both frames also have a foundation in previous studies emphasizing the journalistic practice of marginalizing protests as violent, and treating police as stabilizing agents.[89]
- A "Michael Brown as criminal" frame, dismissing him as deviant. This frame included references to the claim that Brown robbed a store; discussion of toxicology reports that Brown had marijuana in his system during the shooting; and references to Brown as "no angel," in reference to a prominent media editorial portraying him as dangerous.[90] References to Brown and marijuana, and to the robbery, were disseminated by officials, including Ferguson Police and the St. Louis County coroner's office.[91] The frame had the potential to undermine the protests. If Brown was a criminal threat, why take seriously protests of his death? This line of reasoning, although embraced by conservative pundits, ignored the deeper

grievances at work in Ferguson due to police misconduct.[92] Still, a cursory engagement with this frame could pre-empt a deeper analysis of the causes underlying the protests.

In contrast to the critical frames, we constructed three more frames that were supportive of the protesters and drawn from political actors sympathetic to BLM. These frames include the following:

- A "peaceful protests" frame, overlapping with the reality that the overwhelming majority of protesters were non-violent. This frame included: references to peaceful rallies and protest; discussions of non-violence in Ferguson; and reporting on marches, rallies, vigils, or demonstrations.[93] The news-consuming public, which generally abhors violence, is likely to look at this frame more sympathetically than depictions of protesters as dangerous. This frame is founded on the recognition of Governor Nixon's assessment that only a small number of protesters engaged in violence.[94]
- A "police brutality" frame, portraying Ferguson police and the National Guard as fueling distrust and engaging in violence against the city's citizens. This depiction turns the "police protection" frame on its head, reversing notions that police in minority communities simply "protect and serve." This framework included: explicit discussion of police brutality; references to protesters' chant against police of "hands up, don't shoot," a statement lending itself to a depiction of police as violent and dangerous; reporting on militarized local police and military-style weapons used by police and National Guard forces; and discussions about state violence, in reference to police and National Guard activities.[95] This frame is drawn from grievances expressed by Ferguson residents, discussed in reporting referenced earlier in this chapter.[96] It is based on the DOJ's report, which referenced excessive use of force against black city residents by Ferguson police. It is also grounded in previous studies spotlighting the police brutality against protesters and people of color.[97]
- A "race/racial injustice" frame, which drew attention to racial aspects at work in the Ferguson protests and related to Brown's death. This frame contradicts efforts to depict the U.S. as "post-racial," instead drawing attention to ongoing racism. The frame includes: discussions of race, racism, racial issues, black individuals in Ferguson, or racist/racially motivated thinking or behavior as related to Ferguson, Brown, and the protests; references to racial stereotyping; reporting on racial profiling, and police efforts to racially discriminate; discussion of injustice in Ferguson and the need for justice following Brown's death; references to the need to investigate Brown's death; reporting on segregation more broadly; and reporting that referenced civil rights.[98] The "race/racial injustice"

frame is based on community grievances, as discussed in on-the-ground reporting during the protests, and in the DOJ's Ferguson report, which spotlighted racial profiling and discrimination.

Media coverage of Brown's death and the Ferguson protests cannot be classified as strongly favorable to, or critical of, the protesters. Table 3.1 documents the mixed nature of media content. For the three critical frames, one of them – "police protect and serve" – appeared in most stories for 10 of 11 outlets, while a second – "protester violence" – appeared most of the time in all 11 outlets. However, the "Michael Brown as criminal" frame did not appear in most stories across any of the venues. Two of the three favorable frames toward protesters – "peaceful protests" and "race/racial injustice" – appeared in most stories for all 11 outlets, despite the "police brutality" frame never appearing once in most pieces from any venue. Averaged across all outlets, "police protect and serve" appeared in 66 percent of stories, compared to 70 percent of stories for "protester violence," 17 percent for "Michael Brown as criminal," 65 percent for "peaceful protests," 25 percent for "police brutality," and 81 percent for "race/racial injustice."

Table 3.1 Coverage of Michael Brown's Death and the Ferguson Protests (August 9–25, 2014)

News Outlet (# of articles/segments)	Police Protect and Serve	Pro-tester Violence	Brown as Criminal	Peaceful Protests	Police Brutality	Race/Racial Injustice
Frames Critical of the Ferguson Protests (% of stories appearing in)				*Frames Favorable to the Ferguson Protests (% of stories appearing in)*		
New York Times	59	67	9	69	27	81
ABC News	63	59	16	61	22	67
CBS New	64	66	22	58	18	80
NBC News	62	66	9	74	21	57
Fox News	69	78	38	77	25	94
MSNBC	86	82	25	89	48	96
CNN	67	70	16	89	20	78
St. Louis Post-Dispatch	66	69	10	68	20	78
NPR	50	66	16	60	16	82
Associated Press	64	67	12	74	25	86
CNN.com	81	82	17	81	28	94

Source: *Nexis Uni* academic database

These findings have serious implications for coverage of Ferguson. Protesters were regularly humanized in the news, lending legitimacy to their cause. And the issues of race and racism were a constant theme, providing context to a major component of the protesters' agenda. But police brutality was neglected in the news. The media did poorly in spotlighting institutional racism in the criminal justice system. Despite weak efforts at providing context for protesters' distrust of police, these findings are positive for BLM because racism and peaceful protest were routinely covered.

On the other hand, media coverage of Ferguson was misleading and stereotypical. The myth of police as a stabilizing force in minority communities was routinely perpetuated in most stories for 10 of 11 media venues. And the stereotype of protesters as violent was regularly disseminated in every news outlet, despite most-all demonstrators being non-violent. Still, journalists did not consistently marginalize the protests by portraying Brown as a criminal. The question of excessive force against people of color, while not embraced, was not dismissed out of hand. Considering these findings, we expect that increased consumption of news on Ferguson produced growing support for protesters, at least in recognizing the problem of societal racism. In contrast, those paying greater attention to the news should be no more likely to express distrust of police, considering the omission of the "police brutality" frame from most stories.

To test the above predictions, we examined public attentiveness to news on Brown's shooting and the Ferguson protests. We drew on *Pew*'s August 2014 survey, asking Americans how closely they followed "the police shooting of an African American teen and protests in Ferguson, Missouri." *Pew* also asked respondents if they believed "this case raises important issues about race that need to be discussed," or if "the issue of race is getting more attention in this case than it deserves," and if respondents agreed "in the aftermath of the police shooting in Ferguson" that "the police response has gone too far" or "has been about right." We utilize "regression" analysis to measure whether news consumption is associated with opinions of Brown's shooting and the protests, controlling for respondents' ideology, party, gender, age, income, education, race, and geographic background (urban or non-urban residence).

Figure 3.1 provides estimates for the power of each factor in predicting opinions of Ferguson, controlling for all other factors included in our analysis.[99] Greater attention to news is significantly associated with recognition that the protests and shooting raised important questions about race. This finding was expected considering coverage emphasized the problem of racism. Media consumption was a more powerful predictor of attitudes about Ferguson, compared to respondents' income, gender, age, and race.

But media consumption was less powerful than party (identifying as a Democrat) or ideology (identifying as a liberal). In contrast, greater

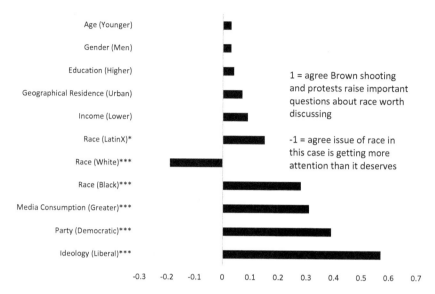

Figure 3.1 Media Effects on Attitudes toward the Ferguson Protests
Source: *Pew Research Center*, August 2014 poll
Statistical Significance Levels: *** = 0.1% ** = 1% * = 5%
Controls: gender, age, education, race, income, political party, ideology, geographic residence

media consumption was *not* associated with concerns that the police response to the Ferguson protests went "too far." This finding was also expected, considering journalists neglected the police brutality frame.

These findings suggest there was room for BLM activists to maneuver in media discourse. Protesters challenged racism in law enforcement, while spotlighting police repression. BLM transformed the national discussion on race, despite a longstanding official source bias in the news.

Intersectionality and Ferguson

Americans define themselves at the intersections of multiple identities. With Ferguson, we analyze how race and ethnicity, gender, class, age, and geographical location interacted to influence opinions of protests against racism in policing. Figure 3.2 documents how intersecting identities appeared to impact assessments of whether Brown's shooting and ensuing protests raised questions about race in America that were worth considering. The data reveal that intersectionality is a useful analytical lens for understanding mass opinion. Twelve of the intersectional identities from Figure 3.2 were significant predictors of public attitudes; only five were not.

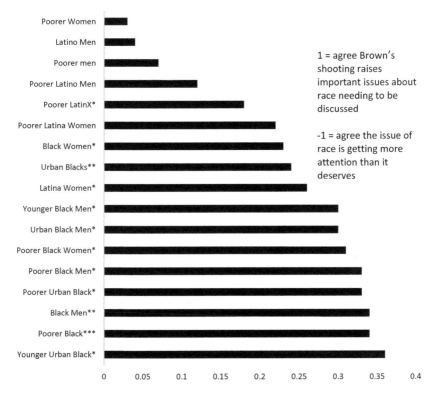

Figure 3.2 Intersecting Identities and the Ferguson Protests
Source: *Pew Research Center*, August 2014 poll
Statistical Significance Levels: *** = 0.1% ** = 1% * = 5%
Controls: gender, age, education, race, income, political party, ideology, geographic residence

The interaction between gender and income (men and women making less than $50,000 a year) was not a significant predictor of attitudes. Neither were interactions between ethnicity and gender for Latino men, or ethnicity, income, and gender for poorer Latino men. These findings aside, all other identity groups were significant in predicting how Americans viewed Ferguson. LatinX Americans were at times more sympathetic, including Latina women and poorer LatinX respondents. Being black, at the intersection of numerous identities, was important too. Whereas white Americans (Figure 3.1) were more likely to reject racial lessons to be learned from Ferguson, numerous black intersectional identities (Figure 3.2) speak to disadvantages faced by these groups in the U.S. Lower income, by itself, was not associated with sympathy toward the protests (Figure 3.1). Rather, income, interacting with other identities, mattered. Disadvantaged groups, at the intersections of race, gender, class, age, and geographic-based identities, were historically neglected and suppressed by a white, affluent, patriarchal power structure.

Individuals fitting the intersectional profiles in Figure 3.2 are also those who have historically been treated with suspicion and a heavy hand by police. They have been disproportionately left behind in a plutocratic political culture depicting poverty among people of color as resulting from personal pathologies, rather than a consequence of a political-economic system producing growing inequality and declining living standards.

The findings from Ferguson reveal the power of movements in impacting political discourse on policing. We now turn to a second case: the death of Freddie Gray in Baltimore, to seek additional confirmation for our findings.

Freddie Gray and the Baltimore Uprising

On April 12, 2015, Freddie Gray was arrested by officers of the Baltimore Police Department (BPD) for possessing an illegal switchblade. Gray reportedly made eye contact with two bike patrol officers, prior to fleeing from police, who followed in foot pursuit. The officers used a taser to subdue Gray, loading him into a police wagon. Gray was removed from the wagon, unconscious, badly injured, and in cardiac arrest. He suffered a severe neck injury, with three fractured vertebrae, a crushed voice box, and a severed spine.[100] Gray fell into a coma and died after arriving at a local trauma center.[101] His death was ruled a homicide by the state medical examiner's office, leading to charges against six Baltimore police officers for second-degree assault and involuntary manslaughter.[102] Charges were dropped against three of them, and the other three received not-guilty verdicts. The DOJ announced it would not bring charges against the officers.[103] Despite the failed prosecutions, Baltimore paid out $6.4 million in a settlement to Gray's family.[104]

Gray's death was as a catalyst event, uniting protesters against police brutality. It sparked demonstrations from late April through early May 2015, which were marked by non-violent protest and rioting.[105] Much public attention was drawn to looting in the Mondawmin neighborhood in northwest Baltimore, where Gray's funeral took place, and where business establishments were destroyed.[106] But the protests were about more than looting. Mass public anger, the DOJ concluded in its report on Baltimore, stemmed from routine violations of the public trust due to police activities. The DOJ reported:

> BPD makes stops, searches, and arrests without the required justification; uses enforcement strategies that unlawfully subject African Americans to disproportionate rates of stops, searches and arrests; uses excessive force; and retaliates against individuals for

their constitutionally protected expression. The pattern of practice results from systemic deficiencies that have persisted within BPD for many years and has exacerbated community distrust of the police, particularly in the African American community.[107]

The Baltimore protests were rooted in frustrations in an era of plutocracy and rising inequality. The unemployment rate for the city in 2015 was 13.9 percent, eight percentage points higher than the nation. In the neighborhoods of Sandtown-Winchester and Harlem Park, where Gray lived and was arrested, and which saw protests following his death, economic distress was more severe. With a black population of 96.6 percent, the household poverty rate was 35.4 percent, compared to a national average of 11.3 percent. The unemployment rate was 24.2 percent, compared to a national rate of 5.5 percent, while 51.2 percent of residents earned less than $25,000 a year, compared to 23.3 percent of Americans.[108] The stress weighed heavily on protesters, as reporting identified economic grievances shared by neighborhood residents during the demonstrations. These included concerns with residential segregation, home foreclosures, a dilapidated housing stock, white flight from older, now disproportionately black neighborhoods, a lack of well-paying jobs, inadequate school funding, and aggressive policing – symbolized in Gray's death.[109] While some Americans were celebrating the "economic recovery," residents of Sandtown-Winchester and Harlem Park endured the consequences of a "free market" economy downplaying the plight of poor people of color.

Social Media, the News Media, and Baltimore

As with Ferguson, activists in Baltimore used social media to organize. *Twitter* and *Facebook* were a convenient way to communicate information for mobilizing rallies.[110] These venues were used to coordinate assistance for those impacted by looting, for example in community clean-up efforts, for feeding children who missed free school lunches, and for finding churches to shelter the displaced.[111] Social media were tools of empowerment, aiding activists in disseminating messages, and helping to reframe the protests as an uprising, rather than driven by lawlessness and looting.[112]

As with Ferguson, social media cut in favor of and against demonstrators. BPD used *Twitter*, drawing on its 113,000 followers, to steer the debate, releasing media advisories warning residents about the violence and looting. It issued updates on injured police officers, drawing attention to parts of the city BPD felt were in danger due to looting and fires. BPD deplored as "violent criminals" those who threw rocks at police and engaged in property destruction. The announcements appealed to parents, advising them to keep children indoors, while demanding that demonstrators remain non-violent.[113] BLM activists were not the only ones using social media in the battle for public opinion.

In contrast to Ferguson, coverage of the Baltimore protests was more sympathetic to the demonstrators than their critics. This finding suggests the growing effectiveness of BLM in impacting media discourse. Activists utilized the media to cultivate support for their goals, temporarily bucking the trend of media bias in favor of official voices.

We used *Nexis Uni*, examining 11 media outlets, to understand how Baltimore was framed. We included the *Baltimore Sun* to measure local news coverage. We examined the period from April 18, when protests began, through May 3, 2015, the day before National Guard forces began withdrawal from Baltimore.[114] For the 11 outlets, we analyzed more than 1,800 stories, segments, and other articles, including all pieces referencing "Freddie Gray" and "Baltimore."

We examined six major frames for understanding the Baltimore protests, three sympathetic to demonstrators, and three antagonistic. These frames were drawn from those previously used, although some were altered to focus on facts on the ground in Baltimore. We included police "protect and serve" and "protester violence" frames, which were preferred ways of covering the protests by officials, threatening to undermine demonstrations by depicting police as protecting the residents of Baltimore, and protesters as threatening them.[115] We added a "Freddie Gray as deviant" frame to match rhetoric from political and law enforcement officials that referenced Gray as having a switchblade, to his being handcuffed, and having "fled unprovoked" from police, in reference to a statement issued by BPD. Discussions of the weapon, his handcuffing, and his fleeing arguably play into a narrative suggesting BPD were simply "doing their job," and had good cause to arrest Gray.

On the other side, we include "peaceful protester," "police brutality," and "race/racial injustice" frames. The "peaceful protester" frame is vital in that even critics of the protests, including Maryland Governor Larry Hogan, admitted 95 percent of protesters were non-violent.[116] The "police brutality" and "race/racial injustice" frames have their foundation in grievances of protesters, which were documented in the DOJ's report on BPD police misconduct.

Table 3.2 documents the effectiveness of BLM in cultivating support from the media on issues of police brutality, institutional racism, and humanizing the black victims of police violence. Sustained criticisms of the protesters were less frequent in Baltimore than Ferguson. The "protect and serve" frame appeared in most stories for two outlets – *MSNBC* and *Fox News* – and in about a third of stories or less for 8 of the 11 sources. Similarly, the "protester violence" frame appeared in most stories only for *MSNBC* and *Fox News*, and in a third of stories or less for 9 of 11 sources. The "Freddie Gray as deviant"

Table 3.2 Media Coverage of the Baltimore Protests and the Death of Freddie Gray (4/18–5/3/2015)

News Outlet	Police Protect and Serve[1]	Protester Violence[2]	Gray as Deviant	Peaceful Protest[3]	Police Brutality[4]	Race/Racial Injustice[5]
New York Times	26	18	9	38	66	68
Baltimore Sun	33	15	12	47	55	56
Associated Press	30	14	25	47	60	71
NPR	33	11	11	33	70	78
CNN.com	26	13	17	52	75	75
ABC News	13	6	0	38	75	63
CBS News	40	13	8	51	63	71
NBC News	34	15	9	55	62	81
CNN	34	22	9	53	71	68
MSNBC	72	61	24	87	91	96
Fox News	65	61	4	63	83	85

The first two columns are under the heading "Frames Critical of the Baltimore Protests (% of stories appearing in)" and the last three columns are under "Frames Favorable to the Baltimore Protests (% of stories appearing in)".

Source: *Nexis Uni* academic database

Notes:

1 The "police protect and serve" framework included any references in news stories on Baltimore and Freddie Gray to the "National Guard," to "martial law," to a "curfew," to the use of crowd control via "tear gas," "rubber bullets," "combat gear," "riot gear," or "armor/body armor."
2 The "protester violence" framework includes references in stories on "Baltimore" and "Freddie Gray" to "riot/riots," "rioting," "loot/looting," to "violent" acts and "violence," to "unrest," "vandalism" or efforts to "vandalize," to "chaos" or to the "burning" of the city or buildings that were "burned," or to "thugs" engaged in rioting, in the words of Baltimore Mayor Stephanie Rawlings-Blake. For Blake's comment, see: Elizabeth Chuck, "Baltimore Mayor Stephanie Rawlings-Blake under Fire for 'Space' to Destroy Comment," *NBC News*, April 28, 2015, https://www.nbcnews.com/storyline/baltimore-unrest/mayor-stephanie-rawlings-blake-under-fire-giving-space-destroy-baltimore-n349656
3 The "peaceful protester" framework includes references in stories on "Baltimore" and "Freddie Gray" to "peaceful" actions and to "peaceful protest (s)," to "non-violent" actions or "non-violence" in the protests, to "rally(ies)," "demonstration (s)," "vigil (s)," and "march (es)." We also included language referring to Freddie Gray as "unarmed," contradicting claims that he was a danger to police. References to Gray as no danger to police fit within a broader framework in which protesters and Gray were depicted in non-violent terms.
4 The "police brutality" framework includes references in stories on "Baltimore" and "Freddie Gray" to police "misconduct," to "police brutality," to the need for "body cameras" to monitor police, to an "investigation" of the six officers involved in Gray's death, to an "independent commission" set up to investigate Gray's death and BPD, to the lack of "probable cause" police officers had in pursuing and arresting Gray, and to the "criminal charges" against the six police officers, or to them being "charged" or "charges" being brought against them.
5 The "race/racial injustice" framework included any references in news stories on "Freddie Gray" and "Baltimore" to "injustice" regarding his case, to the need for "justice," to the importance of "civil rights," and general references to "race," "racial profiling," "racial" matters, "racism," or to "black" politics as related to the protests and Gray.

frame was infrequent, suggesting opposition to the protests was not localized around Gray as an individual. The deviance frame appeared a quarter of the time in the *Associated Press*; but for the other 10 outlets, it appeared less often.

Favorable frames dominated the news, disrupting traditional racist notions that police protect and serve, while poor people of color threaten social order. The "peaceful protest" frame was less common in news on Baltimore than Ferguson. It appeared in a majority of stories and articles for 6 of 11 news sources. Even in the other five outlets, the peaceful protest narrative was common, appearing in a third to under half of all articles. As with Ferguson, the "race/racial injustice" frame was dominant, suggesting journalists engaged in a serious discussion of racism in policing. A point of departure between Ferguson and Baltimore was the "police brutality" frame, which was more common in the latter. This frame appeared in most news stories and articles for all 11 outlets. Perhaps the blatantly violent suppression of Gray, evident when looking at the types of injuries he sustained, prompted reporters to emphasize police brutality. In comparison, Brown's death in Ferguson was less clearcut, with competing accounts of him as an aggressor and a victim. Still, the police brutality frame was dominant in Baltimore, and tipped the scales in coverage in favor of protesters.

The findings from Baltimore speak to an emerging movement that was rapidly gaining public attention. Fueled by grievances and strain felt in poor minority communities due to repressive policing, citizens reached a boiling point, with the death of Gray inciting mass rebellion. Despite the chronic journalistic bias favoring official sources, Baltimore demonstrated it is possible, with great effort, to reverse hegemonic trends in the news, and to force a national discussion oriented toward citizens' interests. The opening of the media to citizen grievances was episodic in this case and with Ferguson, although themes related to police brutality, racism, and peaceful protest broke through to the public. Due to this positive coverage, consumption of news on Baltimore should produce growing support for the protesters.

To assess the impact of coverage on public opinion, we analyzed data from *Pew*'s late-April-to-early-May poll on Gray's death and the Baltimore protests. The survey asked Americans how closely they paid attention to news on "unrest in Baltimore following the death of African-American man Freddie Gray." *Pew* also asked whether "tensions between the African-American community and the police" accounted for "violence and unrest in Baltimore." As with Ferguson, we control for respondents' ideology, party, gender, age, income, education, and race.

Figure 3.3 shows that greater media attention and lower income, more than other factors, were the strongest predictors of recognition that poor community–police relations were driving the protesters. This result suggests sympathetic coverage of mass protests was vital to cultivating

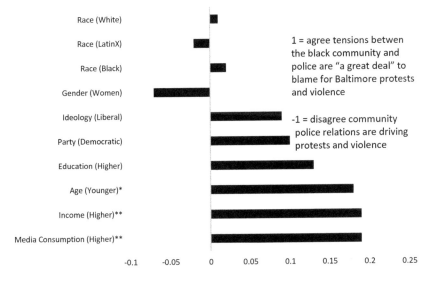

Figure 3.3 Media Consumption and Opinions of Baltimore Protests
Source: *Pew Research Center*, April–May 2015 poll
Statistical Significance Levels: *** = 0.1% ** = 1% * = 5%
Controls: gender, age, education, race, income, political party, ideology

public support. The media may typically favor government perspectives, but social movements can exploit cracks in the system to impact discourse on issues of significance to citizens.

Intersectionality and Baltimore

As with Ferguson, intersectionality was significant in Baltimore to understanding the protests. To provide estimates of its impact, we examined a national survey from the *Public Religion Research Institute* (PRRI) from late April to early May 2015, coinciding with the Baltimore uprising. The poll did not include measures for respondents' geographic location of residence and for LatinX Americans, although measures were available for race (black/whites), income, gender, party, ideology, and age. The *PRRI* poll asked Americans their opinions of police treatment of people of color, regarding whether "police officers generally treat blacks and other minorities the same as whites." This question is a sufficient proxy measure for Americans' opinions about the notion that police are "color-blind" in their conduct. Figure 3.4 provides estimates for how race, income, gender, and age individually and jointly impacted public opinion of the criminal justice system among various subgroups. Income, age, and gender by themselves had

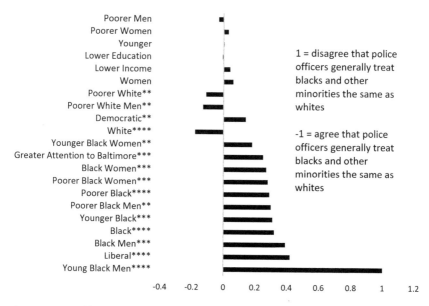

Figure 3.4 Public Opinion and the Question of "Color-Blind" Policing
Source: *Public Religion Research Institute* poll, April–May 2015
Statistical significance levels: *** = 0.1% ** = 1% * = 5%
Controls: gender, age, education, race, income, political party, ideology, media attention

little impact on public opinion. Race was significant, with white Americans more likely to agree that blacks and whites are treated the same by police, and blacks more likely to disagree. Other factors were also significant, with liberals, Democrats, and those paying greater attention to news on the Baltimore protests more likely to disagree that the criminal justice system is color-blind.

The intersections of multiple identities were also significant. Poorer whites and poorer white men were more likely to agree police are color-blind, but poorer men and poorer women were no more likely to feel one way or another on this question. These findings show that class and race interact to impact policing-related opinions among whites. Lower income interacted with white identity to encourage reactionary attitudes. Here, the concept of "intersectional prejudice" is validated, with poorer whites more likely to embrace negative views of police protests.

As with Ferguson, intersecting identities mattered among less privileged groups when examining age, race, income, and gender. Many identities examined in Figure 3.4 were significant predictors of attitudes about policing. These findings will not surprise those living in poor minority communities, whose experiences speak to the impact of intersecting oppressions on identity and political beliefs.

Young black men and women, and poorer black men and women, who (generally speaking) are more economically marginalized than whites, are treated much differently by law enforcement, and have less charitable views of police.

Assessing the Impact of BLM

To this point, we assessed the impacts of the Ferguson and Baltimore protests. It is also important to examine the impact of BLM more generally. Evidence suggests BLM's influence on news coverage varied over time. Drawing on *Nexis Uni*, Figure 3.5 provides a longitudinal view of coverage in the *New York Times*. The period of analysis begins in February 2012, when the movement was founded following Trayvon Martin's death, through February 2018 – six years later, after many protest episodes against police shootings of black men. BLM had zero visibility in the news in 2012 and 2013, and little visibility in 2014. It was not until 2015 to 2016 that the movement gained momentum in media discourse.

Figure 3.5 includes a summary of major events in the news during the months when BLM coverage spiked. This event analysis suggests coverage of BLM was heavily defined through elite political agendas and bottom-up pressures.

Numerous top-down pressures impacted how BLM was discussed. These top-down pressures included: the onset of the DOJ investigation into Eric Garner's death in New York City (12/2014) and Hillary Clinton's call for a DOJ inquiry into the death of Laquan McDonald in Chicago (12/2015); efforts of the 2016 presidential election candidates to discuss BLM (8/2015); coverage of potential grand jury indictments for the deaths of Eric Garner in New York City (12/2014) and Freddie Gray in Baltimore (12/2015); Trump's victory in the 2016 presidential election (11/2016) and Trump's defense of white supremacists who engaged in hate rhetoric and violence in Charlottesville, Virginia (8/2017); and the city of New Orleans' decision to remove confederate post-Civil War monuments (4/2017).

In contrast, bottom-up pressures also accounted for coverage of BLM. These events included: protests of a grand jury's refusal to indict New York City police officers for the death of Eric Garner (12/2014); protests against the shooting of four BLM activists at a Minneapolis demonstration (12/2015); protests of the police shooting of Laquan McDonald in Chicago (12/2015); protests of the shooting of nine church parishioners by a white male in Raleigh, North Carolina (6/2015); protests of the police shootings of Alton Sterling in Baton Rouge, Louisiana (7/2016) and Philando Castile in St. Paul, Minnesota (7/2016); the shooting of five Dallas police officers during a BLM protest (4/2016); campus protests against racial discrimination in higher education (12/2015; 4/2017); and protests against white supremacy in Charlottesville, North Carolina (8/2017).

144 *Black Lives Matter*

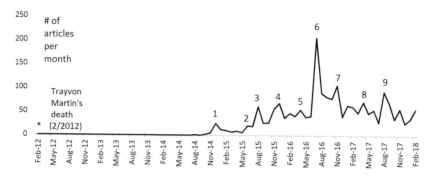

Figure 3.5 *New York Times* Coverage of BLM (2/2012–2/2018)

Month Coverage of BLM Spiked	Major Events in the News
1. 12/2014	DOJ investigation of Eric Garner's death by NYC police begins; no indictment of officers involved in Garner's death; failed indictment sparks protests nationwide
2. 6/2015	White man kills nine black parishioners in Charleston SC church shooting; protests ensue in response to shooting
3. 8/2015	2016 Democratic and Republican presidential candidates address BLM
4. 12/2015	Emerging university protests against racial discrimination; Hillary Clinton calls for federal inquiry into Laquan McDonald shooting by Chicago Police following protests; Baltimore trial of six police officers begins over Freddie Gray's death; Minneapolis protests continue over four whites who killed five BLM activists
5. 4/2016	2016 presidential candidates discuss BLM; Bill Clinton crime bill (from 1990s) is protested by BLM activists
6. 7/2016	Alton Sterling shot by Baton Rouge police; Philando Castile shot by St. Paul suburb police officer; protests in 88 cities over Castile and Sterling shootings; five police officers killed in Dallas BLM protest
7. 11/2016	Donald Trump wins presidential election; protests ensue, involving BLM activists
8. 4/2017	New Orleans removes confederate monument; campus free speech conflicts between BLM activists and right-wing speakers
9. 8/2017	Charlottesville, VA white supremacy protest erupts in violence, spawns counter-protests; Trump defends white supremacists

Source: *Nexis Uni* academic database

The largest spike in coverage of BLM – coinciding with the deaths of Alton Sterling and Philando Castile in April 2016 – speaks to the power of protest following critical catalyst events. These deaths held symbolic value for the public. With Sterling, Baton Rouge police fired numerous shots into his back, killing him, after police responded to reports that Sterling was illegally selling CDs and that he threatened a man outside a convenient store with a gun. Castile was pulled over in a St. Paul suburb, and informed the police officer that he had a legal handgun. After he reached for his billfold in his pocket to provide ID, the officer shot him numerous times, with Castile's girlfriend and her daughter in the car. The officer claimed Castile was reaching for his gun, despite Castile informing him this was not the case. Both shootings incited protests, in part due to the graphic documentation of the deaths via bystander cell phones. The growth in coverage of BLM in relation to these events is evidence of the power of protest to direct attention to concerns about racism and police brutality.

BLM's disruptive power was apparent as it broke into the national consciousness, at a time when the public was becoming increasingly critical in its understanding of race relations in America. Figure 3.6 documents growing coverage of BLM in the *New York Times*, along with rising public concern with race and opinions of BLM. Recognition that race relations in the U.S. were "generally bad" increased from 2013 through 2016 among both whites and blacks, at the same time that

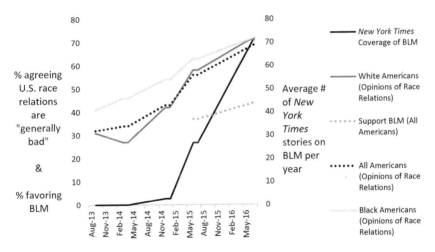

Figure 3.6 Media Coverage and Public Opinion of Race Relations and BLM (2013–2016)
Source: *Nexis Uni* (New York Times analysis)
CBS–New York Times and Pew Research Center polls
Note: The *CBS–New York Times* polls are drawn from a time series available at: Polling Report, "CBS/New York Times Poll," *Pollingreport.com*, 2018, http://www.pollingreport.com/race.htm. The specific polls were conducted on August 7–11, 2013, March 26–30, 2014, August 19–20, 2014, December 6–9, 2014, and July 8–12, 2016. The questions on Black Lives Matter are drawn from the *Pew Research Center's* question archive, and were from polls conducted on May 3, 2016 and August 21, 2017

protests in Ferguson, Baltimore and elsewhere occurred and as coverage of BLM grew. Support for BLM grew during this time. It is difficult to conclude from this data that BLM coverage caused growing recognition of racial problems in America or growing support for BLM. Fortunately, our argument for the impact of BLM does not rely on this data alone, as our case studies provide evidence that civil rights activists impacted coverage and public consciousness.

Other measures of public opinion also suggest BLM influenced political discourse and public opinion. One late-2016 poll found 62 percent of Americans felt BLM had an impact on "race relations in America."[117] A *Pew* survey from early 2016 found 52 percent believed BLM was "helping blacks achieve equality in this country."[118] An *Associated Press* poll from late 2016 found three-quarters of Americans agreed the "Black Lives Matter campaign," as seen in protests of the "deaths of blacks in encounters with police," were important to them personally.[119] Finally, a mid-2017 *Pew* survey found 55 percent supported BLM, compared to 34 percent who were opposed.[120]

While the above evidence suggests BLM had an impact on public opinion, how much of an impact did it have compared to other factors? To answer this question, we examined the strength of attachment to BLM and partisan attachments to the Democratic Party, in predicting opinions about societal racism and racism in policing. By comparing public attachment to an elite force – Democratic partisanship – with attachment to BLM, we assess how much each factor mattered in impacting public thought. We draw on a *CNN/ORC* poll from September 2016 to address BLM's impact, which asked Americans:

- How serious a problem do you think racial discrimination against blacks is in this country?"
- "In general, do you think that the country's criminal justice system treats whites and blacks equally, or does it favor whites over blacks?"

Additionally, the poll asked what Americans thought of BLM. We measure the association between support for BLM and self-identification with the Democratic Party on one hand, and racial attitudes on the other, controlling for ideology, gender, age, education, race, and income.

As Figure 3.7 documents, attachment to BLM was more strongly associated with opinions that racial discrimination is a serious problem, compared to partisanship. Figure 3.8 demonstrates that attachment to BLM, alongside attachment to liberal ideology, are both more strongly associated with opinions that police favor whites over blacks, compared to partisanship. These findings suggest that a principled ideological commitment to BLM, rather than partisanship, was the prime factor associated with public opinion of racism and

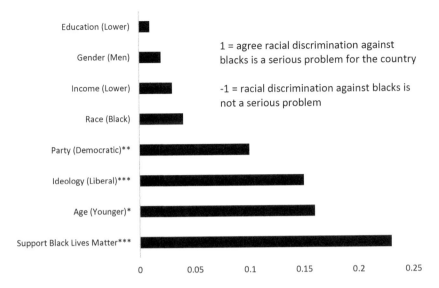

Figure 3.7 Black Lives Matter and Attitudes toward Racism
Source: CNN/ORC poll, September 2016
Statistical Significance Levels: *** = 0.1% ** = 1% * = 5%
Controls: gender, age, education, race, income, political party, ideology

discrimination in America. Political scientists stress the importance of political institutions and parties in influencing public opinion, but the evidence here suggests this emphasis is too parochial, particularly during periods of protest, disruption, and upheaval.

One might question the relationships documented in Figures 3.7 and 3.8, and whether support for BLM causes progressive racial attitudes, or whether those attitudes cause support for BLM. We argue that both causal processes are at work. Based on our case studies, it is obvious that progressive racial attitudes drove support for BLM in Ferguson and Baltimore among protesters. But as the polling above suggests, most Americans also recognized BLM had an effect on public opinion. The movement spoke to a broader sense of public anger with injustice in poor communities of color. For example, one late-2016 *CNN* survey found nearly half of white Americans – 47 percent – expressed support for BLM, while 48 percent of more affluent whites (earning more than $50,000 a year) also indicated support.[121] There was little BLM could contribute directly in a monetary sense to these individuals, and yet tens of millions of white Americans and higher-income whites voiced solidarity with BLM, signaling their opposition to racial profiling and police violence against people of color.

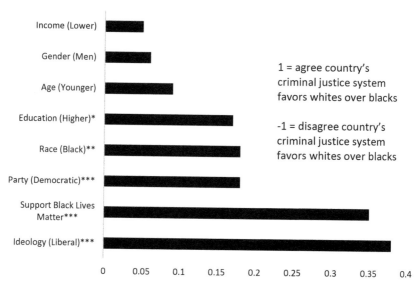

Figure 3.8 Black Lives Matter and Opinions of Racial Prejudice in Criminal Justice System
Source: CNN/ORC poll, September 2016
Statistical Significance Levels: *** = 0.1% ** = 1% * = 5%
Controls: gender, age, education, race, income, political party, ideology

BLM appealed to large numbers of Americans who recognized the movement was motivated by more than people of color spotlighting abuse. BLM was also driven by a larger purpose – shared principles of equality, democracy, and equal rights. BLM sought to address more than violence against African Americans. It directed attention to the disconnect between the popular norm that all Americans be treated equally, and the realities of racial profiling and discrimination that persist in poor minority communities. It was this broader purpose that resonated with tens of millions of Americans, via the recognition from 50 percent of Americans in 2015 that BLM is "mostly a non-violent, civil rights campaign," rather than a movement that "mostly advocates violence to make its point" (35 percent shared this sentiment).[122] The reference in the question to "civil rights" made it clear that much of the support behind BLM was motivated not only by a concern with police abuse, but also by a commitment to equality. The findings here can be interpreted independent of causal processes as well. Progressive racial attitudes and support for BLM exist independently of Democratic partisanship, and the association between racial attitudes and movement attachment is stronger than that between partisanship and racial attitudes. This means movements cannot simply be reduced to manifestations of elite power over mass consciousness.

The Strengths (and Limits) of BLM

BLM expanded its appeal throughout the 2010s among whites and people of color. It highlighted police brutality and institutional racism. It was a model of decentralized, leaderless resistance, addressing grievances across dozens of localities in which BLM was active. As McNall writes of Ferguson:

> Who was in charge or who "owned" the movement? National groups such as the NAACP and Rev. Al Sharpton's National Action Network were on the scene as well as the New Black Panther Party and the Nation of Islam. Local political leaders and civil rights activists and church leaders helped to organize the protests. The Black Lawyers for Justice turned out wearing "peacekeeper" t-shirts to provide a barrier between the police and protesters. In the early Ferguson protests, local groups such as the Organization for Black Struggle, Hands Up, Don't Shoot, Missourians Organizing for Reform and Empowerment, and the Justice for Michael Brown Leadership Coalition took the lead. For every group, different goals and policies materialized. All however, would embrace the larger issue of racial profiling and civil rights.[123]

Some might criticize decentralization as handicapping a movement. But this feature of BLM did not hamstring activists in cities like Chicago, Baltimore, New York, and Ferguson, who articulated grievances to local officials and secured concessions from political leaders, reforming police departments.

BLM was resilient over time, sustaining itself over many years, despite critics. This is more than can be said for other uprisings, including Occupy Wall Street and Madison. BLM's efforts to draw attention to racial oppression received support from both whites and blacks, both of which became increasingly sympathetic to recognizing the poor state of race relations in America. As documented in Figure 3.9, the movement built support by drawing on intersecting identities of black Americans. The data, drawn from a *CNN/Kaiser* poll from October 2015, show a strength of BLM was its ability to speak to multiple dimensions of oppression, including class, race, age, and gender (geographic location was not included in the survey), and to younger, poorer black men.

BLM also spoke to sexual identity politics among people of color. The Toronto chapter of BLM prioritized expanding black rights via

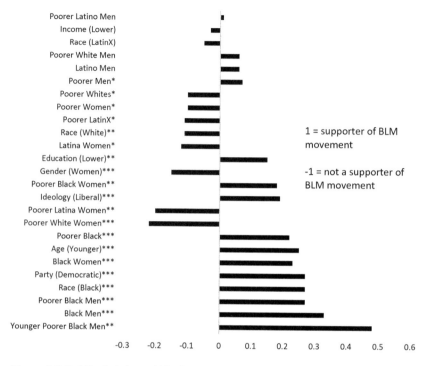

Figure 3.9 Public Opinion of Black Lives Matter
Source: *CNN/Kaiser Family Foundation* poll, October 2015
Statistical Significance Levels: *** = 0.1% ** = 1% * = 5%
Controls: gender, age, education, race, income, political party, ideology

demands for funding black pride events and for increased hiring of black trans women in the workplace.[124] This prioritization of queer and trans identity within the struggle for black liberation was longstanding, tracing back to Cullors and Garza's advocacy of queer political activism at BLM's founding.[125]

BLM did not appeal to everyone. As Figure 3.9 documents, opposition was more common across intersecting identities for white and LatinX respondents. A lack of economic privilege among whites was associated with reduced support for BLM among poorer women, poorer whites, and poorer white women, although the movement was more likely to be supported by poorer men. These outcomes suggest the rightward mobilization of less affluent white Americans, as related to BLM.

Poorer LatinX respondents, Latina women, and poorer Latina women were less likely to endorse BLM, while Latino men and poorer Latino men were not significantly more likely to support or oppose BLM. Lower support among LatinX respondents reveals a limitation of the movement. In restricting its message to black lives, BLM limited its appeal to other people of color, despite LatinX Americans agreeing minorities are targeted via racial profiling and police brutality.[126] The divide between black and LatinX Americans might have been overcome with a relabeling of the movement as "Brown Lives Matter." LatinX Americans are similar to black Americans in holding distrust of law enforcement. This is clear from examining the results of Figure 3.10, drawn from *Pew*'s August 2014 survey on American policing.

Respondents were asked about their level of "confidence" that "police in my community will refrain from using excessive force on suspects." Since the language of the question was not biased in favor of black or LatinX individuals, responses reflected a wider suspicion of police across racial/ethnic groups. We see that overlapping identities related to race

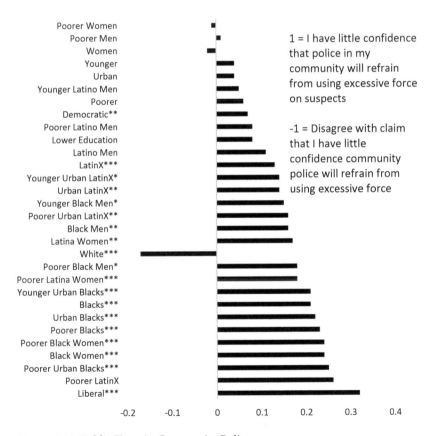

Figure 3.10 Public Trust in Community Police
Source: *Pew Research Center* poll, August 2014
Statistical Significance Levels: *** = 0.1% ** = 1% * = 5%
Controls: gender, age, education, race, income, political party, ideology

(black and LatinX individuals), gender, age, geographical location, and class were significant in stoking public distrust of law enforcement. But BLM restricted its support base by focusing on police violence against black Americans, so the movement received weaker support from LatinX Americans.

Civil rights activists may have built greater support if BLM focused on improving the conditions of poor Americans, across LatinX and black identities. And a progressive alliance between BLM and Fight for $15, although explicitly embraced by BLM supporters like Keeanga-Yamahtta Taylor, never materialized during the mid-to-late 2010s. Such an alliance would have helped address poverty in black communities, in addition to the broader issues of inequality and plutocratic politics.

Policy Change

By highlighting BLM's limitations, we do not mean to dismiss the movement's achievements. Its policy successes were significant. Large protests in Chicago, Baltimore, Ferguson, and New York City pressured municipal and national officials to address racial biases endemic in policing. The protests pressured federal officials to address racial profiling, and they had a significant impact, seen in the DOJ's response of initiating investigations of police forces in Chicago, Baltimore, and Ferguson. With these municipalities being called out by activists and the federal government, local officials were pressured to introduce policing reforms.

Planned reforms were made explicit in the proposals put forward by city officials across all four cities. Baltimore and Chicago entered into agreements with the DOJ, including the introduction of monitoring regimes to combat racial profiling and police brutality, and introducing community policing strategies. These strategies are defined by a partnership between local residents and police, encouraging the establishment of neighborhood watch groups as a tool for empowering citizens to monitor illegal activities. They rely on increased use of foot patrols via beats, in which police officers develop ties with communities, and improve communication via town hall meetings and other interactions in which community members' concerns are voiced to police.[127]

With Ferguson, reforms went deeper than community policing, considering the massive gulf between the city's white political and policing structures, and a majority black community. The city was pressured to commit to: (1) replacing the old city police chief and city manager with black officials, in response to protesters' opposition to a white police and city hall political structure that was running a revenue-making scheme against blacks via excessive ticketing; (2) the replacement of four City Council members with new representatives, to root out supporters of the city's discriminatory practices; (3) the firing of a top court clerk, who had a history of trafficking in racist emails; (4) the passage of sales and utility taxes to offset a budget deficit that emerged after Ferguson pulled back on discriminating against city residents to gather revenues; (5) the removal or resignation of nearly two-dozen police officers, a number of whom were spotlighted for troubled histories in their engagements with community members; and (6) the introduction of body cameras for increased surveillance of, and transparency related to, police activities.[128] Pressure from protesters had an impact in Ferguson by reducing discrimination, as municipal court revenues from tickets and fines fell from $2.7 million in 2014 to $500,000 in 2016.[129]

Contrary to elitist notions that political reforms come from the top down, it was clear from the beginning that the Obama administration and local governments were reluctant partners in BLM's fight for racial justice. Protests in Ferguson, Chicago, New York, and Baltimore preceded political changes by local governments. Protests pressured the federal government and DOJ to take action against municipalities guilty of racial profiling and police brutality. Before declaring support for BLM, the Obama administration's initial reactions to protests in Ferguson were limited, as seen in: (1) the President's announcement that the U.S. is "a nation built on the rule of law," meaning citizens should accept grand jury decisions that exonerate police officers from criminal charges for killing black men; and (2) Obama's denigrating of protesters as obnoxious.[130] Obama saw BLM protesters as uninterested in civil dialogue, via his paternalistic advice that they "seek some understanding rather than simply holler at each other" in response to police shootings, and to "heal rather than wound each other."[131] These pronouncements were tone deaf and elitist, considering that progressive changes historically emerge following fierce citizen attacks on and disruptions of the status quo, with protesters unapologetically articulating what were seen (at the time) as radical political demands. Aside from Obama's intransigence, BLM activists later struggled with opposition from the Trump administration – seen in Attorney General Jeff Session's resistance to using the DOJ to investigate public complaints against local police forces.[132]

Conclusion

This chapter provides several lessons. The first is that progressive movements serve as an independent political force, speaking to the collective grievances of disadvantaged and oppressed groups. They pressure governments for political change. BLM pressured government to address the problem of racism. The movement eventually benefitted from Democratic Party support, from an Obama administration that was initially hostile to its goals, but grew more supportive over time. Second, citizens used media to transform public opinion, despite the official source bias in the news. Third, citizens are increasingly rebelling against poverty and racism, demonstrating that plutocratic control of government produces counter-mobilization in disadvantaged communities aimed at disrupting the status quo. Anger in poor minority communities is economically driven by those left behind in an era of deindustrialization, white flight, and growing inequality. But identities are not only about economics. Other factors influence identity formation. This point is apparent in the fourth lesson of this chapter, which highlights intersectionality as a force impacting consciousness. Prejudice and discrimination are about more than class divisions, as we must look at how communities experience oppression via class, race, gender, age, and geographic-based identities.

Repressive "crime control" policies have negative effects on democracy. Racially discriminatory interactions with police, the courts, and prisons depress faith in government, while reducing political participation.[133] BLM confronted this discrimination, recognizing its toxic impact on society. BLM's push for democratic accountability had a significant impact on public opinion and politics. Without this movement, the problem of racism in policing would have remained under the radar of popular discourse, with little chance of political change.

Notes

1 CNN, "Trayvon Martin Shooting Fast Facts," February 8, 2018, https://www.cnn.com/2013/06/05/us/trayvon-martin-shooting-fast-facts/index.html
2 Leo Benedictus, "How Skittles Became a Symbol of Trayvon Martin's Innocence," *The Guardian*, July 15, 2013, https://www.theguardian.com/world/shortcuts/2013/jul/15/skittles-trayvon-martin-zimmerman-acquittal; Tess Owen, "It Looks Like George Zimmerman Sold the Gun that Killed Trayvon Martin for $138,900," *Vice*, May 18, 2016, https://news.vice.com/article/george-zimmerman-auction-sold-gun-that-killed-trayvon-martin; Serge F. Kovaleski, "Martin Spoke of 'Crazy and Creepy' Man Following Him, Friend Says," *New York Times*, May 18, 2012, http://www.nytimes.com/2012/05/19/us/trayvon-martins-friend-tells-what-she-heard-on-phone.html.
3 CNN, "Trayvon Martin Shooting Fast Facts," 2018.
4 Michael Tesler, *Post-Racial or Most-Racial? Race and Politics in the Obama Era* (Chicago: University of Chicago Press, 2016).
5 Krissah Thompson and Scott Wilson, "Obama on Trayvon Martin: 'If I Had a Son, He'd Look Like Trayvon,'" *Washington Post*, March 23, 2012, https://www.washingtonpost.com/politics/obama-if-i-had-a-son-hed-look-like-trayvon/2012/03/23/gIQApKPpVS_story.html?utm_term=.60d95ecdb753.
6 Mychal Denzel Smith, "A Q&A with Alicia Garza, Co-Founder of #BlackLivesMatter," *The Nation*, March 24, 2015, https://www.thenation.com/article/qa-alicia-garza-co-founder-blacklivesmatter/.
7 Patrisse Cullors, "On Trayvon Martin's Birthday, We Remember His Life and Why We Fight for Black Lives," February 5, 2018, https://www.nbcnews.com/think/opinion/trayvon-martin-s-birthday-we-remember-his-life-why-we-ncna844711.

8 Alicia Garza, Patrisse Cullors, and Opal Tometi, "An Interview with the Founders of Black Lives Matter," *Ted*, 2016, https://www.ted.com/talks/alicia_garza_patrisse_cullors_and_opal_tometi_an_interview_with_the_founders_of_black_lives_matter.
9 Keeanga-Yamahtta Taylor, *From #BlackLivesMatter to Black Liberation* (Chicago: Haymarket Books, 2016): 166.
10 Taylor, *From #BlackLivesMatter to Black Liberation*, 2016: 167.
11 Al Baker, J. David Goodman, and Benjamin Mueller, "Beyond the Chokehold: The Path to Eric Garner's Death," *New York Times*, June 13, 2015, https://www.nytimes.com/2015/06/14/nyregion/eric-garner-police-chokehold-staten-island.html; Matt Apuzzo, Adam Goldman, and William K. Rashbaum, "Justice Dept. Shakes Up Inquiry into Eric Garner Chokehold Case," *New York Times*, October 24, 2016, https://www.nytimes.com/2016/10/25/nyregion/justice-dept-replaces-investigators-on-eric-garner-case.html.
12 Andy Newman, "The Death of Eric Garner, and the Events that Followed," *New York Times*, December 3, 2014, https://www.nytimes.com/interactive/2014/12/04/nyregion/04garner-timeline.html.
13 Jessica Glenza, "Activists Want NYPD Officer Charged as Eric Garner Death Is Ruled a Homicide," *The Guardian*, August 2, 2014, https://www.theguardian.com/world/2014/aug/02/campaigners-nypd-officer-charges-eric-garner-homicide.
14 Newman, "The Death of Eric Garner, and the Events that Followed," 2014; Marc Santora, "Mayor de Blasio Announces Retraining of New York Police," *New York Times*, December 4, 2014, https://www.nytimes.com/2014/12/05/nyregion/mayor-bill-de-blasio-retraining-new-york-police-dept-eric-garner.html.
15 Annie Sweeney and Jason Meisner, "A Moment-by-Moment Account of What the Laquan McDonald Video Shows," *Chicago Tribune*, November 25, 2016, http://www.chicagotribune.com/news/ct-chicago-cop-shooting-video-release-laquan-mcdonald-20151124-story.html; Aryn Braun and Max Greenwood, "The Laquan McDonald Case: A Timeline of the Past Year," *Medill News Service*, November 25, 2015, http://news.medill.northwestern.edu/chicago/the-laquan-mcdonald-case-a-timeline-of-the-past-year/.
16 Sweeney and Meisner, "A Moment-by-Moment Account of What the Laquan McDonald Video Shows," 2016.
17 Brandon E. Patterson, "10 Things You Should Know about the Killing of Laquan McDonald by Police," *Mother Jones*, December 1, 2015, https://www.motherjones.com/politics/2015/12/laquan-mcdonald-chicago-police-shooting-video-explainer/.
18 A. J. Vicens, "Cop Who Shot Black Teen in 'Fetal Position' Finally Charged with Murder," *Mother Jones*, November 24, 2015, https://www.motherjones.com/politics/2015/11/laquan-mcdonald-police-shooting-jason-van-dyke-first-degree-murder/; *NBC Chicago*, "Dash-Cam Video Released Showing Laquan McDonald's Fatal Shooting," *NBC Chicago*, November 24, 2015, https://www.nbcchicago.com/news/local/Police-Release-Disturbing-Video-of-Officer-Fatally-Shooting-Chicago-Teen-352231921.html.
19 Bernard E. Harcourt, "Cover-up in Chicago," *New York Times*, November 30, 2015, https://www.nytimes.com/2015/11/30/opinion/cover-up-in-chicago.html; Nausheen Husain, "Laquan McDonald Timeline: The Shooting, The Video, and the Fallout," *Chicago Tribune*, October 20,

156 *Black Lives Matter*

2017, http://www.chicagotribune.com/news/laquanmcdonald/ct-graphics-laquan-mcdonald-officers-fired-timeline-htmlstory.html.
20 Husain, "Laquan McDonald Timeline," 2017.
21 Pew Research Center, "American Trends Panel Poll," 2017.
22 Paul M. Sniderman and Edward G. Carmines, *Reaching beyond Race* (Cambridge, MA: Harvard University Press, 1999); William Julius Wilson, *The Declining Significance of Race: Blacks and Changing American Institutions* (Chicago: University of Chicago Press, 1980); Richard J. Payne, *Getting beyond Race: The Changing American Culture* (New York: Basic Books, 1998); Shelby Steele, "Obama's Posts-Racial Promise," *Los Angeles Times*, November 5, 2008, http://www.latimes.com/opinion/opinion-la/la-oe-steele5-2008nov05-story.html; Daniel Schorr, "A New, 'Post-Racial' Political Era in America," *NPR*, January 28, 2008, https://www.npr.org/templates/story/story.php?storyId=18489466.
23 Eduardo Bonilla-Silva, *Racism without Racists: Color-Blind Racism and the Persistence of Racial Inequality in America* (Lanham, MD: Rowman & Littlefield, 2017); Michael K. Brown, Martin Carnoy, Elliott Currie, Troy Duster, David B. Oppenheimer, Marjorie M. Schultz, and David Wellman, *White-Washing Race: The Myth of a Color-Blind Society* (Berkeley, CA: University of California Press, 2005); Catherine R. Squires, *The Post-Racial Mystique: Media and Race in the Twenty-First Century* (New York: New York University Press, 2014); Julius Bailey, *Racial Realities and Post-Racial Dreams: The Age of Obama and Beyond* (Peterborough, Canada: Broadview Press, 2015); Paul L. Street, *Racial Oppression in the Global Metropolis: A Living Black Chicago History* (New York: Routledge, 2007).
24 Mark Peffley and Jon Hurwitz, *Justice in America: The Separate Realities of Blacks and Whites* (Cambridge: Cambridge University Press, 2010).
25 Michael Tesler and David O. Sears, *Obama's Race: The 2008 Election and the Dream of a Post-Racial America* (Chicago: University of Chicago Press, 2010); Donald R. Kinder and Allison Dale-Riddle, *The End of Race? Obama, 2008, and Racial Politics in America* (New Haven, CT: Yale University Press, 2012).
26 Paul L. Street and Anthony R. DiMaggio, *Crashing the Tea Party: Mass Media and the Campaign to Remake American Politics* (New York: Routledge, 2018); Christopher S. Parker and Matt A. Barreto, *Change They Can't Believe in: The Tea Party and Reactionary Politics in America* (Princeton, NJ: Princeton University Press, 2014); Tesler, *Post-Racial or Most-Racial?* 2016.
27 George Yancy, *Black Bodies, White Gazes: The Continuing Significance of Race in America* (Lanham, MD: Rowman & Littlefield, 2016); Eddie Glaude Jr., *Democracy in Black: How Race Still Enslaves the American Soul* (New York: Broadway Books, 2017); Bonilla-Silva, *Racism without Racists*, 2017; Grace Carroll Massey, Mona Vaughn Scott, and Sanford M. Dornbusch, "Racism without Racists: Institutional Racism in Urban Schools," *The Black Scholar* 7, no. 3 (1975): 10–19; Shirley Better, *Institutional Racism: A Primer on Theory and Strategies for Social Change* (Lanham, MD: Rowman & Littlefield, 2008); Stephen M. Caliendo, *Inequality in America: Race, Poverty, and Fulfilling Democracy's Promise* (Boulder, CO: Westview Press, 2017); Holona L. Ochs, "'Colorblind' Policy in Black and White: Racial Consequences of Disenfranchisement Policy," *Policy Studies Journal* 34, no. 1 (2006): 81–93.

28 Douglas S. Massey and Nancy A. Denton, *American Apartheid: Segregation and the Making of the Underclass* (Cambridge, MA: Harvard University Press, 1993); James H. Carr and Nandinee k. Kutty, eds. *Segregation: The Rising Costs for America* (New York: Routledge, 2008); Robert O. Self, *American Babylon: Race and the Struggle for Postwar Oakland* (Princeton, NJ: Princeton University Press, 2005); Arnold R. Hirsch, *Making the Second Ghetto: Race and Housing in Chicago, 1940–1960* (Chicago: University of Chicago Press, 1998); Thomas J. Sugrue, *The Origins of the Urban Crisis: Race and Inequality in Postwar Detroit* (Princeton, NJ: Princeton University Press, 2014); Matthew D. Lassiter, *The Silent Majority: Suburban Politics in the Sunbelt South* (Princeton, NJ: Princeton University Press, 2007); Kevin M. Kruse, *White Flight: Atlanta and the Making of Modern Conservatism* (Princeton, NJ: Princeton University Press, 2007).

29 Erica Frankenberg and Gary Orfield, *The Resegregation of Suburban Schools: A Hidden Crisis in American Education* (Cambridge, MA: Harvard University Press, 2012); Jonathan Kozol, *Shame of the Nation: The Restoration of Apartheid Schooling in America* (New York: Broadway Books, 2006); Paul L. Street, *Segregated Schools: Educational Apartheid in Post-Civil Rights America* (New York: Routledge, 2006).

30 Sabrina Tavernise, "Income Gap Grows between Rich and Poor, Studies Say," *New York Times*, February 9, 2012, http://www.nytimes.com/2012/02/10/education/education-gap-grows-between-rich-and-poor-studies-show.html.

31 Eduardo Porter, "A Simple Equation: More Education = More Income," *New York Times*, September 10, 2014, https://www.nytimes.com/2014/09/11/business/economy/a-simple-equation-more-education-more-income.html.

32 Michelle Alexander, *The New Jim Crow: Mass Incarceration in the Age of Colorblindness* (New York: The New Press, 2010).

33 Elizabeth Hinton, *From the War on Poverty to the War on Crime* (Cambridge, MA: Harvard University Press, 2016).

34 Sarah Shannon, Christopher Uggen, Jason Schnittker, Melissa Thompson, Sara Wakefield, and Michael Massoglia, "The Growth, Scope, and Spatial Distribution of People with Felony Records in the United States, 1948–2010," *Demography* 54, no. 5 (2017): 1795–1818.

35 Nicole Flatow, "Police Made More Arrests for Drug Violations than Anything Else in 2012," *New York Times*, September 17, 2013, http://thinkprogress.org/justice/2013/09/17/2627601/people-arrested-drug-abuse-violations-2012/.

36 NAACP, "Criminal Justice Fact Sheet," 2017, http://www.naacp.org/criminal-justice-fact-sheet/.

37 Charles R. Epp, Steven Maynard-Moody, and Donald P. Haider-Markel, *Pulled over: How Police Stops Define Race and Citizenship* (Chicago: University of Chicago Press, 2014).

38 Heather Mac Donald, *The War on Cops: How the New Attack on Law and Order Makes Everyone Less Safe* (New York: Encounter Books, 2017).

39 NAACP, "Criminal Justice Fact Sheet," 2017; Federal Bureau of Investigation, "Crime in the United States 2016: Arrests by Race and Ethnicity," *Department of Justice*, 2016, https://ucr.fbi.gov/crime-in-the-u.s/2016/crime-in-the-u.s.-2016/topic-pages/tables/table-21.

40 Kent Willis, "Fear of the Truth Drives Dodge of Racial Profiling Study," *ACLU Virginia*, August 23, 2000, https://acluva.org/en/press-releases/fear-truth-drives-dodge-racial-profiling-study; Sharon LaFraniere and

Andrew W. Lehren, "The Disproportionate Risks of Driving While Black," *New York Times*, October 24, 2015, https://www.nytimes.com/2015/10/25/us/racial-disparity-traffic-stops-driving-black.html.

41 LaFraniere and Lehren, "The Disproportionate Risks of Driving While Black," 2015.

42 Timothy Williams, "Study Supports Suspicion that Police Are More Likely to Use Force on Blacks," *New York Times*, July 7, 2016, http://www.nytimes.com/2016/07/08/us/study-supports-suspicion-that-police-use-of-force-is-more-likely-for-blacks.html.

43 Quoctrung Bui and Amanda Cox, "Surprising New Evidence Shows Bias in Police Use of Force But Not in Shootings," *New York Times*, July 11, 2016, http://www.nytimes.com/2016/07/12/upshot/surprising-new-evidence-shows-bias-in-police-use-of-force-but-not-in-shootings.html.

44 David R. Dow, "Death Penalty, Still Racist and Arbitrary," *New York Times*, July 8, 2011, http://www.nytimes.com/2011/07/09/opinion/09dow.html.

45 Ed Pilkington, "Research Exposes Racial Discrimination in America's Death Penalty Capital," *The Guardian*, March 13, 2013, https://www.theguardian.com/world/2013/mar/13/houston-texas-death-row-black-inmates; Dow, "Death Penalty, Still Racist and Arbitrary," 2011.

46 Edward P. Morgan, *What Really Happened to the 1960s: How Mass Media Culture Failed American Democracy* (Lawrence, KS: University Press of Kansas, 2010); Christian Davenport, *Media Bias, Perspective, and State Repression: The Black Panther Party* (Cambridge: Cambridge University Press, 2009).

47 Robert M. Entman and Andrew Rojecki, *The Black Image in the White Mind: Media and Race in America* (Chicago: University of Chicago Press, 2001).

48 Martin Gilens, *Why Americans Hate Welfare: Race, Media, and the Politics of Antipoverty* Policy (Chicago: University of Chicago Press, 2000).

49 Jack Glazer, *Suspect Race: Causes and Consequences of Racial Profiling* (New York: Oxford University Press, 2014).

50 Devon W. Carbado and Mitu Gulati, *Acting White? Rethinking Race in "Post-Racial" America* (New York: Oxford University Press, 2015).

51 Nicholas J. G. Winter, *Dangerous Frames: How Ideas about Race and Gender Shape Public Opinion* (Chicago: University of Chicago Press, 2008).

52 Frank D. Gilliam Jr., "The 'Welfare Queen' Experiment: How Viewers React to Images of African-American Mothers on Welfare," *Nieman Reports*, June 15, 1999, http://niemanreports.org/articles/the-welfare-queen-experiment/; Gilens, *Why Americans Hate Welfare*, 2000.

53 Paul M. Kellstedt, *The Mass Media and the Dynamics of American Racial Attitudes* (Cambridge: Cambridge University Press, 2003).

54 Tali Mendelberg, *The Race Card: Campaign Strategy, Implicit Messages, and the Norm of Equality* (Princeton, NJ: Princeton University Press, 2001).

55 Shanto Iyengar and Frank D. Gilliam Jr., "Prime Suspects: The Influence of Local Television News on the Viewing Public," *American Journal of Political Science* 44, no. 3 (2000): 560–573.

56 Antoine J. Banks, *Anger and Racial Politics: The Emotional Foundation of Racial Attitudes in America* (New York: Cambridge University Press, 2014).

57 Joe Soss, Richard C. Fording, and Sanford F. Schram, *Disciplining the Poor: Neoliberal Paternalism and the Persistent Power of Race* (Chicago: University of Chicago Press, 2011).

58 Kellstedt, *The Mass Media and the Dynamics of American Racial Attitudes*, 2003.
59 Morgan, *What Really Happened to the 1960s*, 2010; Frances Fox Piven and Richard Cloward, *Poor People's Movements: Why They Succeed, How They Fail* (New York: Vintage Books, 1978).
60 Doug McAdam and Karina Kloos, *Deeply Divided: Racial Politics and Social Movements in Postwar America* (New York: Oxford University Press, 2014).
61 Doug McAdam, *Political Process and the Development of Black Insurgency, 1930–1970* (Chicago: University of Chicago Press, 1999); Charles Tilly and Sidney Tarrow, *Contentious Politics* (New York: Oxford University Press, 2015).
62 Morgan, *What Really Happened to the 1960s*, 2010; Taeku Lee, *Mobilizing Public Opinion: Black Insurgency and Racial Attitudes in the Civil Rights Era* (Chicago: University of Chicago Press, 2002); Frances Fox Piven, *Challenging Authority: How Ordinary People Change America* (Lanham, MD: Rowman & Littlefield, 2006).
63 Charlton McIlwain and Stephen M. Caliendo, *Race Appeal: How Candidates Invoke Race in U.S. Political Campaigns* (Philadelphia, PA: Temple University Press, 2011).
64 Daniel Q. Gillion, *The Political Power of Protest: Minority Activism and Shifts in Public Policy* (Cambridge: Cambridge University Press, 2013).
65 Regina G. Lawrence, *The Politics of Force: Media and the Construction of Police Brutality* (Berkeley, CA: University of California Press, 2000).
66 Christopher J. Lebron, *Black Lives Matter: A Brief History of an Idea* (New York: Oxford University Press, 2017); Taylor, *From #BlackLives Matter to Black Liberation*, 2016.
67 Maxwell Burkey and Alex Zamalin, "Patriotism, Black Politics and Racial Justice in America," *New Political Science* 38, no. 3 (2016): 371–389; Adam Dahl, "Black Disembodiment in the Age of Ferguson," *New Political Science* 39, no. 3 (2017): 319–332.
68 Monica Davey, Michael Wines, Erik Eckholm, and Richard A. Oppel Jr., "Raised Hands, and the Doubts of a Grand Jury," *New York Times*, November 29, 2014, https://www.nytimes.com/2014/11/30/us/raised-hands-and-the-doubts-of-a-grand-jury-.html.
69 Kimberly Kindy and Sarah Horwitz, "Evidence Supports Officer's Account of Shooting in Ferguson," *Washington Post*, October 23, 2014, https://www.washingtonpost.com/politics/new-evidence-supports-officers-account-of-shooting-in-ferguson/2014/10/22/cf38c7b4-5964-11e4-bd61-346aee66ba29_story.html?utm_term=.728061c96c6f.
70 Davey et. al, "Raised Hands, and the Doubts of a Grand Jury," 2014.
71 Davey et. al, "Raised Hands, and the Doubts of a Grand Jury," 2014.
72 Jon Swaine, Paul Lewis, and Dan Roberts, "Grand Jury Decline to Charge Darren Wilson for Killing Michael Brown," *The Guardian*, November 25, 2014, https://www.theguardian.com/us-news/2014/nov/24/ferguson-police-darren-wilson-michael-brown-no-charges.
73 Editorial, "The Death of Michael Brown: Racial History Behind the Ferguson Protests," *New York Times*, August 12, 2014, https://www.nytimes.com/2014/08/13/opinion/racial-history-behind-the-ferguson-protests.html.
74 United States Department of Justice Civil Rights Division, "Investigation of the Ferguson Police Department," *United States Department of Justice*, March 4, 2015, https://www.justice.gov/sites/default/files/opa/

press-releases/attachments/2015/03/04/ferguson_police_department_report.pdf.
75 Cassandra Vinograd, "Shooting of Michael Brown Sparks Riots in Ferguson, Missouri," *NBC News*, August 11, 2014, https://www.nbcnews.com/storyline/michael-brown-shooting/shooting-michael-brown-sparks-riots-ferguson-missouri-n177481.
76 Julie Bosman and Alan Blinder, "Midnight Curfew in Effect for Ferguson," *New York Times*, August 16, 2014,https://www.nytimes.com/2014/08/17/us/ferguson-missouri-protests.html.
77 Wesley Lowery, "Police Use Tear Gas on Crows in Ferguson, Mo., Protesting Teen's Death," *Washington Post*, August 12, 2014, https://www.washingtonpost.com/news/post-nation/wp/2014/08/12/police-use-tear-gas-on-crowd/?utm_term=.75d807007494.
78 Taylor, *From #BlackLivesMatter to Black Liberation*, 2016: 155.
79 Amy Goodman and Juan González, "'Negro Spring': Ferguson Residents, Friends of Michael Brown Speak Out for Human Rights," *Democracy Now!*, August 21, 2014, https://www.democracynow.org/2014/8/21/negro_spring_ferguson_residents_friends_of.
80 Dhyana Taylor, Dayana Morales Gomez, Jacob Kerr, Matt Ramos, and Yujia Pan, "Watch the Ferguson Protests Unfold on Social Media, Again," *Huffington Post*, August 9, 2015, https://www.huffingtonpost.com/entry/ferguson-tweets_us_55c4bf72e4b0d9b743dbc93f.
81 Rubina Madan Fillion, "How Ferguson Protesters Use Social Media to Organize," *Wall Street Journal*, November 24, 2014, https://blogs.wsj.com/dispatch/2014/11/24/how-ferguson-protesters-use-social-media-to-organize/.
82 Kristina Cooke, "U.S. Police used Facebook, Twitter Data to Track Protesters: ACLU," *Reuters*, October 11, 2016, https://www.reuters.com/article/us-social-media-data/u-s-police-used-facebook-twitter-data-to-track-protesters-aclu-idUSKCN12B2L7.
83 Craig Timberg and Elizabeth Dwoskin, "Facebook, Twitter, and Instagram Sent Feeds that Helped Police Track Minorities in Ferguson and Baltimore, Report Says," *Washington Post*, October 11, 2016, https://www.washingtonpost.com/news/the-switch/wp/2016/10/11/facebook-twitter-and-instagram-sent-feeds-that-helped-police-track-minorities-in-ferguson-and-baltimore-aclu-says/?utm_term=.9eb7d8e2f073.
84 Raf Sanchez and David Lawler, "Ferguson: Timeline of Events Since Michael Brown's Death," *Telegraph*, August 10, 2015, https://www.telegraph.co.uk/news/worldnews/northamerica/usa/11242108/Ferguson-timeline-of-events-since-Michael-Browns-death.html.
85 Newspaper and online news articles, in addition to broadcast programs, are relatively easier to analyze since stories examined tended to emphasize a single issue. But cable media programs transcripts were significantly different, in that these outlets typically include programs that are an hour long or more and focus on many different topics. To protect against false positives in terms of including news stories that were not germane to our analysis, we searched for key words in each of our frameworks within 50 words of the two main words/phrases we used to identify stories for analysis – "Ferguson" and "Michael Brown." We undertook a close examination of each framework and the key words used, to ensure that we did not include stories with key words that were not relevant to our analysis of the Ferguson protests and Michael Brown's death. We repeated this

process for each frame examined in both the Ferguson and Baltimore protest case studies.

We looked at references in the news to police efforts to "protect" or provide "protection" to Ferguson residents; references to the importance of community "safety"; discussion of the "National Guard" being called into or operating in Ferguson, and to its (and Ferguson Police's) efforts to pacify violence via its adoption of a "curfew" and "martial law," and its reliance on "tear gas," "rubber bullets," and other "combat/riot gear" and body "armor" necessary for adequate crowd control; and reporting of "arrest(s)" or individuals who were "arrested" in the process of policing the protest zones.

86 Ralph Ellis, Jason Hanna, and Shimon Prokupecz, "Missouri Governor Imposes Curfew in Ferguson, Declares Emergency," *CNN.com*, August 16, 2014, https://www.cnn.com/2014/08/16/us/missouri-teen-shooting/index.html; Jon Swaine and Rory Carroll, "Missouri National Guard to Be Deployed at Ferguson Protests," *The Guardian*, August 18, 2014, https://www.theguardian.com/world/2014/aug/18/ferguson-missouri-michael-brown-national-guard-deployed.

87 This framework relied on specific key words, including discussion of "riots," "rioting," "looting," and efforts to "loot" stores in Ferguson; reporting of "violent" behavior or "violence" more broadly on the part of city residents; references to "vandalism" and efforts to "vandalize" private property and businesses; discussion of "chaos," "anarchy," and "anarchist(s)" protesters set on destabilizing Ferguson; and broad references to "unrest" at a time of protest and riots.

88 Chico Harlan, Wesley Lowery, and Jerry Markon, "After Night of Violence in Ferguson, Nixon Moves to Prevent More Destruction," *Washington Post*; November 25, 2014, https://www.washingtonpost.com/politics/ferguson-takes-stock-after-rage-over-grand-jury-decision/2014/11/25/ef06c696-7493-11e4-bd1b-03009bd3e984_story.html; Monica Davey, John Eligon, and Alan Blinder, "Missouri Tries Another Idea: Call in the National Guard," *New York Times*, August 18, 2014, https://www.nytimes.com/2014/08/19/us/ferguson-missouri-protests.html.

89 Todd Gitlin, *The Whole World Is Watching: Mass Media in the Making and Unmaking of the New Left* (Berkeley, CA: University of California Press, 1980); Melvin Small, *Covering Dissent: The Media and the Anti-Vietnam War Movement* (New Brunswick, NJ: Rutgers University Press, 1994); Morgan, *What Really Happened to the 1960s*, 2010; Anthony R. DiMaggio, *When Media Goes to War: Hegemonic Discourse, Public Opinion, and the Limits of Dissent* (New York: Monthly Review Press, 2010).

90 This framework relied on specific key words, including references to the claim that Brown had "robbed" or engaged in a "robbery" prior to the altercation with police; reporting that Brown had tried to "steal," or had "stole" or "stolen" from a convenience store prior to the shooting; discussion of toxicology reports that Brown had marijuana in his system at the time of the shooting; and references to Brown as "no angel," in reference to a prominent media editorial that portrayed him as a dangerous figure.

91 Mark Berman and Wesley Lowery, "Ferguson Police Say Michael Brown Was a Robbery Suspect, Identify Darren Wilson as Officer Who Shot Him," *Washington Post*, August 15, 2014, https://www.washingtonpost.com/news/post-nation/wp/2014/08/15/ferguson-police-releasing-name-of-officer-who-shot-michael-brown/?utm_term=.ff9462ada794; Elizabeth Spayd, "An Ill Chosen Phrase: 'No Angel,' Brings a Storm of Protest,"

New York Times, August 25, 2014, https://publiceditor.blogs.nytimes.com/2014/08/25/an-ill-chosen-phrase-no-angel-brings-a-storm-of-protest/; Julia Lurie, "What Do We Know So Far from Mike Brown's Autopsies?", *Mother Jones*, August 18, 2014, https://www.motherjones.com/crime-justice/2014/08/mike-brown-autopsy-baden-doj-explained/.

92 Rush Limbaugh, "The Ferguson, Missouri Story: Drive-by Politicians, Drive-by Agitators, and Drive-by Media Attempting to Cash in on Narratives," *Rushlimbaugh.com*, August 15, 2014, https://www.rushlimbaugh.com/daily/2014/08/15/the_ferguson_missouri_story_drive_by_politicians_drive_by_agitators_and_drive_by_media_attempting_to_cash_in_on_narratives/.

93 The keywords for this framework included references to Ferguson and "peaceful" rallies and "peaceful protest"; a discussion of "non-violence" and "non-violent" resistance in Ferguson; reporting on "march(es)," "rallies" and efforts to "rally," to "vigil(s)," or to "demonstration(s)" and efforts to "demonstrate."

94 Yamiche Alcindor, Aamer Madhani, and Doug Stanglin, "Hundreds of Peaceful Protesters March in Ferguson," *USA Today*, August 19, 2014, https://www.usatoday.com/story/news/nation/2014/08/14/ferguson-missouri-police-clashes-shooting-anonymous/14046707/; Rob Crilly, "Michael Brown Shooting: Peaceful Protests after Second Death in Ferguson," *Telegraph*, August 20, 2014, https://www.telegraph.co.uk/news/worldnews/northamerica/usa/11044995/Michael-Brown-shooting-peaceful-protests-after-another-death-in-Ferguson.html.

95 The key words in this analysis included the following: explicit discussion of "police brutality"; references to protesters' chant against police of "hands up, don't shoot," a statement lending itself to a depiction of police as violent and dangerous; reporting on "militarized" local police, to "militarization" of police forces, and to "military-style" weapons used by police and National Guard forces; and general discussions about "state violence," in reference to police and National Guard activities in Ferguson.

96 Goodman and González, "'Negro Spring,'" 2014.

97 Leonard N. Moore, *Black Rage in New Orleans: Police Brutality and African American Activism from World War II to Hurricane Katrina* (Baton Rouge, LA: Louisiana State University Press, 2010); Lesley J. Wood, *Crisis and Control: The Militarization of Protest Policing* (London: Pluto Books, 2014); Luis A. Fernandez, *Policing Dissent: Social Control and the Anti-Globalization Movement* (New Brunswick, NJ: Rutgers University Press, 2009).

98 The key words used in this analysis include any discussion of "race," "racism," "racial" issues, "black" individuals, or "racist/racially" motivated thinking or behavior as related to Ferguson, Brown, and the protests; references to racial "stereotype(s)" or "stereotyping"; reporting of "racial profiling," police efforts to racially "discriminate" or to racially "discriminatory" behavior, or to racial "discrimination" more broadly; discussion of "injustice" in Ferguson and the need for "justice" following Brown's death; references to "investigate" Brown's death or to an "investigation"; reporting on "segregation" more broadly; and reporting that makes any reference to "civil rights."

99 As with the rest of this book, we utilize binary and ordered logistic regression to estimate whether each independent variable is a significant predictor of my dependent variable, after controlling for all other statistical factors. Again, we use the Clarify statistical program, measuring the

first difference between the predicted impact of the independent variable at its lowest value, from the predicted value of the independent variable at its highest value, on the dependent variable, after controlling for all other independent variables and holding them constant at their means. This method allows us to generate interpretable, standardized coefficients describing the predictive power of each independent variable on the dependent variable.

100 Scott Dance, "Freddie Gray's Spinal Injury Suggests 'Forceful Trauma,' Doctors Say," *Baltimore Sun*, April 21, 2015, http://www.baltimoresun.com/health/bs-hs-gray-injuries-20150420-story.html.

101 Baltimore CBS Local, "Timeline: Freddie Gray's Arrest to His Fatal Spinal Cord Injury," *CBSnews.com*, June 23, 2016, http://baltimore.cbslocal.com/2016/06/23/timeline-freddie-grays-arrest-to-his-fatal-spinal-cord-injury/.

102 Derek Hawkins and Lynh Bui, "Medical Examiner Concluded Freddie Gray's Death Was 'Not an Accident,'" *Washington Post*, June 10, 2016, https://www.washingtonpost.com/local/public-safety/trial-resumes-for-officer-facing-murder-charge-in-freddie-grays-death/2016/06/09/3368bce8-2e7b-11e6-9b37-42985f6a265c_story.html?utm_term=.7c39a66cc581; Michael Pearson, Steve Almasy, and Ben Brumfield, "Freddie Gray Death Ruled Homicide; Officers Charged," *CNN.com*, May 2, 2015, https://www.cnn.com/2015/05/01/us/freddie-gray-baltimore-death/index.html.

103 Rebecca R. Ruiz, "Baltimore Officers Will Face No Federal Charges in Death of Freddie Gray," *New York Times*, September 12, 2017, https://www.nytimes.com/2017/09/12/us/freddie-gray-baltimore-police-federal-charges.html; William J. Gorta, "Freddie Gray Dies after Spine Injured in Police Custody: Lawyer," *NBCNews.com*, April 20, 2015, https://www.nbcnews.com/news/us-news/healthy-baltimore-man-dies-after-being-restrained-police-n344506.

104 Yvonne Wenger and Mark Puente, "Baltimore to Pay Freddie Gray's Family $6.4 Million to Settle Civil Claims," *The Baltimore Sun*, September 8, 2015, http://www.baltimoresun.com/news/maryland/freddie-gray/bs-md-ci-boe-20150908-story.html.

105 Erik Ortiz, "Freddie Gray: From Baltimore Arrest to Protests, a Timeline of the Case," *NBC News*, May 1, 2015, https://www.nbcnews.com/storyline/baltimore-unrest/timeline-freddie-gray-case-arrest-protests-n351156; Holly Yan and Dana Ford, "Baltimore Riots: Looting, Fires Engulf City after Freddie Gray's Funeral," *CNN.com*, April 28, 2015, https://www.cnn.com/2015/04/27/us/baltimore-unrest/index.html; Ray Sanchez, Ralph Ellis, and Faith Karimi, "Baltimore Protests Largely Peaceful," *CNN.com*, May 3, 2015, https://www.cnn.com/2015/05/03/us/freddie-gray-balitmore-protests/index.html.

106 Sheryl Gay Stolberg, "Baltimore Enlists National Guard and a Curfew to Fight Riots and Looting," *New York Times*, April 27, 2015, https://www.nytimes.com/2015/04/28/us/baltimore-freddie-gray.html.

107 U.S. Department of Justice Civil Rights Division, "Investigation of the Baltimore City Police Department," *U.S. Department of Justice*, August 10, 2016, https://www.justice.gov/opa/file/883366/download.

108 Jana Kasperkevic, "Freddie Gray's Neighborhood Compared to the U.S.," *The Guardian*, April 28, 2015, https://www.theguardian.com/us-news/2015/apr/28/freddie-gray-neighborhood-baltimore-poverty-unemployment.

109 Michael Keller, E. Tammy Kim, Tom Kutsch, and Lam Thuy Vo, "Baltimore: The Divided City Where Freddie Gray Lived and Died," *Al Jazeera America*, April 29, 2015, http://america.aljazeera.com/articles/2015/4/29/bal

timore-protests-race-and-poverty-freddie-gray.html; Pam Fessler, "2 Years after Unrest, Baltimore's Youth Are 'Still Fighting for the Basics,'" *National Public Radio*, April 27, 2017, https://www.npr.org/2017/04/27/525723203/2-years-after-unrest-baltimores-youth-are-still-fighting-for-the-basics.

110 Meghan McCorkell, "Social Media Plays Major Role in Freddie Gray Protests," *Baltimore CBS Local*, April 30, 2015, http://baltimore.cbslocal.com/2015/04/30/social-media-plays-major-role-in-freddie-gray-protests/.

111 Tanzina Vega, "How Baltimore Police, Protesters Battle on Twitter," *CNN.com*, April 28, 2015, https://www.cnn.com/2015/04/28/politics/baltimore-riot-social-media/index.html.

112 Vega, "How Baltimore Police, Protesters Battle on Twitter," 2015.

113 Vega, "How Baltimore Police, Protesters Battle on Twitter," 2015.

114 Ralph Ellis, "National Guard Plans Exit from Baltimore," *CNN.com*, May 5, 2015, https://www.cnn.com/2015/05/04/us/freddie-gray-baltimore-protests/index.html.

115 Eyder Peralta, "Amid Riots, Maryland Governor Will Deploy National Guard to Baltimore," *National Public Radio*, April 27, 2015, https://www.npr.org/sections/thetwo-way/2015/04/27/402639082/seven-officers-hurt-in-clashes-with-baltimore-police; Ian Duncan, "National Guard Activated in Response to Baltimore Violence; State of Emergency Declared," Baltimore Sun, April 27, 2015, http://www.baltimoresun.com/news/maryland/bs-md-freddie-gray-national-guard-20150427-story.html; Stolberg, "Baltimore Enlists National Guard and a Curfew to Fight Riots and Looting," 2015.

116 Baltimore CBS Local, "Gov. Hogan Declares State of Emergency, Activates National Guard," *CBSNews.com*, April 27, 2015, http://baltimore.cbslocal.com/2015/04/27/gov-hogan-puts-maryland-national-guard-on-notice/.

117 Harvard Institute of Politics, "Young Americans' Attitudes toward Politics and Public Service Survey," *GfK Knowledge Networks*, October 7–17, 2016.

118 *Pew Research Center*, "Racial Attitudes in America Survey," February 2016.

119 Associated Press, "December 2015 Poll," GfK Knowledge Networks, December 2015.

120 *Pew Research Center*, "August 2017 Poll," August 2017.

121 CNN/ORC, "2016 Presidential Debates/Trump's Taxes/Racial Discrimination/Protests," *Roper Center*, September 28–October 2, 2016.

122 PBS/Marist, "PBS Newshour/Marist Poll," *iPoll*, September 10–15, 2015.

123 Scott G. McNall, *Cultures of Defiance and Resistance: Social Movements in 21st-Century America* (New York: Routledge, 2018): 98–99.

124 James Kirchick, "Politics on Parade: How Black Lives Matter Halted a Gay Pride Parade in Toronto," *Los Angeles Times*, July 6, 2016, http://www.latimes.com/opinion/op-ed/la-oe-kirchick-gay-pride-black-lives-matter-20160705-snap-story.html.

125 McNall, *Cultures of Defiance and Resistance*, 2018: 95.

126 Darren K. Carlson, "Racial Profiling Seen as Pervasive, Unjust," *Gallup*, July 20, 2004, http://news.gallup.com/poll/12406/racial-profiling-seen-pervasive-unjust.aspx.

127 Aamer Madhani, "Chicago Vows Police Reforms Even if DOJ Doesn't Press for Them," *USA Today*, March 15, 2017, https://www.usatoday.com/story/news/2017/03/14/chicago-vows-police-reforms-doj-aversion-to-consent-decrees/99189210/; Kevin Rector, "Baltimore Police Struggle to Redefine Image amid Scrutiny and Violence," *Baltimore Sun*, April 30, 2016, http://www.baltimoresun.com/news/maryland/baltimore-

city/bs-md-ci-police-walk-along-20160430-story.html; Oliver Laughland, "Baltimore and U.S. Justice Department Announce Police Reform Agreement," *The Guardian*, January 12, 2017, https://www.theguardian.com/us-news/2017/jan/12/baltimore-justice-department-police-reform-agreement.

128 Jon Swaine, "Ferguson Removes City Manager after Damning Justice Department Report," *The Guardian*, March 11, 2015, https://www.theguardian.com/us-news/2015/mar/11/ferguson-removes-city-manager-after-damning-justice-department-report; Matt Pearce, "Ferguson Police Chief Steps Down; Official Calls It 'Long Overdue,'" *Los Angeles Times*, March 11, 2015, http://www.latimes.com/nation/la-na-ferguson-police-chief-20150311-story.html; Mariah Stewart, "For the First Time, Ferguson Has a Majority Black City Council," *Huffington Post*, February 24, 2016, https://www.huffingtonpost.com/entry/ferguson-majority-black-city-council_us_56ce22a3e4b0871f60e9f554; German Lopez, "Ferguson and the Feds Have an Agreement on Policing Reform," *Vox.com*, March 16, 2016, https://www.vox.com/2016/1/28/10858766/ferguson-police-reforms; Jennifer S. Mann, "Ferguson Court Clerk Fired over Racist Email Is Now Working in Another Nearby Court," *St. Louis Post-Dispatch*, August 8, 2015, http://www.stltoday.com/news/local/govt-and-politics/ferguson-court-clerk-fired-over-racist-email-is-now-working/article_fd10bf70-ba5d-5fa1-bf75-fa6c1dc62a3e.html; Associated Press, "Voters in Ferguson, Missouri, Approve 2nd Tax Increase," *Fox2now.com*, August 3, 2016, http://fox2now.com/2016/08/03/voters-in-ferguson-missouri-approve-2nd-tax-increase/; Stephen Deere, "2 Years Later, Ferguson Protests Have Produced Some Change," *St. Louis Post-Dispatch*, August 7, 2016, http://www.stltoday.com/news/local/crime-and-courts/years-later-ferguson-protests-have-produced-some-change/article_7cd4d141-e912-5893-83d8-fecee2d6922d.html; *CNN Wire*, "Three Officers Fired, Resigned or Retired over Questionable Police Actions in Ferguson," *CBS6TV.com*, August 31, 2014, http://wtvr.com/2014/08/31/ferguson-officers-fired-over-questionable-actions/comment-page-1.

129 Deere, "2 Years Later, Ferguson Protests Have Produced Some Change," 2016.

130 Barack H. Obama, "Transcript: Obama's Remarks on Ferguson Grand Jury Decision," *Washington Post*, November 24, 2014, https://www.washingtonpost.com/politics/transcript-obamas-remarks-on-ferguson-grand-jury-decision/2014/11/24/afc3b38e-744f-11e4-bd1b-03009bd3e984_story.html?utm_term=.1c53389889de; Michael D. Shear and Liam Stack, "Obama Says Movements Like Black Lives Matter 'Can't Just Keep on Yelling,'" *New York Times*, April 23, 2016, https://www.nytimes.com/2016/04/24/us/obama-says-movements-like-black-lives-matter-cant-just-keep-on-yelling.html.

131 Shear and Stack, "Obama Says Movements Like Black Lives Matter 'Can't Just Keep on Yelling,'" 2016.

132 Devlin Barrett, "Justice Department Ends Program Scrutinizing Local Police Forces," *Washington Post*, September 15, 2017, https://www.washingtonpost.com/world/national-security/justice-department-ends-program-scrutinizing-local-police-forces/2017/09/15/ee88d02e-9a3d-11e7-82e4-f1076f6d6152_story.html?utm_term=.29df15f72cbc.

133 Amy Lerman and Vesla M. Weaver, *Arresting Citizenship: The Democratic Consequences of American Crime Control* (Chicago, IL: University of Chicago Press, 2014).

4 Populism in the 2016 Election

The 2016 presidential election stoked heated discussions among friends, family, and acquaintances across the nation. Republican Presidential candidate Donald Trump's rise was accompanied by a growing anti-intellectualism, via the administration's "alternative facts" and contempt for evidence-based reasoning. Other developments included an intensification of discriminatory rhetoric against minorities and immigrants, attacks on the press, and the reliance of tens of millions on reactionary propaganda for information – with the rising popularity of Trump's *Twitter* feed preferred to conventional news sources.

Trump's politics are populist in nature, although the Republican Party has no monopoly on populism. This chapter examines two different forms of populism: Trumpism on the right and left-wing populism via the rise of Bernie Sanders' political "revolution." Populism has taken many historical forms, and its qualities vary depending on the case.[1] Trump's populism is top-down, with little evidence of a social movement behind it. Sanders' populism is a fusion of grassroots and top-down developments, in that he is the symbolic inheritor of a social uprising – the economic justice movement, via the Madison protests, Occupy Wall Street, and Fight for $15. Both Trump's and Sanders' populism have affected American politics and public opinion. Trump's populism reinforces the politics of plutocracy, while Sanders' opposes it.

Sanders' populism is a progressive reaction to rising inequality. It spotlights a political-economic system seen by leftists as corrupt and plutocratic. It is driven by the grievances of disadvantaged peoples, particularly younger Americans and poorer whites. In contrast, Trump's base is mainly driven by a cultural backlash against demographic change. This populism is anemic, relying on the personality of Trump, rather than drawing on a grassroots social movement. It derives its support from whites and middle-to-upper-class conservatives and Republicans. It is antagonistic toward people of color, women, the poor, and poor people of color. Trump's populism is authoritarian, enhancing corporate power, while assaulting progressive political agendas.

I challenge scholarly and journalistic claims that economic anxiety causes Americans to embrace right-wing values. Recent scholarship makes this point, claiming the rise of economic stress fuels right-wing insurgency in the U.S. and abroad.[2] This chapter demonstrates this is not the case. There is little evidence economic insecurity led voters to support Trump; instead, it was linked to identification with Sanders' campaign and left social movements.

I also analyze populism relating to intersectionality. For Sanders' campaign, public support was significant among poor whites, while he struggled to reach poor people of color. Trump's populism appealed to more affluent groups, including middle-to-higher-income whites. For white male Trump supporters, suspicion of immigrants drove opposition to welfare spending for the poor. Trump's populism demonstrates plutocratic politics is alive and well, with tens of millions being mobilized on the right to fight a re-emerging culture war. Business interests benefit from government policies enhancing the power of the wealthy. The rise of plutocracy, however, is not unchallenged. The prominence of Sanders' 2016 and 2020 campaigns – particularly among younger Americans disillusioned with the political-economic status quo – suggests populist forces matter to Democratic Party politics.

Populism: A Background

Social scientists are not all of one mind on populism. But there are traits upon which many agree. One is the claim that individuals in rebellion are malcontents who oppose what they see as a corrupt status quo. Kazin argues that the American populist movement of the late nineteenth and early twentieth centuries built "a grand coalition of outsiders" against plutocratic politics, coalescing around the Populist Party. This alliance included southern, Midwestern, and western farmers, who joined with urban laborers, to combat industrial monopolies and financial elites.[3] The hope was "the David of populism would be able to convince enough Americans to join in toppling the Goliath of concentrated wealth and corrupt state power."[4] Populists offered "a collection of demands" for progressive taxation, coinage based on silver and gold standards, nationalization of the railroads, prohibition, and anti-trust reforms to break up monopolies of the "Gilded Age."[5]

Efforts to transcend historical periods and movements have produced some agreement on defining populism. It includes efforts to separate masses of people on one side, and those controlling political, economic, and social institutions on the other.[6] Mudde and Kaltwasser discuss populism via portrayals of "the people" as "pure" in comparison to "elites" who are self-serving and "corrupt."[7] But defining "the people" in an unbiased way is impossible, since right- and left-wing populists construct definitions of "worthy" and "unworthy" based on ideology.[8]

For example, Sanders' populism includes progressive-left activists, in contrast to Trump's, which centers on conservative supporters.

Populism encompasses left- and right-wing politics. This is why Mudde and Kaltwasser refer to it as a "thin" theory of politics.[9] Galston maintains, "populism is sometimes regarded less as a distinctive ideology than as an emotion-laden stances ... unlike the great 'isms' of the twentieth century, populism lacks an elaborated theory and canonical texts."[10] Populism, in relying on emotional appeals, is often defined by nationalistic attachments.[11] Patriotic expressions are seen in Trump's promise to "Make America Great Again," and Sanders' call to "protect the nation from plutocracy."[12] Competing uses of nationalism demonstrate populism's malleability across the world.[13]

Populism is associated with perceptions of "personalistic" connection between citizens and a "charismatic strongman [or woman]" taking on the political "establishment."[14] The outsider "strongman" phenomenon was evident in Trump's rise to power. As documented by *Gallup* in the 2016 primary election, three of the top reasons why Americans preferred Trump included the perceptions that he was a "strong" leader, that he was a political "outsider," and that he was a "successful businessman."[15] Trump reinforced these images by exuding confidence on the campaign trail, with his bragging about his polling numbers, and his eccentric attacks on competing candidates.[16] These attacks condemned political elites, via Trump's promise to "drain the swamp" in Washington and his attacks on "Lyin' Ted" Cruz and "Crooked Hillary."[17]

Populism may take on a theatrical, performative flavor.[18] This point is demonstrated through Trump's bombastic speeches and *Twitter* postings, fostering public attachment to his "brand" of in-your-face politics. Theatricality is part of Trump's history as a media personality, a role that catapulted him to the top of the Republican primary, as media outlets latched onto his antics to enhance their ratings.

While millions of Americans felt a strong emotional connection to Trump, that relationship was heavily mediated. Most Trump voters never saw the candidate in the flesh. Once he became president, public access to Trump was even more restricted. The limited public exposure to Trump speaks to the mediated nature of modern populism – noted in previous works.[19] Still, Trump's reliance on social media to communicate with supporters fostered a sense of a "direct" connection with a president who utilized technology to communicate in a way unfiltered by traditional news.

Despite being judged by non-partisan fact-checkers to be one of the most untruthful candidates, Trump's ignorance was seen as a strength by many supporters, or at least not as a roadblock to supporting his candidacy.[20] Disregard for facts and evidence-based reasoning leads populists to target those outside the leader's support base. As Galston writes, "the politics of blame provides fertile ground for demagogues who know how to play on people's hopes and fears" who send the message to supporters that "we should set aside the subtleties of experts and rely on ordinary citizens' common sense."[21]

The notion that ordinary citizens can lead campaigns for social change is longstanding in America. On the left, union leader and socialist Eugene Debs was an important figure in the emerging labor movement. Nearly a century later, he became a source of inspiration for Sanders' "political revolution." Others helped to mobilize the right, such as radio personality Charles Coughlin (in the 1930s), who trafficked in anti-Semitic and fascist views demonizing Jewish people as a pernicious political-economic force. This anti-Semitism became a focal point of the revival of American fascism with the "alt-right" white supremacist movement, while Debs and Sanders invoked populist appeals of empowering citizens and democratizing society. Populists' scapegoating of minorities suggests their ideologies can be used for persecution. As academics recognize, populism can be a positive or negative force, democratically mobilizing the public or empowering anti-Semites, xenophobes, and other reactionaries.[22]

Bernie Sanders and the 2016 Election

Bernie Sanders' political career spans decades. He is a self-described "socialist," independent, and Democratic Party ally. Sanders' activism reaches back to the 1960s, when he joined the Young People's Socialist League, and participated in civil rights activism as a student. Sanders' post-collegiate career was working-class; he worked as a teacher, filmmaker, and writer, among other jobs.[23] His political career began in the 1980s, when he was elected mayor of Burlington, Vermont, an office he held for most of the decade. Sanders was later elected to the U.S. House of Representatives, serving Vermont from the late 1980s through the late 1990s. He won Vermont's U.S. Senate seat in 2006, holding the position for the next decade and during his 2016 and 2020 runs for president.

Sanders built a reputation as a progressive, and regularly voted with the Democratic Party. He voted against authorizing the Iraq War, and for withdrawal of U.S. troops.[24] He opposed the 2008 Wall Street bank bailout and the Bush administration's "Patriot Act," supported immigration reform and minimum wage increases, and opposed financial deregulation.[25] Sanders embraces an older form of liberalism, via Franklin Roosevelt's "New Deal" and Lyndon Johnson's "Great Society," which prioritizes business regulations, civil rights, and combating poverty. Sanders' politics are to the left of most Democratic officials, and are closer to the Scandinavian political model, which endorses higher taxes on the rich and a strong welfare state.

Sanders' decision to run for president was motivated by a populism that is concerned with economic inequality and attacks the wealthy for dominating politics. Sanders challenges the hegemonic notion that business elites are entitled to rule, as reflected in support for Trump's candidacy because of his "success" as a "businessman." In the speech announcing his presidential campaign, Sanders spoke to all these concerns:

> This country today has more serious crises than at any time since the Great Depression. For most Americans, their reality is they're working longer hours for lower wages ... they're earning less money than they used to despite a huge increase in technology and productivity ... 99 percent of all new income generated in this country is going to the top 1 percent, who own almost as much wealth as the bottom 90 percent. That type of economics is not only immoral and wrong, but is unsustainable ... the major issue is how we create an economy that works for all of our people, rather than a small number of billionaires ... We now have a political situation in which billionaires are able to buy elections and candidates.[26]

Sanders' platform and writings articulate a progressive populist vision for transformation, including: spending to rebuild aging infrastructure, coupled with the creation of a youth jobs program; opposition to free trade and support for repeal of NAFTA; income parity between men and women; free college tuition for public colleges and universities, paid for with a tax on Wall Street; expanded Social Security and disability benefits; creation of nationalized health care; passage of an Employee Free Choice Act to encourage re-unionization via streamlined workplace rules for voting to form a union; cancellation of all college debt, support for a "Green New deal"; restoration of the Glass–Steagall anti-monopoly rules for Wall Street banks; new banking regulations to prevent banks from trafficking in speculative "derivatives" investments; investment in renewable energy and funding for high-speed mass rail transit; a ban on fracking and the introduction of a carbon tax on fossil fuels; removing "big money" from politics via the repeal of the *Citizens United* Supreme Court case; paid family/vacation and medical leave for public and private sector employees; a reworking of the tax code, with increases in income taxes, corporate taxes, estate, capital gains, and dividends taxes on the wealthy; a ban on future oil pipelines; immigration reform via a path to citizenship for undocumented immigrants; and criminal justice reform, including an end to the "War on Drugs," the death penalty, and for-profit prisons, and increased funding to address the opioid epidemic.[27]

Sanders' "democratic socialism" has received sustained media attention. He speaks with reverence for socialist labor leader Eugene Debs, whom Sanders called "a revolutionary, and probably the most effective and popular leader the American working-class has ever had."[28] Sanders' "socialism" was subject to derision from conservatives and others depicting him as a threat to free enterprise.[29] Utilizing *Nexis Uni*, I find that Sanders' "socialism" appeared in more than four dozen *New York Times* articles in the first six months of 2016, during the primary season. A review of all U.S. news outlets included in *Nexis Uni* finds more than 1,400 stories, features, articles, op-eds, editorials, and letters to the editor in U.S. media covering Sanders' "socialism" during this period.

Despite his socialist rhetoric, Sanders is a reformist liberal. His politics overlap with western and northern European "social democrats," who support a liberal political-economic agenda. At no point during his campaign did Sanders advocate for socialism, defined by government ownership of the economic means of production, or by a decentralized "libertarian socialism," with workers expropriating the means of production, exercising democratic ownership and workplace control. These two economic systems stand at the center of competing libertarian and authoritarian socialist visions.

Sanders' socialist rhetoric radically differs from that of historical socialists. Deb's 1905 speech, "Revolutionary Unionism," called for "unification of laborers" to "assert their combined power" to "break the fetters of wage slavery."[30] Debs spoke of the businessperson, who "holds the exploited wage worker in utter contempt … No master ever had any respect for his slave, and no slave ever had, or ever could have, any real love for his master." "Prostitution," Debs argued, "is a part, a necessary part, of capitalist society." He wanted workers to "assume control of every industry," and for the means of economic production to be "transferred from the idle capitalist to the workers to whom it rightfully belongs."[31]

Deb's speeches conveyed a militant anti-capitalism, in contrast to Sanders' populism in the 2016 election. Consider, for example, Sanders' Iowa "Caucus Night Speech":

> What the American people understand is this country was based and is based on fairness. It is not fair when the top one-tenth of one percent today owns almost as much wealth as the bottom 90 percent. It is not fair when the 20 wealthiest people in the country own more wealth than the bottom half of America. So are you guys reader for a radical idea? Well, so is America. And that radical idea is, we are going to create an economy that works for working families, not just the billionaire class.[32]

Sanders announced it was "Wall Street's time to help the middle-class," to the cheers of supporters. Drawing on themes of economic insecurity, he spoke of "starvation wages" among the working poor.[33] This language is powerful in directing attention to growing inequality, worker insecurity, and mass anger with the political-economic status quo. But there was nothing in these comments to suggest support for revolutionary socialism. The reformism of Sanders' campaign was lost in media discourse. Another analysis using *Nexis Uni* finds that, while Sanders' emphasis of "socialism" appeared in more than four dozen articles in the *New York Times* in the first half of 2016, his ideology as a "social democrat" appeared in only four stories. Similarly, while all other U.S. media examined in *Nexis Uni* addressed Sanders' "socialism" in more than 1,400 pieces, discussion of Sanders as a social democrat appeared in just 46 stories.

Despite the misrepresentation of socialism, Sanders will be remembered for his importance to American populism and movement building. His 2016 and 2020 presidential campaigns represented the culmination of years of unrest that began with Madison, continued with Occupy, and culminated with Fight for $15. Sanders articulated his campaign's place in relation to mass movements for "social and economic justice," stating "real change" "always occurs from the bottom up – when tens of millions of people say 'enough is enough' and become engaged in the fight for justice."[34]

Sanders referenced contemporary movements as inspiring his "revolution." He made Madison a focal point of his 2016 campaign, as he framed Governor Walker's efforts to "deny the rights of workers to come together in collective bargaining" as far-right "extremism."[35] Sanders was a supporter of the Madison protests when they occurred; he embraced collective bargaining rights and depicted the uprising as an inspiration, sparking a national movement for democratic change. Sanders reflected:

> The fact that so many tens and tens of thousands of people in Wisconsin came together – the trade union movement, environmentalists, women, progressives – creates a strong progressive base in general, which I think is going to be useful in the fight forward for the middle-class and working families in this country, for environmental sanity, and for equal rights for all.[36]

Occupy's language was central to Sanders' 2016 campaign. References to wealthy elites and the "one percent" appeared in nearly all Sanders' speeches during the primary.[37] These references continued in the 2020 primary. Such language revealed a rejection of hegemonic notions that government should serve business interests, but cannot afford to aid American workers. The resonance of Occupy with millions of Americans was situated within a historical narrative that spotlighted growing inequality, and sought to disrupt the status quo of rising corporate power and inequality:

> This election is about ending the grotesque level of income and wealth inequality that we currently experience ... It is not moral, not acceptable and not sustainable that the top one-tenth of one percent now own almost as much wealth as the bottom 90 percent, or that the top 1 percent in recent years has earned 85 percent of all new income. That is unacceptable. That must change.[38]

Citizen protest was the vehicle through which Sanders opposed inequality. Sanders' book, *Guide to Political Revolution*, references Fight for $15 as a force vital to workers reasserting their power in the economy.[39] And Sanders played an important symbolic role by promoting worker strikes for higher wages. In 2017, for example, Sanders amplified public exposure for Fight for $15 by supporting labor rallies and strikes: "we have to increase the minimum wage, and second we have to build strong trade unions."

> Today unions are the only shot for workers to take back the country and fight against corporate interests that have rigged the system against them ... let's show them how we can help working Americans, because that's what it takes. All of us, coming together, organizing, and fighting for $15 and union rights.[40]

Sanders and the Media

The relationship between Sanders' 2016 campaign and the media was at best lukewarm. Sanders' politics were outside of the mainstream views of a Democratic Party that for decades embraced "free trade" policies that contributed to growing inequality. Still, Sanders built up enough goodwill by caucusing with the party on legislative items so as to develop a tactical alliance with party officials, even if most preferred Hillary Clinton to win the primary. Considering this complex relationship, and the longstanding media bias in favor of the major parties, we might expect Sanders would receive significant attention in the news, even if it was not as much as that provided to establishment candidates.

A comprehensive analysis of coverage of the 2016 presidential election is beyond the scope of this study. Instead, I draw on research completed by *Media Tenor*, in coordination with Harvard University's Shorenstein Center, examining the primary season, assessing the tone and volume of coverage devoted to each candidate. Sanders received the most favorable coverage, with most stories covered being positive in tone. In contrast, Donald Trump, Ted Cruz, and Hillary Clinton received majority negative coverage. But positive coverage for Sanders was modest, at 54 percent of all reporting on his campaign, Furthermore, the other major candidates were not far behind, with favorable coverage ranging from 47 to 49 percent. But tone of coverage is not the whole story. Sanders received the *least* news attention compared to these other candidates. The Republican race captured 63 percent of all election coverage, compared to the Democratic race, which accounted for 37 percent. And as the Shorenstein report summarized:

> Sanders struggled to get the media's attention. Over the course of the primary season, Sanders received only two-thirds of the coverage afforded Clinton. Sanders' coverage trailed Clinton's in every week of the primary season. Relative to Trump, Sanders was truly a poor cousin. He received less than half of the coverage afforded Trump. Sanders received even slightly less coverage than Cruz, despite the fact that Cruz quit the race and dropped off the media's radar screen five weeks before the final contests.[41]

The neglect of Sanders' campaign meant that, despite receiving more positive coverage, he was not seen as a "serious" candidate on par with other frontrunners. In a plutocratic political system in which progressives are deemed outside the bounds of legitimate discourse, reporters had little interest in granting Sanders additional coverage.

Considering Sanders' conferred status as a second-tier candidate, one would expect that attention to election news did not exert much impact on public opinion of his campaign. This prediction is confirmed by survey data from *Pew*, which asked Americans about their attention to election news in 2016. Those following news closely were not significantly more likely to support *or* oppose Sanders' candidacy, compared to those not following election news.[42] In contrast, as I document in this chapter, attention to election news was consistently associated with increased support for Trump. In sum, the Sanders campaign struggled to break through to the public via the media. Attention to Sanders was limited, likely reducing his chances of defeating Clinton.

Assessing Sanders' Appeal

Despite Sanders' limited media exposure, by addressing serious economic grievances shared by many Americans, he built a large base of support, even if he did not defeat Clinton. And he consistently polled among the three most popular Democratic primary candidates in 2020. Various progressive attitudes were central to driving Sanders' support. Drawing on the January and March 2016 *Pew* surveys, I find that Sanders' supporters (Sanderists) were concerned with a plethora of social, economic, and foreign policy issues. As depicted in Figure 4.1, Sanderists assigned greater priority to social spending – via their concern that Medicare remain financially sound and their interest in improving the educational system. They also prioritized criminal justice reform – echoing Sanders' support for combating racism in policing. Sanderists' opposition to revising the nation's tax system is unsurprising, considering the dominant paradigm in the plutocratic era is tax cuts for the wealthy. It is likely that the "magic elixir" of tax cuts for the rich as a cure-all for economic problems is what Sanders supporters were negatively responding to here. Finally, Sanderists were strongly anti-militarist, via their opposition to efforts to "strengthen the military," which typically occurs through increasing military budgets. This anti-militarist sentiment overlaps with Sanders' foreign policy positions, which included opposition to the Iraq War and opposition to Republican efforts to increase military spending.[43] All of the attitudes above are significant predictors of Sanders support, after controlling for all the policy attitudes included in Figure 4.1.

A second January *Pew* survey provides additional insights on Sanders supporters, as conveyed in Figure 4.2. Again, Sanderists demonstrated eclectic priorities, with their heightened concern for climate change and gun reform, and their opposition to the "War on Terror." Climate change was a serious issue for Sanders' campaign, as he called for a reinstatement of the Paris Accord, and the introduction of a carbon tax on fossil fuels, reinvestment in renewable energy, and a fracking ban.

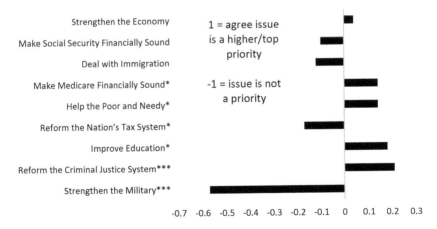

Figure 4.1 Policy Priorities of Sanders Supporters: I
Source: *Pew Research Center* survey, January 2016
Statistical Significance Levels: *** = 0.1% ** = 1% * = 5%

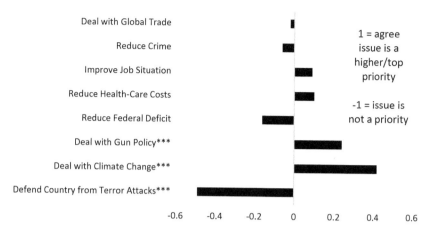

Figure 4.2 Policy Priorities of Sanders Supporters: II
Source: *Pew Research Center* survey, January 2016
Statistical Significance Levels: *** = 0.1% ** = 1% * = 5%

Finally, Figure 4.3 draws on a March *Pew* survey. Significant predictors of Sanders support included support for same-sex marriage, recognition that immigrants strengthen the U.S. by contributing their hard work and talents, and agreement that undocumented immigrants should legally remain in the country. These attitudes overlapped with Sanders' own liberal social positions. Economically, Sanders supporters echoed the candidate's populist rhetoric. They agreed corporations make excessive profits, and that the economic system is rigged against the 99 percent via the conclusion that "hard work and determination" no longer guarantee success for most Americans. Sanderists also aligned with his Medicare-for-all agenda, agreeing the government should ensure all Americans have health insurance. Finally, Sanderists were more likely to agree the nation should protect the environment. All the attitudes described above for Figures 4.2 and 4.3 are significant, after controlling for other attitudes analyzed in the January and March surveys.

What little research was done on Sanders' populism questions whether his campaign represented a leftist rebellion. Achen and Bartels dismiss as "greatly exaggerated" that Sanders' "surprising success in the primary race" was "because of his liberal policy positions." They seem suspicious of progressive populism as driven by policy concerns:

> Many analysts have argued that Sanders's surprising support signals a momentous shift to the left among Democrats. But wishing does not make it so. Decades of social-scientific evidence show that voting behavior is primarily a product of inherited partisan

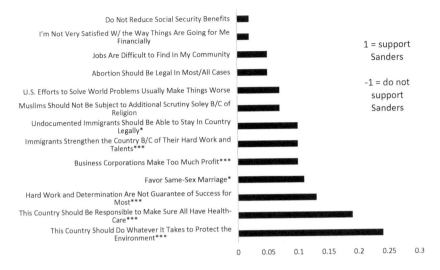

Figure 4.3 Political Attitudes and Sanders Support
Source: *Pew Research Center* survey, March 2016
Statistical Significance Levels: *** = 0.1% ** = 1% * = 5%

loyalties, social identities and symbolic attachments ... The notion that elections are decided by voters carefully weighing competing candidates' stands on major issues reflects a strong faith in American political culture that citizens can control their governments from the voting booth. We call it the "folk theory" of democracy.

This "folk theory," they argue, has little to do with the real world of politics. Achen and Bartels point to National Election Study evidence that Sanders and Clinton supporters were minimally different in their political attitudes, casting doubt on Sanders' "populist" support.[44]

To assess these claims, I examined survey data covering the 2016 presidential election. Figure 4.4 compares Clinton supporters and Sanderists on eight political attitudes from *Pew*'s March 2016 survey. Sanderists were more likely to accept Sanders' populism, as related to feelings that business corporations make too much profit, and that hard work no longer guarantees of success, while these views were not more likely to be held by Clinton supporters. Sanderists were also more likely than Clinton supporters to be anti-militarist, via rejection of greater military spending and opposition to the "War on Terror."

Sanderists were less strongly attached to other leftist views compared to Clinton supporters. They were less driven by concern with improving education, that government should aid the poor and needy, and that

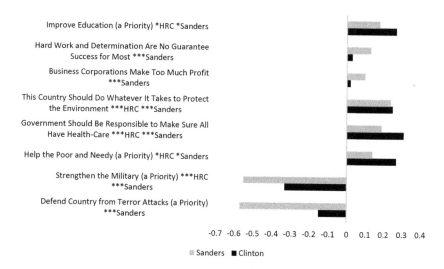

Figure 4.4 Sanders' Populism? Comparing Supporters of Competing Democratic Presidential Candidates
Source: *Pew Research Center* survey, March 2016
Statistical Significance Levels: *** = 0.1% ** = 1% * = 5%

government should ensure all Americans have health insurance. For climate change, Clinton supporters and Sanderists were almost equally energized. A first glance at these findings may lead one to agree Sanders' campaign did not seriously deviate from Democratic Party politics.

A closer look at the 2016 election, however, undermines the Achen-Bartels narrative. Sanderists' political beliefs overlapped significantly with the main political views advocated by their candidate. He supported nationalized health care, and his supporters were more likely to support it too. They were anti-militarist, and Sanders opposed foreign wars and increased military spending. Sanders proposed free college tuition, and his followers supported his vision for strengthening education. Sanderists were more likely to embrace environmental conservation, along with Sanders. Finally, Sanders advocates were more likely to be critical of the wealthy and feel government should help the needy, overlapping with Sanders' support for progressive taxation on the rich and redistribution of resources to the masses via greater welfare spending.

What of the claim that Sanders and Clinton supporters are not consistently different in their beliefs? This is less an indictment of Sanderists – whose politics matched their preferred candidate – than a disconnect between Clinton and her supporters. Clinton's platform deviated in numerous ways from her supporters' preferences. Clinton was *not* an advocate of national health care, instead supporting Obama's

Affordable Care Act. The ACA left millions uninsured. On foreign policy, Clinton and Sanders diverged, with the former supporting the Iraq War, and the latter opposing it. On combating poverty, Clinton supported raising the minimum wage to $12 an hour, in contrast to Sanders' commitment to Fight for $15. A $3 difference may seem modest, but Sanders' longstanding commitment to Fight for $15, compared to Clinton's non-support, suggests a significant divide between the two concerning their role in supporting social movements.[45] Clinton is a supporter of "free trade" agreements, while Sanders opposes them. It was only after pressure from Trump and Sanders that Clinton jettisoned that support.[46] Clinton also favored Wall Street deregulation, while Sanders supported new regulations on speculative investments and breaking up the big banks. Finally, Sanders supported free college tuition, while Clinton only embraced this idea late in the primary – likely to cultivate support from Sanderists during the general election.

The key difference between Sanders and Clinton supporters was that the former recognized their progressive preferences were better represented by Sanders. There may be numerous reasons why many progressives chose Clinton. Perhaps they wanted to be part of the historic election of the first female president, or they saw her as a more "electable" candidate because of Sanders' rhetorical commitment to "socialism." Whatever the reason(s), there is little evidence that Sanders' campaign was not a deviation from the Democratic status quo.

There is also the question of what demographic factors drove support for Sanders. *Pew*'s April 2016 monthly survey reveals Sanders was more likely to be supported by younger Americans (18–29 years old), independents (more so than Republicans or Democrats), men and women, whites, liberals, moderates, and conservatives, and individuals at all education and income levels. Figure 4.5 assesses which factors most strongly drove Sanders support. For one, it had little to do with Democratic partisanship or favorable views from Democrats, undermining Achen and Bartel's claim that voters were motivated by partisanship over policy. Rather, ideology was one of the most powerful predictors of Sanders support. Furthermore, his economic populism resonated with many Americans, considering Sanders was more likely to receive support from poorer white men and women and younger Americans – three groups suffering from economic insecurity in the modern era.

While Sanders' populism had wide appeal, it had limits. Figure 4.5 suggests Sanders struggled in attracting support from minority groups, while generating little excitement from those affected by intersectional oppression. Black and LatinX Americans were less likely to support Sanders, as were Latina and black women, in addition to poorer Latina women. These findings may be explained by the relative priorities of Sanders himself. His 2016 campaign did not seriously commit to building a broad-based coalition by uniting Americans

180   Populism in the 2016 Election

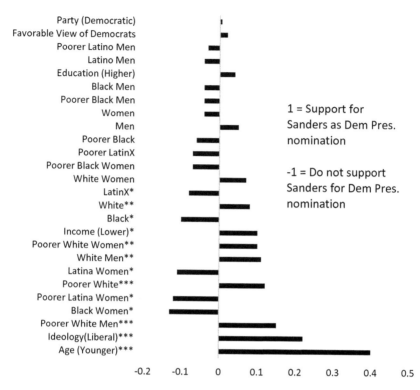

Figure 4.5 Intersectionality, Identities, and the Sanders Campaign
Source: *Pew Research Center* survey, April 2016
Statistical Significance Levels: *** = 0.1% ** = 1% * = 5%
Controls: gender, age, education, race, income, political party, ideology

across racial, gender, and class lines. His *Guide to Political Revolution* barely discussed issues of gender inequality and oppression, while only addressing state violence against poor people of color near the end of the book. He also failed to even reference intersectional identities and their importance to politics. Sanders seemed to recognize his failure in his 2020 campaign, which placed a greater emphasis on racism in America and civil rights activism, and recruited a more racially diverse staff, to reach out to people of color.[47]

Sanders' 2016 campaign was not as successful as it could have been in uniting disadvantaged groups. To overcome institutional opposition to his progressive visions within the Democratic Party, Sanders needed to build a groundswell of support among the masses of progressive, liberal, and Democratic Americans. This was a tall order considering Sanders was never formally a Democrat, and claims independence from the party.[48] Nonetheless, his failure to win the primary provided a clue for how future progressive candidates could win the nomination – by building a broad coalition across disadvantaged groups.

Despite Sanders' limits, his economic proposals are likely to benefit future progressive candidates set on building a coalition for political transformation. As documented in Chapter 2, progressive proposals such as raising the minimum wage to $15, coupled with re-unionization, receive significant intersectional support from disadvantaged groups and poorer Americans. This point is further validated by my analysis of public opinion on Medicare-for-all – a major point of emphasis for Sanders. Figure 4.6 draws on *CNN* polling from 2016, measuring public support for Medicare-for-all, documenting its popularity among poorer whites (men and women), black and LatinX Americans, poorer Americans (men and women), poorer black and LatinX Americans (men and women), liberals, and Democrats. Support from these groups is needed

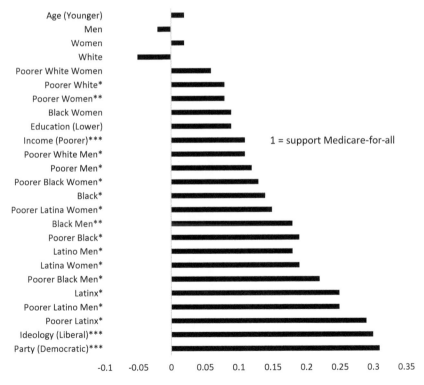

Figure 4.6 Public Support for Medicare-for-All
Source: *CNN* survey, February 2016
Statistical Significance Levels: *** = 0.1% ** = 1% * = 5%
Controls: gender, age, education, race, income, political party, ideology

for Sanders' vision of a mass mobilization for progressive change to materialize.

Younger Americans were at the forefront of the Sanders "revolution." As addressed in Figure 4.5, younger individuals were significantly more likely to support Sanders. And as addressed in Figure 4.7, younger Americans concerned with improving U.S. education and reducing health-care costs were more likely to support Sanders, compared to other Americans. These findings reflect the grievances shared by the millennial generation, via rapidly rising student loan debt, skyrocketing costs of health care, and declining prospects for well-paying careers among college graduates. These economic anxieties need to be addressed if Sanders-style populism is to succeed. And Sanders' presidential bid in 2016 was unique, appealing to large numbers of disaffected youth. More than 70 percent of young Americans voting in the primaries chose Sanders, surpassing the youth voter surge for Obama in 2008.[49]

Sanders' call for revolution was well received by millennials. Polling from the 2010s suggests the rise of countercultural values among America's youth. *Pew*'s April 2010 survey found 45 percent of Americans aged 18–29 supported socialism, compared to 35 percent of 30–44 year olds, 24 percent of 45–64 year olds, and 15 percent of those 65 and older.[50] These results suggest young Americans are serious about systemic economic alternatives, considering the dominant public understanding of "socialism" centers on movement toward societal equality.[51]

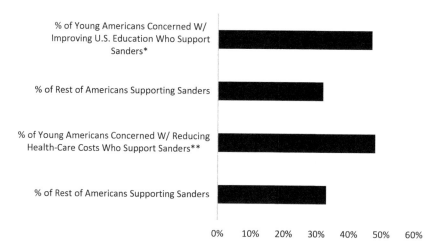

Figure 4.7 Economic Insecurity and Young Sanders Supporters
Source: *Pew Research Center* survey, January 2016
Statistical Significance Levels: *** = 0.1% ** = 1% * = 5%
Controls: gender, age, education, race, income, political party, ideology

Furthermore, only 49 percent of 18–29 year olds supported capitalism, compared to 62 percent of 30–44 year olds, 62 percent of 45–64 year olds, and 67 percent of those 65 and older. Age is a significant predictor of opinions toward capitalism and socialism, after controlling for respondents' gender, education, race, income, party, and ideology.[52]

Assessing Sanders' "Political Revolution"

A final assessment of the "Bernie" phenomenon is difficult as of this writing (late 2019), considering that the effects of social movements take years to understand, and since his second presidential campaign was still underway. Signs of Sanders' impact were apparent less than two years after his first presidential run. The primary election results suggested that attacks on Sanders as an unelectable candidate who lacked serious electoral prospects were exaggerated. Sanders won more than 13 million votes (43 percent of the total), compared to 16.9 million by Clinton (55 percent).[53] As Sanders reflected near the end of the primaries, he won 22 states and finished within two percentage points or less of Clinton for another five states. In sum, the race between Clinton and Sanders was competitive, if not neck and neck.[54]

The mainstreaming of Sanders' progressive agenda was evident in polling, with 24 percent of Democrats saying Sanders' status as a "democratic socialist" made him more electable, compared to 9 percent who said it made him less so, and 66 percent who said it made "no difference."[55] In other words, 90 percent of Democrats felt the "socialism stigma" was irrelevant to their political calculations.

Regarding policy, Americans felt Sanders was *more* qualified than other candidates to deal with economic issues. Fifty-eight percent of Democrats said Sanders would do the best job addressing inequality.[56] A plurality of Democrats – 47 percent – felt Sanders would be better at reining in Wall Street.[57] On welfare policy, 34 percent thought Sanders' policies would best help lower-income people, compared to 23 percent who said the same of Clinton, and 12 and 10 percent respectively who said Donald Trump and Ted Cruz.[58] Finally, 52 percent supported Sanders' "single-payer" universal health-care system.[59]

More generally, 50 percent of Americans in January 2016 held a favorable view of Sanders.[60] Sanders' numbers were higher than those for Trump and Clinton, who held 40 and 45 percent ratings respectively.[61] This polling suggests that notions of "electability" are constructed in political-media discourse, independently from public support for candidates. Journalists decided that Trump and Clinton ran more "serious" campaigns based on the attention they gave both candidates, but those decisions were made independently of public opinion. These findings also provide evidence of Sanders' mass appeal. If

Trump won the presidential election with a 40 percent favorability rating, it was possible for Sanders to prevail with a 50 percent rating.

Sanders' campaign impacted Democratic politics following Clinton's 2016 loss. Her defeat raised questions about conventional notions of electability. Clinton was widely supported by the Democratic establishment, and viewed as the more serious candidate by journalists, but she was defeated by one of the least popular, most controversial presidential candidates in history. Clinton's loss, however, was accompanied by an opening of the party to the Sanders wing's progressive politics. This was evident with the "Better Deal" legislative agenda embraced in 2017 by Democratic Congressional leaders Chuck Schumer and Nancy Pelosi, which called for a $15 an hour minimum wage – a proposal endorsed by 19 Democratic presidential primary candidates in 2019. It was apparent in the support in 2017 from most House Democrats (104) and more than a third of Senate Democrats (17) for legislation establishing a "Medicare-for-all."[62] It was also evident in the support from 100 House Democrats in 2019 for Alexandria Ocasio Cortez's "Green New Deal," which called for federal initiatives to establish higher education for all, free housing, universal health care, and a full shift to renewable energy by 2030.[63] Finally, the rise of Elizabeth Warren and Andrew Yang's campaigns, as reflected in their support for progressive policies such as Medicare-for-all and universal basic income, suggests that the leftist wing of the party grew significantly between 2016 and 2020.

Sanders made progress promoting reform within the Democratic Party. As Cloward and Piven argue in *Poor People's Movements*, major parties grant "symbolic" and "material concessions" to disruptive social movements during times of instability and turbulence.[64] Neither type of concession should be taken for granted. Symbolic recognition of progressive goals suggests serious changes in the political culture are occurring, translating into growing legitimacy for left movements. Material concessions are also vital, since symbolic victories by themselves do not better the lives of working Americans. On symbolic and material levels, Sanders and the progressive movements he drew on demonstrate that reforms are possible when government faces mass pressure from below.

Populism on the Right: The Rise of Trump

Donald Trump came to his political career late in life, becoming president at 70 years old. Raised in New York City, Trump earned an economics degree from the University of Pennsylvania, before beginning a career in real estate. His business investments involved construction and renovation, casinos, golf courses, and licensing his "brand name" to various products. Trump raised his profile through mass media exposure, as a businessman on the New York cultural scene, as an author ("The Art of the Deal"), as host of "reality TV" programs "The Apprentice" and "Celebrity Apprentice," and as the owner of the Miss USA and Miss Universe beauty pageants. Through a combination of investments and inheritance, Trump became one of the wealthiest people in the world, with assets of more than $3 billion.[65]

Trump did not receive sustained *political* attention until the 2012 and 2016 presidential elections. He flirted with running in 2012 but did not become a presidential candidate until 2016. He will be remembered for his involvement in the Obama "birther" conspiracy, when he insinuated many times that the former president was not a U.S. citizen.[66] Relying on incendiary rhetoric and his status as a media "personality," Trump quickly bested almost all the candidates running in a crowded Republican 2016 primary race. Although he lost the popular vote to Clinton by nearly 3 million votes, he had enough electoral votes to win the election.[67]

Trump is not a typical Republican. He lacks the polish associated with professional politicians. He "shoots from the hip" without filtering his messages to avoid offending others. The plain-spoken Trump is seen by many to be a leader for the "common man." In populist terms, the cultivation of this image means he projects himself as "one of us," not an "elite" from Washington who is "out of touch" with "ordinary people."

One of the best representations of Trump's plain-spoken populism was captured in an analysis of his early speeches as president – his first 30,000 words while in office. Using various lexicological analyses to analyze his speech patterns, researchers classified Trump as the least sophisticated of modern presidents. He used the least "unique words" in appealing to the public, preferring basic English, using the least syllables per word of any president. Trump was judged to speak at a fourth-grade level.[68] In the era of *Twitter* communication of 280 characters or less, Trump mastered the "art" of disseminating messages with as little nuance and sophistication as possible. Examples from Trump's tweets and other comments provide context:

- "FAKE NEWS: A TOTAL POLITICAL WITCH HUNT!" in response to investigations of Trump's alleged ties to the Russian government.[69]
- "I will be announcing my decision on Paris Accord, Thursday at 3 PM. The White House Rose Garden. MAKE AMERICA GREAT AGAIN!"[70]
- "I love the White House, one of the most beautiful buildings (homes) I have ever seen. But Fake News said I called it a dump – TOTALLY UNTRUE."[71]

- "Crooked Hillary said that I want guns brought into the school classroom. Wrong!"[72]
- "Wow, Lyin' Ted Cruz really went wacko today. Made all sorts of crazy charges. Can't function under pressure – not very presidential. Sad!"
- "I will be phenomenal to women. I want to help women."[73]
- "I have a great relationship with African Americans, as you possibly have heard. I just have great respect for them. And they like me. I like them."[74]
- "Our country is in serious trouble. We don't have victories anymore. We used to have victories, but we don't have them. When was the last time anybody saw us beating, let's say, China, in a trade deal? They kill us. I beat China all the time. All the time."[75]
- "I am very highly educated. I know words. I have the best words."[76]

These quotes reveal a simple, populist rhetorical style, defined by short sound bites, monosyllabic words, and the disavowing of complex vocabulary or nuance.

Trump's simplistic language has been highly effective at encouraging tens of millions on the right to support this president. Condemnations of Trump as "stupid" or "boorish" because of his simplicity and lack of refinement fall flat for Americans who view his "straight-shooter" approach as a virtue. For millions of conservatives, Trump is one of them – a cheeseburger-eating patriot and a "common man" who drops his "g's" and tells it "like it is," fighting fat cats and Washington corruption. This is quite different from Sanders' populism, which rejects anti-intellectualism, while calling on "the people" to demand progressive change.

Trump's use of simple language, coupled with his Manichean framing of the world between black and white, "smart" and "dumb," good and evil – means he is well situated as a right-wing populist. By consolidating conservative support around his presidency, he has nurtured an authoritarian streak in American politics, marked by a "personalized" sense of "direct" communication with "the people," and contempt for the media and political officials. This authoritarianism is evident in the reliance of 60 million Americans on Trump's *Twitter* feed for their information about the world, and millions of Republicans' preference for Trump's *Twitter* communications as their primary source of news.[77]

Populism and Plutocracy

Populism and manipulation are not synonymous, although the former is useful in pursuing the latter. One consequence of Trump's populism is it has masked the intensification of plutocratic politics, lending a "common" face to governance, while policies enriching the wealthy continue. Despite Trump's efforts to build an image as a freedom-loving "average Joe," his administration was anything but. As the *Washington Post* reported following his 2016 victory, Trump's appointees called back to the "Gilded Age" of politics, with extreme wealth recruited to control the levers of government:

> Trump is putting together what will be the wealthiest administration in modern American history. His announced nominees for top positions include several multimillionaires, an heir to a family mega-fortune and two Forbes-certified billionaires, one of whose family is worth as much as industrial tycoon Andrew Mellon was when he served as Treasury Secretary nearly a century ago. Many of the Trump appointees were born wealthy, attended elite schools and went on to amass even larger fortunes as adults. Their collective wealth in many ways defies Trump's populist campaign promises. But the group also amplifies Trump's own campaign pitch: that Washington outsiders who know how to navigate and exploit a "rigged" system are best able to fix that system for the working-class.[78]

The irony of the wealthiest individuals in history serving as protectors of the working-class was lost on tens of millions of Americans of modest means who voted for a populist candidate promising to "bring back jobs" and "Make America Great Again." For this group, embrace of a "benevolent" billionaire and his promise to save the "working man" speak to the effectiveness of hegemonic propaganda in molding citizens' minds.

The Trump administration's bias toward the wealthy ran contrary to campaign promises to improve the lives of working-class Americans. Trump lamented the decline of manufacturing jobs, invoking the notion of a lost greatness:

> Right now, 92 million Americans are on the sidelines, outside the workforce, and not part of our economy. It's a silent nation of jobless Americans.
>
> Look no further than the city of Flint, where I just visited. The jobs have been stripped from this community, and its infrastructure has collapsed. In 1970, there were more than 80,000 people in Flint working for GM – today it is less than 8,000. Now Ford has announced it is moving all small car production to Mexico. It used to be cars were made in Flint and you couldn't drink the water in Mexico. Now, the cars are made in Mexico and you can't drink the water in Flint. We are going to turn this around … Jobs can stop

leaving our country, and start pouring in. Failing schools can become flourishing schools. Crumbling roads and bridges can become gleaming new infrastructure. Inner cities can experience a flood of new jobs and investment. And rising crime can give way to safe and prosperous communities. All of these things, and so much more, are possible. But to accomplish them, we must replace the present policy of globalism – which has moved so many jobs and so much wealth out of our country – and replace it with a new policy of Americanism.[79]

Following his 2016 electoral victory, Trump delivered his inaugural address, offering an "America First" doctrine, and promising an economy reinvigorated by 25 million new jobs within a decade.[80] His address relied on populist appeals and attacks on the political establishment:

Today's ceremony has very special meaning. We are not merely transferring power from one Administration to another, or from one party to another – but we are transferring power from Washington, D.C. and giving it back to you, the American People ... For too long, a small group in our nation's Capital has reaped the rewards of government while the people have borne the cost. Washington flourished – but the people did not share in its wealth. Politicians prospered – but the jobs left, and the factories closed. The establishment protected itself, but not the citizens of our country ... At the center of this movement is a crucial conviction: that a nation exists to serve its citizens ... America will start winning again, winning like never before. We will bring back our jobs. We will bring back our borders. We will bring back our wealth, and we will bring back our dreams.[81]

Trump's reference to a "movement" for change resonated with millions of Americans. But Trump's populism was also anemic; it had little to do with movement building. The president may have enjoyed delivering speeches and campaigning in front of large audiences. But speeches are a form of top-down communication. They are not central to movement building, which involves community members coming together, organizing, and building a vision for change. Movements rely on community meetings, demonstrations and rallies, leafleting, marches, civil disobedience, shared displays of solidarity, canvassing neighborhoods, and engaging in framing campaigns to influence political discourse. Trump's speeches, in contrast, were designed to elect one individual to office. Trump relied on the passive support of voters, who were never called upon to organize a grassroots rebellion.

Trump promised to "drain the swamp" of corruption in Washington, but his policies solidified plutocratic politics.[82] His decision to withdraw the U.S. from the Paris Agreement, in addition to his rollback of Obama-era environmental regulations, were a boon for oil companies and fossil-fuel polluters, to the detriment of environmental sustainability. His effort to repeal "Obamacare" would have eliminated insurance and subsidies for tens of millions of Americans, while granting additional tax relief to wealthy households.[83] His tax cuts targeted high-income earners, placing greater strain on federal budgets, and creating additional pressure to cut spending for popular social programs.[84] In short, Trump's folksy populism was belied by his economic policies.

Reactionary Populism in the Culture War

Trump made a considerable effort to fuel the culture war. Some of his comments and actions traced back to years before his presidential bid, but most of the examples below are from the 2016 campaign or after. They include sleights against Native Americans;[85] claims that black and Latin American immigrants are unwelcome;[86] associating foreign travel with disease;[87] his many flirtations with white supremacists;[88] his support for the racist "birther" conspiracy;[89] his claims that undocumented immigrants are animals, drug dealers, and rapists;[90] his associations of Islam with terrorism;[91] and his blatant misogyny via judging women's value by their looks and his bragging about sexual assault.[92] This list demonstrates Trump's bigoted statements and racially/ethnically discriminatory behavior. Trump's prejudice was well documented in the 2016 election and before – meaning that those who voted for Trump were either supportive of his bigotry or tolerated it.

Trump and the Media

Trump's relationship with the media is more complicated than he recognizes. He has relied heavily on news and social media to communicate with the public. Furthermore, Trump is supported by right-wing media, serving as foot soldiers for disseminating his messages. Still, Trump has developed a caustic relationship with journalists, who he claims are biased in their reporting.[93] And many journalists are uncomfortable covering the Trump administration.[94] They see themselves as "objective" professionals, and that commitment puts them in a difficult position covering the administration's many obvious falsehoods.

While journalists display a bias toward official sources, they risk their credibility by allowing Trump to go unchallenged making false claim after false claim, especially when these claims are so clumsy they can be disproven with simple google searches or consulting fact-checking websites. But reporters also amplified Trump's claims, while corporate media profited from growing audiences due to their coverage of Trump's incendiary comments. While the relationship between Trump and reporters was at times conflictual in the 2016 campaign, journalists played a major role in Trump's rise to political power.

Trump's 2016 campaign was consistently reported on in negative ways. *Media Tenor* and Harvard's Shorenstein Center found, depending on the outlet examined, that positive reporting on Trump ranged from 10 percent to a quarter of all coverage. Clinton's coverage was also negative, with positive reporting ranging from 20 to almost 50 percent of all coverage. From these statistics, one could conclude reporters' discomfort with Trump and his falsehoods made them critical of his campaign. After all, Trump was the least truthful of the final candidates in the 2016 primaries, with 77 percent of his statements deemed false by *Politifact*.[95] But there is an alternative interpretation of this data, one embraced by the Shorenstein Center, claiming news coverage was actually sympathetic to Trump. Negativity has long been a dominant feature of U.S. news, as related to elections. Negative campaigning is dominant in America, while mudslinging is the norm. In this environment, negativity could be seen as reinforcing the Republican Party's anti-government rhetoric. As Thomas Patterson, author of the Shorenstein report, argued:

> An irony of the press's critical tendency is that it helps the right wing. Although conservatives claim that the press has a liberal bias, the media's persistent criticism of government reinforces the right wing's anti-government message. For years on end, journalists have told news audiences that political leaders are not to be trusted and that government is inept. And when journalists turn their eye to society, they highlight the problems and not the success stories. The news creates a seedbed of public anger, misperception, and anxiety – sitting there waiting to be tapped by those who have a stake in directing the public's wrath at government.[96]

Following Patterson's claims, one can imagine a political scenario in which negative news worked to Trump's benefit: Republicans and conservatives, after years of right-wing media and Republican officials demonizing journalists, dismiss negative coverage of Trump as "liberal bias." With this negativity discounted, Trump benefits from the increased volume of coverage – $2 billion in free media publicity – that he received, to the detriment of Cruz, Sanders, and Clinton.[97] Since all the candidates were framed negatively, critical reporting toward Trump is not a liability, relative to how news audiences see him compared to other candidates. Trump's campaign gains steam, because "there is no such thing as bad publicity" when one seeks to win political office.

Trump's campaign was the most covered of all presidential candidates. This dominance was evident in national newspapers such as the *New York Times* and *Washington Post* before the November election. In the *New York Times*, Trump was mentioned in the headlines of 58 front-page features, compared to Clinton's 25 features, translating into 132 percent greater attention in the months before election day. In the *Washington Post*, there were 39 front-page features mentioning Trump in its headlines, compared to 24 for Clinton, translating into 63 percent greater coverage.[98]

The amplification of Trump's campaign relates to a pro-business bias in the media favoring increased ratings, audiences, and profits. This bias was displayed by *CBS* President Les Moonves in relation to journalists' fixation on the Trump "circus," which he admitted "may not be good for America," but is "damn good for *CBS*." Moonves reflected on Trump's saturation level attention:

> Who would have expected the ride we're all having right now ... The money's rolling in and this is fun ... I've never seen anything like this, and this is going to be a very good year for us. Sorry. It's a terrible thing to say, But, bring it on, Donald. Keep going ... I'm not taking a side, I'm just saying for us, economically, Donald Trump's place in this election is a good thing.[99]

Left out of Moonves' reflection was recognition that Trump's monopolization of the news meant less exposure for other candidates.

Contrary to Trump's attacks on journalists, his campaign developed a symbiotic relationship with the press. Trump relied on the media for increased exposure and to reach supporters. And corporate media improved their bottom line by drawing attention to the Trump spectacle. Trump shrewdly fed the media monster with a steady stream of controversial tweets, dwarfing competing candidates in media exposure. Trump was a media creation, even before his days as a presidential candidate – as a business celebrity, and entertainer. These points are obscured in Trump's demonizing of the media.

A second dimension of news coverage relates to Trump's populism. I examined how effective Trump was in conveying that he was leading a populist uprising against the Washington establishment. In question are: (1) How much attention did Trump's populism receive in the media? and (2) Was Trump's populism covered in a way suggesting he was challenging business-as-usual politics in Washington? On both counts, Trump successfully projected himself as a populist opposed to the status quo.

The volume of coverage of Trump's populism compared favorably to modern social movements. Utilizing *Nexis Uni*, I classified news coverage as emphasizing a populist theme if stories on Trump included references to populism, rebellion, insurgency, anti-establishment politics, the Tea Party, or the working-class.[100] Table 4.1 examines *New York Times* coverage of Trump's populism compared to Black Lives Matter, the Tea Party, Occupy Wall Street, Fight for $15, and the 2017 Women's March in D.C. Trump's populism appeared regularly in the news, in 95 articles on average per month in 2016, and 56 articles per month in 2017. The 2016 average is higher-than-average monthly coverage of Black Lives Matter from 2015 through 2017, and of the Tea Party and Occupy in 2016, and Fight for $15 in 2015 and 2016. Other social movements were covered more than Trump's populism, including the Tea Party in 2010, Occupy in 2011 and 2012, and the Women's March in 2017.

Media coverage included sustained attention to Trump's populism. An examination with *Nexis Uni* finds that, in 2016, references to Trump's populism appeared in more than 13,000 articles, news stories, features, op-eds, editorials, and letters to the editor across U.S. newspapers, radio outlets, online news sources, cable news, and broadcast media outlets. This meant nearly 1,100 pieces per month. In sum, compared to major social movements, Trump's populism was a regular topic of discussion in the media.

Trump's populism was described in the news using various terms suggesting a mutiny against the political status quo. Figure 4.8 provides

Table 4.1 *New York Times* Coverage of Trump Populism and Modern Social Movements

Event	Articles per Month
Trump Rebellion (2016)	95
Trump Rebellion (2017)	56
Black Lives Matter (2015)	27
Black Lives Matter (2016)	75
Black Lives Matter (2017)	55
Tea Party (2010)	117
Tea Party (2016)	53
Occupy Wall Street (10/17/2011–3/31/2012)	216
Occupy Wall Street (2016)	8
Fight for $15 (2015)	3
Fight for $15 (2016)	3
Women's March (Jan–Feb 2017)	177

Source: *Nexis Uni* academic database

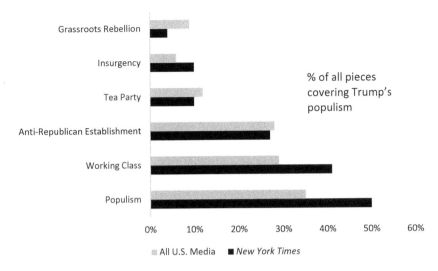

Figure 4.8 Media Coverage of Trump's Populism (1/1–12/31/2016)
Source: *Nexis Uni* academic database

an assessment of these terms. Using *Nexis Uni*, I estimated the percentage of all articles in the *New York Times* and other media referencing some version of Trump's populism, as a percentage of all pieces discussing Trump's populism.

References to grassroots resistance, rebellion, or insurgency against the status quo were the least common to appear, as were references to the Tea Party. Other themes were more common, including references to opposition to the Republican establishment, the working-class, and Trump as a populist, or to populism more generally. Then there is the sustained discussion of Trump's appeal to the working-class – a regular theme in the news.

The working-class narrative reinforced the populist notion that Trump represented Americans suffering under economic stress.[101] The *Atlantic* magazine wrote of "The Billionaire Candidate and His Blue-Collar Following," while the *New York Times* emphasized "What Donald Trump Might Do for Working-Class Families."[102] The *Washington Post* reported on "Rallying Blue-Collar Workers in Cincinnati" in support of Trump, as he "Blames Democrats for Obstructing his Agenda."[103] The *Atlantic* argued that "class, not ideology, has boosted Trump's unconventional rise," while the *New York Times* reported after the 2016 election that Trump was elected "in [a] stunning repudiation of the establishment," culminating with "an explosive, populist, and polarizing campaign … it was a decisive demonstration of power by a largely overlooked coalition of mostly blue-collar white and working-class voters who felt that the promise of the United States had slipped their grasp amid decades of globalization and multiculturalism."[104]

Right-wing media were strong boosters of Trump's populism. *Fox News*' Tucker Carlson called Trump "shocking, vulgar, and right," while lambasting Republicans for "trade deals that eliminated jobs while enriching their donors."[105] Radio host Rush Limbaugh warned:

> The establishment is simply offended that Trump won. They are offended that they haven't been able to stop him … They're offended that he tweets. They're offended that he's enjoying himself. They're offended that he gets away with everything they've thrown at him. They're offended his tax cuts are working. They're offended that he dared attack Obamacare. They are offended that he continues to attack Crooked Hillary, Crazy Bernie. They can't stand it, and the objective is to get rid of this guy no matter what else.[106]

Fox News host Sean Hannity considers himself and the president to be personal friends, hosting Trump for interviews, sharing meals and advice, and defending him from attacks.[107] Hannity condemns Republicans as "a dead party. They are morally corrupt, they are weak. They are ineffective, they're visionless, and they have no identity."[108]

Not all media treated Trump's populism the same. Some were bigger boosters of his agenda. Figure 4.9 details this variation; the *Wall Street Journal*, *ABC*, *CBS*, and *NBC* were least likely to refer to Trump and

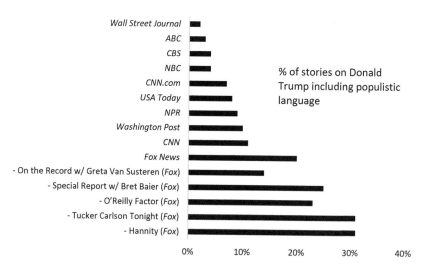

Figure 4.9 Varied Coverage of Trump's Populism by Venue (1/1–12/31/2016)
Source: *Nexis Uni* academic database

his supporters using populist terms. *CNN*, *CNN.com*, *USA Today*, *NPR*, and the *Washington Post* were more likely to use such terms. *Fox News* hosts were the biggest proponents of populist language.

Right-wing media are key Trump supporters. They defended the president when other reporters criticized him for his commitment to "alternative facts" – those running contrary to verifiable facts. The Trump administration benefitted from an ascendant American right, via a large conservative apparatus that was decades in the building. This apparatus emerged in the 1970s and 1980s, with the rise of conservative think tanks, in backlash against the progressive movements of the 1960s and against New Deal liberalism.[109] The right-wing backlash further developed in the 1980s with the rise of the Reagan presidency and the growth of conservative think tanks, in the 1990s and 2000s with the rise of far-right media, and in the 2010s with the Tea Party and Trump's populism, with Trump's rise assisted by right-wing media and *Twitter*.

If the media were central to building support for Trump, we should find that attention to the news produced growing support for Trump's candidacy. I analyze *Pew* polls from mid-to-late 2016 and early 2017, measuring how media attention was related to attitudes toward Trump. Figure 4.10 draws on *Pew*'s June, August, and October 2016 polls, documenting how greater attention to election news was associated with increased support for Trump, after controlling for respondents' race, income, gender, age, education, ideology, and party. It was not until early

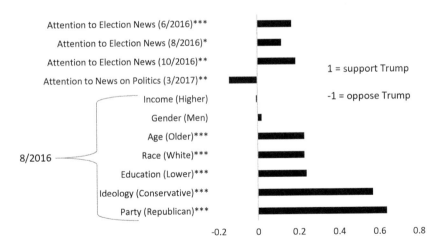

Figure 4.10 Media Consumption and Public Attitudes toward Trump
Source: *Pew Research Center* surveys, June/August/October 2016; March 2017
Statistical Significance Levels: *** = 0.1% ** = 1% * = 5%
Controls: gender, age, education, race, income, political party, ideology

196   *Populism in the 2016 Election*

2017, when Trump took power, that attention to the news was associated with growing opposition to the president. These findings suggest that the relationship between the press and Trump was mixed during his campaign and first year in office. But the media boosted support for the president during the election, likely due to the heavy attention to his candidacy and the sympathetic coverage of Trump's populism.

A look at media effects for far-right sources suggests these outlets were also significant in building Trump support. According to Figure 4.11, attention to "mainstream" outlets such as *CNN* and *NPR* was associated with increased opposition to Trump in late 2016, while consumption of right-wing sources such as Limbaugh's radio program, *Fox News*, Sean Hannity specifically, and to the "alt-right" *Breitbart News* were associated with increased support. These results suggest conservative attacks on the media for undermining Trump are deeply exaggerated. There is some evidence that media consumption produced growing opposition to the president in early 2017, but the findings from 2016 suggest a mutually reinforcing, symbiotic relationship between Trump and the media. Trump's campaign was aided by all the free media he received, which improved the financial bottom lines of media corporations craving the sensationalistic, negative news coverage Trump was happy to provide. The Trump administration quickly began to attack mainstream journalists once in office, which may explain the growing opposition to Trump that came with increased attention to the news, as reporters defended themselves against the president's attacks.[110]

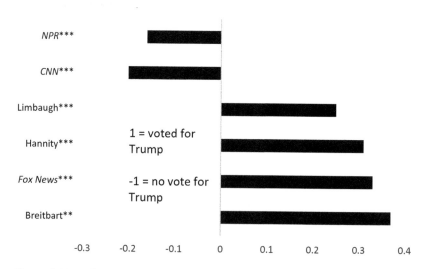

Figure 4.11 Right-Wing Media Consumption and Trump Support
Source: *Pew Research Center* Survey, November 2016
Statistical Significance Levels: *** = 0.1% ** = 1% * = 5%
Controls: gender, age, education, race, income, political party, ideology

Trump and the Public: Right-Wing Populism and Its Supporters

Much ink was spilled by journalists and academics to understand why tens of millions of Americans supported Trump's populism. My analysis of *Pew*'s October 2016 monthly survey finds Trump receives less support from younger Americans, from those 18–29 and 30–49 years old, compared to those 50 and older. Over a third of Trump supporters come from households with incomes under the national average of $56,516.[111] The largest single group of supporters are those earning more than $100,000 a year, who make up nearly a third of his base. Trump supporters are almost entirely moderate to conservative, heavily leaning toward the latter. Two-thirds are Republicans; another third are independents. Most Trump supporters have modest educational achievements, with high school degrees (or less) or a few years of college. This statistic explains why so many journalists frame Trump's base as "blue-collar" and "working-class." Trump supporters are a nearly equal mix of men and women, and the large majority are white, as he receives little support among LatinX Americans, and virtually no support from blacks.

Trump supporters are strongly conservative. On "family values," 68 percent believe "children with two parents are better off if one parent stays home." Only 40 percent agree an increased number of people "of different races and ethnicities make the U.S. a better place to live." Just 24 percent agree whites "have advantages blacks don't have," and only 6 percent feel racial discrimination is "the main reason blacks can't get ahead." On immigration, just 43 percent say undocumented immigrants are no more likely to commit serious crimes, and 79 percent favor building a wall between the U.S. and Mexico. Fifty-seven percent agree Muslims should be subjected "to greater scrutiny to prevent terrorism." And 68 percent agree free trade is "a bad thing for the U.S." Similarly, discontent was apparent in their perceived quality of life, with 81 percent agreeing "life is worse today than 50 years ago" for "people like them." Just 25 percent agree climate change is real and human-caused.[112] On economic policy, Trump supporters are conservative. An overwhelming 83 percent agree government is "almost always wasteful and inefficient," and 87 percent want a "smaller government with fewer services." Just 21 percent agree government "should do more to help the needy"; only 17 percent feel government regulation of business is "necessary to protect the public interest."[113]

Many Trump supporters hold reactionary racial attitudes. Sixty-one percent agree Obama was born in another country – in line with Trump's "birther" conspiracy.[114] And 66 percent think Obama is a Muslim.[115] Fifty-eight percent hold unfavorable views of Islam.[116] Two-thirds agree "immigrants are a burden on our country because they take our jobs, housing, and health care."[117] Most agree with

198 Populism in the 2016 Election

Trump's claim that Mexican immigrants are criminals and rapists, while nearly half agree blacks are "lazier" than whites.[118] After calling Trump supporters "deplorables" during the run-up to the November election, Clinton apologized, rejecting "grossly generalistic" characterizations.[119] But majorities of Trump supporters share bigoted, racist, and xenophobic values. Drawing on Truman's disturbance theory, his supporters hold shared "grievances." They are disturbed by demographic shifts in the U.S. As I document in this chapter, many are uncomfortable with women asserting themselves against patriarchal, misogynist power structures. They view Muslims as a security threat. They see immigrants from Mexico and Latin America as deviants who drain societal resources. They hold negative views of blacks, depicting them as lazy, violent, and unworthy of aid. They seek to "Make America Great Again" by strengthening power structures that advantage affluent whites, while relegating other groups to second-class status.

From these findings, it is difficult to tell what attitudes are driving support for Trump's populism. Reactionary economic *and* social values are associated with Trump's support base. To understand what factors drive Trump's appeal, I analyzed *Pew* surveys from 2016. Figures 4.12 and 4.13 summarize my findings from the primary period. Figure 4.12 reveals economic concerns about health-care costs, the deficit, and improving the "job situation" in the nation were not significant predictors of Trump support. Neither were concerns with reducing crime and protecting the environment.

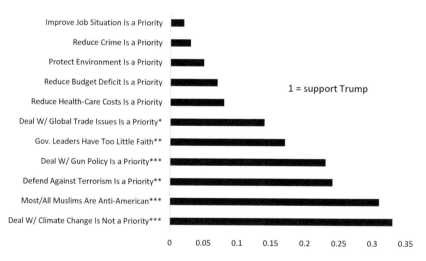

Figure 4.12 Attitudinal Predictors of Trump Support in the Primaries: I
Source: *Pew Research Center* survey, January 2016
Statistical Significance Levels: *** = 0.1% ** = 1% * = 5%

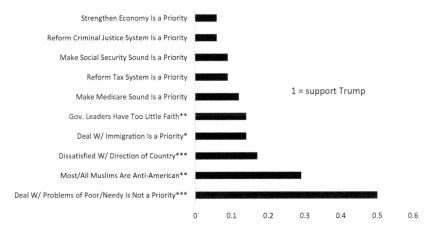

Figure 4.13 Attitudinal Predictors of Trump Support in Primaries: II
Source: *Pew Research Center* survey, January 2016
Statistical Significance Levels: *** = 0.1%   ** = 1%   * = 5%

The only economic concern associated with Trump support related to global trade issues, and it was the weakest of all the significant attitudinal predictors. Predictors of Trump support were largely socially related, including a concern with gun policy, feelings that Muslims are anti-American, the belief that government leaders have "too little faith," and concern with defending the nation against terrorism, which is linked to Islamophobia among Trump's supporters. The only other significant predictor – agreement that climate change is not a priority – was economically and socially relevant, socially in that environmental sustainability is vital to interpersonal human relations, and economic because efforts to limit global warming require government regulations of fossil fuel companies. The attitudes in Figure 4.12 were significant predictors of Trump support, after controlling for all other attitudes included in the analysis.

The results from Figure 4.13 echo the above findings. Economic factors, including concern with the economy, concern with improving education, support for making Social Security sound, support for reforming the tax system, and agreement that Medicare reform should be a priority, were not associated with Trump support. Only one social issue – support for reforming the criminal justice system – was insignificant in predicting support. In contrast, three of the five social factors that predicted support were significant, including feelings that government leaders have too little faith, agreement that dealing with immigration is a priority, and feelings that Muslims are anti-American. Only one economic factor – disinterest in government aiding the poor and needy – predicted Trump support.

200   Populism in the 2016 Election

My analysis of *Pew*'s August 2016 survey provides similar results to those above. Figure 4.14 finds that five of the six factors that predict Trump support are socially related. These include: animosity toward Muslims, opposition to accepting Syrian refugees, agreement that undocumented immigrants should leave the country, feelings that abortion should be illegal, agreement that too much attention is paid to racial issues in America, and feelings that Clinton was treated less critically than Trump in the 2016 election, *because* she is a woman. Two economic attitudes effectively predict Trump support: agreement with cutting taxes on wealthier Americans, and feelings that free trade harms the country. Concern about losing one's job is not a predictor of Trump support. These results suggest economic attitudes play *some* role in motivating Trump support.

But support is heavily motivated by far-right cultural attitudes – for example, the claim that women have an advantage in presidential races over men, despite all presidents historically being men. This "reverse sexism" position was developed by reactionary males who embrace the "men's rights" movement, which imagines men are systematically repressed by feminists and a power structure committed to assaulting masculinity.[120]

Finally, Figure 4.15 provides additional evidence of the primacy of cultural attitudes. Only two economic attitudes – opposition to raising the minimum wage and resistance to government regulation of business – are associated with Trump approval. Four economic attitudes – opposition to environmental regulations, concern with the lack of well-paying jobs in America, disinterest in the gap between rich and poor, and feelings that

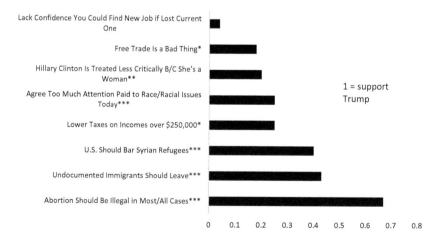

Figure 4.14 Attitudinal Predictors of Trump Support in the General Election: I
Source: *Pew Research Center* survey, August 2016
Statistical Significance Levels: *** = 0.1% level ** = 1% level * = 5% level

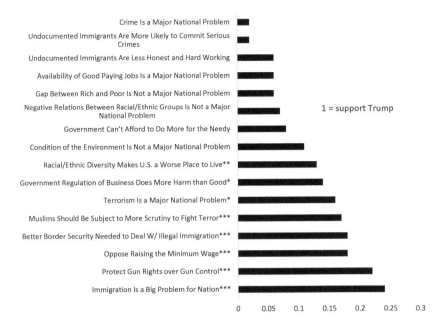

Figure 4.15 Attitudinal Predictors of Trump Support in the General Election: II
Source: *Pew Research Center* survey, August 2016
Statistical Significance Levels: *** = 0.1% level ** = 1% level ** = 5% level

government cannot afford to help the needy – are not associated with Trump support. Of the eight significant predictors of Trump approval, six are socio-cultural. Support for increased scrutiny of Muslims in the name of fighting terror, concern that terrorism is a major problem, agreement immigration is a major problem, support for increased border security, agreement that gun rights need to be protected, and feelings that racial and ethnic diversity leave the country worse off are all significant predictors of Trump support.

While opposition to gun regulations is one of the stronger predictors of Trump support, (Figure 4.15), anxiety over gun control is linked to racism and xenophobia among whites. As documented in Figure 4.16, white Americans opposing new gun regulations and agreeing "an increasing number of people of many different races, ethnic groups, and nationalities in the U.S. make this country a worse place to live," are significantly more likely to embrace Trump. This relationship is strong; although not as powerful as partisanship, it is about equal to ideology, and stronger than age, education, income, and gender in driving Trump support. This interaction of factors is more powerful than any other

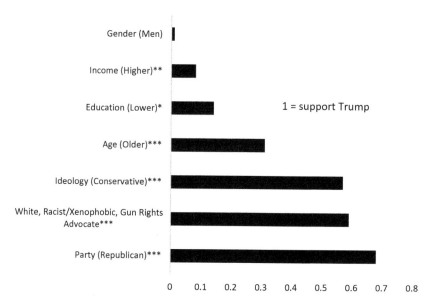

Figure 4.16 Prejudice and Trump Support: White Racism, Xenophobia, and Gun Ownership
Source: *Pew Research Center* poll, August 2016
Statistical Significance Levels: *** = 0.1% ** = 1% * = 5%
Controls: gender, age, education, income, political party, ideology

attitudinal factor in this chapter – save opposition to abortion – in predicting pro-Trump attitudes. The association between xenophobia, racism, white identity, and opposition to gun control fits within a reactionary paradigm in which conservative whites see racial diversity and immigration as threats to white identity, and in which gun ownership provides "protection" from the "threat" of people of color. The "minorities as a threat" narrative, as discussed in Chapter 3, has long been driven by reporting associating "black" with poverty, crime, and deviance.

In summarizing the findings thus far, only 7 of 21 survey questions covering economic issues are significant predictors of pro-Trump attitudes. In other words, economics is somewhat important in describing his rise to power. In contrast, 17 of 25 socio-cultural questions are significantly associated with Trump support. Economic attitudes are significant to Trump's base, but they are not the main factor motivating his supporters. And there is no evidence here that progressive attitudes regarding inequality are associated with Trump support, contrary to notions that Trump appealed to both the left and the right due to his rhetoric on job loss and outsourcing.

Populism in the 2016 Election 203

The populism of the early 2010s – driven by the Tea Party – was primarily economic, with right-wing social values playing a secondary role. By the late 2010s, the American right fell in line behind Trump's reactionary populism. While plutocratic policies guide Trump's policy agenda, they are not as salient in driving his base, which has internalized racist, sexist, Islamophobic, and xenophobic views. There is evidence, however, that socio-cultural and economic attitudes work together in defining Trump supporters. For example, xenophobic attitudes played a role in undermining support for the welfare state, as reinforced by Figure 4.20 – drawn from *Pew*'s August 2016 survey. It shows Trump supporters who oppose immigration, in addition to white Trump supporters and white male Trump supporters opposing immigration, are more likely to feel government cannot afford to assist the poor and needy. As with the Tea Party, these results speak to the persistence of intersectional prejudice that drives conservative thought. Race, gender, Trump support, and xenophobia interact in significant ways to encourage opposition to government efforts to assist the poor. This finding echoes the right's claim that "lazy" and poor immigrants take advantage of welfare, preferring "free benefits" to hard work. The relative privilege of Trump supporters appears to drive reactionary views on immigration and welfare. This is seen via greater opposition among higher-income Americans and older Americans (Figure 4.17), who tend to be financially better off than young Americans.

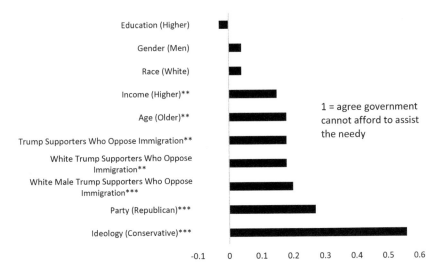

Figure 4.17 Intersecting Identities: Trump Support, Gender, Race, Immigration, and Welfare Attitudes

Source: *Pew Research Center* survey, August 2016
Statistical Significance Levels: *** = 0.1% ** = 1% * = 5%
Controls: gender, age, education, race, income, political party, ideology

The Myth of Trump's Economic Populism

What about the claim that Trump voters are angry because of economic insecurities? An exhaustive analysis of surveys suggests this narrative is heavily exaggerated. To assess the economic populism thesis, I reviewed data from *Pew* and other surveys throughout 2016 onward, searching for evidence that Trump's base was driven by financial insecurity. There is little to indicate this is the case. Figure 4.18 examines the self-designated class status of Trump supporters, revealing they are not more likely than non-supporters to identify as lower-class or lower middle-class, after controlling for respondents' gender, age, education, race, party, and ideology. Most consider themselves "middle-class," like the rest of America. A mistake in the Trump-populism narrative is the common assumption that, because individuals do not have a four-year degree or better, and because many hold non-white-collar "working-class" jobs, they are economically distressed. This assumption is baseless without evidence that they earn low incomes or suffer from economic distress.

"Working-class" is an amorphous term, vaguely suggesting modesty in one's economic position. Individuals may identify as "working-class" and have lower levels of formal education, but earn the median household income or above. According to *Pew*'s October 2016 national survey, only a third of Trump supporters earn less than $50,000 a year, and the largest

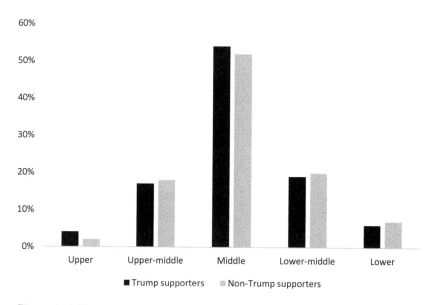

Figure 4.18 Trump Supporters' Economics: Self-Designated Class Status
Source: *Pew Research Center* survey, January 2016

single group of supporters earn more than $100,000. Furthermore, as we see in polls across numerous years, income is not a consistent predictor of Trump support – further evidence of the exaggerated claim that Trump supporters are motivated by economic insecurity.[121]

One limitation of Figure 4.18 is that it measures attitudes toward Trump as a function of class status via lower-middle- and lower-class designations. Neither exactly fit the alternative "working-class" designation. To address this issue, I examined an *ABC News* survey from March 2016 including a measure of "working-class" identity. Respondents identifying as working-class or white working-class were *not* more likely to say they were voting for Trump, after controlling for respondents' party, ideology, gender, age, and education. Figure 4.19 shows the relationship between being white and working-class, and identification with Trump is weak and not statistically significant. Other factors such as party and education are more powerful in predicting Trump support. Reportedly, working-class whites who voted in both 2012 and 2016 were modestly more likely than non-working-class whites who voted in both elections to favor Obama in 2012, but swing toward Trump in 2016.[122] But this is an extremely small group of people, compared to the adult population overall, and compared to the voting population. And as I document in this chapter, the attempt to link financially insecure white working-class Americans to Trump is difficult when self-designated "working-class" whites are no more likely than other Americans to support Trump. Furthermore, the narrative that "white working-class insecurity" fuels Trumpism is unsustainable

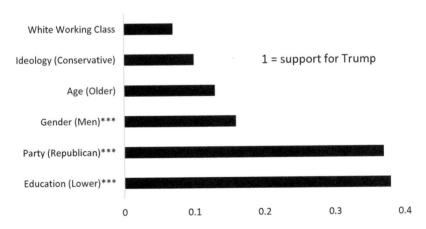

Figure 4.19 Trump and the White Working Class
Source: *ABC News* poll, March 2016
Statistical Significance Levels: *** = 0.1% level ** = 1% level **= 5% level
Controls: gender, age, education, political party, ideology

when neither individuals suffering from economic insecurity, nor those living in working-class areas suffering from higher rates of manufacturing job loss, are more likely to support Trump.

And while white working-class Americans are statistically more likely to be in the lower-income category than other Americans, they are not significantly more likely to support Trump.[123] If Trump benefitted from some working-class support in 2016, that does not mean these individuals were more likely to be economically insecure. More specifically, there is little evidence that anger over losing a manufacturing job was a significant driver of support for Trump. On the one hand, individuals living in counties that experienced higher job losses due to outsourcing of manufacturing were more likely to support Trump than Clinton.[124] On the other hand, these same counties were no more likely to vote Republican and for Trump in 2016, compared to voting Republican and for Romney in 2012.[125] So county-level data provides no evidence of a "Trump effect" related to manufacturing, since Trump gained no votes from these areas compared to Romney's vote totals in 2012. Furthermore, the very limited county-level data suggesting a Republican-Trump advantage is suspect for another reason. Counties are clumsy, broad statistical measures, since they include large numbers of people living in different communities, and who are more and less affluent, economically. In an era of record inequality and growing residential segregation by income and wealth, it is unwise to assume that counties are uniform in their economic demographics.

A more precise examination of geographic regions by "commuting areas" and zip codes finds no evidence of a connection between manufacturing job loss and Trump voting. To the contrary, areas harmed by such job loss were more likely to see greater *opposition* to Trump.[126] Coupled with the failure to find evidence of a significant link between economic insecurity and Trump support in national surveys, these findings are troubling. They provide little compelling evidence of a connection between working-class insecurity and Trump support.

Higher voting for Trump in large metropolitan areas that experience manufacturing job loss can be explained by the political demobilization of working-class and disadvantaged individuals. Democrats lost 3.5 times as many votes as Republicans gained from the 2012 to the 2016 presidential elections from those living in "rustbelt areas" hit hardest by deindustrialization.[127] In large regions (counties) harmed by outsourcing, the demobilization of voting among working-class Americans means the further empowerment of more affluent individuals also in these areas who support Trump. The reality is that Trump did not gain working-class votes from those harmed by outsourcing; Democrats lost them. The Democrats' failure to retain blue-collar votes likely relates to the party's support for free trade, which enabled manufacturing job outsourcing.

Concerns with free trade played some role in mobilizing Trump support. My analysis (Figure 4.14) finds antagonistic feelings toward free trade are a significant predictor of Trump support, but these feelings exist independently of individuals being harmed by such trade. My analysis of *Pew*'s March 2016 survey finds the perception that free trade has hurt an individual and his/her family is a significant predictor of Trump support.[128] A third of Trump supporters, compared to less than 20 percent of non-supporters, claim free trade has harmed them. But these findings are misleading. As described above, *Gallup*'s national survey of Trump supporters finds outsourcing encourages *opposition* to Trump when looking at the highest quality data, based on examining "commuting areas" and zip codes.

Trump supporters have exaggerated the extent to which they are impacted by outsourcing. An estimated 5 million Americans lost manufacturing jobs in the U.S. between 2000 and the mid-2010s.[129] In contrast, 40 percent of adults surveyed by *Pew* in October 2016 said they supported Trump; among them, a third (33 million people) claimed they were personally hurt by free trade. This represents more than a 6.5:1 discrepancy between Americans who lost jobs to free trade in the last decade-and-a-half and those claiming to be harmed.

Other survey data also undermines the claim that Trump supporters are economically disadvantaged. Via the August 2016 *Pew* survey, I examine attitudes toward Trump among various economic subgroups. Figure 4.20 shows that poorer white men and women – earning less than a $50,000 household income a year – are no more likely to support Trump. Poorer men and women are more likely to *oppose* Trump, after controlling for age, education, race, party, and ideology. Relatively more privileged groups, however, are more likely to support Trump, including affluent whites (earning over $75,000 a year), older men (50 and older), affluent white men, and affluent older white men. Other groups more likely to support Trump include Republican older white men, Republican older affluent white men, conservative older white men, and conservative older affluent white men. These results speak to intersectional forms of affluence, and how they reinforce support for right-wing populism.

Other data findings from the *Pew* surveys reveal little evidence of economic insecurity among Trump's base:

- Trump supporters were not more likely to be unemployed or to say they have poor personal finances (10/2016).
- They were not more likely to be concerned with improving the job situation of the country, or with improving the economy (1/2016).
- They were not more likely to show concern that there is a lack of "good-paying jobs" in America, nor were they more likely to be concerned about inequality and poverty (8/2016). Concern with

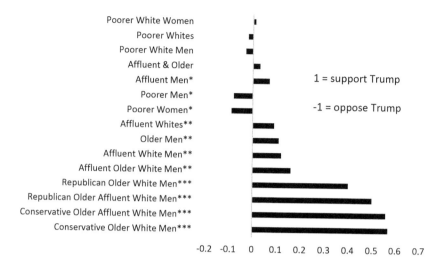

Figure 4.20 Intersecting Identities and Trump Support
Source: *Pew Research Center* survey, August 2016
Statistical Significance Levels: *** = 0.1% level ** = 1% level * = 5% level
Controls: gender, age, education, race, income, political party, ideology

these problems should be paramount for Trump's supporters, if they are concerned with factory workers who are unemployed or otherwise harmed by outsourcing.
- They were significantly more likely to be disinterested in government dealing with the problems of the poor and needy (1/2016), to oppose raising the minimum wage for the working poor, and to support tax cuts for Americans earning over $250,000 a year (8/2016).
- Finally, Republican Americans and Republican-leaning independents, 90 percent of whom in early 2018 approved of Trump, show little sign of being more impacted by negative economic developments.[130] They were not more likely to say their households' financial circumstances were affected "a lot" by growing food and consumer goods prices, growing gas prices, a shortage of available jobs, or changes in the stock market, and *less* likely to say they were negatively affected by changing real estate values and growing health-care costs (3/2018).[131]

Many previous academic studies provide similar conclusions, with little indication that Trump voters suffer from economic insecurity.[132] But this does not mean they are free from economic anxiety. Some surveys suggest economic discontent partly motivated Trump's base. My analysis of *Pew*'s March 2016 survey reveals Trump supporters were significantly more likely than non-supporters to say they were dissatisfied with their financial situation.[133] Exit polling data from the 2016 election revealed Trump voters were more likely than Clinton voters to feel the economy was in only fair or poor shape. Trump voters were almost four times more likely than Clinton voters to say their families' financial situations were "worse" in 2016 than in the past.[134] And Trump supporters were more likely than other Americans to agree working people like them have a harder time nowadays making ends meet than working people did in decades past.[135]

There are two potential explanations for these expressions of financial anxiety. One is that Trump supporters display a narcissistic fixation on their own finances, despite being mostly middle- to middle-upper-class in income, not suffering from cost-of-living, real estate, or employment-related stresses, and being well-off compared to disadvantaged groups. They may *feel* persecuted due to the prevalence of right-wing media rhetoric portraying conservatives and whites as victims of societal repression. Paranoid feelings of persecution do not have to involve deception. Trump supporters, despite being generally well off, have internalized the rhetoric of a Trump administration that rode to power on a wave of populist rhetoric emphasizing white America's decline.

The above narrative explains the radical transformation of Trump supporters' economic attitudes following his ascension to the presidency. While Trump supporters were more likely to be angry about the economy and the state of the nation in mid-2016, their opinions transformed by 2017 to 2018, once Trump was in office. Whereas dissatisfaction with the economy and the state of the nation were significant predictors of Trump support in 2016, strong satisfaction with the nation's state and the condition of the economy predicted support for the president by 2017 and 2018.[136] This rapid shift in beliefs had little to do with the actual state of the economy, since economic growth rates (in GDP change) were only slightly higher in Trump's earlier years than in the post-recession Obama years, and median household wealth was actually lower when Trump was in office, compared to Obama.[137] Rather, the shift was most likely the product of Trump's own rhetoric, via his consistent bragging about economic growth and his flagrantly false claim that he was presiding over "the greatest economy in the history of our country."[138]

A second possibility is that Trump supporters are in *relatively* worse financial positions than in the past, despite scholars' failure to identify how this has occurred. One could imagine Trump supporters angry over the 2008 economic housing collapse, with losses in retirement savings and in the value of their homes, which were probably over-valued prior to the housing crash. One could link such economic anxiety to right-wing efforts to scapegoat the poor, people of color, Muslims, immigrants, and women, with Trump supporters looking for an easy target on which to take out their economic frustrations. But there is little evidence to back up the declining economic fortunes thesis in relation to economic experiences of Trump supporters in the half-decade run-up to Trump's 2016 victory. This point is reinforced by Mutz's 2018 study, concluding that changes in self-reported personal finances, employment status, and personal income between 2012 and 2016 were not significantly associated with Trump support.[139] Furthermore, there is little evidence of the "retirement anxiety" thesis, since Trump supporters are no more likely to say they worry about retirement, compared to non-supporters.[140]

I expand on Mutz's analysis with an assessment of the August–September 2016 *CNN–Kaiser Family Foundation* survey, which included numerous measures of fluctuations in individuals' financial and economic status in the year run-up to the 2016 election. I examine each of these financial circumstances and their potential impact on public opinion, controlling for respondents' gender, age, education, race, party, and ideology. I also look at the intersection of economic insecurity and race – examining white Americans citing various financial problems, to measure whether "white insecurity" is relevant to Trump support. According to Figure 4.21, almost all the measures of financial insecurity were statistically unrelated to Trump support.[141] Reliance on welfare benefits, including Medicaid, food assistance, government aid with paying medical bills, and unemployment benefits, were unrelated to Trump support, among all Americans and whites. Individuals' concerns that it was getting harder to "get ahead financially," provide for "a secure retirement," "find a good job," and secure "a good education" were also unrelated to Trump support among all Americans and whites. Trump support was unrelated among whites and all respondents to accumulating credit card debt, to the postponing of dental or medical care, to having lost a job or suffered from reduced work hours, and to unexpected losses in individuals' retirement funds, education-related savings, and long-term savings. My findings overlap with other research showing Trump supporters were no more likely to report poorer health conditions.[142] Finally, Trump supporters (among whites and all Americans) were *less* likely to say they borrowed money from friends or relatives. They also had higher incomes than non-Trump supporters. Of the 28 individual measures of financial insecurity for whites and all Americans in Figure 4.21, just two – concern with the ability to afford health-care costs (for all Americans and for whites) were significant predictors of Trump support.[143] But these findings must be qualified. While Trump supporters were more likely to cite concerns about medical costs, they were *not* more likely to put off medical or dental care, or to claim they were unhealthy. This suggests that, while Trump's base was more likely to complain about health-care costs, they were not more likely to be harmed by rising costs.

Figure 4.21 The Myth of Rising Insecurity and Trump Voting
Source: *CNN/Kaiser Family Foundation* poll, August–September 2016
Statistical Significance Levels: *** = 0.1% ** = 1% * = 5%
Controls: gender, age, education, race, political party, ideology

The lessons from these findings are four-fold. First, the main drivers of Trump support are entirely unrelated to economic insecurity among whites and Americans more broadly. Rather, support for Trump is heavily driven by partisanship and ideology. Trump supporters fit the standard profile of conservatives who identify with the Republican Party and have above-average incomes.

Second, although pundits are too quick to equate "working-class" and lower formal education with economic insecurity and support for Trump, an analysis of the *CNN/Kaiser* poll from Figure 4.21 shows that factory workers were *not* statistically more likely to support Trump, after controlling for other factors. Figure 4.21 demonstrates that less-educated

212 Populism in the 2016 Election

Americans and *white* factory workers are both statistically more likely to support Trump. But white factory workers are significantly more likely to be economically prosperous, as documented in Figure 4.22. White factory workers are less likely to come from households earning under $20,000 a year, and somewhat more likely to earn between $50,000 and 75,000 a year compared to other Americans. While large numbers of white factory workers have modest incomes, they are not disadvantaged compared to other households.

Third, it is time to start looking at other measures of stress, outside of economic insecurity, when describing Trump's base. Figure 4.21 provides evidence that Americans (and whites specifically) who work additional hours at their jobs or take a second job are significantly more likely to support Trump. This increased occupational stress among whites was linked to reactionary socio-cultural attitiudes in the *CNN/Kaiser* survey, for example, the feeling that immigrants exert a harmful impact on society because they "take" American "jobs, housing, and health care." This conclusion is verified in Figure 4.21, which shows whites who reported job-related stress (increased work hours), and who embraced attacks on immigrants, were more likely to support Trump. The intersection of race, occupational stress, and reactionary social attitudes was significant in driving Trump's appeal.

Finally, to the extent that Trump's supporters have expressed economic anxiety, it was largely related to abstract grievances that had little tangible connection to their financial circumstances, and were probably driven by Trump's own fearmongering rhetoric. In Figure 4.21, Trump supporters (among whites and the broader public) were significantly more likely to express concerns that their children will be worse off in the future than at the time Trump supporters were surveyed. And as

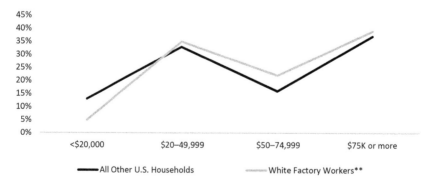

Figure 4.22 Are White Factory Workers Financially Insecure?
Source: CNN/Kaiser Family Foundation survey, August–September 2016
Statistical Significance Levels: *** = 0.1% ** = 1% * = 5%
Controls: gender, age, education, race, political party, ideology

previously discussed, their generalized economic anxiety was apparent in Trump supporters' heightened anxiety (prior to Trump taking office) with the poor state of the economy and their own personal finances, assessments which apparently existed indpendently of their actual finances.

Trump has drawn on a nostalgic commitment to lost greatness on the part of white, relatively affluent, conservative Americans. He romanticized a return to the "good old days," in which white men felt free to say almost anything they pleased, even if their comments were offensive to people of color, women, and other minority groups. America's "lost" greatness, Trump promised, could be recovered by assaulting the "enemies" of the republic, including political correctness, immigrants, women, Muslims, liberals, and people of color insistent on asserting their rights through protest. These "grievances" on the part of white voters had little to do with financial insecurity. Rather, this prejudice has been stoked by decades of hateful rhetoric on the right, from political officials, conservative activists, and media pundits. This prejudice stands at *the* core of Trump's populism, as it appeals to the public and the need to "Make America Great Again." Considering these points, it is fitting that Trump supporters' economic anxiety would rapidly evaporate following his assumption of the presidency, at a time when Trump began to actively discriminate in his policies against people of color, and as he endlessly celebrated the (allegedly) unprecedented nature of the "Trump economic recovery."

Trump and "the Fascist Creep"

Henry Giroux warns the Trump administration represents a fascistic threat to democracy.[144] These claims should not be taken lightly, as words like fascism and authoritarianism are sometimes thrown around with little regard for their meaning.[145] Cavalier use of these terms threatens to dilute their value. Still, there are concerns regarding statements and actions of the president, which validate anxiety over rising authoritarianism, and a "creeping fascism."[146]

One red flag is the growing popularity of political and media discourse that pits empirically based facts against "alternative facts" – the latter popularized by the Trump administration after his advisor Kelly Anne Conway argued with a journalist over the White House's inflated estimates of crowd turnout at Trump's inauguration.[147] The notion that facts are malleable, to be manipulated at will for partisan purposes, reveals an attack on enlightenment principles of truth and knowledge. The rise of authoritarianism involves efforts to intimidate journalists. This strategy has been embraced by the president and his staff, who regularly attack reporters for pedaling "fake news," in response to journalists emphasizing the brazen falsehoods propagated by

Trump. This is quite a charge to level at reporters, considering Trump's campaign was one of the least truthful of all the 2016 candidacies. And Trump's efforts to control and intimidate journalists go beyond rhetorical attacks, including the restricting of reporters' access to White House press briefings.[148] Concerns about authoritarianism also arise when members of the Trump administration talk of criminalizing the reporting of classified intelligence, despite legal protections that guarantee reporters this right.[149]

Another issue is Trump's support for violence against critics. Trump speaks fondly of violence against leftist protesters, congratulating a supporter at a campaign rally for physically attacking one of his critics. He offered to pay the attacker's legal fees – a symbol of his support for authoritarian suppression of dissent.[150] He laughs about supporters who call for murdering immigrants.[151] Trump speaks of the "good old days" when protesters were assaulted by police, while speaking in veiled sentiments about his supporters among police, the military, and armed vigilantes taking action against his critics.[152] This authoritarian streak was reinforced when Trump commended fascists as "very fine people" after white supremacist violence in Charlottesville, Virginia, which injured more than a dozen protesters and resulted in one murder.[153] These expressions have the potential to encourage violence, when one in five Trump supporters endorse violence against civilians in pursuit of political and other causes.[154] Support for obedience to authority and for crushing dissent are embraced by many Trump supporters, as shown in numerous studies.[155]

Public anxiety over authoritarianism and fascism is stoked by the growing radicalism on the right, whose supporters endorsed repressive policies under Trump, as seen in various surveys. As one national survey from 2017 found, nearly half of Republicans agreed government should "shut down" media outlets deemed by Trump to be "broadcasting stories that are biased or inaccurate." Similarly, more than half of Republicans felt news outlets should be fined for reporting alleged falsehoods, and that the media are "the enemy of the people."[156]

A second sign of authoritarianism and fascism is expressed in the blind trust millions bestow on government officials as the primary means through which citizens become politically "informed." Three-quarters of Republicans said they trusted Trump more than *CNN*, the *New York Times*, and the *Washington Post*, to provide them with information. An equal number of Republicans say they trust Trump over conservative media, including the *National Review* and the *Weekly Standard*. More than half have greater trust for Trump than *Fox News*.[157] Millions believe they can get more accurate information about the political world from Trump's *Twitter* feed than from the media. The belief that legitimate news comes from Trump instead of from the news suggests many Americans would rather be propagandized than informed.

A third warning sign is evident via public support for the roll-back and destruction of American elections. Fifty-two percent of Republicans agreed that postponing the 2020 presidential election was acceptable if Trump said it was necessary to combat voter fraud. Similarly, 56 percent of Republicans agreed shutting down elections was acceptable if Congress agreed.[158] The concern with voter fraud preoccupied Trump since he lost the popular vote in 2016. Trump claimed the popular vote was stolen from him, despite failing to present evidence.[159] Voter fraud is rare in U.S. politics, contrary to Trump's claim.[160]

Finally, authoritarianism and fascism were apparent in Trump's attacks on the rule of law. In declaring a "national emergency" to confiscate federal funds for his border wall, he ignored Congress's power to determine how taxpayer dollars are allocated. The wall was justified under racist and xenophobic pretenses, via Trump's unsubstantiated claims that immigrants endanger national security via diseases, drugs, and rape, and by Trump and Donald Trump Jr.'s dehumanization of immigrants, comparing them to animals.[161] The national emergency was accompanied by the introduction of what were described as "dangerous" "concentration-camp"-style conditions in detention facilities, via the denial of legal representation, health care, and basic goods such as toothpaste and soap to unauthorized immigrants in detention.[162]

The rise of Trump's populism raises concerns for democracy. The power of the "creeping fascist" metaphor is that it does not frame the nation as fascist or not-fascist, but as falling into fascism incrementally as right-wing leaders and media push politics further to the right over time. While the rise of left-wing social movements and protest during the 2010s meant there was a countervailing power against creeping fascism, these movements had not yet succeeded by the late 2010s in building a broad-based coalition capable of keeping political power in Washington.

Conclusion

Trump supporters made possible a new form of anemic populism, which claims to channel the will of the people, but leaves citizens on the sidelines as spectators. Their political role is to validate the rise of elite right-wing political forces, led by a commander in chief who flirts with fascism and embraces prejudice. In the 2016 election, Trump supporters were more likely to be "low information voters," knowing less than others about politics, and mobilized by appeals to social and cultural bigotry.[163] These findings are problematic for those concerned with Trump's populism and the future of democracy. Poorly informed voters who make decisions based on prejudice and authoritarian values are difficult to trust as safeguards of the rule of law, when it comes to rolling back plutocracy, and in holding political leaders accountable for abuses of power. Despite the dangers associated with Trump's populism, the rise of leftist movements means there is still a check on reactionary political forces. With the ascendance of left- and right-wing populism in the last decade, American politics is more polarized. The problem of intensifying extremism, via the election of Trump and the rise of the "alt-right" white supremacy movement, translates into a growing authoritarian danger, with the specter of fascism undermining democratic freedoms.

Notes

1 Federico Finchelstein, *From Fascism to Populism in History* (Berkeley, CA: University of California Press, 2017).
2 Barry Eichengreen, *The Populist Temptation: Economic Grievance and Political Reaction in the Modern Era* (New York: Oxford University Press, 2018).
3 Elizabeth Sanders, *Roots of Reform: Farmers, Workers, and the American State, 1877–1917* (Chicago: University of Chicago Press, 1999).
4 Michael Kazin, *The Populist Persuasion: An American History* (Ithaca, NY: Cornell University Press, 2017): 28.
5 Kazin, *The Populist Persuasion*, 2017: 29–32.
6 Cas Mudde and Cristobal Rovira Kaltwasser, *Populism: A Very Short Introduction* (New York: Oxford University Press, 2017): 5.
7 Mudde and Kaltwasser, *Populism*, 2017: 6.
8 Mudde and Kaltwasser, *Populism*, 2017: 9.
9 Mudde and Kaltwasser, *Populism*, 2017.
10 William A. Galston, *Anti-Pluralism: The Populist Threat to Liberal Democracy* (New Haven, CT: Yale University Press, 2018): 35.
11 Mudde and Kaltwasser, *Populism*, 2017: 14.
12 Daniel White, "Bernie Sanders' Speech to Supporters," *Time*, June 17, 2016, http://time.com/4372673/bernie-sanders-speech-text-read-transcript/.
13 Hans-Georg Betz, *Radical Rightwing Populism in Western Europe* (New York: Palgrave, 1994); Daniel Stockemer, *The Front National in France: Continuity and Change under Jean-Marie Le Pen and Marine Le Pen* (New York: Springer, 2017); Eirikur Bergmann, *Nordic Nationalism and Rightwing Populist Politics: Imperial Relations and National Sentiments* (New York: Palgrave, 2016); Gabriella Lazaridis, *Understanding the Populist Shift: Othering in a Europe in Crisis* (New York: Routledge, 2016); Harold D. Clarke, Matthew Goodwin, and Paul Whiteley, *Brexit: Why Britain Voted to Leave the European Union* (New York: Cambridge University Press, 2017); Gabriella Lazaridis, *The Rise of the Far Right in Europe: Populist Shifts and "Othering"* (New York: Palgrave, 2016); Tjiske Akkerman, Sarah L. de Lange, and Matthijs Rooduijn, eds., *Radical Rightwing Populist Parties in Western Europe: Into the Mainstream?* (New York: Routledge, 2016); Ruth Wodak, *The Politics of Fear: What Rightwing Populist Discourses Mean* (Thousand Oaks, CA: Sage, 2015); Carlos de la Torre and Cynthia J. Arnson, eds., *Latin American Populism in the Twenty-First Century* (Baltimore, MD: Johns Hopkins University Press, 2013); Sebastian Edwards, *Left Behind: Latin America and the False Promise of Populism* (Chicago: University of Chicago Press, 2010); Federico Finchelstein, *The*

Ideological Origins of the Dirty War: Fascism, Populism, and Dictatorship in Twentieth Century Argentina (New York: Oxford University Press, 2017); Jeffery R. Webber, *From Rebellion to Reform in Bolivia: Class Struggle, Indigenous Liberation, and the Politics of Evo Morales* (Chicago: Haymarket Books, 2011); Eduardo Elena, *Dignifying Argentina, Peronism, Citizenship, and Mass Consumption* (Pittsburgh, PA: University of Pittsburgh Press, 2011); Ryan Brading, *Populism in Venezuela* (New York: Routledge, 2015); Robert R. Barr, *A Resurgence of Populism in Latin America* (New York: Lynne Rienner, 2017).

14 Mudde and Kaltwasser, *Populism*, 2017: 63; Kurt Weyland, "Clarifying a Contested Concept: Populism in the Study of Latin American Politics," *Comparative Politics* 34, no. 1 (2001): 1–22; Benjamin Moffit, *The Global Rise of Populism: Performance, Political Style, and Representation* (Stanford, CA: Stanford University Press, 2016).

15 Frank Newport and Lydia Saad, "Trump Support Built on Outsider Status, Business Experience," *Gallup*, March 4, 2016, http://news.gallup.com/poll/189773/trump-support-built-outsider-status-business-experience.aspx.

16 Nick Gass, "Donald Trump's Polling Obsession," *Politico*, December 10, 2015, https://www.politico.com/story/2015/12/trump-polls-216640.

17 Trevor Hughes, "Trump Calls to 'Drain the Swamp' of Washington," *USA Today*, October 18, 2016, https://www.usatoday.com/story/news/politics/elections/2016/2016/10/18/donald-trump-rally-colorado-springs-ethics-lobbying-limitations/92377656/; Jessica Estepa, "It's Not Just 'Rocket Man.' Trump has a Long History of Nicknaming His Foes," *USA Today*, September 21, 2017, https://www.usatoday.com/story/news/politics/onpolitics/2017/09/21/its-not-just-rocket-man-trump-has-long-history-nicknaming-his-foes/688552001/.

18 Moffitt, *The Global Rise of Populism*, 2016: 5.

19 Margaret Canovan, "People, Politicians, and Populism," *Government and Opposition* 19, no. 3 (1984): 312-327; Moffitt, *The Global Rise of Populism*, 2016, 98.

20 Tessa Stuart, "Who Is the Biggest Liar in the 2016 Election?", *Rolling Stone*, December 15, 2015, https://www.rollingstone.com/politics/news/ben-carson-donald-trump-are-the-least-truthful-candidates-20151215; Aaron Sharockman, "The Truth (So Far) behind the 2016 Campaign," *Politifact*, June 29, 2016, http://www.politifact.com/truth-o-meter/article/2016/jun/29/fact-checking-2016-clinton-trump/.

21 Galston, *Anti-Pluralism*, 2018: 34.

22 For the claim that left-wing populism is vital to empowerment and democracy, see: Lawrence Goodwyn, *Democratic Promise: The Populist Movement in America* (New York: Oxford University Press, 1976); and Ernesto Laclau and Chantal Mouffe, *Hegemony and Socialist Strategy: Towards a Radical Democratic Politics* (London: Verso, 1985). For a discussion of the dangers of right-wing populism as related to extremism, xenophobia, and antisemitism, see the classic work: Seymour Martin Lipset, *Political Man: The Social Bases of Politics* (Baltimore, MD: Johns Hopkins University Press, 1981).

23 Nicole Gaudiano, "6 Things to Know about Bernie Sanders," *USA Today*, April 29, 2015, https://www.usatoday.com/story/news/nation-now/2015/04/29/bernie-sanders-president-2016-vermont/26561211/.

24 Philip Bump, "How the Presidential Hopefuls Voted on Iraq – and Why It Matters," *Washington Post*, May 14, 2015, https://www.washington

post.com/news/the-fix/wp/2015/05/14/only-a-third-of-the-114th-congress-was-around-for-the-iraq-vote-but-a-lot-of-presidential-candidates-were/?noredirect=on&utm_term=.a80340d10436; Bernie Sanders, "Senate Approves Iraq Withdrawal, Sanders and Leahy Ask Bush to Reconsider Veto Threat," *Sanders.senate.gov*, March 29, 2007, https://www.sanders.senate.gov/newsroom/press-releases/senate-approves-iraq-withdrawal-sanders-and-leahy-ask-bush-to-reconsider-veto-threat.

25 U.S. Senate, "Vote Summary: H.R. 2 (Fair Minimum Wage Act of 2007)," *U.S. Senate*, January 24, 2007, https://www.senate.gov/legislative/LIS/roll_call_lists/roll_call_vote_cfm.cfm?congress=110&session=1&vote=00023; Derek Willis, "The Senate Votes that Divided Hillary Clinton and Bernie Sanders," *New York Times*, May 27, 2015, https://www.nytimes.com/2015/05/28/upshot/the-senate-votes-that-divided-hillary-clinton-and-bernie-sanders.html; Bernie Sanders, "Bernie Sanders 1999 Opposes Repeal of Glass-Steagall Act," *C-Span*, July 1, 1999, https://www.c-span.org/video/?c4570935/bernie-sanders-1999-opposes-repeal-glass-steagall-act; Will Cabaniss, "The Fact-Checker's Guide to Viral Graphics Contrasting Hillary Clinton, Bernie Sanders," *Politifact*, September 2, 2015, http://www.politifact.com/punditfact/article/2015/sep/02/11-examples-hillary-clinton-and-bernie-sanders-hol/.

26 Daniel White, "Read Bernie Sanders' Speech to Supporters," *Time*, June 17, 2016, http://time.com/4372673/bernie-sanders-speech-text-read-transcript/.

27 Bernie Sanders, *Bernie Sanders Guide to Political Revolution* (New York: Henry Holt, 2017); Anthony DiMaggio, "Sanders' Socialism: Neutering a Radical Tradition," *Counterpunch*, February 29, 2016, https://www.counterpunch.org/2016/02/29/sanders-socialism-neutering-a-radical-tradition/.

28 James Hohmann, "The Daily 202: Bernie Sanders has a Eugene V. Debs Problem," *Washington Post*, January 22, 2016, https://www.washingtonpost.com/news/powerpost/wp/2016/01/22/the-daily-202-bernie-sanders-has-a-eugene-v-debs-problem/?utm_term=.9aa98cab1a79.

29 Sam Frizell, "Here's How Bernie Sanders Explained Democratic Socialism," *Time*, November 19, 2015, http://time.com/4121126/bernie-sanders-democratic-socialism/; Kevin D. Williamson, "Bernie's Strange Brew of Nationalism and Socialism," *National Review*, July 20, 2015, https://www.nationalreview.com/2015/07/bernie-sanders-national-socialism/; Paul Starr, "Why Democrats Should Beware Sanders' Socialism," *Politico*, February 22, 2016, https://www.politico.com/magazine/story/2016/02/bernie-sanders-2016-socialism-213667; Marian Tupy, "Bernie Is Not a Socialist and America Is Not Capitalist," *The Atlantic*, March 1, 2016, https://www.theatlantic.com/international/archive/2016/03/bernie-sanders-democratic-socialism/471630/.

30 Eugene V. Debs, "Revolutionary Unionism," *Marxists.org*, November 25, 1905, https://www.marxists.org/archive/debs/works/1905/revunion.htm.

31 Debs, "Revolutionary Socialism," 1905.

32 Jeff Stein, "Here's the Full Text of Bernie Sanders's Iowa Speech," *Vox*, February 2, 2016, https://www.vox.com/2016/2/2/10892752/bernie-sanders-iowa-speech.

33 Stein, "Here's the Full Text of Bernie Sanders's Iowa Speech," 2016.

34 White, "Read Bernie Sanders' Speech to Supporters," 2016.

35 Patrick Marley, "Bernie Sanders Tells Madison Crowd He Seeks 'Political Revolution,'" *Milwaukee Journal Sentinel*, July 1, 2015, http://archive.

jsonline.com/news/statepolitics/bernie-sanders-tells-madison-crowd-he-seeks-political-revolution-b99530702z1-311345541.html/.
36 John Nichols, "Bernie Sanders Talk about His Distaste for Scott Walker and His Respect for Bob La Follette," *The Cap Times*, March 29, 2016, https://madison.com/ct/news/opinion/column/john_nichols/john-nichols-bernie-sanders-talks-about-his-distaste-for-scott/article_876dbc90-e141-5c69-a5a7-49159551f8d2.html.
37 Kate Linthicum, "Occupy Movement Protesters Fight on – Now in Support of Bernie Sanders," *Los Angeles Times*, February 1, 2016, http://www.latimes.com/nation/politics/la-na-0201-sanders-occupy-20160201-story.html.
38 Will Drabold, "Read Bernie Sanders' Speech at the Democratic Convention," *Time*, July 26, 2016, http://time.com/4421574/democratic-convention-bernie-sanders-speech-transcript/.
39 Sanders, *Bernie Sanders Guide to Political Revolution*, 2017: 27.
40 Bernie Sanders, "Labor Day: Bernie Sanders Fights for $15," *Fight for 15*, 2017, https://fightfor15.org/labor-day-bernie-sanders-video-splash-page/.
41 Thomas E. Patterson, "News Coverage of the 2016 Presidential Primaries: Horse Race Reporting Has Consequences," *Shorenstein Center on Media, Politics, and Public Policy/Media Tenor*, July 2016, https://shorensteincenter.org/news-coverage-2016-presidential-primaries/.
42 *Pew Research Center*, "American Trends Panel Wave, November 2016," November 29–December 12, 2016. No relationship is observed, after controlling for respondents' gender, age, education, race, income, political party, and ideology.
43 Niv Elis, "Sanders Blasts GOP Push to Increase Military Spending," *The Hill*, September 21, 2017, http://thehill.com/policy/finance/351765-sanders-blasts-gop-push-to-increase-military-spending.
44 Christopher H. Achen and Larry M. Bartels, "Do Sanders Supporters Favor His Policies?", *New York Times*, May 23, 2016, https://www.nytimes.com/2016/05/23/opinion/campaign-stops/do-sanders-supporters-favor-his-policies.html.
45 Kshama Sawant, "Hillary Was Nowhere to Be Seen in the Fight for 15 – I Should Know," *The Nation*, April 18, 2016, https://www.thenation.com/article/hillary-was-nowhere-to-be-seen-in-the-fight-for-15-i-should-know/.
46 Michael A. Memoli, "Hillary Clinton Once Called TPP the 'Gold Standard.' Here's Why, and What She Says about the Trade Deal Now," *Los Angeles Times*, September 26, 2016, http://www.latimes.com/politics/la-na-pol-trade-tpp-20160926-snap-story.html.
47 Daniel Marans, "Bernie Sanders Struggled with Black Voters. His Campaign is Working Overtime to Fix that," *Huffington Post*, March 6, 2019, https://www.huffpost.com/entry/bernie-sanders-black-voters_n_5c7ec096e4b0e62f69e71c49.
48 Nicole Gaudiano, "Sen. Bernie Sanders: 'I Am an Independent,'" *USA Today*, October 23, 2017, https://www.usatoday.com/story/news/politics/onpolitics/2017/10/23/bernie-sanders-i-am-an-independent/792186001/.
49 Jeff Stein, "Sanders Is Beating Obama's 2008 Youth Vote Record. And the Primary's Not Even over," *Vox*, June 2, 2016, https://www.vox.com/2016/6/2/11818320/bernie-sanders-barack-obama-2008.
50 Anthony DiMaggio, "Youth in Revolt: Why Millennials Are the Key to Future Social Transformation," *Truthout*, September 16, 2017, http://www.truth-out.org/opinion/item/41951-youth-in-revolt-why-millennials-are-the-key-to-future-social-transformation.

220 *Populism in the 2016 Election*

51 Frank Newport, "The Meaning of 'Socialism' to Americans Today," *Gallup*, October 4, 2018, https://news.gallup.com/opinion/polling-matters/243362/meaning-socialism-americans-today.aspx.
52 DiMaggio, "Youth in Revolt," 2017.
53 Nate Silver, "Was the Democratic Primary a Close Call or a Landslide?", *FiveThirtyEight*, July 27, 2016, http://fivethirtyeight.com/features/was-the-democratic-primary-a-close-call-or-a-landslide/.
54 Katie Reilly, "Read Bernie Sanders' Speech Vowing to Continue His Nomination Fight," *Time*, June 8, 2016, http://time.com/4361146/bernie-sanders-democratic-primary-speech-transcript/.
55 Harvard University, "Young Americans' Attitudes toward Politics and Public Service Survey," *iPoll*, October 30–November 9, 2016.
56 *CBS News*, "CBS News Poll, November 2015," *iPoll*, November 14, 2015.
57 Bloomberg, "Bloomberg Poll, November 2015," *iPoll*, November 15–17, 2015.
58 CNBC, "CNBC All-America Economic Survey, March 2016," *iPoll*, March 21–24, 2016.
59 Harvard University, "Young Americans' Attitudes toward Politics and Public Service Survey," 2016.
60 CNN, "CNN/ORC International Poll, January 2016," *iPoll*, January 21–24, 2016.
61 Polling Report, "CNN Poll, January 2016," *Pollingreport.com*, January 21–24, 2016, http://www.pollingreport.com/trump_fav.htm; Polling Report, "CNN/ORC Poll, October 2016," *Pollingreport.com*, October 20–23, 2016, http://www.pollingreport.com/hrc.htm.
62 Nika Knight, "For First Time Ever, Majority of House Democrats Support 'Medicare-for-All' Bill," *Common Dreams*, April 27, 2017, https://www.commondreams.org/news/2017/04/27/first-time-ever-majority-house-dems-support-medicare-all-bill; Bernie Sanders, "17 Senators Introduce Medicare for All Act," *Sanders.senate.gov*, September 13, 2017, https://www.sanders.senate.gov/newsroom/press-releases/17-senators-introduce-medicare-for-all-act.
63 Ledyard King, "Biggest Obstacle to Passage of Green New Deal? Democratic Lawmakers," *USA Today*, March 20, 2019, https://readersupportednews.org/news-section2/318-66/55589-focus-biggest-obstacle-to-passage-of-green-new-deal-democratic-lawmakers.
64 Frances Fox Piven and Richard Cloward, *Poor People's Movements: How They Succeed, Why They Fail* (New York: Vintage, 1978): 32.
65 Jennifer Calfas, "President Trump's Net Worth Tumbled Last Year: Here's What Changed," *Time*, March 6, 2018, http://time.com/money/5188095/donald-trump-net-worth-2018/.
66 Gregory Krieg, "14 of Trump's Most Outrageous 'Birther' Claims – Half from after 2011," *CNN.com*, September 16, 2016, https://www.cnn.com/2016/09/09/politics/donald-trump-birther/index.html.
67 Gregory Krieg, "It's Official: Clinton Swamps Trump in Popular Vote," *CNN.com*, December 22, 2016, https://www.cnn.com/2016/12/21/politics/donald-trump-hillary-clinton-popular-vote-final-count/index.html.
68 Nina Burleigh, "Trump Speaks at a Fourth-Grade Level, Lowest of Last 15 U.S. Presidents, New Analysis Finds," *Newsweek*, January 8, 2018, http://www.newsweek.com/trump-fire-and-fury-smart-genius-obama-774169.
69 Matthew Nussbaum, "The Definitive Trump-Russia Timeline of Events," *Politico*, March 3, 2017, https://www.politico.com/trump-russia-ties-scandal-guide/timeline-of-events.

70 Donald J. Trump, "I will be announcing my decision on Paris Accord, Thursday at 3:00 P.M. The White House Rose Garden. MAKE AMERICA GREAT AGAIN!", *Twitter.com*, May 31, 2017, https://twitter.com/realdonaldtrump/status/870083798981111808?lang=en.
71 Donald J. Trump, "I love the White House, one of the most beautiful buildings (homes) I have ever seen. But Fake News said I called it a dump - TOTALLY UNTRUE," *Twitter.com*, August 2, 2017, https://twitter.com/realdonaldtrump/status/892920397162848257?lang=en.
72 Donald J. Trump, "Crooked Hillary said that I want guns brought into the school classroom. Wrong!", *Twitter.com*, May 21, 2016, https://twitter.com/realdonaldtrump/status/734231223002894337?lang=en.
73 Rebecca Kaplan, "Donald Trump: 'I Will Be Phenomenal to Women,'" *Face the Nation*, August 9, 2015, https://www.cbsnews.com/news/donald-trump-i-will-be-phenomenal-to-the-women/.
74 Anderson Cooper, "Interview with Donald Trump," *Anderson Cooper 360 Degrees*, July 22, 2015, http://www.cnn.com/TRANSCRIPTS/1507/22/acd.01.html.
75 Andy Buchanan, "30 of Donald Trump's Wildest Quotes: On Winning," *CBSnews.com*, June 2015, https://www.cbsnews.com/pictures/wild-donald-trump-quotes/25/.
76 Donald J. Trump, "'I Have the Best Words,'" *Washington Post*, April 5, 2017, https://www.washingtonpost.com/video/trump-i-have-the-best-words/2017/04/05/53a9ae4a-19fd-11e7-8598-9a99da559f9e_video.html.
77 Anthony DiMaggio, "Fascism Here We Come: The Rise of the Reactionary Right and the Collapse of the Left," *Counterpunch*, August 15, 2017, https://www.counterpunch.org/2017/08/15/fascism-here-we-come-the-rise-of-the-reactionary-right-and-the-collapse-of-the-left/; Julian Joyce, "Trump, Twitter, and His 'Filter Bubble,'" *BBC News*, November 30, 2017, http://www.bbc.com/news/world-us-canada-42187596.
78 Jim Tankersley and Ana Swanson, "Donald Trump Is Assembling the Richest Administration in Modern American History," *Washington Post*, November 30, 2016, https://www.washingtonpost.com/news/wonk/wp/2016/11/30/donald-trump-is-assembling-the-richest-administration-in-modern-american-history/?utm_term=.ecc8b1ef4b37.
79 Tessa Berenson, "Read Donald Trump's Speech on Jobs and the Economy," *Time*, September 15, 2016, http://time.com/4495507/donald-trump-economy-speech-transcript/.
80 Heather Long, "Trump Vows 25 Million Jobs, Most of Any President," *CNN.com*, January 20, 2017, http://money.cnn.com/2017/01/20/news/economy/donald-trump-jobs-wages/index.html.
81 Donald J. Trump, "The Inaugural Address," *WhiteHouse.gov*, January 20, 2017, https://www.whitehouse.gov/briefings-statements/the-inaugural-address/.
82 Astead W. Herndon, "Trump Promised to 'Drain the Swamp.' So What's Happening with His Cabinet?", *Boston Globe*, April 16, 2018, https://www.bostonglobe.com/news/politics/2018/04/16/trump-promised-drain-swamp-what-happening-with-his-cabinet/7AzbPVU8rV4cAXwTAwB5dM/story.html.
83 Tami Luhby, "32 Million People Would Lose Coverage If Obamacare Was Repealed," *CNN.com*, June 30, 2017, http://money.cnn.com/2017/06/30/news/economy/obamacare-repeal-trump/index.html.
84 Marc Morial, "Trump's Tax Cuts Are a Feast for Wealthy and Gruel for Working Families," *The Hill*, November 21, 2017, http://thehill.com/opin

ion/finance/361378-trumps-tax-cuts-are-a-feast-for-wealthy-and-gruel-for-working-families.
85 Dan Merica, "At a Navajo Veterans' Event, Trump Makes 'Pocahontas' Crack," *CNN.com*, November 28, 2017, https://www.cnn.com/2017/11/27/politics/trump-pocahontas-navajo-code-talkers/index.html.
86 David Leonhardt and Ian Prasad Philbrick, "Donald Trump's Racism: The Definitive List," *New York Times*, January 15, 2018, https://www.nytimes.com/interactive/2018/01/15/opinion/leonhardt-trump-racist.html; Patrick Wintour, Jason Burke, and Anna Livsey, "'There's No Other Word But Racist': Trump's Global Rebuke for 'Shithole' Remark," *The Guardian*, January 13, 2018, https://www.theguardian.com/us-news/2018/jan/12/unkind-divisive-elitist-international-outcry-over-trumps-shithole-countries-remark.
87 Leonhardt and Philbrick, "Donald Trump's Racism," 2018.
88 Z. Byron Wolf, "Trump Blasts 'Breeding' in Sanctuary Cities. That's a Racist Term," *CNN.com*, April 25, 2018, https://www.cnn.com/2018/04/18/politics/donald-trump-immigrants-california/index.html; Eric Bradner, "Trump Retweets Fake, Racially Charged Crime Data from Non-Existent Group," *CNN.com*, November 23, 2015, https://www.cnn.com/2015/11/22/politics/donald-trump-black-crime-police-retweet/; Julie Hirschfeld Davis, "Trump Calls Some Unauthorized Immigrants 'Animals' in Rant," *New York Times*, May 16, 2018, https://www.nytimes.com/2018/05/16/us/politics/trump-undocumented-immigrants-animals.html; Melissa Chan, "Donald Trump Refuses to Condemn KKK, Disavow David Duke Endorsement," *Time*, February 28, 2016, http://time.com/4240268/donald-trump-kkk-david-duke/; Leonhardt and Philbrick, "Donald Trump's Racism," 2018.
89 Krieg, "14 of Trump's Most Outrageous 'Birther' Claims – Half From after 2011," 2016.
90 Tal Kopan, "What Donald Trump Has Said about Mexico and Vice Versa," *CNN.com*, August 31, 2016, https://www.cnn.com/2016/08/31/politics/donald-trump-mexico-statements/index.html.
91 Jenna Johnson and Abigail Hauslohner, "'I Think Islam Hates Us': A Timeline of Trump's Comments about Islam and Muslims," *Washington Post*, May 20, 2017, https://www.washingtonpost.com/news/post-politics/wp/2017/05/20/i-think-islam-hates-us-a-timeline-of-trumps-comments-about-islam-and-muslims/?utm_term=.dd96ecd05cb2; Jenna Johnson, "Trump Calls for 'Total and Complete Shutdown of Muslims Entering the United States,'" *Washington Post*, December 8, 2015, https://www.washingtonpost.com/news/post-politics/wp/2015/12/07/donald-trump-calls-for-total-and-complete-shutdown-of-muslims-entering-the-united-states/?utm_term=.c87bb936eeff; Elizabeth Landers, "Trump Retweets Anti-Muslim Videos," *CNN.com*, November 30, 2017, https://www.cnn.com/2017/11/29/politics/donald-trump-retweet-jayda-fransen/index.html; Lauren Carroll, "Fact-Checking Trump's Claim that Thousands in New Jersey Cheered When World Trade Center Tumbled," *Politifact*, November 22, 2015, http://www.politifact.com/truth-o-meter/statements/2015/nov/22/donald-trump/fact-checking-trumps-claim-thousands-new-jersey-ch/.
92 Donald J. Trump, "Transcript: Donald Trump's Taped Comments about Women," *New York Times*, October 8, 2016, https://www.nytimes.com/2016/10/08/us/donald-trump-tape-transcript.html.
93 Maya Rhodan, "Trump Is Threatening to 'Take Away' Reporters' Credentials. He Told TIME He Wouldn't Do that," *Time*, May 9, 2018, http://time.com/5270968/donald-trump-reporters-credentials-media/; Julie

Hirschfield Davis and Michael M. Grynbaum, "Trump Intensifies His Attacks on Journalists and Condemns F.B.I. 'Leakers,'" *New York Times*, February 24, 2017, https://www.nytimes.com/2017/02/24/us/politics/white-house-sean-spicer-briefing.html.

94 Mallory Shelbourne, "Tapper Mocks Team Trump on 'Alternative Facts,'" *The Hill*, January 23, 2017, http://thehill.com/homenews/media/315723-tapper-mocks-team-trump-on-alternative-facts; Libby Nelson, "Anderson Cooper Asked Donald Trump 4 Times about His Sexual Assault Bragging. Trump Kept Dodging," *Vox*, October 9, 2016, https://www.vox.com/2016/10/9/13222094/donald-trump-presidential-debate-leaked-tape-questions.

95 Tom Kertscher, "The Final Five – on the Truth-o-Meter," *Politifact*, March 27, 2016, http://www.politifact.com/wisconsin/article/2016/mar/27/final-five-truth-o-meter/.

96 Thomas E. Patterson, "Coverage of the 2016 General Election: How the Press Failed the Voters," *Shorenstein Center on Media, Politics, and Public Policy/Media Tenor*, December 2016, https://shorensteincenter.org/wp-content/uploads/2016/12/2016-General-Election-News-Coverage-1.pdf?x78124.

97 Nicholas Confessore and Karen Yourish, "$2 Billion Worth of Free Media for Donald Trump," *New York Times*, March 15, 2016, https://www.nytimes.com/2016/03/16/upshot/measuring-donald-trumps-mammoth-advantage-in-free-media.html.

98 Anthony DiMaggio, "Bigotry for Profit and 'Fun': Traversing the Wasteland of U.S. Election News," *Counterpunch*, October 10, 2016, https://www.counterpunch.org/2016/10/10/87468/.

99 Paul Bond, "Leslie Moonves on Donald Trump: 'It May Not Be Good for America, But It's Damn Good for CBS," *Hollywood Reporter*, February 29, 2016, https://www.hollywoodreporter.com/news/leslie-moonves-donald-trump-may-871464.

100 Using the *Nexis Uni* database, I searched for all English language articles in North America, and operating out of American states, that referenced "Donald Trump." Of that universe of stories, I then tabulated how many pieces included a reference to Trump within 25 words of discussions of "populism" or "populist" politics, to "insurgency" or "insurgent" politics, to "grassroots" politics and "rebellion," to the "Tea Party," to "anti-establishment" or anti-"Republican establishment" politics, and finally references to the "working-class" or "white working-class."

101 Michael McQuarrie, "The Revolt of the Rust Belt: Place and Politics in the Age of Anger," *British Journal of Sociology* 68, no. 1 (2017): 120–152; Stephen L. Morgan and Jiwon Lee, "The White Working Class and Voter Turnout in U.S. Presidential Elections, 2004–2016," *Sociological Science* 4 (2017): 656–685; Stephen L. Morgan and Jiwon Lee, "Trump Voters and the White Working Class," *Sociological Science* 5 (2018): 234–245; Justin Gest, *The New Minority: White Working Class Politics in an Age of Immigration and Inequality* (New York: Oxford University Press, 2016).

102 Ronald Brownstein, "The Billionaire Candidate and His Blue-Collar Following," *The Atlantic*, September 11, 2015, https://www.theatlantic.com/politics/archive/2015/09/the-billionaire-candidate-and-his-blue-collar-following/432783/; Claire Cain Miller, "What Donald Trump Might Do for Working-Class Families," *New York Times*, November 29, 2016, https://www.nytimes.com/2016/11/29/upshot/what-donald-trump-might-do-for-working-class-families.html.

103 Damian Paletta and David Nakamura, "Rallying Blue-Collar Workers in Cincinnati, Trump Blames Democrats for Obstructing His Agenda," *Washington Post*, June 7, 2017, https://www.washingtonpost.com/politics/rallying-blue-collar-workers-in-cincinnati-trump-blames-democrats-for-obstructing-his-agenda/2017/06/07/af92c186-4baa-11e7-bc1b-fddbd8359dee_story.html?utm_term=.cfeddf7a502f.

104 Matt Flegenheimer and Michael Barbaro, "Donald Trump Is Elected in Stunning Repudiation of the Establishment," *New York Times*, November 9, 2016, https://www.nytimes.com/2016/11/09/us/politics/hillary-clinton-donald-trump-president.html; Brownstein, "The Billionaire Candidate and His Blue-Collar Following," 2015.

105 Tucker Carlson, "Donald Trump Is Shocking, Vulgar, and Right," *Politico*, January 28, 2016, https://www.politico.com/magazine/story/2016/01/donald-trump-is-shocking-vulgar-and-right-213572.

106 Rush Limbaugh, "The Establishment Is Out to Get Trump and Every Day Is a Trap," *Rushlimbaugh.com*, February 20, 2018, https://www.rushlimbaugh.com/daily/2018/02/20/the-establishment-is-gunning-for-trump-and-every-day-is-a-trap/.

107 *CNN.com*, "Sean Hannity's 'Bromance' with Trump," *Anderson Cooper 360*, https://www.cnn.com/videos/politics/2018/04/17/sean-hannity-trump-relationship-kaye-pkg-ac.cnn/video/playlists/fox-news-host-sean-hannity/.

108 Rebecca Savransky, "Hannity: GOP Is a 'Dead Party,'" *The Hill*, December 5, 2017, http://thehill.com/homenews/media/363320-hannity-gop-is-dead-party.

109 Jason Stahl, *Right Moves: The Conservative Think Tank in American Political Culture since 1945* (Chapel Hill, NC: University of North Carolina Press, 2016).

110 Brian Stelter, "White House Press Secretary Attacks Media for Accurately Reporting Inauguration Crowds," *CNN.com*, January 21, 2017, http://money.cnn.com/2017/01/21/media/sean-spicer-press-secretary-statement/index.html; Anthony DiMaggio, "Media Ban! Making Sense of the War between Trump and the Press," *Counterpunch*, February 27. 2017, https://www.counterpunch.org/2017/02/27/media-ban-making-sense-of-the-war-between-trump-and-the-press/; Anthony DiMaggio, "Journalism under Assault: Trump's Crackdown on the News, and Where We Go from Here," *Counterpunch*, August 7, 2017, https://www.counterpunch.org/2017/08/07/journalism-under-assault-trumps-crackdown-on-the-news-and-where-we-go-from-here/.

111 Tami Luhby, "The Middle Class Gets a Big Raise … Finally!", *CNN.com*, September 13, 2016, http://money.cnn.com/2016/09/13/news/economy/median-income-census/index.html.

112 Lawrence C. Hamilton, "On Renewable Energy and Climate, Trump Voters Stand Apart," *University of New Hampshire Carsey Reseach*, Winter 2017, https://scholars.unh.edu/cgi/viewcontent.cgi?referer=&httpsredir=1&article=1292&context=carsey.

113 Samantha Smith, "6 Charts that Show Where Clinton and Trump Supporters Differ," *Pew Research Center*, October 20, 2016, http://www.pewresearch.org/fact-tank/2016/10/20/6-charts-that-show-where-clinton-and-trump-supporters-differ/.

114 Anthony DiMaggio, "White Supremacist America: Trump and the 'Return' of Rightwing Hate Culture," *Counterpunch*, September 16, 2016, https://

www.counterpunch.org/2016/09/16/white-supremacist-america-trump-and-the-return-of-right-wing-hate-culture/.
115 DiMaggio, "White Supremacist America," 2016.
116 DiMaggio, "White Supremacist America," 2016.
117 DiMaggio, "White Supremacist America," 2016.
118 German Lopez, "Polls Show Many – Even Most – Trump Supporters Really Are Deeply Hostile to Muslims and Nonwhites," *Vox*, September 12, 2016, https://www.vox.com/2016/9/12/12882796/trump-supporters-racist-deplorables; DiMaggio, "White Supremacist America," 2016.
119 Catherine Lucey, "Clinton Says 'Deplorables' Comment Is 'Grossly Generalistic,'" *Associated Press*, September 11, 2016, https://www.apnews.com/97d6e5c7188845888bba36957160b675.
120 Mariah Blake, "Mad Men: Inside the Men's Rights Movement – and the Army of Misogynists and Trolls It Spawned," *Mother Jones*, January/February 2015, https://www.motherjones.com/politics/2015/01/warren-farrell-mens-rights-movement-feminism-misogyny-trolls/.
121 Income is not a significant predictor of attitudes toward Trump in the August 2016 *Pew* survey, after controlling for respondents' gender, age, education, race, ideology, and political party. Other research into the early Trump years finds, for example in numerous polls from 2018, that income was also statistically unrelated to Trump support. See: Anthony DiMaggio, "The 'Trump Recovery': Behind Right-Wing Populism's Radical Transformation," *Counterpunch*, August 9, 2019, https://www.counterpunch.org/2019/08/09/the-trump-recovery-behind-right-wing-populisms-radical-transformation/.
122 Morgan and Lee, "Trump Voters and the White Working Class," 2018.
123 In *ABC News'* March 2016 poll, identification with a working-class status is significantly associated with one's income level, after controlling for respondents' gender, age, education, race, political party, and ideology.
124 Richard Florida, "The Geography of the Republican Primaries," *CityLab*, April 12, 2016, https://www.citylab.com/equity/2016/04/the-geography-of-the-republican-primaries/477693/.
125 Caroline Freund, "The Working Class's Role in Trump's Election," *Vox*, June 1, 2017, https://voxeu.org/article/working-class-s-role-trump-s-election.
126 Jonathan Rothwell, "Economic Hardship and Favorable Views of Trump," *Gallup*, July 22, 2016, https://news.gallup.com/opinion/polling-matters/193898/economic-hardship-favorable-views-trump.aspx; Jonathan T. Rothwell and Pablo Diego-Rosell, "Explaining Nationalist Political Views: The Case of Donald Trump," *SSRN*, August 15, 2016, https://papers.ssrn.com/sol3/papers.cfm?abstract_id=2822059.
127 Konstantin Kilibarda and Daria Roithmayr, "The Myth of the Rust Belt Revolt: Donald Trump Didn't Flip Working-Class White Voters. Hillary Clinton Lost Them," *Slate*, December 1, 2016, http://www.slate.com/articles/news_and_politics/politics/2016/12/the_myth_of_the_rust_belt_revolt.html.
128 The relationship between feelings that free trade has hurt individuals and their families and support for Trump is statistically significant at the 0.1 percent level, after controlling for respondents' gender, age, race, education, income, ideology, and political party.
129 Heather Long, "U.S. Has Lost 5 Million Manufacturing Jobs since 2000," *CNN.com*, March 29, 2016, http://money.cnn.com/2016/03/29/news/economy/us-manufacturing-jobs/index.html.

130 Gallup, "Donald Trump Job Approval by Party Identification," *Gallup.com*, January 29–February 4, 2018, http://news.gallup.com/poll/203198/presidential-approval-ratings-donald-trump.aspx.

131 *Pew Research Center*, "Positive Views of Economy Surge, Driven by Major Shifts among Republicans," March 22, 2018, http://www.people-press.org/2018/03/22/positive-views-of-economy-surge-driven-by-major-shifts-among-republicans/.

132 David Norman Smith and Eric Hanley, "The Anger Games: Who Voted for Donald Trump in the 2016 Election," *Critical Sociology* 44, no. 2 (2018): 195–212; Brian F. Schaffner, Matthew MacWilliams, and Tatishe Nteta, "Understanding White Polarization in the 2016 Vote for President: The Sobering Role of Racism and Sexism," *Political Science Quarterly*, 133, no. 1 (2018): 9–34; Alan I. Abramowitz, "It Wasn't the Economy Stupid: Racial Polarization, White Racial Resentment, and the Rise of Trump," in *Trumped: The 2016 Election that Broke All the Rules*, eds. Larry Sabato, Kyle Kondik, and Geoffrey Skelley (Lanham, MD: Rowman & Littlefield, 2017); Nicholas Carnes and Noam Lupu, "It's Time to Best the Myth: Most Trump Voters Were Not Working Class," *Washington Post*, June 5, 2017, https://www.washingtonpost.com/news/monkey-cage/wp/2017/06/05/its-time-to-bust-the-myth-most-trump-voters-were-not-working-class/?utm_term=.45f7d2197ad1; Niraj Chokshi, "Trump Voters Driven by Fear of Losing Status, Not Economic Anxiety, Study Finds," *New York Times*, April 24, 2018, https://www.nytimes.com/2018/04/24/us/politics/trump-economic-anxiety.html; Daniel Cox, Rachel Lienesch, and Robert P. Jones, "Beyond Economics: Fears of Cultural Displacement Pushed the White Working Class to Trump," *Public Religion Research Institute*, May 9, 2017, https://www.prri.org/research/white-working-class-attitudes-economy-trade-immigration-election-donald-trump/; Jeff Manza and Ned Crowley, "Ethnonationalism and the Rise of Donald Trump," *Contexts*, 17, no. 1 (2018): 28–33; Richard C. Fording and Sanford F. Schram, "The Cognitive and Emotional Sources of Trump Support: The Case of Low-Information Voters," *New Political Science* 39, no. 4 (2017): 670–686; Anthony DiMaggio, "Election Con 2016: New Evidence Demolishes the Myth of Trump's 'Blue-Collar' Populism," *Counterpunch*, June 16, 2017, https://www.counterpunch.org/2017/06/16/93450/; Anthony DiMaggio, "Donald Trump and the Myth of Economic Populism: Demolishing a False Narrative," *Counterpunch*, August 16, 2016, https://www.counterpunch.org/2016/08/16/donald-trump-and-the-myth-of-economic-populism-demolishing-a-false-narrative/; Tyler T. Reny, Loren Collingwood, and Ali Venanzuela, "Vote Switching in the 2016 Election: How Racial and Immigration Attitudes, Not Economics, Explains Shifts in White Voting," *Public Opinion Quarterly*, 83 (1) 2019: 91–113.

133 For the March 2016 *Pew* survey, the relationship between dissatisfaction with one's finances and support for Trump is statistically significant at the 1 percent level, after controlling for respondents' gender, age, education, race, income, ideology, and political party.

134 Jon Huang, Samuel Jacoby, Michael Strickland, and K. K. Rebecca Lai, "Election 2016: Exit Polls," *New York Times*, November 8, 2016, https://www.nytimes.com/interactive/2016/11/08/us/politics/election-exit-polls.html.

135 Gest, *The New Minority*, 2016.

136 DiMaggio, "The 'Trump Recovery,'" 2019.

137 DiMaggio, "The 'Trump Recovery,'" 2019.
138 Glenn Kessler, "President Trump's Repeated Claim: 'The Greatest Economy in the History of Our Country,'" *Washington Post*, September 7, 2018, https://www.washingtonpost.com/politics/2018/09/07/president-trumps-repeated-claim-greatest-economy-history-our-country/.
139 Diana Mutz, "Status Threat, Not Economic Hardship, Explains the 2016 Presidential Vote," *Proeedings of the National Academy of Sciences of the United States of America*, April 23, 2018, 1–10.
140 DiMaggio, "The 'Trump Recovery,'" 2019.
141 In this survey, Trump support was measured by a survey question that asked Americans whether they were willing to vote for Trump for president, or whether they were against voting for him.
142 DiMaggio, "The 'Trump Recovery,'" 2019.
143 Figure 4.21 is a composite representation of two different regressions I ran, one for all Americans, and one for white Americans, in terms of assessing their levels of economic anxiety and support for Trump. For simplicity's sake, I combine the results into one table, making it easier to consider all of my findings at once.
144 Henry A. Giroux, *American Nightmare: Facing the Challenge of Fascism* (San Francisco, CA: City Lights, 2018); Henry A. Giroux, *The Public in Peril: Trump and the Menace of American Authoritarianism* (New York: Routledge, 2017); Paul L. Street, "American Style Totalitarianism in the Age of Trump," *Truthdig*, December 22, 2017, https://www.paulstreet.org/american-style-totalitarianism-age-trump/; Anthony DiMaggio, "Fascism Here We Come: The Rise of the Reactionary Right and the Collapse of the Left," *Counterpunch*, August 15, 2017, https://www.counterpunch.org/2017/08/15/fascism-here-we-come-the-rise-of-the-reactionary-right-and-the-collapse-of-the-left/.
145 For a severe misrepresentation of fascism, see: Jonah Goldberg, *Liberal Fascism: The Secret History of the American Left, from Mussolini to the Politics of Change* (New York: Crown Forum, 2009).
146 Alexander Reid Ross, *Against the Fascist Creep* (Oakland, CA: AK Press, 2017).
147 Eric Bradner, "Conway: Trump White House Offered 'Alternative Facts' on Crowd Size," *CNN.com*, January 23, 2017, https://www.cnn.com/2017/01/22/politics/kellyanne-conway-alternative-facts/index.html.
148 Sabrina Siddiqui, "Trump Press Ban: BBC, CNN, and Guardian Denied Access to Briefing," *The Guardian*, February 25, 2017, https://www.theguardian.com/us-news/2017/feb/24/media-blocked-white-house-briefing-sean-spicer.
149 Joanna Walters, "'Trump Has Declared War': Journalists Denounce Any Attack on Press Freedom," *The Guardian*, May 21, 2017, https://www.theguardian.com/us-news/2017/may/21/trump-threat-reporters-press-freedom.
150 Chuck Todd, "Will Donald Trump Pay Supporter's Legal Fees?", *NBC News*, March 13, 2016, https://www.nbcnews.com/meet-the-press/video/will-donald-trump-pay-supporter-s-legal-fees-643448899613.
151 William Cummings, "'Only in the Panhandle,' Trump Chuckles When Audience Member Suggests Shooting Migrants," *USA Today*, May 10, 2019, https://www.usatoday.com/story/news/politics/onpolitics/2019/05/09/trump-chuckles-shooting-migrants/1150160001/.
152 Eric Levitz, "Donald Trump Misses the 'Old Days' When You Were Allowed to Beat up Protesters," *New York Daily Intelligencer*, February 23,

2016, http://nymag.com/daily/intelligencer/2016/02/trump-on-protester-id-like-to-punch-his-face.html.
153 Rosie Gray, "Trump Defends White-Nationalist Protesters: 'Some Very Fine People on Both Sides,'" *The Atlantic*, August 15, 2017, https://www.theatlantic.com/politics/archive/2017/08/trump-defends-white-nationalist-protesters-some-very-fine-people-on-both-sides/537012/.
154 Anthony DiMaggio, "The Shutdown as Fascist Creep: Profiling Right-Wing Extremism in America," *Counterpunch*, January 4, 2019, https://www.counterpunch.org/2019/01/04/the-shutdown-as-fascist-creep-profiling-right-wing-extremism-in-america/.
155 Smith and Hanley, "The Anger Games," 2018; Matthew MacWilliams, "The One Weird Trait that Predicts Whether You're a Trump Supporter," *Politico*, January 17, 2016, https://www.politico.com/magazine/story/2016/01/donald-trump-2016-authoritarian-213533.
156 *The Economist*, "Most Republicans Trust the President More than They Trust the Media," August 3, 2017, https://www.economist.com/news/united-states/21725822-there-also-broad-support-shutting-down-outlets-perceived-biased-most-republicans.
157 *The Economist*, "Most Republicans Trust the President More than They Trust the Media," 2017.
158 *CBS*, "Poll: Majority of Republicans Would Back 2020 Election Delay If Trump Proposed It," *Face the Nation*, August 10, 2017, https://www.cbsnews.com/news/poll-majority-of-gop-would-back-2020-election-delay-if-trump-proposed-it/.
159 Michael Tackett and Michael Wines, "Trump Disbands Commission on Voter Fraud," *New York Times*, January 3, 2018, https://www.nytimes.com/2018/01/03/us/politics/trump-voter-fraud-commission.html.
160 Robert Schlesinger, "The Voter Fraud Fraud," *US News and World Report*, May 5, 2017, https://www.usnews.com/opinion/thomas-jefferson-street/articles/2017-05-05/study-finds-little-voter-fraud-evidence-in-key-2016-jurisdictions; Brennan Center for Justice, "Debunking the Voter Fraud Myth," January 31, 2017, https://www.brennancenter.org/analysis/debunking-voter-fraud-myth.
161 Michelle Ye Hee Lee, "Donald Trump's False Comments Connecting Mexican Immigrants and Crime," *Washington Post*, July 8, 2015, https://www.washingtonpost.com/news/fact-checker/wp/2015/07/08/donald-trumps-false-comments-connecting-mexican-immigrants-and-crime/?utm_term=.65253adf2c0c; Abigail Simon, "People Are Angry President Trump Used This Word to Describe Undocumented Immigrants," *Time*, June 19, 2018, http://time.com/5316087/donald-trump-immigration-infest/; Jessica Durando, "Donald Trump Jr. Compared Border Wall to Zoo Fences that Hold Animals in Instagram Post," *USA Today*, January 9, 2019, https://www.usatoday.com/story/news/politics/2019/01/09/donald-trump-jr-compares-border-wall-zoo-instagram-post/2523385002/.
162 Paul Street and Anthony DiMaggio, "A Mostly Serious Response to the Semi-Satirical Ken Silverstein on Trump's Second Term," *Counterpunch*, July 5, 2019, https://www.counterpunch.org/2019/07/05/a-mostly-serious-response-to-the-semi-satirical-ken-silverstein-on-trumps-second-term/.
163 Richard C. Fording and Sanford F. Schram, "The Cognitive and Emotional Sources of Trump Support: The Case of Low-Information Voters," *New Political Science* 39, no. 4 (2017): 670–686.

5 The Anti-Trump Uprising and Beyond

On November 12, 2016, I traveled to Easton, Pennsylvania to attend a protest of Donald Trump's presidential victory. The streets were flooded with hundreds of activists expressing their outrage. The hostility reflected a visceral, spontaneous anger, perhaps best reflected in one placard reading: "WTF did you do?" in response to Americans voting for Trump. The meeting at Centre Square was heavily policed following a series of anonymous death threats, with law enforcement cordoning off the mass of Trump protesters from dozens of Trump supporters. Participation was diverse, including a mix of whites and people of color, and men and women of all ages. Trump's election united a plethora of social groups seeking to disrupt the president's plutocratic agenda.

The protesters reflected various concerns. The demonstrators carried placards with disparate grievances, including anger at the Electoral College for electing Trump over the popular vote, opposition to bigotry and hate, concerns with the rights of minority groups, and anxiety about the future of democracy. Some grievances were economic; one protester lamented Trump's ties being manufactured in China, contrary to his promise to bring jobs back to America. Other demonstrators carried placards reading "No Guac for Immigrant Haters," "Trump KKK Go Away," "No Unity with Islamophobia, Racism, Misogyny, Anti-Semitism," "Trans Lives Matter," and "Black Lives, Reproductive Rights, Immigrant, Refugees' Lives Matter." All were united in opposition to Trump. Following Truman's disturbance theory, protesters felt they had something to lose from Trump administering his reactionary agenda.

Protesters lamented Trump's social agenda as driven by hate. One declared: "Hate Can't Make America Great Again." Onlookers honked in support of the protesters, as the latter chanted "Love Trumps Hate!" This message revealed protesters' empathy with those who were the target of Trump's reactionary rhetoric. This empathy drove protests of Trump's travel ban, the Deferred Action for Childhood Arrivals (DACA) repeal, and Republicans' attempted repeal of the Affordable Care Act (ACA).

The Easton protest was one of many across the country. Thousands more participated in other cities, including New York, Boston, Chicago,

Los Angeles, Austin, Denver, Philadelphia, Portland, Oregon, San Francisco, Seattle, and Washington D.C.[1] Opposition to prejudice was articulated across the nation, with protesters expressing anxiety about the future of American democracy.[2]

This chapter examines anti-Trump protests following the 2016 election. I analyze protests of Trump's travel ban; Tax Day rallies against Trump's failure to release his tax returns; the March(es) for Science; and protests of the ACA repeal effort. I also examine the MeToo movement. My analyses rely on first-person experience with rallies as a participant-observer in cities throughout eastern Pennsylvania and the Lehigh Valley, and in Washington D.C., from late 2016 through late 2017. I provide statistical analyses, measuring how these uprisings were covered in the news, and how they were received by the public.

Americans are living through a second renaissance of mass protest, comparable to that of the 1960s and early 1970s. Following the 2008 economic crash, we have seen a large number of movements: the Tea Party, the Madison protests, Occupy, BLM, Fight for $15, the anti-Trump uprising, and #MeToo, among others. Some movements are reactionary in orientation; others are progressive. On the left, the anti-Trump uprising was reactive; its participants opposed what they saw as the worst parts of the Trump agenda. This contrasts with BLM, Occupy, and Fight for $15, which offered positive agendas. Because of the liberal-establishment nature of the anti-Trump protests, this movement, while including millions of Americans, did not offer a vision for progressive change.

The anti-Trump protests had mass appeal. Each part of this movement has its own appeals and goals, while MeToo moved beyond Trump, drawing on mainstream values in favor of gender equality. The Trump uprising mobilized with the help of the media. And favorable news coverage helped build public support. But the uprising also struggled because of its lack of support from the political system following the Republican takeover of Congress and the executive. MeToo also altered political discourse, public opinion, and politics, while facing institutional challenges.

Some of the anti-Trump protests were motivated by opposition to plutocracy. The Trump administration is the most economically elitist in modern history. Its agenda caused anxiety among disadvantaged groups via the effort to repeal the ACA and considering Trump's regressive tax policies. MeToo was indirectly relevant to concerns over plutocracy, as it spotlighted sexism in structures dominated by affluent men.

Protests against Trump had varied relevance with regard to intersectionality. The protests spoke to various groups, and individuals at the intersections of those groups, because of the movement's recognition of oppression across multiple dimensions of identity. Protests of the ACA repeal were significant to intersectionality because they addressed the needs of many groups in danger of losing health care. MeToo, on the other hand, saw only modest success in appealing to poorer women and poorer people of color, although it is better received by older women. This likely relates to the white professional faces that dominated the movement in the media, despite poor women of color also suffering from discrimination.

A Second Renaissance of Protest

The 2010s were defined by instability and change. Record inequality meant a growing number of Americans were strained and struggling to pay for basic goods such as health care, education, and other needs. To use Truman's terminology, Americans became increasingly disturbed at the state of the nation and their place in it. With growing political distrust, protest became the norm, and was mainstreamed as a primary way for citizens to seek redress. The 1960s and 1970s were also a period of upheaval. The anti-war movement, civil rights protests, the fight for women's rights, consumer rights, and the rise of environmentalism all challenged the established order, transforming politics. These movements produced civil rights legislation, environmental protections for clean air and water, the labeling of consumer goods and passage of regulations for automobile safety, affirmative action hiring for women and the establishing of reproductive rights, and an end to the Vietnam War. These movements demonstrate how citizens exercise political power through organizing and challenges to the status quo.

The late 2000s and 2010s also saw many movements, with no sign of public anger abating by the end of the decade. It is difficult to gauge the effects of these movements without years of hindsight. Nonetheless, this chapter provides a "first cut" at a scholarly history of the movements that defined the second half of the 2010s, including their impacts.

The 2017 Women's Marches

On January 21, 2017, I attended the Women's March in Washington D.C. against Donald Trump's inauguration. I have participated in demonstrations in our nation's capital for 20 years, alongside tens to hundreds of thousands in favor of reproductive rights, in opposition to war, supporting environmental conservation, and for global economic justice. But I never saw a protest this large in my time as an activist. The metro was packed with demonstrators, making it difficult to get into the city. Once I arrived at the national mall, I struggled to get off the train, waiting for half an hour in the tunnel near 12th Street and Independence by the Washington Monument. The crowds did not ease once outside of the station, as the protest was so large that it was difficult to move. When the march began, frequent stops of 15 to 20 minutes were normal, considering the massive crowds and the feeder marches coming together, inundating the capital. After an hour of congestion, the "march" devolved into masses of people struggling to move. One estimate put attendance at half a million to a million people, with millions more rallying across the nation.[3]

Like the protests immediately following Trump's election, the Women's March was eclectic. Based on conversations with fellow marches, I saw the crowd was a mix of seasoned activists and first-time protesters, and was diverse in age, race and ethnicity, and gender. Despite scuffles between police and demonstrators at the periphery of the protest zone, the march was peaceful, despite protests shutting down the mall and surrounding streets. The sheer magnitude of this protest, coupled with the diversity of participants, spoke to the mass public appeal and mainstreaming of protest in America.

The D.C. march was diverse in its speakers, which included Hollywood actresses, women's and reproductive rights activists, gay, lesbian, and transgender activists, feminists, civil rights organizers, left intellectuals, immigrant rights and Native American activists, labor organizers, television entertainers, religious leaders, and environmentalists. They stressed the importance of human dignity, empathy with disadvantaged groups, human rights under attack, the risks accompanying a political agenda driven by prejudice, misogyny, and hate, and the need for grassroots protest. Many topics were addressed: racism and mass incarceration, LGBTQ rights, discriminatory immigration policies against poor people of color, the risks to civil liberties under Trump, climate change, Islamophobia, reproductive rights, the need for adequate school funding and the dangers of market-based education reforms, and the need for economic justice via universal health care, a higher minimum wage, and a rollback of plutocratic politics.

Demonstrators articulated a wide range of beliefs. Some themes were broadly applied – seen in various placards – via calls for "human dignity for all" and unity "against hate," attacks on sexism as "a social disease," support for "social justice," the claim that "women's rights are human rights," support for open borders via the declaration that "no human being is illegal," and the re-articulation of the principle that "Black Lives Matter." Feelings of empowerment were palpable, seen in chants such as "This is what democracy looks like!", "The people united will never be defeated," and "Love not hate makes America great." Policy stances were articulated in conversations I had with demonstrators, including support for safe and legal abortions, opposition to a U.S.–Mexican wall, demands for cutting carbon emissions, and support for raising wages for the poor.

Many demonstrators were allied with the Hillary Clinton wing of the Democratic Party. One protester carried a sign reading "Proud nasty woman," echoing speaker and actress Ashley Judd's celebration of Clinton's campaign. Others spoke of Clinton as "the people's choice." Some portrayed Trump as a puppet of Russian President

Vladimir Putin, echoing Democratic rhetoric. Other protesters avoided partisan affiliations, articulating their general opposition to Trump. Most were not explicitly partisan, although as I show in this chapter, attachment to Democrats was a dominant characteristic of protesters.

Whether through chants, placards, speakers, or conversations with demonstrators, the Women's March was reactive in nature. There was little effort from speakers to articulate a progressive vision, and most protesters' comments revealed a picture of liberals on the defensive. This reactive "agenda" was seen in support for Planned Parenthood against government funding cuts, warnings against Trump to keep his "hands off our health care," opposition to "feeble minded fascists" and a "ridiculous plutocrat" president, anger over Trump's contempt for the press, displeasure with his militant nationalism, and a general anxiety, focused on the feeling that Trump was trying to "turn back" the clock to the 1950s era of gender expectations and power dynamics.

The protest was not radical, but liberal. Protests of U.S. militarism were sparse. Concerns about U.S. saber rattling against China, Russia, and Syria were infrequent. The popular protest during the Bush years of "no war for oil" was not present, despite continued militarism in the Middle East. Themes of inequality, corporate greed, and plutocracy were not highly salient, but were present. Some protesters indirectly spoke to these concerns, calling on Trump to release his tax returns and condemning attacks on the welfare state. But an explicit emphasis on economic issues was not readily apparent.

Despite these limits, the D.C. march had mass appeal. The demonstrators committed to empathetic politics, via attempts to protect women, minorities, indigenous peoples, and immigrants from discrimination. Opposition to intersectional oppression was apparent in the comments from left intellectual Angela Davis, one of the rally's speakers. Davis, known for her emphasis on combating discrimination across class, gender, and racial lines, spoke of resistance to Trump as a reflection of liberatory politics. She recognized the plight of native peoples fighting to protect their land from environmental degradation. Her appeals were explicitly intersectional:

> This is a women's march. And this women's march represents the promise of feminism as against the pernicious powers of state violence. An inclusive and intersectional feminism that calls upon all of us to join the resistance to racism, to Islamophobia, to anti-Semitism, to misogyny, to capitalist exploitation. Yes, we salute the Fight for $15. We dedicate ourselves to collective resistance to the billionaire mortgage profiteers and gentrifiers. Resistance to the health care privateers, to the attacks on Muslims and immigrants, to the attacks on disabled people, and state violence perpetrated by the police and

through the prison industrial complex. Resistance to institutional gender violence, especially against trans-women of color.[4]

The march's focus on protecting at-risk groups spoke to the importance of empathy in the movement. As I document in this chapter, most Trump protesters were white, meaning Trump's immigration policies, his dismissal of police brutality in black communities, and his attacks on Muslim immigrants did not directly impact them. Protesters were motivated by collective opposition to oppression. They united in resistance to an administration that rose to power via a conservative backlash against social change. The opposition to growing ethnic and racial diversity, to immigration of non-Caucasian peoples, to the ascendance of gay, lesbian, and trans rights, and to the racism, misogyny, and classism in Trump's campaign, were primary foci of the protests. The protests sent a message to political elites that much of the public was unwilling to normalize discrimination and bigotry. These protests offered no concrete political agenda, but were motivated by humanistic principles, including freedom to dissent, equal rights, justice, and democracy.

The D.C. Women's March had a significant impact on public consciousness. The demonstrations received sustained news coverage. A search of *Nexis Uni* finds there were more than 4,400 media segments, op-eds, editorials, letters to the editor, and other pieces in U.S. news outlets referencing the "Women's March" in the last two weeks of January 2017. This high volume of attention meant presidential critics had a mass platform to influence public opinion. The exposure worked in favor of protesters. A large majority of Americans – 86 percent – followed news on the Women's Marches.[5] When Americans were asked how they felt about marches in D.C. and across the country, 61 percent said they supported them, compared to 29 percent opposed.[6] This support was coupled with public distrust of Trump, as *Gallup* polling revealed 52 percent of Americans disapproved of the president by late January 2017.[7] The Trump protests did not forward an agenda for change, but they resonated with the public, since most Americans were already antagonistic toward the president.

Opposing Trump's Travel Ban and the DACA Repeal

In February 2017, Trump issued an executive order mandating a 90-day travel ban against seven Muslim-majority countries: Iran, Libya, Iraq, Syria, Somalia, Sudan, and Yemen. He claimed the ban was necessary to combat terrorism, although he provided no evidence of a threat from these countries. Critics felt the ban was based on Trump's Islamophobia, which he displayed in the 2016 campaign.[8] This assessment drew on Trump's December 2015 call for a "total and complete shutdown of

Muslims entering the United States," to combat those with "a great hatred toward Americans."[9] The religious intent of the action was affirmed by Trump's advisor Rudy Giuliani, who explained the president sought his counsel on how to "legally" implement a "Muslim ban" after Trump's executive order was thrown out in the federal courts.[10]

Trump inflamed progressives when he announced in September 2017 that he was ending the DACA initiative implemented under Obama. It allowed for those who immigrated illegally as children to apply for renewable two-year deference of deportation, while becoming eligible to work legally in the U.S. DACA was a step short of the "Dream Act," which proposed a path to citizenship for unauthorized immigrants. Nonetheless, DACA provided protection for more than 740,000 beneficiaries by late 2016.[11]

I participated in anti-travel ban and anti-DACA repeal protests in early-to-late 2017 throughout the Lehigh Valley, in Allentown and Bethlehem, Pennsylvania. At Lehigh University, where I teach, students rallied in early February, after Trump issued the ban, in solidarity with those affected. While dozens of students were impacted, the crowd included faculty, staff, administration, and unaffected students. The protest conveyed opposition to xenophobia and Islamophobia. Speakers stressed the importance of cultural diversity and the need to live in a nation free from racial, ethnic, and religious discrimination. Students unaffected by the ban empathized with those affected, letting those from Muslim-majority countries know they were not alone. The solidarity evident in these rallies showed Trump protests were about building a movement based on just governing principles.

Protests occurred across the country against Trump's ban. Thousands demonstrated in Los Angeles, San Francisco, New York, Dallas, Raleigh, Seattle, Houston, Portland, and Atlanta, and at airports where about 100 travelers from Muslim-majority countries were detained.[12] Rallies took place at Boston's Copley Square, Battery Park in Manhattan, and outside the White House.[13] One concern was that refugees – already the victims of war – were unfairly discriminated against.[14] Many see the U.S. as a force for good, opening its borders to the "poor," "tired," "huddled masses yearning to breathe free," and providing opportunities for those seeking a better life. Trump's ban made it clear this dream was not open to millions of Muslims. While several federal courts issued injunctions against Trump's travel ban, the U.S. Supreme Court allowed it to move forward.[15]

Trump's decision to rescind DACA sparked protests across the nation. I attended protest events in September 2017 in Pennsylvania against DACA's repeal, including one in Allentown organized by local community justice groups, and another organized by students of my university. The main concern was with demonstrating solidarity with those impacted by DACA's elimination. Although most protestors were unaffected directly by the repeal, students, faculty, and administrators united in empathy with those impacted. Speakers called on the audience to do all they could to help those affected, while demanding the revocation of the honorary degree bestowed on the president by Lehigh University An overwhelming majority of university faculty voted to revoke the degree in a sign of protest against the DACA repeal and Trump more generally.[16]

Trump's DACA decision drew others to action. In Washington D.C., 250 demonstrators with red, white, and blue balloons and American flags marched from the White House to the Justice Department and the Immigration and Enforcement Office, chanting "Shame on you, Donald Trump," and "Up, up with education; down, down with deportation."[17] In New York, demonstrators were arrested outside Trump Tower after blocking traffic on Fifth Avenue, chanting "Whose streets? Our streets!"[18] In Chicago, a thousand protesters marched, chanting in Spanish and English, with placards and shirts reading "Protection for all" and "Coming out of the shadows."[19] Protesters in Pennsylvania, Wyoming, Arizona, Washington D.C., and Minnesota rallied at the offices of their members of Congress to support DACA.[20]

Although DACA's elimination and travel ban protests received national news attention, they did not stop Trump's immigration agenda. Trump imposed his travel ban and DACA was revoked.[21] But the protests also reflected rising public anger with Trump's far-right agenda. Public support for protesters was evident in numerous surveys. Regarding DACA in 2018 – nearly 9 in 10 said the children of unauthorized immigrants should be able to stay in the U.S. if they were employed or attending school.[22] A January 2017 poll found 55 percent opposed Trump's executive order imposing a 90-day ban on immigration from Muslim-majority countries; the same number opposed a revised ban two months later.[23] While these protests did not have a policy impact, they were part of a broader uprising aimed at disrupting Trump's reactionary agenda, mobilizing the public against the president.

Tax Day Protests and the March(es) for Science

Demonstrations against Trump's refusal to release his tax returns and the March(es) for Science across the country were both economically focused. I attended the April 15, 2017 Tax Day rally at Payrow Plaza in Bethlehem, Pennsylvania, where hundreds of activists gathered to demand transparency from the president on his tax returns. Demonstrators lamented wealthy Americans for not paying a fair share of the tax burden. Participants expressed anger over the ACA repeal effort, coupled with Republican tax cuts for the wealthy. One speaker highlighted the negative implications of the affluent not paying taxes, and its impact on communities' ability to provide quality education.

Suspicion of Trump and wealthy Americans not paying taxes reflected public anxieties over plutocratic dominance of politics.

The Tax Day protest included liberals and progressives. Liberal Democratic state and local officials used the rally to promote their political initiatives and candidacies. This elitist aspect of the rally was somewhat limited by grassroots concerns from demonstrators with the declining responsibility of the wealthy in paying taxes. The suspicion that Trump was hiding something by not releasing his tax returns was widespread, as was the feeling that the wealthy were forcing the masses to pay taxes, while reducing their own burdens. The greatest applause was reserved for speakers addressing education and tax reform, rather than for Democratic electoral candidates. Demonstrators opposed Trump's bombing of Syria and his threats against North Korea, and rallied against a state initiative from Republicans to eliminate local property taxes, while supporting greater education spending.

Protesters gathered in more than 100 cities echoing the concerns in Bethlehem.[24] Activists demanded Trump demonstrate openness in his finances, allowing citizens to assess whether he retained conflicts of interest in his business ties with other countries.[25] In New York City, one organizer reflected:

> We need to see Trump's tax returns as a matter of transparency. If we're going into a tax reform debate, we need to know if what Trump wants to do is going to benefit himself, since he tends to do things that help him and not necessarily others.[26]

Democratic officials called on Trump to release his tax returns, framing his refusal as a good governance issue.[27] This focus on the collective good contrasted with Tea Party Tax Day rallies. While the Tea Party opposed contributing taxes to helping the needy, Tax Day protesters embraced the prism of collectivity. The Tax Day rally was driven by protesters pursuing a common good. And their concerns resonated with the public. Most Americans believe the wealthy do not pay their fair share in taxes.[28] Between two-thirds and three-quarters believed Trump should make his returns public.[29] Most rejected a Republican tax plan heavily tilted toward the wealthy.[30]

The tax protesters saw limited policy success. As of late 2019, Trump had not released his tax returns. Republicans passed a tax bill that mainly benefitted wealthy Americans.[31] It produced a large federal deficit, placing greater pressure on the federal government, as growing debt is used by Republicans to argue for spending cuts against popular social programs.

One week after the Tax Day rallies, Americans participated in the March(es) for Science, linking tax-related themes with concerns about the decline of education. I attended the March for Science rally in

Bethlehem, which saw a turnout of more than 1,000, where grievances were articulated against the right's assault on science. There was an environmental presence at the gathering, with activists linking the Republican rejection of climate science to the failure of the education system to inform the public on this issue. One placard read: "Science is the antidote to alternative facts," juxtaposing activists' commitment to science and Trump's contempt for evidence-based reasoning. Other protesters bemoaned the conservative effort to politicize science by equating it with liberalism.

Many themes were articulated by speakers. One emphasized how political officials jeopardize human sustainability and endanger the future by refusing to address climate change. Another theme was the fear of state and federal budget cuts for education spending, which endangered quality learning experiences for America's youth. A final grievance was against efforts to cut federal funding for scientific research, which was viewed as anti-intellectual and harmful to developing human knowledge.

Activists also came together throughout the nation and world in 600 Earth Day rallies on April 22, 2017.[32] The gatherings were described by organizers as "political but nonpartisan," reflecting scientifically minded individuals' efforts to avoid framing scientific inquiry as "liberal."[33] Activists protested Trump's effort to silence scientists in federal agencies and politicize issues such as climate change, human reproductivity, and sex education.[34] The protests coincided with Trump's call for $54 billion in cuts to government programs, coupled with increased military spending.[35] In Washington D.C., demonstrators at the Capitol building chanted "Save the EPA" and "Save the NIH" in response to Trump's call to cut 18 percent of the funding from the National Institutes of Health and 31 percent from the Environmental Protection Agency (EPA), while reducing the latter's workforce by 25 percent.[36] In total, 100,000 people demonstrated in D.C., 70,000 in Boston, 60,000 in Chicago, 50,000 each in San Francisco and Los Angeles, and thousands more in other cities.[37]

The March for Science's website laid main concerns for the rallies, including: recognition of "the many ways that science serves our communities and our world"; support for scientists' efforts to "reach out to their communities" to "support and safeguard the scientific community"; the embrace of science as a "vital feature of a working democracy," providing "insight into the world," protecting "the common good," and helping individuals "to think critically, ask questions, and evaluate truth based on the weight of evidence." The website encouraged political officials to use evidence-based reasoning in policymaking and "make use of peer-reviewed evidence and scientific consensus, not personal whims and decrees," to avoid the perversion of science via its manipulation "by special interests"; and to oppose efforts "to further restrict scientists' ability to research and communicate their findings."[38]

The Anti-Trump Uprising and Beyond 239

The March(es) for Science saw mixed success. For government scientific funding, the proposed cuts proposed by Trump were reversed in Congress' 2018 budget, which increased funding for the NIH, NASA, the USDA, and scientifically oriented agencies and programs, although the EPA saw a reduction in funding.[39] But the Trump administration muzzled federal scientists through intimidation, restricting the EPA from using the words "climate change," and through an order from the administration for USDA and EPA scientists not to communicate with the media.[40] Finally, the Trump administration withdrew from the Paris Agreement on climate change, and rolled back Obama-era environmental regulations.[41]

The March(es) for Science, however, successfully appealed to the public. They received extensive news coverage, as an analysis utilizing *Nexis Uni* finds that the rallies appeared in more than 1,100 articles, stories, op-eds, editorials, letters to the editor, and other features in newspapers and online news venues over the last two weeks of April 2017. Coverage consistently conveyed protesters' main concerns. In Figure 5.1, my analysis of *New York Times* coverage using *Nexis Uni* finds attention to concerns with scientific funding appeared in about a third of stories, while references to climate change and other environmental concerns materialized in about half of articles. References to the Trump administration, proposed cuts in scientific funding, his longstanding antagonism toward scientific reasoning, and other scientific concerns appeared in about two-thirds of articles. My analysis of all newspaper and online news venues included in *Nexis*

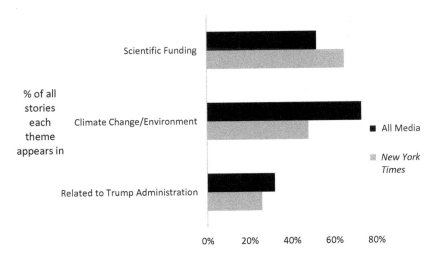

Figure 5.1 Media Coverage of March for Science Concerns
Source: *Nexis Uni* academic database

Uni and covering the March(es) for Science included references to Trump in more than half of stories, to climate change and the environment three-quarters of the time, and to scientific funding one-third of the time.[42] In short, the reporting on the marches was favorable, regularly conveying protesters' concerns.

The public was sympathetic to activists' grievances. Americans express positive feelings about science. Two-thirds believe science has a "mostly positive effect on society"; just 4 percent say it has a "mostly negative" impact.[43] Nearly 8 in 10 believe "science has made life easier for most people," while 71 percent say "government investment" in scientific research "pays off in the long run."[44] Nearly three-quarters of Americans agreed with the demonstrators that it was a "bad idea" to cut federal funding for scientific research.[45] Large numbers of Americans believed the March(es) for Science had a positive impact. While 44 percent of respondents felt "the protests, marches, and demonstrations about science held this April" would "make no difference" to "public support for science," an equal number believed they would "help" build support. Just 7 percent felt the events would "hurt" the cause.[46] Forty-nine percent agreed the marches created pressure to address climate change; the same number agreed they would "encourage policymakers to rely more on the advice of scientific experts."[47] Forty-eight percent believed the marches would assist in "raising support for government funding of science," while 59 percent felt the marches would "encourage scientists to be more active in civic and public affairs."[48] These feelings suggest the March(es) for Science significantly impacted mass political discourse.

The March(es) for Science demonstrators utilized the media to increase public knowledge of attacks on science, encouraging Americans to oppose these campaigns. Polling from May 2017 found that 61 percent of Americans followed news on the March(es) for Science.[49] Of those paying attention, 48 percent said the information they were exposed to encouraged them to support "the goals of the protests, marches and demonstrations about science."[50] These data confirm activists' success in raising their concerns with tens of millions of Americans, while increasing support for these concerns.

The rise of the Trump administration, and its suspicion of science, posed a threat to evidence-based inquiry. In 2017, more than half of Republicans agreed higher education was harmful to society – a serious sign of declining intellectualism on the right.[51] The March(es) for Science alone could not roll back this development. Many Americans demonstrate low levels of scientific knowledge, evident in the most extreme findings that one in four do not know the Earth revolves around the sun, and that only a quarter of Americans in the late 2010s recognized almost all climate scientists agree global warming is "mostly due to human activity."[52] These findings suggest the battle for scientific literacy would continue, despite the positive impact of the March(es) for Science.

Opposing "Obamacare" Repeal

Since the ACA was passed, Republicans fixated on its repeal. Republicans in the House of Representatives voted dozens of times to repeal the ACA before the party's takeover of the Senate and Trump's victory in 2016. In early 2018, repeal of the ACA appeared likely. But hopes of repeal were stymied by growing protest and opposition. Large numbers of working, middle-class, and poorer Americans challenged a repeal plan that would cost an estimated 22 million people their health coverage following the elimination of the ACA.[53]

In the Spring and Summer of 2017, I participated in public actions in Allentown, Pennsylvania seeking to pressure Republican Senator Pat Toomey and Republican Representative Charlie Dent not to repeal the ACA. One event in April, coordinated by Pennsylvania Health Access Network, met outside Dent's office to deliver a petition reflecting constituents' opposition to repeal. Dozens of activists voiced their support for Congress' reauthorization of the ACA state exchange subsidies, while protesting Trump's executive order shortening the period to enroll in the federal health exchange. Speakers articulated anxieties over the prospect of a repeal of the ACA's prohibition on private insurers denying health care due to "pre-existing conditions." Fears were highly personalized – for example, the concern that Medicaid cuts would hurt services for drug addicts, and that repeal would hurt young Americans on their parents' insurance. Speakers at this event and others told stories of how their health improved due to ACA assistance, after suffering major sicknesses. These stories contribute to the conclusion that citizens are pushed to action by personal grievances and threats to their well-being.

In early July, I attended a rally at Toomey's office with hundreds of other demonstrators, protesting Toomey's refusal to hold town halls to discuss health care, and opposing his support for the ACA repeal. The central theme of the rally was greed. Protesters felt Republicans were prioritizing financial benefits for the wealthy, while taking them from the needy. This grievance was based on the plan to repeal the ACA's tax on families making more than $250,000 a year, which funded benefits going to millions using the health-care exchanges. The class warfare angle was evident in chants and placards, including: "Trumpcare kills the poor to pay the rich," "Medicaid not millionaires," "Healthcare, not wealth care," "No tax cuts for the wealthy, trickle-down [economics] does not work," and "The only minority destroying America is the rich." These messages revealed activists' strong class consciousness, via their judgment that Trump sided with wealthy Americans over the disadvantaged in a conflict with life and death stakes.

Speakers at the rally voiced many criticisms of Republicans. An activist from Planned Parenthood warned the ACA repeal would hurt poor people and poor women of color – speaking to the intersectionality of the health-care protests. Intersectional considerations were also apparent in comments from a community religious leader lamenting any repeal written behind closed doors and benefitting affluent white men standing to gain from the repeal's lowering of taxes on high-income earners. But activists' motivations transcended intersectionality. Their support for the ACA was limited, as demonstrators recognized it was a flawed policy, but that it was better than the Republican repeal and eliminating insurance for tens of millions. Instead, most supported establishing health-care as a public good. This sentiment was reflected in chants that "health-care is a human right" and in the widespread applause from the crowd when a speaker discussed the need for national health-care. Other indications of empathy with the needy were expressed by speakers who supported increasing health-care spending and emphasized the harm that would be visited on children with the ACA repeal.

A final theme from the rally was the disconnect between the public and Republican officials. Demonstrators expressed resentment over Americans being forced to pay taxes, but being denied benefits by the ACA repeal. There was anger directed at Senator Toomey, who was deemed a coward for refusing to meet with constituents about his support for repeal. Finally, there was recognition that rallies like this one mattered, not because Toomey would listen to protesters, but because protests were necessary to mobilize against unresponsive political leaders.

Public responses suggested the tide was turning against Republicans. Demonstrators benefitted from endless honking from drivers-by – a sign of mass solidarity with those seeking to protect Americans from losing health care. And a mass groundswell was apparent from the wide variety of groups participating. The event brought together different segments of America in pursuit of a common purpose. Groups involved included a labor contingent via the Service Employees International Union (SEIU), a feminist component from Planned Parenthood and "Women's March Pennsylvania" (a feminist group built out of the anti-Trump protests), a minority voice from "Make the Road Pennsylvania," an immigrants rights group, and a religious community organization presence via "POWER Northeast" (Pennsylvanians Organized to Witness, Empower, and Rebuild), which lobbied "to interrupt oppressive and inequitable systems that have historically negatively impacted black, Latino/a, working-class, and poor communities in the Lehigh Valley."

The protests in Allentown overlapped with demonstrations across the country. On the Capitol grounds in Washington D.C., activists rebelled in a march called "Linking Together: March to Save Our Care," including groups such as Planned Parenthood, SEIU, and the American Civil Liberties Union (ACLU).[54] Activists occupied more than a dozen House and Senate office buildings, with 80 arrested on misdemeanor charges of "crowding" and "obstructing" public spaces.[55] Sit-ins occurred in

Republican congressional offices in Kentucky and Tennessee, and outside offices in Arizona, Florida, Ohio, Arkansas, and elsewhere.[56] In Miami, activists pressured Senator Marco Rubio to "vote no on wealthcare," while "die-ins" occurred on the lawn outside Rubio's office and at a county courthouse in Bloomington, Indiana, in solidarity with those at risk of losing health care.[57] Protesters gathered outside Republican Senate Majority Leader Mitch McConnell's office in Fort Wright Kentucky, accompanied by "Mitch, you're killing us" signs.[58] In Chicago, hundreds gathered in Federal Plaza to celebrate the seventh anniversary of the ACA. The SEIU invited local and state Democrats to speak, who pledged to oppose the repeal effort.[59]

The protests against ACA repeal were the most successful of the anti-Trump demonstrations. Health-care activists benefitted from significant public support. Based on Figure 5.2, *Gallup* polling revealed support for the ACA reached its highest in 2017, at the time that millions realized they were in danger of losing health care. By April 2017, 55 percent of Americans approved of the ACA, with 41 percent disapproving. By the end of the year, 56 percent agreed it was "the responsibility of the federal government to make sure all Americans have health insurance," a sentiment running contrary to Republican repeal efforts. Eighty percent of Americans in 2017 disapproved of how Republicans were "handling" health-care reform.[60] Only 33 percent favored the Republican health plan, which repealed

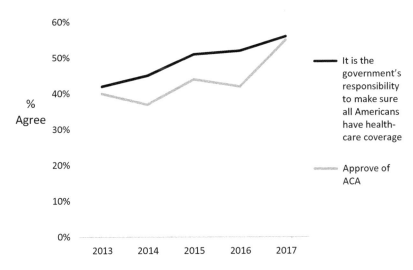

Figure 5.2 Shifting Public Opinion on the Affordable Care Act (2013–17)
Source: *Gallup* Polling, 2013–17
Drawn from Polling Report

the ACA's mandate that all Americans have insurance, and eliminated the subsidies to purchase insurance.[61] Most Americans wanted the government to go further than the ACA, with 57 percent favoring "a national health plan – or Medicare-for-all – in which all Americans would get their insurance from a single government plan."[62]

The ACA's popularity meant serious pressure on Republicans not to repeal the law. Based on the September 2017 *Pew* poll, represented in Figure 5.3, the law was more likely to be supported by liberals, Democrats, black and LatinX Americans, and the more highly educated. It also had intersectional appeal. Disadvantaged groups were more likely to embrace the ACA, including poorer LatinX and poorer black Americans, poorer Latino/Latina men and women, and poorer black women. It is likely that millions in these groups understood the Republican plan would harm their ability to secure affordable care. In

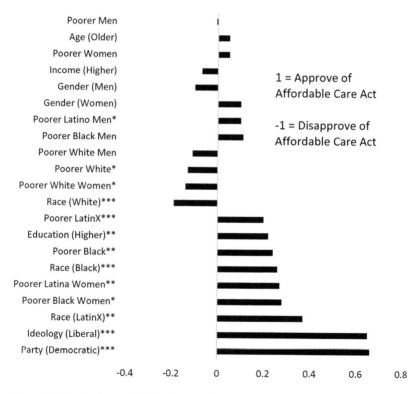

Figure 5.3 Attitudes on Health Care Reform
Source: *Pew Research Center* poll, February 2017
Statistical Significance Levels: *** = 0.1% ** = 1% * = 5%
Controls: gender, age, education, race, income, political party, ideology

contrast, white Americans, poorer whites, and poorer white women were more likely to disapprove of the ACA. But these findings must be qualified. A closer look at the *Pew* survey finds these groups were not more likely to support repeal. Most whites, poorer whites, and poorer white women said they wanted legislators to modify the law. Poorer Americans had an interest in opposing repeal, which was likely to reduce their access to care. The public's commitment to the ACA was apparent at demonstrations, as I met numerous activists drawing on their own experiences with the law in helping them secure life-saving care. In short, the movement to stop the ACA repeal benefitted from mass support, with most Americans recognizing the dangers of eliminating insurance for tens of millions, and with many activists having personal stakes motivating their protests.

Activists across the nation pressured Congress. These protests led to concerns among legislators about an electoral backlash. Demonstrations across the country, attacks on Republican legislators at town hall meetings, and angry calls to members of Congress from constituents all meant serious pressure on Republicans to abandon repeal, and by late 2017, the Republican attempt to dismantle the ACA had failed.[63]

House Republicans passed repeal legislation, but the Senate had difficulties passing a bill. Nine Senate Republicans voted against a "repeal and replace" bill, with those opposing it being impacted by constituent pressure.[64] Senators Dean Heller, Susan Murkowski, and Susan Collins referenced constituent pressure and worries over Medicaid cuts as driving their "no" votes.[65] Jerry Moran and Mike Lee opposed the proposal as inadequate in achieving lower health-care costs for constituents.[66] Lindsey Graham and John McCain felt the plan would create greater instability in insurance markets, harming their constituents.[67] Tom Cotton worried about a backlash from voters.[68] Bob Corker admonished Republicans for supporting a repeal that would reduce taxes on the wealthy, while denying Medicaid funding to the poor. The "no" votes from these Senators meant Republicans failed to pass a repeal and replace bill.[69]

The Democratic Party was too weak to effectively resist the repeal effort. The responsibility fell on protesters and constituents who risked losing their health care. Constituents' success in fighting the repeal speaks to the power of protest. When effectively mobilized, citizens can achieve outcomes that at first appear unlikely, as happened with the ACA. Few Americans probably predicted a Republican failure on health-care reform, considering the energy the party dedicated to fighting the ACA. Most party members opposed the law and saw Trump's election as their opportunity to eliminate it. Their failure was a milestone moment in the anti-Trump movement. It was a policy victory at a time when Republicans and Trump were openly assaulting liberal government policies.

The Strengths and Limits of the Anti-Trump Protests

Trump's rise produced a mass mobilization against right-wing politics. The counter-backlash against Trump's cultural backlash is captured in Figure 5.3, tracking growing opposition to a wall on the U.S.–Mexico border and to the deportation of undocumented immigrants, rising support for a path to citizenship for undocumented immigrants, and increasingly favorable views of Muslims.[70]

The case studies in this chapter suggest anti-Trump protests resonated with the public, but were less effective at the policy level. The Women's March and March(es) for Science received extensive coverage, providing Trump's opponents with a mass platform to disseminate their concerns. Demonstrators' grievances resonated with large segments of the public. And since the protests were reactive, in opposition to a president already opposed by most Americans, the anti-Trump demonstrations did not face the same uphill battle to transform public opinion faced by movements like BLM.[71] BLM sought to build mass awareness of racism in America. The anti-Trump protests were less ambitious, seeking to stifle the most reactionary proposals of the Republican Party. As discussed in previous chapters, it took years for BLM to gain majority support. In contrast, from the beginning of the anti-Trump protests, most Americans agreed with the movement and opposed the president.

The protests were supported by the Democratic Party establishment. The January 2017 Women's Marches were endorsed by Hillary Clinton and other Democrats, who embraced a liberal agenda on criminal justice

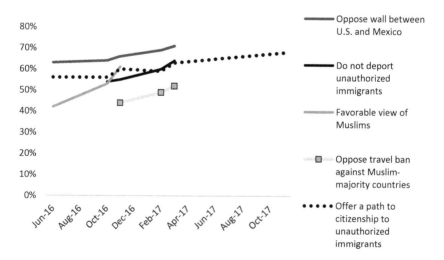

Figure 5.4 The Counter-Backlash against Trump's Right-Wing Politics
Source: *CNN, Quinnipiac, Washington Post* polls

The Anti-Trump Uprising and Beyond 247

reform, opposition to sexism and racism, immigration reform, and health-care.[72] By mid-2017, Clinton declared she was an "activist citizen and part of the resistance."[73] Trump's travel ban was denounced by Democrats, who presented legislation to block his executive order.[74] Similarly, Trump's rescinding of DACA was condemned by Democrats, who pushed legislation protecting those at risk of deportation.[75] Democrats also joined the protests of Trump's refusal to release his tax returns, and supported legislation forcing the president to make publicly available his financial records.[76] Democrats opposed the ACA repeal; not a single party member in the House or Senate voted for the three repeal bills presented in mid-2017.[77]

Because Trump was disliked by most Americans, this made it easier for protesters to gain public support. And Democratic sympathy likely aided the movement in gaining media attention. Movements have a greater chance of success when a country's "political opportunity structure" is sympathetic to its values. But the Democratic partisanship of the protests also meant that they struggled to achieve policy successes when Republicans controlled Congress and the White House. So the "political opportunity structure" framework also explains the limits of the anti-Trump protests, as there was little chance Republicans would side with demonstrators over the president.

Despite the movement's failures, demonstrators mobilized large numbers of people and connected with most Americans on various policy issues. By early 2018, 15 percent of Americans indicated they had "taken part in a protest march or demonstration" of some kind since Trump was elected.[78] Of those protesters, more than two-thirds said the protest(s) were against Trump.[79] Tens of millions of Americans claimed active participation in the anti-Trump movement. These Americans stood to the left of the public, although there was a strong overlap between Trump protesters' attitudes and mass opinion. Table 5.1 summarizes *Pew*'s June–July 2017 survey, asking Americans who attending anti-Trump protests about their political attitudes.

Those who attended protests of Trump were to the left of other Americans by ten percentage points or more for all nine questions. In seven of the nine questions, most anti-Trump protesters and other Americans shared leftist attitudes. These findings speak to public support for the anti-Trump movement.

The movement was different in numerous ways compared to all Americans and to those holding unfavorable views of Trump. According to *Pew*'s June–July 2017 survey, anti-Trump protesters were not very different from all Trump opponents and all respondents regarding their age. The protesters hailed from various income levels, although they were more likely to be concentrated at higher incomes (over $150,000 a year) than all respondents and all Trump opponents. Protesters were more likely to be women, highly educated, liberal, and

Table 5.1 Anti-Trump Protesters: Socio-Political Attitudes

Attitudes (% agreeing with each attitude)	Anti-Trump Protesters	Rest of Americans
Stricter environmental laws are worth the cost	94	59
Inequality is a very big problem	84	44
There are significant obstacles that make it harder for women to get ahead than men	89	54
The economic system favors powerful interests	92	63
Poor people have hard lives because government benefits don't go far enough to help them live decently	90	52
Immigrants today strengthen our country because of their hard work and talents	98	69
Government regulation of business is necessary to protect the public interest	86	51
Hard work and determination no longer guarantee success	70	35
Business corporations make too much profit	86	56

Source: *Pew Research Center*, June–July 2017

Democratic, compared to all respondents and all Trump opponents. But most Americans in the *Pew* survey – 60 percent – held an unfavorable view of Trump, suggesting the main political message of demonstrators was well received by the public.

Pew's June–July survey provides evidence of what factors were most important in driving opposition to Trump. In Figure 5.5, resistance to Trump was fueled by education, race and ethnicity, partisanship, ideology, and various intersectional identities. Highly educated Americans were more likely to oppose Trump, as were Democrats and liberals. Among historically disadvantaged groups, opposition was higher among younger Americans, LatinX and black Americans, poorer LatinX and black Americans (making under $50,000 a year), poorer black women, and poorer Latino/a men and women. Opposition to Trump across class, race/ethnic, and gender lines should be expected considering the president's many insults against disadvantaged groups. His attacks on poor "shithole countries," his reported sexual assault against women, his practice of rating women based on physical appearance, and his derogatory comments toward Muslims, LatinX individuals, and other minority groups were poorly received by many Americans, and by marginalized racial and ethnic groups.[80]

Figure 5.5 also assesses participation in anti-Trump protests compared to Democratic partisanship in predicting Trump opposition.

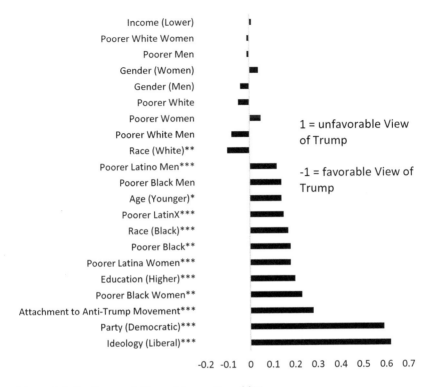

Figure 5.5 Predictors of Opposition to Donald Trump
Source: *Pew Research Center* poll, June–July 2017
Statistical Significance Levels: *** = 0.1% ** = 1% * = 5%
Controls: gender, age, education, race, income, political party, ideology

In previous chapters, I documented how attachment to BLM, Madison, and Occupy were more powerful than Democratic Party attachment in predicting progressive attitudes on issues related to race, labor, jobs, and inequality. In contrast, participation in the anti-Trump movement is much *less powerful* in predicting opposition to Trump than Democratic partisanship.

I have argued that progressive movements seek to upend the status quo and are *the* driving factor in pushing for progressive societal transformation. These movements struggle at first, because they have little support from major political parties, and must rely on street protests, disruption, and civil disobedience to gain attention. But when these movements finally break through into mass discourse, they pressure government to grant concessions, as we saw with BLM, the Sanders "Revolution" (fueled by Madison, Occupy, and Fight for $15), and with the Sanders campaigns pulling the Democratic Party to the left.

In contrast, the anti-Trump movement was instantly embraced by Democratic officials and elevated to a serious movement in political-media discourse. Its reactive nature, however, meant it failed where other left movements have not, in offering a progressive agenda for change. This point is not meant to dismiss the movement's significance. The anti-Trump protests represented an important moment in history and were a mass movement against the rise of right-wing political power. But the movement was fundamentally different from progressive movements in that its politics were more establishment-oriented. Under these circumstances, the movement was relatively less significant in impacting public opinion than Democratic partisanship.

The Democratic Party mobilized against Trump after his election. In 2017, Democratic officials' main goal was to oppose Trump and the Republicans' policy agenda. But the protests of Trump did not offer messages distinct from those offered by Democratic officials. In other words, the movement drew much of its appeal from Democratic Party elites. This is not to say that the movement was entirely reliant on Democrats. This was not the case. As Figure 5.4 documents, attachment to the anti-Trump protests was independently associated with opposition to Trump, after controlling for partisanship. Still, it is difficult to argue the movement represented an independent effort to transform politics when it has been embraced by the Democratic Party since its inception.

The anti-Trump protests benefitted from and contributed to the mainstreaming of protest. The protests were seen in a positive light during Trump's first year. One *Pew* February 2017 survey found nearly all Americans – 91 percent – agreed "the right to non-violent protest" is "very important to maintaining a strong democracy."[81] A second survey from August found just 21 percent felt the U.S. had "gone too far in expanding the right to protest or criticize government."[82] In another sign of the mainstreaming of protest, 42 percent of Americans in May 2017 said they were "likely" to "attend a political rally, speech, or organized protest about global warming" "if a person you like and respect asked you to," compared to 34 percent who said they would not.[83] This sentiment suggested significant public support for the anti-Trump protests, considering the importance of climate change to the movement. The above survey results, when combined, provide some evidence of an independent impact of the protests on public opinion, as the anti-Trump movement spoke to the public in a broad sense, and in a way that was not entirely dependent on Democratic partisanship.

Although the movement was dependent on elite support, it demonstrated the power of solidarity in driving opposition to Trump. As I witnessed firsthand with these protests, activists understood they were part of something bigger than protesting a president. The movement developed its own inertia, serving as a symbol for a deeper commitment to empathy with groups that Trump discriminated against. Protests of the ACA repeal were not simply about preserving a law; they demonstrated that people, when united in mass, can impact politics for the betterment of fellow Americans. The anti-Trump movement transcended a transactional approach to protest; individuals did not demonstrate simply to oppose a president's policies. They understood they were part of something bigger than themselves or a policy issue – they were exercising power through unified action, fighting for equality, democracy, human rights, and just governance. In the process, they built a mass movement that made history.

Beyond the Anti-Trump Protests: #MeToo

The rise of #MeToo was a long time coming. The warning signs were apparent more than a decade before its rise in the class action sexism lawsuit against Walmart that was brought before the Supreme Court. Despite 1.5 million women joining the suit, and despite evidence of gender bias in company job ads, in hiring for management positions and tolerance of sexual harassment of women in the workplace, the Supreme Court dismissed the case in 2011.[84] Downplaying countless stories of discrimination from lawsuit participants, the late Justice Antonin Scalia assaulted the very notion of women joining in mass to fight sexism in the workplace. In the court's majority decision, Scalia wrote that women involved in the suit failed to demonstrate "a common answer to the crucial question, why was I disfavored?" Scalia lamented that the case involved "literally millions of employment decisions" and the plaintiffs had not demonstrated there was "some glue holding the alleged reasons for all those decisions together."[85] This conclusion was probably puzzling to women's rights advocates, considering the "glue holding" the incidents together seemed clear: sexism and discrimination. Scalia frustrated progressives who hoped the Supreme Court would take the problem of misogyny in the workplace seriously. Scalia's comments about more than a million women failing to identify a common thread in their experiences suggested the judge was skeptical of the entire idea of collective action against sexism.

The history of #MeToo traces back to the mid-2000s, when feminist activist Tarana Burke adopted the phrase on *MySpace* to spotlight sexism, and for women to share stories about sexual abuse. The campaign was meant to provide "empowerment through empathy" to the survivors of sexual violence, while drawing attention to sexual abuse. As Burke explained:

> I am a survivor of sexual violence myself. When I was starting to figure out what healing looked like for me, I realized the most powerful interactions I had were among survivors. Non-survivors

said, "Oh my gosh that happened to you?" or, "That's awful, are you ok?" People mean well when they do that, a lot of times its genuine, but it's also disconnecting. It feels like you're an other, it's "othering." One of the worst things about experiencing sexual trauma is feeling like you're all alone. If you work up the courage to tell somebody, and they "other" you, that can also feel like an additional burden. Instead, when people say, "This happened to me too, I understand you," a connection happens, it's a very different process. "Me Too" became the way to succinctly and powerfully, connect with other people and give people permission to start their journey to heal.[86]

Burke's efforts did not immediately catch on in mass political discourse. It was not until 2017 that the movement gained steam, after actress Alyssa Milano took to *Twitter* in October to encourage her followers to share the "MeToo" hashtag, to draw attention to sexual assault and discrimination. As Milano wrote: "If all women who have been sexually harassed or assaulted wrote 'Me Too' as a status, we might give people a sense of the magnitude of the problem."[87]

#MeToo quickly caught fire in the Fall of 2017, as high-profile actresses and celebrities voiced support for speaking out against sexual harassment and assault, including Evan Rachel Wood, Lady Gaga, Patricia Arquette, Debra Messing, Ashley Judd, Jennifer Lawrence, Reese Witherspoon, Angelina Jolie, Gwyneth Paltrow, and others.[88] But it took many women working in various professional capacities in Washington, D.C., Hollywood, and in the media coming forward with allegations of sexual abuse and assault for MeToo to captivate the public and raise the problem of sexism to a defining issue. The allegations were many, spotlighting sexual assault and abuse of power by prominent men. Allegations were brought against prominent figures, first concentrating on Hollywood movie producer Harvey Weinstein and comedian Bill Cosby, then others such as comedians/entertainers Louis CK, Ryan Seacrest, Aziz Ansari, Steven Segal, Morgan Freeman, and James Franco, sporting figures such as Alan Nassar, Brett Favre, and Donovan McNabb, Democratic and Republican officials such as Al Franken, Patrick Meehan, John Conyers, Blake Farenthold, and Donald Trump, and journalists, pundits, and media executives such as Matt Lauer, Charlie Rose, Bill O'Reilly, Roger Ailes, and Glenn Thrush.

Allegations against prominent men seemed to come as a surprise to many Americans. Weinstein was identified by numerous women as a sexual predator, with more than 50 offering allegations against him. These charges included multiple counts of rape and unwanted sexual advances such as requests to expose himself to and grope women, threats to commit violence and murder, and using casting as leverage in exchange for sexual acts.[89] Legal charges against former USA Gymnastics coach and

Michigan State University-affiliated doctor Alan Nassar included molestation charges involving 30 females, with one of the charges involving a 13 year old.[90] In total, 140 women came forward to claim Nassar sexually abused them – almost equal to the number of sexual assault and abuse allegations against Bill Cosby, Harvey Weinstein, and Jerry Sandusky combined.[91] Former *Fox News* host Bill O'Reilly paid $13 million to five women not to pursue sexual abuse allegations against him before being fired by the network. The women who came forward included those working on his program and guests, outlining "a wide range of behavior," including "verbal abuse, lewd comments, unwanted sexual advances and phone calls in which it sounded as if Mr. O'Reilly was masturbating."[92]

A resurgent women's rights movement emerged in the late 2010s because of widespread practices of sexism and sexual abuse in American workplaces and society. In October 2017, 54 percent of women admitted they were subjected to "unwanted" and "inappropriate sexual advances" in and outside of the workplace; 95 percent said this behavior went unpunished.[93] A November survey found more than a third of women were "sexually harassed or abused at work."[94] Another survey published by the *New York Times* in February 2018 provided evidence of widespread sexual abuse, summarized in Figure 5.6.[95] While a significant minority of men reported being victimized, women were far more likely to be victims of sexual assault, male-genital flashing, being physically followed, and being exposed to online sexual harassment, unwelcome sexual touching, and verbal sexual harassment. Verbal sexual harassment and unwelcome sexual touching were the most common offenses, with most women subjected to both. These surveys reveal the severity of the nation's history of sexism and sexual abuse, contrary to the widely declared principle of equality.

The rise of MeToo is somewhat unorthodox in terms of assessing whether it represented a social movement. On the one hand, there were not large numbers of rallies with massive turnouts throughout 2017 primarily devoted to this cause. The movement did not include traditional grassroots outreach within communities, engaged in by community activist groups. In line with McFarland's theory of "creative participation," MeToo is an example of citizen activism geared toward social justice, even though it does not conform to previous notions of political engagement via rallies, demonstrations, and street protests.[96] Still, I would argue MeToo is a different sort of movement; it has empowered large numbers of women to step forward to fight sexism, while engaging in public outreach to further its cause, and while militantly challenging a political-economic system that long swept sexism under the rug. Furthermore, MeToo looks more like a social movement if we link it back to certain protests, such as the Women's Marches of early 2017 and 2018 against sexism.

254 *The Anti-Trump Uprising and Beyond*

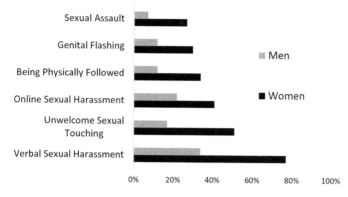

Figure 5.6 Public Experiences with Sexual Assault
Source: *New York Times*, February 2018

One could argue MeToo was a product of Trump's rise to power. Its emergence overlapped with the ascendance of the most openly misogynistic administration in modern history. Trump's assumption of power, despite revelations that he had bragged about sexually assaulting women, angered millions who felt he was unfit to be President. Trump's casual glossing-over of the charges during one of the presidential debates revealed his disinterest in taking sexual assault seriously. And Trump's misogyny was not confined to bragging about grabbing female genitals.[97] It included numerous allegations of sexual assault and harassment, allegations of sexual infidelity involving models and pornographic actresses, Trump's brazen complaints about women's physical appearances, and his rankings of women based on their perceived sexual attractiveness.[98] Democratic calls for Trump to resign overlapped with the rise of MeToo, with pronouncements that both parties should be held accountable regarding sexual assault and harassment.[99]

MeToo was about more than Trump. The movement forwarded a positive progressive agenda, continuing the work of the women's rights movement in fighting against a culture marked by rampant sexism in government and the private sector. As the previous comments from Tarana Burke reveal, MeToo was conceptualized as an empathy-building campaign for women to unite, and draw attention to and combat sexism. It was a mechanism for helping the survivors of sexual assault to cope with their experiences, and assist in recovering from traumatic experiences. Survivors of sexual abuse and assault would understand they were not alone, and had the support of other victims. As with other social movements, MeToo's meaning transcends individual women and their specific grievances. It was also defined by solidarity among the victims of sexual aggression and violence, in addition to others who, while not having experienced sexual discrimination, were interested in fighting misogyny. The campaign against sexism, for millions, was motivated by broader principles of social justice, democracy, human rights, and equality.

MeToo benefitted from sustained attention in the news, providing audiences with information about the problems of sexual abuse and violence. In the last three months of 2017, references to "#MeToo" and "MeToo" appeared in nearly 300 articles in the *New York Times* – according to my analysis drawing on the *Nexis Uni* database. Within the same period, the movement appeared in more than 2,900 articles, features, analyses, op-eds, editorials, and letters to the editor across American newspapers and online news venues. This represents significant and sustained attention.

Previous research finds the women's rights movement benefitted from positive media attention during the height of "second wave" feminism in the 1960s and 1970s, related to coverage of equal rights, women in the workplace and in political roles, and challenging traditional gender roles.[100] This positive coverage continued with MeToo. An analysis of movement coverage finds numerous grievances and concerns from movement supporters were mentioned in the thousands of news stories referenced above. A summary of my analysis – drawing on *Nexis Uni* – is included in Figure 5.7. References to stronger language addressing sexual predators, predation, and sexual violence appeared least often in news content. References to sexual abuse appeared more often, while reporting on sexual harassment was most common. In total, the *New York Times* and other outlets provided significant context – referencing at least one of the frameworks from Figure 5.7 as a matter of standard operating procedure – in 88 percent of *New York Times* articles and 91 percent of pieces in other venues.[101]

Editorials were strongly sympathetic to MeToo. The *Chicago Tribune*'s editors wrote that MeToo "is an angry voice – rightfully so … fed by decades of injustice piling up like kindling." The paper concentrated on the movement's effects:

> Untold numbers of powerful men now must practice their public apologies to all the women they've pawed and compromised, never taking no for an answer. We hope the cascading consequences are a cautionary tale for all men. This egregious behavior no longer merits a wink and a nod, if it ever did.[102]

The *Los Angeles Times* editors directed attention not only to Hollywood professionals and affluent women, but to the less fortunate victims of abuse:

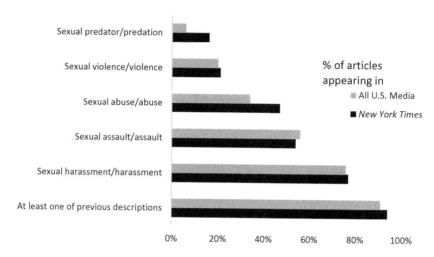

Figure 5.7 MeToo and the Media: Descriptions of the Movement
Source: *Nexis Uni* academic database

There's nothing new about sexual harassment. Women (and to a lesser degree, men) have been experiencing it for as long as there have been workplaces ... But pervasive sexual harassment, and the toll taken on those who are victimized by it, didn't receive the nationwide outpouring of outrage it deserved until this year, when it became a problem of the rich, famous and successful. It took dozens of A-list actresses and internationally known models coming forward to accuse producer Harvey Weinstein of sexual misconduct to spark the backlash that became the #MeToo movement. So far, the headlines have mostly been attached to the stories of women in the high-profile fields of entertainment, media, tech and politics who have alleged various forms of sexual misconduct by powerful and often well-known men. Missing have been the stories of the hotel maids, farmworkers, restaurant servers and others whose economic need and relative powerlessness has often left them without recourse ... If there's to be a second act to this cultural movement — and we hope there will be — it should focus on the plight of lower-wage workers in industries where sexual harassment is also rampant, but where victims have fewer resources than the average movie star. Many of these women are immigrants or women of color, with little protection from retaliation if they complain.[103]

Some commentary emphasized MeToo's political significance. The *New York Times* editors cautiously reflected: "hundreds of long-silent women are calling out powerful, influential men at a remarkable clip and accusing them of sexual misconduct ... this reckoning is all to the good, even if it is far too late." They wrote of the significance of MeToo following a 2013 Supreme Court ruling declaring that Title VII of the Civil Rights Act only makes employers legally culpable for sex- and race-based discrimination by supervisors with the power to hire and fire workers, but not for the behavior of other types of supervisors. The *Times* urged Congress to pass legislation requiring employers to publicly report the sexual harassment claims filed each year, and to reverse the Supreme Court ruling by establishing a "broader and more realistic definition of a supervisor."[104] While each of these editorials focused on different elements of MeToo, they all called on larger principles of equality and resistance to misogyny as worthy goals.

With extensive reporting that provided Americans with access to the multiple grievances driving the movement, one would expect attention to the news would produce increased support for MeToo. Numerous findings confirm this prediction. By December 2017, 92 percent of Americans acknowledged paying attention to MeToo-related allegations in the news.[105] An October 2017 *NBC/Wall Street Journal* poll asked Americans about their attention to "high-profile" news stories on MeToo, and whether being exposed to these stories made respondents more sympathetic to women alleging sexual assault and harassment. Forty-four percent of women said attention to news on MeToo made them "want to share" their "own past experiences" about how they "have been treated as a woman."[106] The same number of men agreed attention to sexual harassment and assault allegations "changed" their "view about how women are treated in society."[107] Similarly, 49 percent of men felt attention to these stories "caused" them "to think about" their "own behavior" and how they "interact with women."[108] Seventy-seven percent of men said reporting on sexual allegations against prominent men "made" them "more likely to speak out" if they "see a woman treated unfairly."[109] A November 2017 *Quinnipiac* survey found 55 percent of respondents – and about an equal number of men and women – felt "recent allegations of sexual harassment in the news these days" gave people "a better understanding of sexual harassment."[110] Finally, 62 percent of Americans – with an almost equal number of men and women agreeing – felt "recent allegations of sexual harassment in the news" contributed to an environment in which "people are more likely to be held accountable for sexual harassment" than in the past.[111] These survey findings suggest that women's rights activists effectively utilized the media to cultivate public support for a renewed campaign against sexism in the workplace and elsewhere. Whether it was most Americans, or a large minority who agreed with the statements above, tens of millions of citizens became increasingly sympathetic to MeToo.

To measure how MeToo appealed to the public, I designed a nationally representative survey, administered in January 2018, asking 1,000 respondents their opinions of the movement. The survey asked whether respondents "agreed" "regarding recent allegations of sexual harassment and assault that have been made against prominent men in entertainment, politics, and the media" whether these acts "are mainly isolated incidents of individual misconduct," or if "they reflect a widespread problem in society."[112] Nearly two-thirds agreed the allegations suggested a "widespread problem in society." Only a minority of Americans – just over a quarter, felt the allegations against prominent men were merely "isolated incidents."

I also examined opinions of MeToo by demographic subgroups. Support for MeToo is widely distributed across different age groups, although those aged 65 and over are the smallest group of supporters. Those agreeing with the movement come from various incomes, with those earning over $100,000 being the largest group. They are almost evenly split between Democrats, independents, and Republicans. About a quarter of supporters have a high-school degree or less, while a third have "some college" or a two-year degree, a quarter have a four-year degree, and less than 20 percent have a graduate or professional degree. More supporters are women – 54 percent – than men. MeToo draws widely from different racial groups, with black and LatinX Americans representing a quarter of movement supporters. Those Americans who are heavily reliant on far-right-wing media – including *Fox News*, Rush Limbaugh, *InfoWars*, *Breitbart.com*, and *Drudge Report* – are a minority of MeToo supporters, with those relying less heavily on these outlets compromising the large majority of movement supporters.

Contrary to my conservative media findings, my analysis of *Pew*'s December 2017 national survey finds that overall media consumption was associated with increased support for MeToo. This should be expected, considering my documentation of how media coverage of MeToo favored the movement by stressing the problems of sexual harassment and discrimination along multiple dimensions. Those paying "a lot" of attention to sexual harassment allegations against prominent men were significantly more likely to agree that this reporting spoke to "widespread problems in society" with sexism, after controlling for respondents' party, ideology, gender, age, education, race, and income.[113] Finally, my analysis of *Pew*'s December 2017 survey finds ideology was also significant in impacting attitudes, with liberal Americans more likely to identify with MeToo compared to moderates and conservatives.[114]

What factors best predicted support for the movement? Drawing on my survey data, Figure 5.8 provides estimates for how each demographic group related to attitudes of MeToo. The factors most strongly associated with movement support included age and gender,

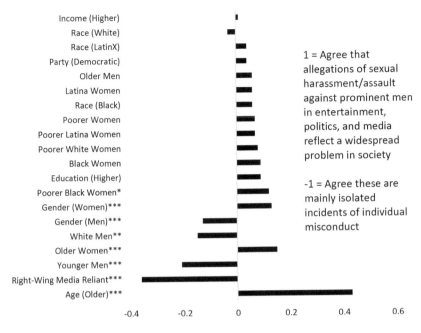

Figure 5.8 Predictors of Support for #MeToo
Source: Author's poll, January 2018
Statistical Significance Levels: *** = 0.1% ** = 1% * = 5%
Controls: gender, age, education, race, income, political party

with older Americans, women, and older women the most strongly linked to movement support. To a lesser extent, poorer black women are also more likely to support MeToo. Some groups are less likely to support, and even more likely to oppose MeToo, including those who rely heavily on right-wing media, younger men, and white men. But some factors are neither positively nor negatively associated with MeToo. These include income, race and ethnicity (white, black, LatinX), and education. My supplemental analysis of *Pew*'s December 2017 survey finds that media attention to sexual harassment charges was about as strong as gender in predicting support for MeToo, after controlling for other demographic factors previously discussed. Heavier media consumers and liberals were each about 20 percent more likely than low media consumers and conservatives to agree MeToo spotlighted societal problems with sexism, while women were 12 percent more likely to agree than men.

The increased appeal of MeToo among women should be no revelation, since women are much more likely to be sexually harassed and assaulted than men. Greater support among older Americans, and older women in particular, is likely due to the cumulative experiences with sexism and discrimination that women face as they age. Having dealt with the problem of misogyny their entire lives, older women are more likely to recognize it as a serious societal problem. It is also not surprising that men are relatively less supportive of MeToo, since they are less likely to face gender-based discrimination, and more likely to be purveyors of such acts. Generally speaking, white men have historically held the dominant position in America in terms of social prestige and holding social, political, and economic leadership positions. Younger men's reduced support for MeToo, however, raises questions. Younger Americans are widely seen as more liberal-to-progressive politically, so it might be expected that they would be more in tune with allegations of sexual abuse. On the other hand, younger men are less likely to be victims of sexual abuse and relatively more likely than younger women to be sexual aggressors, so these factors may be playing into their reduced sympathy toward MeToo. Finally, those who heavily trust and rely on right-wing media were the most antagonistic toward the movement. This is to be expected considering the strong attachment between the far right and sexism under Trump.

Intersectional identities played little role in impacting opinions of MeToo. Outside of poorer black women, other identity groups pertaining to race, gender, and class were not significantly more likely to feel one way or another about the movement. These findings apply to poorer women, older men, black and Latina women, and poorer white and Latina women. The weak role of intersectionality in explaining MeToo attitudes likely relates to the public face of the movement in late 2017, which was largely white Hollywood women. In a plutocratic political system, the interests of affluent whites and affluent white males are elevated above other considerations. The rise of MeToo represented a partial reversal of this trend, via women's challenges to political, economic, and entertainment systems dominated by privileged white men. But those challenging these men were overwhelmingly white professional women working in the entertainment industry. This leadership of MeToo limited the effectiveness of the battle over women's rights.

MeToo's impact can be assessed by examining its effects on public attitudes about sexism, on solidarity building, on MeToo's practical impact on interpersonal relations, and its effects on U.S. political economy. On public opinion, we see significant changes occurring in late 2017 and early 2018. By February 2018, 51 percent of Americans believed the movement against sexual harassment and abuse helped address gender inequality, compared to 20 percent feeling it had a negative impact by treating men unfairly.[115] These results reveal a large majority of Americans – 71 percent – felt the movement had some impact on sex and gender relations in the country. Most Americans in March 2018 – 58 percent – also believed increased attention to workplace sexual harassment because of MeToo was "an appropriate response to a problem that has been ignored for too long," and agreed that "addressing it [harassment] will help women in the workplace."[116] In contrast, only a third agreed attention to sexual abuse had "gone too far" and was "calling into question all interactions between men and women in the workplace, which will hurt people's ability to do their jobs."[117] One-quarter of Americans at the end of 2017 said MeToo or the January Women's March were "personally" the "most significant and important" events of the year.[118] Finally, a plurality – 49 percent – believe MeToo was a "watershed moment" in history "when it comes to sexual harassment in the workplace."[119] The historic importance of the movement was also captured by the feeling of 67 percent of Americans that a "greater focus" on "addressing sexual harassment in the workplace" led to "a long-term change of attitudes about this issue."[120] These results indicate MeToo's rise was a significant moment in modern history – with serious effects on how Americans look at sexual abuse. While the problems of sexism have not disappeared, increased attention to these problems meant that progress was made in holding institutions and individuals accountable for sexual abuse.

MeToo was driven by feelings of solidarity in the pursuit of justice for the women victimized by sexual aggression. The movement altered public discourse by strengthening the notion that citizens have a collective responsibility to acknowledge the sexism endemic in institutions and interpersonal behavior, and to fight sexual abuse. Some attitudes revealed unification across the country, as seen in 52 percent of Americans agreeing that protests of sexual harassment "change[d] the nation for the better," and in the feeling of 72 percent of Americans that sexual harassment was a "serious problem in this country."[121] References to "the nation" and "this country" suggest a common mindset for MeToo supporters, who were part of a larger social justice campaign. The public commitment to justice was apparent among 56 percent of Americans supporting MeToo so that abusers would be "held accountable" for their behavior. Nearly one in five Americans in 2017 agreed the rise of sexual abuse allegations made them "more likely to believe someone who reports sexual harassment" than they were in the past.[122] This represents a significant shift, even if not a seismic one. A final sign that MeToo served to forge collective identities was evident in the sentiment, expressed by 73 percent of women, that MeToo's emergence meant "I would know I'm not alone" in the fight against sexual abuse "because I can see others getting support."[123] The attitudes above demonstrate social movements are not simply mechanical manifestations of individualism. Rather, empathy building is central to movement success, and to the pursuit of common goods.

MeToo altered how individuals interact with each other in the workplace and outside of it. Nearly three-quarters of Americans agreed in 2017 that corporations firing high-profile male professionals over sexual abuse allegations is warranted, suggesting citizens were becoming less tolerant of sexism in the economy.[124] In March 2018, almost a third of women agreed the chance they would sue someone who harassed them grew because of rising protests of sexual harassment.[125] One late 2017 poll found two-thirds of women said "the recent outpouring of accusations" against men for sexual abuse made them "feel more comfortable speaking out and challenging" their abusers, compared to only a third of women who felt MeToo had no effect on their mindset.[126]

Employers and their employees responded to this pressure as well. More than a third of Americans said MeToo led to a push in their workplaces for "increased accountability or penalties for people who engage in improper behavior of a sexual nature."[127] Almost half reflected the movement had the effect in their workplaces of increasing "the training or discussion about what is appropriate behavior" in professional settings.[128] Nearly 30 percent agree MeToo motivated men in work settings to "change their behavior" via their interactions with women.[129] These reported changes are sizable, affecting a third to half of the employed population.

Lastly, MeToo resonated with Americans regarding voting behavior and policy outcomes. It placed pressure on officials accused of sexual harassment and abuse to resign or not to run for re-election, while many voters signaled MeToo impacted how they looked at electoral candidates. Two-thirds of respondents in a December 2017 survey said they would definitely not vote for a political candidate who was accused of multiple acts of sexual harassment.[130] Nearly three-quarters agreed allegations of sexual harassment against a candidate were important to their vote in the 2018 Congressional elections.[131] Sixty percent felt political officials accused of multiple acts of sexual abuse should resign, while 50 percent said Trump should resign due to the multiple sexual allegations against him.[132] A greater number of Americans – 63 percent – supported a Congressional investigation into allegations of sexual harassment and abuse relating to Trump.[133] Furthermore, there was also a tangible impact on political outcomes, with eight Congressmen by January 2018 either resigning or indicating they would not seek re-election due to sexual assault and discrimination allegations.[134] In the states, 32 lawmakers left office or lost election races as a result of MeToo-related accusations, and numerous states passed laws to revise the rules for workplace non-disclosure agreements protecting sexual harassment assailants, for improving the testing of rape kits, and for extending statutes of limitation for those seeking to file civil suits against perpetrators of sexual crimes. Furthermore, MeToo pressured nearly every statehouse to reassess its policies for addressing workplace sexual harassment.[135]

Conclusion

This chapter, by including analyses of many different case studies of protests during Trump's presidency, documented the role of social

The Anti-Trump Uprising and Beyond 263

movements in opposing right-wing politics and sexism. The anti-Trump protests, while resonating with the public, had limited effects on public policy outside of the efforts to stifle the repeal of "Obamacare". Sociologists speak of political opportunity structures as determining how effective left social movements are in influencing policy. In 2017, the federal government was under the control of Republicans, so there were few opportunities for liberal movements to promote policy change. Still, the anti-Trump movement, by drawing on support from the Democratic Party establishment, reached Americans through waves of protests in the streets and sustained media coverage, galvanizing public opposition to Trump, his agenda, and sexism.

The movement stoked the flames of discontent against rising right-wing political power. The protests of Trump's inauguration, and against his immigration, tax, education, and health-care policies, showed many Americans were unwilling to normalize reactionary social and economic policies. These protests helped disrupt the ruling political order. But they were different from leftist movements. BLM and the economic justice movement were politically progressive-to-radical, and struggled to transform American politics at a time when both parties embraced a plutocratic approach to governing. These movements pressured a reluctant government to adopt policies that would benefit large numbers of Americans suffering from racial discrimination, poverty, and growing economic insecurity. In contrast, the broad initial appeal of the anti-Trump movement meant significant space for a close link with the Democratic Party. The close alliance between the movement and Democrats limited the independent power of the anti-Trump protests.

Finally, MeToo created a national discussion about misogyny and sexual abuse in the private sector and in government. And it broadly mobilized women, in addition to other demographic groups. MeToo spotlighted the sexism endemic in American life, using the news to build public support. The movement transformed how men and women interact with each other in professional, political, and personal settings.

Notes

1 Euan McKirdy, Susanna Capelouto, and Max Blau, "Thousands Take to the Streets to Protest Trump Win," *CNN.com*, November 10, 2016, https://www.cnn.com/2016/11/09/politics/election-results-reaction-streets/index.html.
2 Christopher Mele and Annie Correal, "'Not Our President': Protests Spread after Donald Trump's Election," *New York Times*, November 9, 2016, https://www.nytimes.com/2016/11/10/us/trump-election-protests.html.
3 Erica Chenoweth and Jeremy Pressman, "Analysis: In Washington, D.C., It Was the Largest Protest since the Anti-Vietnam War Protests in the 1960's and 1970's. This Is What We Learned by Counting the Women's Marches," *Washington Post*, February 7, 2017, https://www.washingtonpost.com/news/monkey-cage/wp/2017/02/07/this-is-what-we-learned-by-counting-the-womens-marches/?utm_term=.687d3f9fb1d3; Heidi M. Przybyla and

Fredreka Schouten, "At 2.6 Million Strong, Women's Marches Crush Expectations," *USA Today*, January 22, 2017, https://www.usatoday.com/story/news/politics/2017/01/21/womens-march-aims-start-movement-trump-inauguration/96864158/.
4 Angela Davis, "Angela Davis Speaks at Women's March in Washington, DC," *Youtube.com*, January 21, 2017, https://www.youtube.com/watch?v=_LKQRXYyRn8.
5 *Washington Post*, "Washington Post January Poll," *iPoll*, January 25–29, 2017.
6 *Washington Post*, "Washington Post January Poll," 2017.
7 Gallup, "Presidential Approval Ratings – Donald Trump," *Gallup.com*, 2018, http://news.gallup.com/poll/203198/presidential-approval-ratings-donald-trump.aspx.
8 Richard North Patterson, "The Dangerous Path of Trump's Xenophobia," *Boston Globe*, October 2, 2017, https://www.bostonglobe.com/opinion/2017/10/02/the-dangerous-path-trump-xenophobia/Dqc3cxdGm7rsElqJaFRf8M/story.html; Suman Raghunathan, "Trump's Xenophobic Vision of America Is Inciting Racist Violence," *The Nation*, January 27, 2018, https://www.thenation.com/article/trumps-xenophobic-vision-of-america-is-inciting-racist-violence/.
9 Jenna Johnson, "Trump Calls for 'Total and Complete Shutdown of Muslims Entering the United States," *Washington Post*, December 8, 2015, https://www.washingtonpost.com/news/post-politics/wp/2015/12/07/donald-trump-calls-for-total-and-complete-shutdown-of-muslims-entering-the-united-states/?utm_term=.9ef394823702.
10 Amy B. Wang, "Trump Asked for a 'Muslim Ban,' Giuliani Says, and Ordered a Commission to Do It 'Legally,'" *Washington Post*, January 29, 2017, https://www.washingtonpost.com/news/the-fix/wp/2017/01/29/trump-asked-for-a-muslim-ban-giuliani-says-and-ordered-a-commission-to-do-it-legally/?utm_term=.2fd00f604fc3.
11 Philip E. Wolgin, "The High Cost of Ending Deferred Action for Childhood Arrivals," *American Progress*, November 18, 2016, https://www.americanprogress.org/issues/immigration/news/2016/11/18/292550/the-high-cost-of-ending-deferred-action-for-childhood-arrivals/; Emanuella Grinberg and Eliott C. McLaughlin, "Travel Ban Protests Stretch into Third Day from US to UK," *CNN.com*, January 31, 2017, https://www.cnn.com/2017/01/30/politics/travel-ban-protests-immigration/index.html; Esther Yu Hsi Lee, "The Week the Country United against Trump's Xenophobia," *Think Progress*, January 27, 2018, https://thinkprogress.org/muslim-ban-one-year-anniversary-ce90b97d04da/.
12 Lauren Gambino, Sabrina Siddiqui, Paul Owen, and Edward Helmore, "Thousands Protest against Trump Travel Ban in Cities and Airports Nationwide," *The Guardian*, January 29, 2017, https://www.theguardian.com/us-news/2017/jan/29/protest-trump-travel-ban-muslims-airports.
13 Grinberg and McLaughlin, "Travel Ban Protests Stretch into Third Day from US to UK," 2017.
14 Daniel Marans, "Americans Protest Trump's Travel Ban for a Second Weekend," *Huffington Post*, February 4, 2017, https://www.huffingtonpost.com/entry/protests-trump-travel-ban_us_58964933e4b0406131373798.
15 Adam Liptak, "Supreme Court Allows Trump Travel Ban to Take Effect," *New York Times*, December 4, 2017, https://www.nytimes.com/2017/12/04/us/politics/trump-travel-ban-supreme-court.html.

The Anti-Trump Uprising and Beyond 265

16 Michelle Merlin, "Lehigh University Faculty Overwhelmingly Vote to Ask Trustees to Rescind Trump's Honorary Degree," *Morning Call*, February 27, 2018, http://www.mcall.com/news/breaking/mc-nws-lehigh-professors-trump-honorary-degree-20180212-story.html.

17 Lauren Rosenblatt, "Protesters March in Washington to Show Support for DACA," *Los Angeles Times*, September 5, 2017, http://www.latimes.com/politics/la-dreamers-decision-live-updates-protesters-march-on-washington-to-1504637282-htmlstory.html.

18 Meghan Keneally, "DACA Announcement Sparks Protests Nationwide, Dozens Arrested at Trump Tower," *ABC News*, September 6, 2017, http://abcnews.go.com/Politics/arrests-made-daca-protest-york/story?id=49625957.

19 Tony Briscoe, "Hundreds March in Loop to Protest Trump's Decision to End DACA," *Chicago Tribune*, September 6, 2017, http://www.chicagotribune.com/news/local/breaking/ct-trump-daca-announcement-chicago-met-2-20170905-story.html.

20 Carlos Ballesteros, "Dreamers Occupy Senate Building for DACA Rights," *Newsweek*, November 9, 2017, http://www.newsweek.com/daca-dreamers-immigration-protest-senate-706985; Julian Routh, "Demonstrators to 'Occupy' Pittsburg GOP Congressional Offices in Reaction to DACA announcement," *Pittsburgh Post-Gazette*, September 5, 2017, http://www.post-gazette.com/news/politics-state/2017/09/05/President-Donald-Trump-DACA-protest-occupy-Rothfus-Murphy-Congress-Congressmen-Dreamers-immigrants-undocumented/stories/201709050110; Hannah Jones, "Protesters Gather Outside Minnesota Lawmakers' Offices to Support 'Dreamers,'" *Savage Pacer*, March 8, 2018, http://www.swnewsmedia.com/savage_pacer/news/protesters-gather-outside-minnesota-lawmakers-offices-to-support-dreamers/article_5ece0800-0c12-51ed-b77d-c7bddb723aca.html; Ryan Santistevan, "DACA Recipients Continue to Press Flake for 'Clean' Dream Act," *The Arizona Republic*, December 19, 2017, https://www.azcentral.com/story/news/local/phoenix/2017/12/19/daca-recipients-continue-press-jeff-flake-clean-dream-act/963611001/.

21 Ali Rogin and Mariam Khan, "Dreamers Deferred as Congress Lets DACA Deadline Pass," *ABC News*, March 5, 2018, http://abcnews.go.com/Politics/dreamers-deferred-congress-lets-daca-deadline-pass/story?id=53464924.

22 Max Greenwood, "Poll: Nearly 9 in 10 Want DACA Recipients to Stay in U.S.," *The Hill*, January 18, 2018, http://thehill.com/blogs/blog-briefing-room/news/369487-poll-nearly-nine-in-10-favor-allowing-daca-recipients-to-stay.

23 Gallup, "Gallup January 2017 Poll," *iPoll*, January 30–31, 2017; Polling Report, "Quinnipiac University Poll," March 16–21, 2017, *Pollingreport.com*, http://www.pollingreport.com/immigration.htm.

24 Doug Stanglin and Heidi M. Przybyla, "Tax Day Protesters Demand Trump Release His Returns," *USA Today*, April 16, 2017, https://www.usatoday.com/story/news/2017/04/15/tax-day-marches-aim-pressure-trump-release-his-returns/100497026/.

25 *CBS/Associated Press*, "'Tax March' Protests Demand Release of Trump's Tax Returns," *CBSnews.com*, April 15, 2017, https://www.cbsnews.com/news/tax-march-protests-demand-donald-trump-to-release-tax-returns/; Chelsea Bailey and Alex Seitz-Wald, "Demonstrators Demand President Trump Produce Tax Returns," *NBC News*, April 15,

2017, https://www.nbcnews.com/news/us-news/tax-day-demonstrators-demand-president-trump-produce-tax-returns-n746986.
26 Alex Seitz-Wald, "Tax Day Protests to Demand Trump's Returns," *NBC News.com*, April 14, 2017, https://www.nbcnews.com/storyline/democrats-vs-trump/tax-day-protests-demand-trump-s-returns-n746146.
27 Stanglin and Przybyla, "Tax Day Protesters Demand Trump Release His Returns," 2017.
28 Frank Newport, "Majority Say Wealthy Americans, Corporations Taxed Too Little," *Gallup.com*, April 18, 2017, http://news.gallup.com/poll/208685/majority-say-wealthy-americans-corporations-taxed-little.aspx.
29 Quinnipiac University, "American Voters Still Want to See Trump's Tax Returns, Quinnipiac University National Poll Finds," *Quinnipiac University*, February 21, 2018, https://poll.qu.edu/national/release-detail?ReleaseID=2522; Stanglin and Przybyla, "Tax Day Protesters Demand Trump Release His Returns," 2017; Joshua Gillin, "Trump Wrong that Americans Don't Care about His Tax Returns," *Politifact*, January 11, 2017, http://www.politifact.com/truth-o-meter/statements/2017/jan/11/donald-trump/trump-wrong-reporters-are-only-ones-who-care-about/.
30 Anthony DiMaggio, "Fool Me Twice? Americans Reject Trump's Tax Cuts," *Counterpunch*, October 30, 2017, https://www.counterpunch.org/2017/10/30/fool-me-twice-americans-reject-trumps-tax-cuts/.
31 Danielle Kurtzleben, "Here's How GOP's Tax Breaks Would Shift Money to Rich, Poor Americans," *National Public Radio*, November 14, 2017, https://www.npr.org/2017/11/14/562884070/charts-heres-how-gops-tax-breaks-would-shift-money-to-rich-poor-americans.
32 Laura Smith-Spark and Jason Hanna, "March for Science: Protesters Gather Worldwide to Support 'Evidence,'" *CNN.com*, April 23, 2017, https://www.cnn.com/2017/04/22/health/global-march-for-science/index.html.
33 Smith-Spark and Hanna, "March for Science," 2017.
34 Julia Belluz and Umair Irfan, "The Disturbing New Language of Science under Trump, Explained," *Vox*, December 20, 2017, https://www.vox.com/2017/12/20/16793010/cdc-word-ban-trump-censorship-language.
35 Dan Merica, Jeremy Diamond, and Kevin Liptak, "Trump Proposes Defense Spending Boost, $54 Billion in Cuts to 'Most Federal Agencies,'" *CNN.com*, February 27, 2017, https://www.cnn.com/2017/02/27/politics/trump-budget-proposal/index.html.
36 Nicholas St. Fleur, "Scientists, Feeling under Siege, March against Trump Policies," *New York Times*, April 22, 2017, https://www.nytimes.com/2017/04/22/science/march-for-science.html.
37 March for Science, "The Science behind the March for Science Crowd Estimates," *Medium.com*, May 10, 2017, https://medium.com/marchforscience-blog/the-science-behind-the-march-for-science-crowd-estimates-f337adf2d665.
38 Ed Yong, "What Exactly Are People Marching for When They March for Science?", *The Atlantic*, March 7, 2017, https://www.theatlantic.com/science/archive/2017/03/what-exactly-are-people-marching-for-when-they-march-for-science/518763/.
39 Science News Staff, "How Science Fares in the U.S. Budget Deal," *Science*, May 1, 2017, http://www.sciencemag.org/news/2017/05/how-science-fares-us-budget-deal.
40 Dina Fine Maron, "Trump Administration Restricts News from Federal Scientists at USDA, EPA," *Scientific American*, January 24, 2017, https://

www.scientificamerican.com/article/trump-administration-restricts-news-from-federal-scientists-at-usda-epa/.
41 David Roberts, "There's a Huge Gap between the Paris Climate Change Goals and Reality," *Vox*, October 31, 2017, https://www.vox.com/energy-and-environment/2017/10/31/16579844/climate-gap-unep-2017.
42 My examination of news stories and other articles included any articles mentioning the "March for Science" in the *New York Times* and other news venues. Of those stories, I searched for any articles that referenced "Trump," that discussed "climate change," the "environment," or "environmental" issues, and that referenced "funding" for scientific research and education.
43 Lee Rainie, "U.S. Public Trust in Science and Scientists," *Pew Research Center*, June 27, 2017, http://www.pewinternet.org/2017/06/27/u-s-public-trust-in-science-and-scientists/.
44 Cary Funk and Lee Rainie, "Public and Scientists' Views on Science and Society," *Pew Research Center*, January 29, 2015, http://www.pewinternet.org/2015/01/29/public-and-scientists-views-on-science-and-society/.
45 Quinnipiac University, "Quinnipiac University March 2017 Poll," March 3–April 3, 2017, *iPoll*.
46 *Pew Research Center*, "Pew Political Poll, May 2017," *iPoll*, May 3–7, 2017.
47 *Pew Research Center*, "Pew Political Poll, May 2017," 2017.
48 *Pew Research Center*, "Pew Political Poll, May 2017," 2017.
49 *Pew Research Center*, "Pew Political Poll, May 2017," 2017.
50 *Pew Research Center*, "Pew Political Poll, May 2017," 2017.
51 Hannah Fingerhut, "Republicans Skeptical of Colleges' Impact on U.S., But Most See Benefits for Workforce Preparation," *Pew Research Center*, July 20, 2017, http://www.pewresearch.org/fact-tank/2017/07/20/republicans-skeptical-of-colleges-impact-on-u-s-but-most-see-benefits-for-workforce-preparation/.
52 Rainie, "U.S. Public Trust in Science and Scientists," 2017; Scott Neuman, "1 in 4 Americans Thinks the Sun Goes around the Earth, Survey Says," *National Public Radio*, February 14, 2014, https://www.npr.org/sections/thetwo-way/2014/02/14/277058739/1-in-4-americans-think-the-sun-goes-around-the-earth-survey-says.
53 Scott Horsley, "GOP Senate Bill Would Cut Health Care Coverage by 22 Million," *National Public Radio*, June 26, 2017, https://www.npr.org/2017/06/26/534432433/gop-senate-bill-would-cut-health-care-coverage-by-22-million.
54 Patrick Caldwell, "Powerful Scenes from the Health Care Rally Outside Congress," *Mother Jones*, June 28, 2017, https://www.motherjones.com/politics/2017/06/a-health-care-rally-is-underway-outside-congress-follow-the-protests-live/.
55 Emily Karl, Ted Barrett, and Grace Hauck, "80 Arrested on Capitol Hill after Health Care Protests," *CNN.com*, July 10, 2017, https://www.cnn.com/2017/07/10/politics/health-care-protests-capitol-hill/index.html.
56 Heidi M. Przybyla, "Progressives Stage Health Care Sit-ins Outside Republican Lawmaker Offices," *USA Today*, July 6, 2017, https://www.usatoday.com/story/news/politics/2017/07/06/progressives-stage-health-care-sit-ins-outside-republican-lawmaker-offices/454915001/.
57 Tim Stelloh, "Protesters Rail against GOP's Latest Obamacare Repeal Effort," *NBC News*, June 27, 2017, https://www.nbcnews.com/politics/congress/protesters-rail-against-gop-s-latest-obamacare-repeal-effort-n777026.

58 Stelloh, "Protesters Rail against GOP's Latest Obamacare Repeal Effort," 2017.
59 Elyssa Cherney, "Health Care Workers Protest Efforts to Overhaul Obamacare," *Chicago Tribune*, March 23, 2017, http://www.chicagotribune.com/news/local/breaking/ct-health-care-rally-met-20170323-story.html.
60 Polling Report, "Quinnipiac University Poll: July 27–August 1, 2017," *Pollingreport.com*, 2017, http://www.pollingreport.com/health.htm.
61 Polling Report, "NPR/PBS NewsHour/Maris Poll: November 13–15, 2017," *Pollingreport.com*, 2017, http://www.pollingreport.com/health.htm.
62 Polling Report, "Kaiser Family Foundation Poll: June 14–19, 2017," *Pollingreport.com*, 2017, http://www.pollingreport.com/health.htm.
63 Leeron Hoory, "GOP Reps Return Home to Angry Constituents in Health Care Town Halls," *AOL News*, May 9, 2017, https://www.aol.com/article/news/2017/05/09/gop-reps-return-home-to-angry-constituents-in-health-care-town-h/22078406/; Diamond Naga Siu, "Republican Senators Hit by Calls From Voters Worried about Obamacare Repeal Bill," *Politico*, June 27, 2017, http://www.politico.com/story/2017/06/27/republican-health-care-bill-voter-response-239981; Stelloh, "Protesters Rail against GOP's Latest Obamacare Repeal Effort," 2017.
64 Alicia Parlapiano, Wilson Andrews, Jasmine C. Lee, and Rachel Shorey, "How Each Senator Voted on Obamacare Repeal Proposals," *New York Times*, July 28, 2017, https://www.nytimes.com/interactive/2017/07/25/us/politics/senate-votes-repeal-obamacare.html?mcubz=3.
65 Ashley Killough, "Republicans Opposing GOP Health Care Plan Hear from Voters During Recess," *CNN.com*, July 5, 2017, http://www.cnn.com/2017/07/05/politics/republicans-health-care-plan-july-4-holiday/index.html; Charlotte Alter, "How Women Helped Save Obamacare," *Time*, July 29, 2017, http://time.com/4878724/donald-trump-gop-health-care-women/; Eric Bradner, "Nevada's Heller Dogged by Summer of Reversals on Health Care," *CNN.com*, September 21, 2017, http://www.cnn.com/2017/09/21/politics/dean-heller-nevada-health-care/index.html.
66 M. J. Lee, Phil Mattingly, and Ted Barrett, "Latest Health Care Bill Collapses Following Moran, Lee Defections," *CNN.com*, July 18, 2017, http://www.cnn.com/2017/07/17/politics/health-care-motion-to-proceed-jerry-moran-mike-lee/index.html.
67 John Bresnahan, Burgess Everett, Jennifer Haberkorn, and Seung Min Kim, "Senate Rejects Obamacare Repeal," *Politico*, July 28, 2017, http://www.politico.com/story/2017/07/27/obamacare-repeal-republicans-status-241025.
68 Jacob Kauffman, "Update: Senator Cotton Backs Healthcare Repeal without Replacement, Governor Disagrees," *KASU.org*, July 19, 2017, http://kasu.org/post/update-senator-cotton-backs-healthcare-repeal-without-replacement-governor-disagrees.
69 Ed Kilgore, "GOP Senators Begin to Question Health-Care Bill's Tax Cuts for the Rich," *New York Magazine*, July 28, 2017, http://nymag.com/intelligencer/2017/06/gop-senators-question-health-bills-tax-cuts-for-the-rich.html.
70 Anthony DiMaggio, "Americans Are Resisting Trump's Authoritarianism," *Salon.com*, June 18, 2017, https://www.salon.com/2017/06/18/americans-are-resisting-trumps-authoritarianism/.

71 Gallup, "Gallup Daily: Trump Job Approval," *Gallup.com*, 2018, http://news.gallup.com/poll/201617/gallup-daily-trump-job-approval.aspx.
72 Reena Flores, "Hillary Clinton, Democrats Show Support for Women's March on Washington," *CBS News*, January 21, 2017, https://www.cbsnews.com/news/womens-march-on-washington-hillary-clinton-politicians/.
73 Anthony Zurcher, "Hillary Clinton Joins the 'Trump Resistance,'" *BBC News*, May 3, 2017, http://www.bbc.com/news/world-us-canada-39788317; Kristin Fisher, "Hillary Clinton, on Book Tour, Cheers the 'Resistance,'" *Foxnews.com*, September 18, 2017, http://www.foxnews.com/politics/2017/09/18/hillary-clinton-on-book-tour-cheers-resistance.html.
74 Erin Kelly and Eliza Collins, "Democrats Condemn Trump's Revised Travel Order as 'Still a Muslim Ban,'" *USA Today*, March 6, 2017, https://www.usatoday.com/story/news/politics/2017/03/06/democrats-condemn-trumps-revised-travel-order-still-muslim-ban/98805416/; Emily Shugerman, "Democrats Introduce Bill to Block Trump's Travel Ban," *Independent*, November 17, 2017, https://www.independent.co.uk/news/world/americas/us-politics/trump-travel-ban-bill-block-muslim-countries-restrictions-democrats-law-latest-a8061346.html.
75 Tim Murphy, "Democrats Are Using Their State of the Union Plus-Ones to Protest the President," *Mother Jones*, January 30, 2018, https://www.motherjones.com/politics/2018/01/democrats-are-using-their-state-of-the-union-plus-ones-to-protest-the-president/.
76 Heidi M. Przybyla, "With Tax March, Democrats Become Party of Revolt amid Rising Inequality," *USA Today*, April 14, 2017, https://www.usatoday.com/story/news/politics/2017/04/14/tax-march-democrats-become-party-revolt-amid-rising-inequality/100456942/; Andrew Rafferty, "De Blasio and Dems Mock Trump on Tax Day," *NBCnews.com*, April 18, 2017, https://www.nbcnews.com/politics/politics-news/de-blasio-dems-mock-trump-tax-day-n747811; Naomi Jagoda, "House Panel Rejects Measure to Seek Trump's Tax Returns," *The Hill*, September 7, 2017, http://thehill.com/policy/finance/349699-house-panel-rejects-measure-to-seek-trumps-tax-returns.
77 Parlapiano et al., "How Each Senator Voted on Obamacare Repeal Proposals," 2017.
78 *Fox News*, "Fox News Poll, February 2018," *iPoll*, February 10–13, 2018.
79 Associated Press–NORC, "GenForward Survey: August 2017," *iPoll*, August 31–September 16, 2017.
80 Eli Watkins and Abby Phillip, "Trump Decries Immigrants from 'Shithole Countries' Coming to U.S.," *CNN.com*, January 12, 2018, https://www.cnn.com/2018/01/11/politics/immigrants-shithole-countries-trump/index.html; Anna North, "The Summer Zervos Sexual Assault Allegations and Lawsuit against Donald Trump, Explained," *Vox*, March 26, 2018, https://www.vox.com/policy-and-politics/2018/3/26/17151766/summer-zervos-case-trump-lawsuit-sexual-assault-allegations; Mark Makela, "Transcript: Donald Trump's Taped Comments About Women," *New York Times*, October 8, 2016, https://www.nytimes.com/2016/10/08/us/donald-trump-tape-transcript.html; Mattie Kahn, "In Newly Leaked Tapes, Donald Trump Deems Angelina Jolie 'a Seven' and Declares Ivanka is Better Looking than Charlize Theron," *Elle*, September 26, 2017, https://www.elle.com/culture/career-politics/a12474753/donald-trump-ranks-women-hollywood-

tapes/; Kate Snow, "Trump and the Muslim 'Problem,'" *MSNBC.com*, May 11, 2016, https://www.msnbc.com/kate-snow/watch/trump-and-the-muslim-problem-683851843512; BBC, "'Drug Dealers, Criminals, Rapists': What Trump Thinks of Mexicans," *BBC News*, August 31, 2016, http://www.bbc.com/news/av/world-us-canada-37230916/drug-dealers-criminals-rapists-what-trump-thinks-of-mexicans; Jamiles Lartey, "Racism and Donald Trump: A Common Thread throughout His Career and Life," *Guardian*, January 12, 2018, https://www.theguardian.com/us-news/2018/jan/12/racism-and-donald-trump-a-common-thread-throughout-his-career-and-life.

81 *Pew Research Center*, "Pew Research Center Poll, February 2017," *iPoll*, February 7–12, 2017.

82 NPR, "NPR/PBS NewsHour/Maris Poll, August 2017," *iPoll*, August 14–15, 2017.

83 Yale University/George Mason University, "Climate Change in the Latino Mind Survey, May 2017," *iPoll*, May 18–June 8, 2017.

84 Stacy Jones and Grace Donnelly, "Walmart's New Jobs Approach Could Be Undermined by Gender Bias," *Fortune*, April 4, 2017, http://fortune.com/2017/04/04/walmart-jobs-gender-bias/; Al Norman, "Sex Discrimination Wal-Mart: The 'Bitches' Story that Won't Go Away," *Huffington Post*, July 17, 2016, https://www.huffingtonpost.com/entry/sex-discrimination-t-wal-mart-dthe-biktches-story_us_578bbafae4b0b107a24147d3.

85 Adam Liptak, "Justices Rule for Wal-Mart in Class-Action Bias Case," *New York Times*, June 20, 2011, https://www.nytimes.com/2011/06/21/business/21bizcourt.html.

86 Daisy Murray, "'Empowerment through Empathy,' – We Spoke to Tarana Burke, the Woman Who Really Started the 'Me Too' Movement," *Elle*, October 23, 2017, https://www.elle.com/uk/life-and-culture/culture/news/a39429/empowerment-through-empathy-tarana-burke-me-too/.

87 Lisa Respers France, "#MeToo: Social Media Flooded with Personal Stories of Assault," *CNN.com*, October 16, 2017, https://www.cnn.com/2017/10/15/entertainment/me-too-twitter-alyssa-milano/index.html.

88 Tara John, "Tons of Celebrities Are Joining Alyssa Milano's 'MeToo' Protest against Sexual Harassment," *Time*, October 16, 2017, http://time.com/4983731/me-too-alyssa-milano/; Jasmyn Belcher Morris, "Actress Ashley Judd's #MeToo Moment Was Driven by a 'Commitment' to Her Younger Self," *National Public Radio*, March 2, 2018, https://www.npr.org/2018/03/02/589619992/actress-ashley-judds-metoo-moment-was-driven-by-a-commitment-to-her-younger-self; Alanna Vagianos, "Jennifer Lawrence Is Working on a TV Series Inspired by Me Too Movement," *Huffington Post*, February 26, 2018, https://www.huffingtonpost.com/entry/jennifer-lawrence-tv-series-inspired-by-me-too-and-times-up_us_5a9420d6e4b0ee6416a55ad5; Libby Hill, "#MeToo: Reese Witherspoon Says a Director Sexually Assaulted Her When She Was 16," *Chicago Tribune*, October 17, 2017, https://www.chicagotribune.com/la-et-entertainment-news-updates-reese-witherspoon-shares-her-story-of-1508254090-htmlstory.html; Jodi Kantor and Rachel Abrams, "Gwyneth Paltrow, Angelina Jolie, and Others Say Weinstein Harassed Them," *New York Times*, October 10, 2017, https://www.nytimes.com/2017/10/10/us/gwyneth-paltrow-angelina-jolie-harvey-weinstein.html.

89 BBC, "Harvey Weinstein Scandal: Who Has Accused Him of What?", *BBC News*, December 20, 2017, http://www.bbc.com/news/entertainment-arts-41580010.

90 Gretel Kauffman, "Larry Nassar, Former USA Gymnastic Coach, Is Charged with Sexual Assault," *Christian Science Monitor*, February 22, 2017, https://www.csmonitor.com/USA/Justice/2017/0222/Larry-Nassar-former-USA-gymnastic-coach-is-charged-with-sexual-assault.

91 Alanna Vagianos, "140 Women Have Accused Larry Nassar of Abuse. His Victims Think We Don't Care," *Huffington Post*, January 14, 2018, https://www.huffingtonpost.com/entry/larry-nassar-abuse-victims-public-outrage_us_5a58f619e4b03c4189654efe.

92 Joe Otterson, "Bill O'Reilly Scandal Timeline: From Fox News Star to Unemployed," *Variety*, April 19, 2017, http://variety.com/2017/tv/news/bill-oreilly-fired-sexual-harassment-fox-news-timeline-1202372546/.

93 Claire Zillman, "A New Poll on Sexual Harassment Suggests Why 'Me Too' Went So Insanely Viral," *Fortune*, October 17, 2017, http://fortune.com/2017/10/17/me-too-hashtag-sexual-harassment-at-work-stats/.

94 Laura Santhanam, "Poll: A Third of Women Say They've Been Sexually Harassed or Abused at Work," *PBS News*, November 21, 2017, https://www.pbs.org/newshour/nation/poll-a-third-of-women-say-theyve-been-sexually-harassed-or-abused-at-work.

95 Susan Chira, "Numbers Hint at Why #MeToo Took Off: The Sheer Number Who Can Say Me Too," *New York Times*, February 21, 2018, https://www.nytimes.com/2018/02/21/upshot/pervasive-sexual-harassment-why-me-too-took-off-poll.html.

96 Michele Micheletti and Andrew S. McFarland, *Creative Participation: Responsibility-Taking in the Political World* (New York: Routledge, 2011).

97 Makela, "Transcript: Donald Trump's Taped Comments about Women," 2016.

98 North, "The Summer Zervos Sexual Assault Allegations and Lawsuit against Trump, Explained," 2018; Josh Gerstein and Lorraine Woellert, "Trump Subjected to Trifecta of Sex-Scandal Lawsuits," *Politico*, March 20, 2018, https://www.politico.com/story/2018/03/20/trump-sex-scandal-lawsuits-daniels-476728; Kate Briquelet, "Exclusive: Stormy Daniels' Friend Alana Evans: I'm Also Going to Sue Michael Cohen," *The Daily Beast*, March 26, 2018, https://www.thedailybeast.com/exclusive-stormy-daniels-friend-alana-evans-im-also-going-to-sue-michael-cohen; Julie Mazziotta, "Donald Trump's History of Body Shaming: He Rated Female Celebrities on a Scale of 1 to 10," *People*, September 28, 2016, http://people.com/bodies/donald-trump-rated-female-celebrities-on-a-scale-of-1-to-10/; Jessica Estepa, "Donald Trump on Carly Fiorina: 'Look at that Face!'", *USA Today*, September 10, 2015, https://www.usatoday.com/story/news/nation-now/2015/09/10/trump-fiorina-look-face/71992454/.

99 Jennifer Hansler, "These Are the Senators Calling for Trump to Resign over Sexual Misconduct Allegations," *CNN.com*, December 14, 2017, https://www.cnn.com/2017/12/12/politics/trump-resignation-senators/index.html.

100 Kaitlynn Mendes, *Feminism in the News: Representations of the Women's Movement since the 1960s* (New York: Palgrave, 2011); Nayda Terkildsen and Frauke Schnell, "How Media Frames Move Public Opinion: An Analysis of the Women's Movement," *Political Research Quarterly* 50, no. 4 (1997): 879–900; Patricia Bradley, *Mass Media and the Shaping of American Feminism, 1963–1975* (Jackson, MS: University Press of Mississippi, 2005).

101 Using the *Nexis Uni* database, I searched for all stories in the *New York Times* and other newspapers and online venues for references to "sexual

abuse" or "abuse," to "sexual assault" or "assault," to "sexual harassment," "harassment," "harassing," or efforts to "harass" women, to "sexual predator(s)," "sexual predation," or "predation," and to "sexual violence" or "violence" against women.

102 Editorial, "The #MeToo Bonfire," *Chicago Tribune*, October 27, 2017, http://www.chicagotribune.com/news/opinion/editorials/ct-edit-harass-metoo-gender-20171026-story.html.
103 Editorial, "A #MeToo Moment for the Poor and Powerless," *Los Angeles Times*, December 28, 2017, http://www.latimes.com/opinion/editorials/la-ed-low-wage-sex-harassment-20171228-story.html.
104 Editorial, "Will Harvey Weinstein's Fall Finally Reform Men?", *New York Times*, October 28, 2017, https://www.nytimes.com/2017/10/28/opinion/sunday/harvey-weinstein-sexual-harassment.html.
105 *Pew Research Center*, "Pew Research Center Poll November 2017," November 29–December 4, 2017.
106 *NBC News/Wall Street Journal*, "NBC/Wall Street Journal Poll, October 2017," October 23–26, 2017, iPoll.
107 *NBC News/Wall Street Journal*, "NBC/Wall Street Journal Poll, October 2017," 2017.
108 *NBC News/Wall Street Journal*, "NBC/Wall Street Journal Poll, October 2017," 2017.
109 *NBC News/Wall Street Journal*, "NBC/Wall Street Journal Poll, October 2017," 2017.
110 Quinnipiac University, "Quinnipiac University Poll, November 2017," *iPoll*, November 15–20, 2017.
111 Quinnipiac University, "Quinnipiac University Poll, November 2017," 2017.
112 This question wording was drawn verbatim from the *Pew Research Center*'s December 2017 survey on sexual harassment in America. The results from my findings were essentially the same as *Pew*'s, with 60 percent of respondents in my survey saying harassment allegations were indicative of a larger social problem, compared to 66 percent saying the same in *Pew*'s survey.
113 The relationship between media consumption and concern with sexism was statistically significant, at the 0.1 percent level.
114 *Pew*'s December 2017 survey contained identical wording to my own survey. I find that ideology is a significant predictor of attitudes toward MeToo, after controlling for respondents' party, gender, age, education, race, and income.
115 Rebecca Shabad and Stephanie Perry, "Poll: Majority Says #MeToo Movement Has Helped Address Gender Inequality," *NBC News*, March 9, 2018, https://www.nbcnews.com/politics/politics-news/poll-majority-says-metoo-movement-has-helped-address-gender-inequality-n854576.
116 *NBC News/Wall Street Journal*, "NBC News/Wall Street Journal Poll, March 2018," *iPoll*, March 10–14, 2018.
117 *NBC News/Wall Street Journal*, "NBC News/Wall Street Journal Poll," 2018.
118 *NBC News/Wall Street Journal*, "NBC News/Wall Street Journal Poll, December 2017," *iPoll*, December 14–15, 2017.
119 Suffolk University/USA Today, "Suffolk University/USA Today Poll, December 2017," *iPoll*, December 5–9, 2017.
120 *NBC News/Wall Street Journal*, "NBC News/Wall Street Journal Poll, March 2018," 2018.

121 Quinnipiac University, "Quinnipiac University Poll, December 2017," *iPoll*, November 29–December 4, 2017; *ABC News/Washington Post*, "ABC News/Washington Post Poll, January 2018," *iPoll*, January 15–18, 2018.
122 Quinnipiac University, "Quinnipiac University Poll, November 2017," 2017.
123 Anthony DiMaggio, "#MeToo: Women Are Speaking Out, Are We Listening?", *Counterpunch*, December 15, 2017, https://www.counterpunch.org/2017/12/15/me-too-women-are-speaking-out-are-we-listening/.
124 Polling Report, "CNBC All-America Economic Survey," *Pollingreport.com*, December 10–13, 2017, http://www.pollingreport.com/work.htm.
125 Gallup, "Gallup Poll, November 2017," *iPoll*, November 5–11, 2017.
126 *NBC News/Wall Street Journal*, "NBC/Wall Street Journal Poll, October 2017," 2017.
127 *NBC News/Wall Street Journal*, "NBC News/Wall Street Journal Poll, March 2018," 2018.
128 *NBC News/Wall Street Journal*, "NBC News/Wall Street Journal Poll, March 2018," 2018.
129 *NBC News/Wall Street Journal*, "NBC News/Wall Street Journal Poll, March 2018," 2018.
130 Quinnipiac University, "Quinnipiac University Poll, December 2017," *iPoll*, December 6–11, 2017.
131 Quinnipiac University, "Quinnipiac University Poll, December 2017," 2017.
132 CNN, "CNN Poll, December 2017," *iPoll*, December 14–17, 2017.
133 CNN, "CNN Poll, December 2017," 2017.
134 Elise Viebeck, "The #MeToo Movement Roils Capitol Hill as More Allegations Are Made Public," *Washington Post*, January 26, 2018, https://www.washingtonpost.com/powerpost/the-metoo-movement-roils-capitol-hill-as-more-allegations-made-public/2018/01/26/6facf812-02ab-11e8-bb03-722769454f82_story.html?noredirect=on&utm_term=.a0ad37ee9beb.
135 Rebecca Beitsch, "#MeToo Has Changed Our Culture, Now It's Changing Our Laws," *Pew Trusts*, July 31, 2018, https://www.pewtrusts.org/en/research-and-analysis/blogs/stateline/2018/07/31/metoo-has-changed-our-culture-now-its-changing-our-laws.

Conclusion

Throughout this book, I presented evidence that scholars, intellectuals, and Americans more broadly should place greater emphasis on the study of social movements. We need to recognize their primary importance in promoting progressive change. These movements, despite the chronic official source bias in the media, take advantage of news coverage at critical junctures and during periods of disruption and instability, to stake out a space in national political discourse – to pursue their political, economic, and social goals. Progressive movements and populism, more so than right-wing rebellions, rely heavily on grassroots, bottom-up pressure to succeed. Since right-wing protests tend to support concentrated political and economic power, they have the benefit of drawing on the resources of organized political and business interests, which amplifies their messages. In contrast, progressive movements struggle to impact politics, as they oppose plutocracy and concentrated political-economic power.

This book also makes the case that the study of identities, and the intersections of various identities, are key to understanding contemporary social movements. Many on the left and right lambaste terms like "intersectionality," while dismissing or condemning those who adopt identity-based analyses of the world. But the case studies I examined show that it is difficult, if not impossible, to develop a comprehensive, nuanced understanding of modern organizing, activism, and social movements without understanding how identities centered on race, ethnicity, class, and geography (among other identities) function to bring Americans together in pursuit of common interests.

The term "identity politics" is used pejoratively to dismiss leftist intellectuals and activists, who are portrayed as too parochial and self-indulgent in their politics, and as dupes of American political and business elites. But any hope of a serious and sustained progressive movement – one that will build a powerful, broad-based coalition for political change – must consider how different identities matter to how individuals experience the world. This will be the central challenge for those on the left who seek to build such a movement in coming years.

Each progressive movement in this book has its own unique history, strengths, and limitations. Each draws on specific identities, be it professional white women with MeToo, or economically stressed whites in the cases of Occupy and Madison, poorer people of color (and black Americans specifically) with BLM, or poor men and women of all ethnicities and races in Fight for $15. These movements, on their own, each had a significant impact on American politics. But on their own, each of these movements has not succeeded in building a broad-based coalition that can effectively commit to sustained progressive transformation of politics, and to challenging the plutocratic political-economic order. Of course, it is easy to say that various movements and identity groups should work together to effect change. It is much harder to actually do so, especially considering the rise of reactionary political forces such as the Tea Party and Trumpian populism, which were dedicated to driving wedges between groups of Americans, and fomenting increased cultural discord centered on racial, ethnic, gender, and class-based conflicts.

If the challenge on the left is to combat the growing authoritarianism, bigotry, and the creeping fascistic turn in American politics under Trump, the obstacles on the right are also daunting, at least for those committed to democracy, the rule of law, and political equality. Many American conservatives have not embraced the authoritarian "fascist creep" we witnessed under Trump's presidency. Half of Republicans have not embraced positions – as Trump's supporters have – that future elections should be shut down at the command of the President to combat fictitious voter fraud, and that journalists should be censored because of their critical coverage of Trump. And half of Republicans do not agree – as Trump supporters do – that their primary source of information about the world should be the propaganda and distortions emanating from the President's *Twitter* feed. For those conservatives and Republicans who have not embraced authoritarianism, the task that lies ahead is figuring out how to decouple conservatism from the cult of Trump's personality. Conservatives' challenge was made more difficult without the help of right-wing media outlets – which widely embraced the President. But the concern with rising authoritarianism on the right also transcends Trump's presidency, and continues after he is out of office, as the shift toward right-wing extremism among conservatives and Republicans has been a long time coming, as documented by Political Scientists.[1]

Elections as an Instrument of Democracy?

Modern progressive movements had a significant impact on the 2018 and 2020 elections. A transformed political culture that followed MeToo meant the rise of a new generation of female political candidates and victors who were open about their experiences with sexual harassment and assault, and how they impacted their politics. Furthermore, nearly a third of Americans explained that the changing political climate under MeToo made them more likely to vote for female electoral candidates.[2] Two-thirds of women voters going into 2018 were more likely to vote for candidates who supported women's rights, as related to instituting "paid parental leave and enacting harsher penalties for sexual harassment and assault in the workplace."[3]

The anti-Trump movement more generally also resonated with voters. In the 2018 Congressional midterms, anger with the Trump administration was the driving motivation for many voters. The Republican Party lost nearly three-dozen House seats, with two-thirds of voters admitting Trump was a motivating factor in their vote. Of those voters, four in ten said their vote was intended as a protest of Trump, compared to a quarter who said their vote was intended to validate his presidency.[4]

Finally, the 2020 presidential race was also impacted by progressive-left movements. Sanders' 2020 campaign was largely a continuation of the themes he raised in 2016, which drew heavily on the economic justice movement. And Sanders' attempts to expand his appeal to women and people of color by spotlighting systemic racism and sexism were in significant part a response to his previous failure to cultivate mass support from these groups, and his responding to rising protest pressures with regard to recognizing the importance of equal rights for women and minorities. Elizabeth Warren's entrance into the 2020 Democratic primaries further signaled the mainstreaming of progressive values promoted by left social movements.

Social Movements and Democracy

I have argued that progressive social movements, not political parties, are the driving force behind democratic and leftist political reforms. This point was demonstrated repeatedly by my case studies. In instance after instance, progressive causes are given short shrift in politics and discourse, until the emergence of progressive movements, which draw those issues to the forefront of public debate. While protesters' demands are at first seen as radical, exotic, and non-mainstream, their political agendas are eventually embraced by masses of Americans, particularly after increasingly favorable coverage of these movements in the media. Such coverage produces heightened support among regular news consumers, and public opinion then creates pressure on the political system for change.

There must be greater recognition of the power of social movements in enabling political transformation, at least if Americans wish to see their government address popular demands to combat racism, sexism, poverty, and inequality. If Americans rely on the "politics-as-usual" approach of staying home and voting once every four years, without recognizing the need for more direct democracy and additional social movements, we will witness the perpetuation of the sexist, racist, and plutocratic political order that dominates American politics. This book explored a path out of this plutocracy: mass citizen action. Mass participation is not merely important to a democracy – it *is* the heart of democracy. And without a sustained effort to promote progressive change via protest, civil disobedience, and movement building, American society will continue to fail in fulfilling its democratic potential.

Notes

1 Marc J. Hetherington and Jonathan D. Weiler, *Authoritarianism and Polarization in American Politics* (New York: Cambridge University Press, 2009); Richard Hofstadter, *The Paranoid Style in American Politics* (New York: Vintage, 2008).
2 Emily Shugerman, "The #MeToo Movement Takes Office after Winning Elections across the U.S.," *Daily Beast*, November 7, 2018, https://www.thedailybeast.com/the-metoo-movement-takes-office-after-winning-elections-across-the-us.
3 Ashley Kirzinger, "Data Note: How Women Voters Could Influence the 2018 Elections and beyond," *Kaiser Family Foundation*, July 30, 2018, https://www.kff.org/womens-health-policy/poll-finding/data-note-how-women-voters-influence-2018-elections-and-beyond/.
4 Anthony DiMaggio, "In the Wake of the Blue Wave: The Midterms, Recounts, and the Future of Progressive Politics," *Counterpunch*, November 15, 2018, https://www.counterpunch.org/2018/11/15/in-the-wake-of-the-blue-wave-the-midterms-recounts-and-the-future-of-progressive-politics/.

Index

Note: Information in figures and tables is indicated by page numbers in *italics* and **bold**, respectively.

ACA *see* Affordable Care Act (ACA)
activist core 2–3
Adbusters 80–81
Affordable Care Act (ACA) 28, 32–33, 52, 178–179, 241–245, *243–244*
African Americans; *see also* Black Lives Matter Obama and 120; stereotypes of 30; Tea Party and 34
Americans for Prosperity 35
anti-Trump uprising: Affordable Care Act repeal and 241–245, *243–244*; DACA repeal in 234–236; diversity in 229; intersectionality and 233–234; March(es) for Science in 237–240, *239*; #MeToo and 250; Muslim travel ban in 234–236; strengths and limits of 246, 246–251, **248**, *249*; Tax Day protests in 236–237; Women's Marches (2017) in 231–234
Armey, Dick 26

Baltimore 136–143, **139**, *141–142*
Barrett, Tom 70
Beck, Glenn 26, 32
bigotry 46, 47; of Tea Party 29–31
birther conspiracy 31, 185
Black Lives Matter 3, 7–9, 120–154, **132**, *134–135*, **139**, 141, *142*, **144**, *144–145*, *147–148*, *150–151*; Ferguson and 126–136, **132**, *133–134*; Garner and 122–123; impact of 143–149, *145*, *147–148*;

intersectionality and 121, 134–136, *135*; lessons from 121–122; limits of 149–152; Martin and 120–121; media coverage of 37–38, 97; policy change and 152–153; public opinion on *150*; racism and 124–126, *147*; sexual identity politics and 149–150; social media and 128–129; strengths of 149–152
Boston Tea Party 25
Brown, Jerry 99
Brown, Michael 123, 126–136, **132**, *133–134*, 160n85, 161n90
Burke, Tarana 251–252

Carender, Keli 25
Castile, Philando 123, 144–145
classism 27
Clinton, Hillary 176–179, 183–184, 232, 246–247
cognitive liberation 6
color-blind racism 33
Communist Manifesto, The (Marx & Engels) 3
conspiracy theories 31–32
core, activist 2–3
criminal justice 124–125, 175
Cullors, Patricia 120–121, 128
culture war 189
Cuomo, Andrew 99

DACA *see* Deferred Action for Childhood Arrivals (DACA)
Davis, Angela 233–234
"death panels" 32

death penalty 125
Deferred Action for Childhood Arrivals (DACA) 235–236, 247
democracy: elections and 275–276; social movements and 276–277
Democratic Party 9; Madison protests and 79; Tea Party and 29; in Trump opposition 250
demographic change 24–25, 166
Dent, Charlie 241
disturbance theory 5–6, 33, 121
Donegan, Connor 70
Draitser, Eric 55n3
drug war 124

economic insecurity 66
Egypt 70, 80
electability 183
elitism 9
Emanuel, Rahm 123
Engels, Friedrich 3

"fascist creep" 213–215
feminism 34
Ferguson, Missouri 126–136, *132*, *133–134*, 149, 152–153, 160n85, 161n90
Fight for $15 3, 8–9, 64, 70–71, 94–102, *96*, **97**, **98**, *101*, 173, 179; media coverage of 37–38, **97**, **98**
Freedom Works 35
free markets 28–29
free rider problem 5

Garner, Eric 122–123, 143
Garza, Alicia 120–121, 128
Giroux, Henry 213
Giuliani, Rudy 235
Graham, Lindsey 245
Gramsci, Antonio 4
Gray, Freddie 123, 128, 136–143, **139**, *141–142*, 143
Green New Deal 184
gridlock, in Senate 65–66

Hannity, Sean 31
health-care protests 32–33
hegemony 4

identities 2
identity politics 7, 24, 274–275
immigration 197–198
income inequality 64–65

inequality 65–68
intersectionality 2, 16n5, 74, 76, 121; Baltimore uprising and 141–143, *142*; Black Lives Matter and 134–136, *135*; #MeToo and *260*; populism and 167; Sanders and 179–180; Women's March and 233–234
intersectional sexism 33–35
Islamophobia 31–32

Lee, Mike 245
Limbaugh, Rush 31, 34
living wage 94; see also Fight for $15
lobbying, "outside" 10

Madison protests see Walker, Scott
March(es) for Science 237–240, *239*
Martin, Isaac 23n77
Martin, Trayvon 120–121
Marx, Karl 3–4
Marxism 67
McCain, John 245
McDonald, Laquan 123, 143
McKleskey v. Kemp 125
media; see also social media: Baltimore and 137–141, **139**, *141*; Ferguson and 129–134, **132**, *134*, 160n85; Madison protests and 72–80, **73**, *74–78*; March for Science and 239; #MeToo in *256*, 256–257; Occupy Wall Street and 86–91, **88**, **89**; Sanders in 173–174; Tea Party and 35–41, **37**, **41**, *41–42*, 60n75; Trump and 189–196, **192**, *193–196*
Medicare 27–28
#MeToo 3, 7, 251–262, *254*, *256*, *259*
Milano, Alyssa 252
minimum wage see Fight for $15
Moran, Jerry 245
Mosely Braun, Carol 34
Mubarak, Hosni 70, 80
Muslim travel ban 234–236

Nassar, Alan 252–253
9/12 project 26
Nixon, Jay 128

Obama, Barack 24, 27–28, 31–32, *52*, 54, 70, 79, 82, 178–179, 185; see also Affordable Care Act (ACA)
Ocasio Cortez, Alexandria 184

Occupy Wall Street 2–3, 8–9, 37, 68, 70–71, 80–94, **88**, *89*, *91–93*, 172–173
Olson, Mancur 5
O'Reilly, Bill 253
outreach efforts 2
"outside" lobbying strategy 10

Palin, Sarah 26
Pelosi, Nancy 184
Piven, Frances Fox 9–10
pluralism 5
plutocracy 4, 186–189
police violence 122–123
policy process theory 6–7
political discourse 71–72
political opportunity structure 6
political participation 65
political process theory 6
politics: inequality and 65–68
populism 11; background on 167–169; intersectionality and 167; plutocracy and 186–189; reactionary, in culture war 189; of Sanders 166, 168, 170; of Trump 166, 168, 184–189, 191–195, **192**, *193–194*
postmodernism 2
poverty 27–28
progressive societal transformation 1
Putin, Vladimir 232–233

racial priming 125–126
racism 32–33, 46, *47*; Black Lives Matter and 124–126, *147*; criminal justice and 124–125; thought and 125; of Trump supporters 197, *202*
Republican Party: Tea Party and 24, 26, 29, 36, 43, *43*, 50, 55; Trump and 185; whites in 67
resource mobilization 5–7
retrospective voting 66
Rolf, David 95
Romney, Mitt 70

Sanate 65–66
Sanders, Bernie 7, 64, 68; 2016 election and 169–173; appeal of 174–183, *175–178*, *180–182*; Fight for $15 and 96, 98, *98*, 100, 173; legislative history of 169–170; media and 173–174; Occupy Wall Street and 172–173; "political revolution" of 183–184; populism of 166, 168, 170; younger individuals and 182, *182*
Schumer, Chuck 184
segregation 9, 124, 127
Senate, Rick 25–26
sexual identity politics 149–150
social media 86–87, 128–129, 137–141
social movements: hegemony and 4; identity and 6; identity politics and 7; mainstream theories of 4–10, *8*; and "outside" lobbying strategy 10; plutocracy and 4; populism and 11; understanding 2–4
Social Security 27–28
stereotypes, racial 125–126
Sterling, Alton 123, 144–145
strain theory 5
Sustar, Lee 71

Tax Day protests 236–237
taxes: Tea Party and 28–29
Taylor, Keeanga-Yamahtta 121
Tea Party 2, 7, 11, 23n77, 24–55; Affordable Care Act and 32–33, *52*; beliefs of 26–29; bigotry of 29–31, 46, *47*; challenging conventional wisdom on 42–45, *43*; conspiracy theories among 31–32; decline of 44–45; economic issues and 46, *47–48*, 49–50; free markets and 28–29; history of 25–26; intersectional sexism and 33–35; Islamophobia of 31–32; media and 35–41, **37**, **41**, *41–42*, 60n75; motivations of 45–50, *47–48*, *52–53*; poverty and 27–28; as pro-business 28–29; Republican Party and 24, 26, 29, 36, 43, *43*, 50, 55; taxes and 28–29; as white 26–27
Tometi, Opal 120, 128
Toomey, Pat 241
Truman, David 5–6, 33, 121
Trump, Donald 7, 11; *see also* anti-Trump uprising; birtherism and 31, 185; economic populism of, as myth *204*, 204–213, *205*, *208*, *211–212*; and "fascist creep" 213–215; ignorance on part of, as strength 168–169; media

and 189–196, **192**, *193–196*;
populism of 166, 168,
184–189, 191–195, **192**,
193–194; predictors of
opposition to *249*; speech
patterns of 185–186; as
"strongman" 168; supporters
of 197–203, *198–203*, 207–208,
208; support of violence by
214; Tea Party and 25; wealthy
and 187–188

unions 69, *75*, 77, 79

Van Dyke, Jason 123
Vietnam War 7

wage stagnation 64
Walker, Scott 3, 8–9, 64, 67–80, **73**,
74–78, 172
Warren, Elizabeth 184
wealth inequality 64–65
Weinstein, Harvey 252
white male privilege 84
whites: as conservative 67; Tea Party
comprised of 26–27
Women's Marches 231–234, 246–247

xenophobia 32–33, *33*, 46

Yang, Andrew 184

Zimmerman, George 120–121